HEGEL'S
PHILOSOPHY OF
RIGHT

HEGEL'S
PHILOSOPHY OF
RIGHT

TRANSLATED WITH NOTES BY

T. M. KNOX

OXFORD UNIVERSITY PRESS
LONDON   OXFORD   NEW YORK

First published by the Clarendon Press, 1952
First issued as an Oxford University Press paperback, 1967
printing, last digit: 29 28 27 26 25 24
Printed in the United States of America

TRANSLATOR'S FOREWORD

§ 1

THIS book is a translation of the work which Hegel published in 1821* under the double title: *Naturrecht und Staatswissenschaft im Grundrisse* and *Grundlinien der Philosophie des Rechts* (Natural Law and Political Science in Outline; Elements of the Philosophy of Right). The text of that edition is the basis of the translation, but reference has also been made to the editions of Gans (Berlin, 1833 and 1854—the first and third editions of *Hegels Werke*, vol. viii), Bolland (Leyden, 1902), and Lasson (Leipzig, 1921). Lasson has recorded in his edition the results of his collation of previous editions. The translator has tacitly accepted Lasson's corrections of misprints in the first edition and has confined his textual notes to recording (*a*) Hegel's own corrections of his published text (which are printed in *Hegels eigenhändige Randbemerkungen zu seiner Rechtsphilosophie*, hrsg. von G. Lasson, Leipzig, 1930), (*b*) some of Lasson's emendations, and (*c*) certain emendations of his own, most of which are corrections of Hegel's cross-references.

In his editions of the book, Gans intercalated into Hegel's text a number of Additions culled from notes taken at Hegel's lectures; these have been translated here (from Gans's 1833 edition, except where otherwise stated), but in order to distinguish them from what Hegel published himself, they have been relegated to an Appendix. The point in the text where Gans inserted an Addition is here indicated by [A.].

The use of square brackets in the translation indicates that the matter enclosed between them is the translator's.

Hegel subjoins to many of his Paragraphs explanatory notes which are here printed in smaller type and referred to throughout as 'Remarks' in order to distinguish them from the translator's 'Notes'. The latter are exegetical and illustrative only; they fall short of a full commentary and provide no criticism of Hegel's argument.

§ 2

The translator is specially indebted to previous workers in this field, first to F. Messineo,† whose translation has been a valuable

---

* Not 1820, as many writers state. For the circumstances of its publication, see an article on 'Hegel and Prussianism' by the translator in *Philosophy*, January 1940.

† *Hegel: Lineamenti di filosofia del diritto*, tradotti da Francesco Messineo (Bari, 1913).

guide, secondly to J. M. Sterrett* and S. W. Dyde†. The excellent synopsis of Hegel's work by T. C. Sandars in *Oxford Essays*, 1855, is wrongly described in Croce's bibliography as a 'translation'.

Mr. H. A. Reyburn's *Hegel's Ethical Theory* (Oxford, 1921) provides a summary of the whole of Hegel's argument. Many of Hegel's critics misrepresent or misapprehend him, but there is one critic whose work on the *Philosophy of Right* the student of this book will find indispensable, namely Mr. M. B. Foster. See the following books and articles of his: *Die Geschichte als Schicksal des Geistes* (Tübingen, 1929), 'Hegel und die Politik' (in *Die Idee*, 1933), 'The opposition between Hegel and the philosophy of empiricism' (in *Verhandlungen des dritten Hegel-Kongresses in Rom*—Tübingen and Haarlem, 1934), and *The Political Philosophies of Plato and Hegel* (Oxford, 1935).

§ 3

The difficulties of translating the *Philosophy of Right* begin with the title. *Recht* is the German equivalent of *jus*, *droit*, and *diritto* as distinct from *lex*, *loi*, and *legge*. There is no corresponding distinction in English. 'Right' has been selected almost everywhere as perhaps the least confusing rendering of Hegel's meaning, although this leads at times to phrases unnatural in English. For instance, 'science of right' (Paragraph 1) sounds strange to an English ear, but to use the more natural 'jurisprudence' would be to restrict Hegel's meaning unduly. He says (Addition to Paragraph 33) that by *Recht* he means not only civil law, but also morality, ethical life, and world history. The associations of the word 'right' perhaps make it the best equivalent of a term given so wide a sense.

Hegel distinguishes sharply between *wirklich* and *real* (see Note 27 to the Preface) and also between *moralisch* and *sittlich* (see Note 75 to Paragraph 33), and these distinctions must be preserved in the translation. No natural equivalents are available, and some more or less arbitrary choice of rendering must be made. Hence *wirklich* is translated 'actual' and *real* 'real', while *moralisch* is translated 'moral' and *sittlich* 'ethical', even though English usage would require 'real' and 'moral' in certain contexts where, in order to retain Hegel's distinctions, 'actual' and 'ethical' have been used.

---

   * *The Ethics of Hegel*—translated selections from his *Rechtsphilosophie*, with an introduction by J. Macbride Sterrett, D.D. (Boston, 1893).

   † *Hegel's Philosophy of Right* translated by S. W. Dyde, M.A., D.Sc. (London, 1896).

One further avoidance of an obvious English usage may require explanation. Hegel speaks of *Stände* as divided into two Houses. *Stände* in its political meaning has here been translated 'Estates' and not 'Parliament', chiefly because Hegel insists so strongly on the connexion between parliament and the Estates of the Realm, or the social classes, of which it is composed.

Where there is available a well-known English translation of German books cited by Hegel, the title of that translation has been given here in place of the German one.

§ 4

Hegel's terminology causes difficulty to a beginner, and he takes for granted in the *Philosophy of Right* the general conception of philosophy and the general mode of argument expounded in his *Encyclopaedia of the Philosophical Sciences*. The best introduction to the study of any part of his philosophy is probably the smaller *Logic*, i.e. the first part of the *Enc.*, and of this there is an English translation by W. Wallace (Oxford, 1892). The first five chapters of Mr. Reyburn's *Hegel's Ethical Theory* expound the presuppositions of the *Philosophy of Right*. The translator has appended notes on many of Hegel's technicalities as they arise in the text, but it may be useful to supplement these here by adapting and amplifying the exposition of some of his chief terms which Hegel prefixed to his lectures on the history of philosophy and which has recently been published from one of his manuscripts (see *Hegels Geschichte der Philosophie*, hrsg. von J. Hoffmeister—Leipzig, 1938—Lief. 1, pp. 96 ff.).

(i) The thought (*Gedanke*) of a thing.

Philosophy is thinking, the thinking of the universal. The product of thinking is a thought, and this, viewed objectively, we call the 'universal'. But we know that the universal in this sense is abstract and different from the particular. The universal is a form, and its content, the particular, stands contrasted with it.

Now if we go no further than the thought of a thing, than this abstract universal, we remain at the level of the Understanding (*Verstand*), the level of reflection (see Note 61 to Paragraph 21), and the categories of 'essence' (see Note 5 to Paragraph 108). The Understanding (spelt with a capital letter in this translation because it is a technicality which Hegel often uses to mean 'those who remain at the level of the understanding and limit themselves to its

categories') is abstract or formal thinking, the thinking characteristic of the mathematical and empirical sciences or of formal logic,
as well as of those philosophies which adhere to scientific method
instead of abandoning it in favour of reason (*Vernunft*) and the
philosophic method of

(ii) The concept (*Begriff*).

(Wallace, Reyburn, and others translate *Begriff* by 'notion'.)
The defect of the Understanding is that while it correctly distinguishes between form and content, essential and inessential, universal and particular, it fails to synthesize these opposites. Held
apart from one another, however, each of these opposites becomes
an abstraction, and the living whole of reality has not been explained but explained away and killed by being so analysed into its
constituents. What the Understanding fails to recognize is that a
'thought' is not something empty or abstract; it is a determinant,
a determinant of itself. The essence of thought is its concreteness,
and the concrete thought is what Hegel calls the *concept*. When the
thought of a thing is handled philosophically instead of scientific-
ally, it is seen to be inherently concrete, i.e. not a mere abstract
form, but possessed of a content which it has given to itself. In a
sense it is right enough to say that philosophy deals with abstractions, with thoughts abstracted from the sense-perceptions which
are sometimes called 'concrete'; but in another sense this is quite
false, because when the sensuous content is separated from its
universal form, it also becomes an abstraction. Philosophy has to
do not with these two abstractions, held apart from one another,
but with their concrete synthesis, the concept. Its constituents are
not self-subsistent entities, which is what the Understanding takes
them to be, but only 'moments' in an organic whole.

The concept is the thought in so far as the thought determines
itself and gives itself a content; it is the thought in its vivacity and
activity. Again, the concept is the universal which particularizes
itself, the thought which actively creates and engenders itself.
Hence it is not a bare form for a content; it forms itself, gives itself
a content and determines itself to be the form. What is meant by
'concrete' is the thought which does not remain empty but which
is self-determining and self-particularizing.

The concept is thus the inward living principle of all reality.
(The background of Hegel's thought is theological, and the concept is his philosophical equivalent for the wisdom and so for the

creative power of God.) It follows that it is one and the same concept whose self-determining activity the philosopher studies whether in logic (which is the thought of God 'before the creation of nature and a finite spirit'—*Science of Logic*, i. 60), or nature, or man, or human institutions.

(iii) The Idea (*Idee*).

(This word is spelt throughout the translation with a capital letter in order to distinguish it from 'idea' (*Vorstellung*), i.e. from 'whatsoever is the object of the understanding when a man thinks'.)

Just as the thought of a thing, when viewed concretely, is the concept, so the concept, viewed concretely (i.e. in its truth, in its full development, and so in synthesis with the content which it gives to itself), is the Idea. The Idea is the concept in so far as the concept gives reality and existence to itself. To do this, the concept must determine itself, and the determination is nothing external, but is the concept itself, i.e. it is a *self*-determination. The Idea, or reason, or truth, is the concept become concrete, the unity of subject and object, of form and content.

(iv) Development.

Since the concept determines itself, it is alive and active, and its life is a development. The nature of mind is an immanent restless process; mind is self-productive and exists in and through this self-production. Development is from implicit (*an sich*, *potentia*, δύναμις) to explicit (*für sich*, *actus*, ἐνέργεια). To illustrate this process, Hegel frequently uses the analogy of organic growth. The tree—trunk, branches, and fruit—is present in germ in the seed. The seed is the whole life of the tree in its 'immediacy', and that life becomes explicit as its immediacy is mediated through the different stages in the tree's history. Hence as the tree grows, all that happens is that what is implicit becomes explicit; but the development is a genuine development and change, because trunk, branches, &c., do not exist *realiter* in the seed—even a microscope will not detect them there. As the seed grows, it differentiates itself into trunk, branches, leaves, &c., but when its growth is complete, it is a concrete unity (the tree as a whole) and not, as the seed was, an abstract unity, because it is now a differentiated and not an immediate, undeveloped, immature, unity.

It is a development of this sort which we study in the *Philosophy of Right*, and the process is always from immediate, undifferentiated, unity (i.e. bare abstract universality), through difference and particularization, to the concrete unity and synthesis of universal and particular, subject and object, form and content. This synthesis is individuality or concrete universality, or the concept in its truth as Idea. Since the process of its life is a single process, the determinations or particularizations which the concept gives to itself are an organically connected series, and they follow one another in stages of gradually increasing concreteness. The later stages cancel the earlier ones, and yet at the same time the earlier ones are absorbed within the later as moments or elements within them. Hence, although 'ethical life' supersedes 'abstract right' and 'morality', both of these are absorbed into ethical life as its constituents, just as family and civil society are both superseded by and incorporated in the state.

A beginner may perhaps be warned that Hegel's introductory matter, whether his Preface and Introduction or the first few Paragraphs of the three parts of the book, is seldom intelligible without some knowledge of that which it is meant to introduce.

§ 5

Hegel's conception of *civil society* has given rise to misunderstandings. 'Civil society' is used by eighteenth-century writers in contexts where we would now normally speak of 'the state', and Hegel has had his share in this change of linguistic usage. The popularity of the expression 'civil society' in Hegel's Germany was largely due to a translation of Adam Fergus̃on's *Essay on the History of Civil Society* (1767)—or so Rosenzweig says (*Hegel und der Staat*, Munich and Berlin, 1920, vol. ii, p. 118)—but Hooker uses the expression and it is a commonplace of English writers on political theory after him.

Just as the family is an immature kind of state (i.e. a patriarchal community), so civil society is also a kind of state, though one less immature than the family, because particular differences are explicit within it. It is, for example, an eighteenth-century despotism, under which the citizen, unless he were a civil servant, was conscious of the state, if at all, only as something external to him. His interests were civil and economic, not political, and he felt himself to be not a participant in public affairs, but the subject of his prince. His private affairs had no concern with politics, and political difficulties did not concern him. Universal and particular interests were thus distinct, and hence from the point of view of the Understanding, civil society *is* the state. It is an abstract universal which rules and commands the particular.

Civil society is not only a kind of state, the kind about which the Understanding's political theories are true enough, it is a moment in the state proper. It grows up into the state, because the educative influence of civil life (especially the life of trade and commerce) makes men realize that they are by nature not self-seeking individualists but creatures of reason; they have a universal side and so can aline themselves with the universal without sacrifice of freedom. So long as men regard freedom as freedom to pursue selfish whims, society is possible only if external checks are placed on this freedom; government is then an external organization to meet men's necessities. But if they realize that their true freedom consists in the acceptance of principles, of laws which are their own, a synthesis of universal and particular interests becomes possible. It can be actualized, however, only in and through the political institutions whereby the state proper is distinguished from civil society, notably *limited* monarchy, parliament, and freedom of press and public opinion. In civil society, the law which defends security of property and enforces contracts is regarded as an external force; in the state the law receives its content from parliament and so is the law of the citizens themselves.

Hence the transition from civil society to the state is due to education. When men realize that the cleavage between universal and particular which is characteristic of civil society is only an appearance, or in other words when they realize the concrete unity of universal and particular in their own nature, then this leads at once to the objectification of this concrete though differentiated unity in the political institutions which make the state an organic whole. Civil life then remains as an element in the state, but only as a subordinate moment of it (see, e.g., Paragraphs 287, 314, and the third footnote to Paragraph 270). The acquisition of political interests does not mean that economic interests cease.

§ 6

The translation has greatly benefited from the criticisms and suggestions of Mr. G. R. G. Mure, Mr. M. B. Foster, Professor Richard Kroner, and Mr. J. I. McKie. To these and to many other friends who answered his queries on points of translation and exegesis, the translator wishes to record his gratitude. He is solely responsible for any errors that remain. He has tried to be literal and so to allow Hegel to speak for himself; but Hegel prided himself on teaching philosophy to speak German, and the translator is aware that he has been able to make Hegel's philosophy speak English only at the expense of some awkward sentences and cumbersome expressions. Even so, there may be those who will object that his renderings of certain technicalities, such as *an sich* and *für sich*, have not been literal enough.

§ 7

The translator thanks the Delegates of the Clarendon Press for undertaking to publish his work, and especially for persevering with the publication amidst the difficulties of the present time.

In recognition of a pupil's debt to a tutor, and in gratitude for a friendship of twenty years, the translator dedicates his work to R. G. Collingwood, Fellow of the British Academy, sometime Waynflete Professor of Metaphysical Philosophy in the University of Oxford.

T. M. K.

UNITED COLLEGE, ST. ANDREWS,
August 1942

POSTSCRIPT

(i) The reference to Croce's bibliography of Hegel in § 2 of this Foreword is to the French translation. See *Ce qui est vivant et ce qui est mort de la philosophie de Hegel* (Paris, 1910), p. 194.

(ii) References in the Notes to 'all editions' are to all the editions and translations which the translator has seen, i.e. to those enumerated in this Foreword.

TABLE OF CONTENTS

ABBREVIATIONS

KEY TO ABBREVIATED REFERENCES TO BOOKS CITED

Abbreviation	*Full title*
	(A) HEGEL'S WORKS
Aesthetic	*Hegel's Philosophy of Fine Art*, translated by F. P. B. Osmaston, 4 vols., London, 1916.
Enc.	*Encyclopaedia of the Philosophical Sciences.* See Note 2 to the Preface.
Hegels e. R.	*Hegels eigenhändige Randbemerkungen zu seiner Rechtsphilosophie*, hrsg. von G. Lasson, Leipzig, 1930.
History of Philosophy	*Hegel's History of Philosophy*, translated by E. S. Haldane, 3 vols., London, 1892.
Phenomenology	*Hegel's Phenomenology of Mind*, translated by Sir J. B. Baillie, 2nd edn., London, 1931.
Philosophy of History	*Hegel's Philosophy of History*, translated by J. Sibree, 2nd edn., New York, 1900.
Philosophy of Religion	*Hegel's Philosophy of Religion*, translated by the Rev. E. B. Speirs and J. Burdon Sanderson, 3 vols., London, 1895.
Science of Logic	*Hegel's Science of Logic*, translated by W. H. Johnston and L. G. Struthers, 2 vols., London, 1929.
Werke[1] or [2]	*Hegels sämtliche Werke*, neu hrsg. von H. Glockner, Stuttgart, 1927 ff. The pagination quoted is that of the original edition, which is given in the margin of Glockner's reprint.

(B) EDITIONS AND TRANSLATIONS OF THE PHILOSOPHY OF RIGHT

Bolland	*Hegels Grundlinien der Philosophie des Rechts*, hrsg. von G. J. P. J. Bolland, Leyden, 1902.
Gans	*Hegels sämtliche Werke*, vol. viii, Berlin, 1st edn. 1833, 3rd edn. 1854.
Lasson	*Hegels Grundlinien der Philosophie des Rechts*, neu hrsg. von G. Lasson, 2nd edn., Leipzig, 1921.
Messineo	*Hegel: Lineamenti di filosofia del diritto*, tradotti da Francesco Messineo, Bari, 1913.
Sterrett	*The Ethics of Hegel, translated selections from his Rechtsphilosophie*, with an introduction by J. Macbride Sterrett, D.D., Boston, 1893.

Abbreviation	Full title
	(C) OTHER WORKS
Science of Knowledge	Fichte's Science of Knowledge (Wissenschafts-lehre), translated by A. E. Kroeger, London, 1889.
Science of Rights	Fichte's Science of Rights (Grundlage des Naturrechts), translated by A. E. Kroeger, London, 1889. References to numbered sections are omitted in Kroeger's translation, and they are inserted here from J. G. Fichte, Werke, hrsg. von F. Medicus, Leipzig, 1908, vol. ii.
Philosophy of Law	Kant's Philosophy of Law (the first part of his Metaphysik der Sitten), translated by W. Hastie, Edinburgh, 1887.
Kant's Theory of Ethics	Kant's Theory of Ethics, translated by T. K. Abbott, 6th edn., London, 1923.

In quoting from translations of Hegel, the translator in his Notes has made modifications here and there in order to bring the terminology into accordance with that used here.

HEGEL'S
PHILOSOPHY OF
RIGHT

HEGEL'S PHILOSOPHY OF RIGHT

PREFACE

THE immediate inducement to publish this manual is the need for putting into the hands of my audience a text-book for the lectures on the Philosophy of Right which I deliver in the course of my professional duties.[1]* This compendium is an enlarged and especially a more systematic exposition of the same fundamental concepts which in relation to this part of philosophy are already contained in a book of mine designed previously for my lectures—the *Encyclopaedia of Philosophical Sciences* (Heidelberg, 1817).[2]

But this manual was to appear in print and therefore it now comes before the general public; and this was my inducement to amplify here a good many of the Remarks which were primarily meant in a brief compass to indicate ideas akin to my argument or at variance with it, further inferences from it, and the like, i.e. material which would receive its requisite elucidation in my lectures. The object of amplifying them here was to clarify occasionally the more abstract parts of the text and to take a more comprehensive glance at current ideas widely disseminated at the present time. Hence the result has been a number of Remarks rather more extensive than is usually consistent with the style and aim of a compendium. Apart from that, however, a compendium proper has as its subject-matter what is taken to be the closed circle of a science; and what is appropriate in it, except perhaps for a small addition here and there, is principally the assembly and arrangement of the essential factors in a content which has long been familiar and accepted, just as the form in which it is arranged has its rules and artifices which have long been settled. *Philosophical* manuals are perhaps not now expected to conform to such a pattern, for it is supposed that what philosophy puts together is a work as ephemeral as Penelope's web, one which must be begun afresh every morning.

I need hardly say that the chief difference between this manual and an ordinary compendium lies in the method which constitutes their guiding principle. But in this book I am presupposing that philosophy's mode of progression from one topic to another and

* [Numerals so inset refer throughout to the Translator's Notes.]

its mode of scientific proof—this whole speculative way of knowing—is essentially distinct from any other way of knowing. It is
only insight into the necessity of such a difference that can rescue
philosophy from the shameful decay in which it is immersed at the
present time. It is true that the forms and rules of the old logic,
of definition, classification, and syllogism, which include the rules
of discursive thinking, have become recognized as inadequate for
speculative science; or rather their inadequacy has not been recognized; it has only been felt, and then these rules have been thrown
off as if they were mere fetters in order to allow the heart, the imagination, and casual intuition to say what they pleased.[3] And since
reflection and connexions of thought have after all to come on the
scene as well, there is an unconscious relapse into the despised
method of commonplace deduction and argumentation.

Since I have fully expounded the nature of speculative knowing
in my *Science of Logic*,[4] in this manual I have only added an explanatory note here and there about procedure and method. In
dealing with a topic which is concrete and intrinsically of so varied
a character, I have omitted to bring out and demonstrate the chain
of logical argument in each and every detail. For one thing, to
have done this might have been regarded as superfluous where
acquaintance with philosophical method is presupposed; for
another, it will be obvious from the work itself that the whole, like
the formation of its parts, rests on the logical spirit. It is also from
this point of view above all that I should like my book to be taken
and judged. What we have to do with here is philosophical *science*,
and in such science content is essentially bound up with form.

We may of course hear from those who seem to be taking a profound view that the form is something external and indifferent to
the subject-matter, that the latter alone is important; further, the
task of a writer, especially a writer on philosophy, may be said to
lie in the discovery of truth, the statement of truth, the dissemination of truth and sound concepts. But if we consider how this task
is as a rule actually discharged, what we find in the first place is
that the same old stew is continually warmed up again and again
and served round to everybody—a task that will even be meritorious
in educating and stimulating men's hearts, though it might preferably be regarded as the superfluous labour of a busybody—'They
have Moses and the Prophets, let them hear them.'[5] In particular,
we have ample opportunity to marvel at the pretentious tone
recognizable in these busybodies when they talk as if the world had

wanted for nothing except their energetic dissemination of truths, or as if their *réchauffé* were productive of new and unheard-of truths and was to be specially taken to heart before everything else 'to-day' and every day. But in this situation we also find one party giving out truths of this sort only to have them dislodged and brushed aside by truths of just the same sort purveyed by other parties. In this press of truths, there is something neither new nor old but perennial; yet how else is this to be lifted out of these reflections which oscillate from this to that without method, how else is it to be separated from them and proved, if not by philosophic science?

After all, the truth about Right, Ethics, and the state is as old as its public recognition and formulation in the law of the land, in the morality of everyday life, and in religion. What more does this truth require—since the thinking mind is not content to possess it in this ready fashion? It requires to be grasped in thought as well; the content which is already rational in principle must win the *form* of rationality and so appear well-founded to untrammelled thinking. Such thinking does not remain stationary at the given, whether the given be upheld by the external positive[6] authority of the state or the *consensus hominum*, or by the authority of inward feeling and emotion and by the 'witness of the spirit' which directly concurs with it. On the contrary, thought which is free starts out from itself and thereupon claims to know itself as united in its innermost being with the truth.

The unsophisticated heart takes the simple line of adhering with trustful conviction to what is publicly accepted as true and then building on this firm foundation its conduct and its set position in life. Against this simple line of conduct there may at once be raised the alleged difficulty of how it is possible, in an infinite variety of opinions, to distinguish and discover what is universally recognized and valid. This perplexity may at first sight be taken for a right and really serious attitude to the thing, but in fact those who boast of this perplexity are in the position of not being able to see the wood for the trees; the only perplexity and difficulty they are in is one of their own making. Indeed, this perplexity and difficulty of theirs is proof rather that they want as the substance of the right and the ethical not what is universally recognized and valid, but something else. If they had been serious with what is universally accepted instead of busying themselves with the vanity and particularity of opinions and things, they would have clung to what is substantively right, namely to the commands of the ethical order and the state, and would have regulated their lives in accordance with these.

A more serious difficulty arises, however, from the fact that man thinks and tries to find in thinking both his freedom and the basis of ethical life. But however lofty, however divine, the right of thought may be, it is perverted into wrong if it is only this [opining] which passes for thinking and if thinking knows itself to be free only when it diverges from what is *universally* recognized and valid and when it has discovered how to invent for itself some *particular* character.

At the present time, the idea that freedom of thought, and of mind generally, evinces itself only in divergence from, indeed in hostility to, what is publicly recognized, might seem to be most firmly rooted in connexion with the state, and it is chiefly for this reason that a philosophy of the state might seem essentially to have the task of discovering and promulgating still another theory, and a special and original one at that. In examining this idea and the activity in conformity with it, we might suppose that no state or constitution had ever existed in the world at all or was even in being at the present time, but that nowadays—and this 'nowadays' lasts for ever—we had to start all over again from the beginning, and that the ethical world had just been waiting for such present-day projects, proofs, and investigations. So far as nature is concerned, people grant that it is nature as it is which philosophy has to bring within its ken, that the philosopher's stone lies concealed somewhere, somewhere within nature itself, that nature is inherently rational, and that what knowledge has to investigate and grasp in concepts is this actual reason present in it; not the formations and accidents evident to the superficial observer, but nature's eternal harmony, its harmony, however, in the sense of the law and essence immanent within it. The ethical world, on the other hand, the state (i.e. reason as it actualizes itself in the element of self-consciousness), is not allowed to enjoy the good fortune which springs from the fact that it is reason which has achieved power and mastery within that element and which maintains itself and has its home there.* The universe of mind is supposed rather to be left to the mercy of chance and caprice, to be God-forsaken, and the result is that if the ethical world is Godless, truth lies outside it, and at the same time, since even so reason is supposed to be in it as well, truth becomes nothing but a problem. But it is this also that is to

---

* [A.] [See Translator's Foreword, § 1.]

authorize, nay to oblige, every thinker to take his own road, though not in search of the philosopher's stone. for he is saved this search by the philosophizing of our contemporaries,[7] and everyone nowadays is assured that he has this stone in his grasp as his birthright. Now admittedly it is the case that those who live their lives in the state as it actually exists here and now and find satisfaction there for their knowledge and volition (and of these there are many, more in fact than think or know it, because ultimately this is the position of everybody), or those at any rate who *consciously* find their satisfaction in the state, laugh at these operations and affirmations and regard them as an empty game, sometimes rather funny, sometimes rather serious, now amusing, now dangerous. Thus this restless activity of empty reflection, together with its popularity and the welcome it has received, would be a thing on its own, developing in privacy in its own way, were it not that it is philosophy itself which has earned all kinds of scorn and discredit by its indulgence in this occupation. The worst of these kinds of scorn is this, that, as I said just now, everyone is convinced that his mere birthright puts him in a position to pass judgement on philosophy in general and to condemn it. No other art or science is subjected to this last degree of scorn, to the supposition that we are masters of it without ado.

In fact, what we have seen recent philosophical publications[8] proclaiming with the maximum of pretension about the state has really justified anybody who cared to busy himself with the subject in this conviction that he could manufacture a philosophy of this kind himself without ado and so give himself proof of his possession of philosophy. Besides, this self-styled 'philosophy' has expressly stated that 'truth itself cannot be known',[9] that that only is true which each individual allows to rise out of his heart, emotion, and inspiration about ethical institutions, especially about the state, the government, and the constitution. In this connexion what a lot of flattery has been talked, especially to the young![10] Certainly the young have listened to it willingly enough. 'He giveth to his own in sleep'[11] has been applied to science and hence every sleeper has numbered himself among the elect, but the concepts he has acquired in sleep are themselves of course only the wares of sleep.

A ringleader[12] of these hosts of superficiality, of these self-styled 'philosophers', Herr Fries,* did not blush, on the occasion of a

---

* I have borne witness before to the superficiality of his philosophy—see *Science of Logic* (Nuremberg, 1812), Introduction, p. xvii [Eng. tr. vol. i, p. 63].

public festival[13] which has become notorious, to express the following ideas in a speech on 'The state and the constitution': 'In the people ruled by a genuine communal spirit, life for the discharge of all public business would come from below, from the people itself; living associations, indissolubly united by the holy chain of friendship, would be dedicated to every single project of popular education and popular service', and so on. This is the quintessence of shallow thinking, to base philosophic science not on the development of thought and the concept but on immediate sense-perception and the play of fancy; to take the rich inward articulation of ethical life, i.e. the state, the architectonic of that life's rationality—which sets determinate limits to the different circles of public life and their rights, uses the strict accuracy of measurement which holds together every pillar, arch, and buttress and thereby produces the strength of the whole out of the harmony of the parts—to take this structure and confound the completed fabric in the broth of 'heart, friendship, and inspiration'. According to a view of this kind, the world of ethics (Epicurus,[14] holding a similar view, would have said the 'world in general') should be given over—as in fact of course it is not—to the subjective accident of opinion and caprice. By the simple family remedy of ascribing to feeling the labour, the more than millenary labour, of reason and its intellect, all the trouble of rational insight and knowledge directed by speculative thinking is of course saved. On this point, Goethe's Mephistopheles, a good authority!, says something like this, a quotation I have used elsewhere[15] already: 'Do but despise intellect and knowledge, the highest of all man's gifts, and thou hast surrendered thyself to the devil and to perdition art doomed.' The next thing is that such sentiments assume even the guise of piety, for this bustling activity has used any and every expedient in its endeavour to give itself authority. With godliness and the Bible, however, it has arrogated to itself the highest of justifications for despising the ethical order and the objectivity of law, since it is piety too which envelops in the simpler intuition of feeling the truth which is articulated in the world into an organic realm. But if it is piety of the right sort, it sheds the form of this emotional region so soon as it leaves the inner life, enters upon the daylight of the Idea's development and revealed riches, and brings with it, out of its inner worship of God, reverence for law and for an absolute truth exalted above the subjective form of feeling.[16]

The particular form of guilty conscience revealed by the type of

eloquence in which such superficiality flaunts itself may be brought
to your attention here and above all if you notice that when it is
furthest from mind, superficiality speaks most of mind, when its
talk is the most tedious dead-and-alive stuff, its favourite words are
'life' and 'vitalize', and when it gives evidence of the pure selfishness of baseless pride, the word most on its lips is 'people'. But the
special mark which it carries on its brow is the hatred of law. Right
and ethics, and the actual world of justice and ethical life, are
understood through thoughts; through thoughts they are invested
with a rational form, i.e. with universality and determinacy. This
form is law; and this it is which the feeling that stipulates for its own
whim, the conscience that places right in subjective conviction, has
reason to regard as its chief foe. The formal character of the right
as a duty and a law it feels as the letter, cold and dead, as a shackle;
for it does not recognize itself in the law and so does not recognize
itself as free there, because law is the reason of the thing, and reason
refuses to allow feeling to warm itself at its own private hearth.
Hence law, as I have remarked somewhere[17] in the course of this
text-book, is *par excellence* the shibboleth which marks out these
false friends and comrades of what they call the 'people'.

At the present time, the pettifoggery of caprice has usurped the
name of philosophy and succeeded in giving a wide public the
opinion that such triflings are philosophy. The result of this is that
it has now become almost a disgrace to go on speaking in philosophical terms about the nature of the state, and law-abiding men
cannot be blamed if they become impatient so soon as they hear
mention of a philosophical science of the state. Still less is it a
matter for surprise that governments have at last directed their
attention to this kind of philosophy, since, apart from anything
else, philosophy with us is not, as it was with the Greeks for instance, pursued in private like an art, but has an existence in the
open, in contact with the public, and especially, or even only, in the
service of the state.[18] Governments have proved their trust in
their scholars who have made philosophy their chosen field by
leaving entirely to them the construction and contents of philosophy—though here and there, if you like, it may not have been so
much confidence that has been shown, as indifference to learning
itself, and professorial chairs of philosophy have been retained only
as a tradition (in France, for instance, to the best of my knowledge,
chairs of metaphysics at least have been allowed to lapse). Their
confidence, however, has very often been ill repaid, or alternatively,

if you preferred to see indifference, you would have to regard the result, the decay of thorough knowledge, as the penalty of this indifference. Prima facie, superficiality seems to be extremely accommodating, one might say, at least in relation to public peace and order, because it fails to touch or even to guess at the substance of the things; no action, or at least no police action,[19] would thus have been taken against it in the first instance, had it not been that there still existed in the state a need for a deeper education and insight, a need which the state required philosophical science to satisfy. On the other hand, superficial thinking about the ethical order, about right and duty in general, starts automatically from the maxims which constitute superficiality in this sphere, i.e. from the principles of the Sophists which are so clearly outlined for our information in Plato.[20] What is right these principles locate in subjective aims and opinions, in subjective feeling and particular conviction, and from them there follows the ruin of the inner ethical life and a good conscience, of love and right dealing between private persons, no less than the ruin of public order and the law of the land. The significance which such phenomena must acquire for governments is not likely to suffer any diminution as a result of the pretentiousness which has used that very grant of confidence and the authority of a professorial chair to support the demand that the state should uphold and give scope to what corrupts the ultimate source of achievement, namely universal principles, and so even to the defiance of the state as if such defiance were what it deserved. 'If God gives a man an office, he also gives him brains' is an old joke which in these days surely no one will take wholly in earnest.

In the fresh importance which circumstances have led governments to attach to the character of philosophical work, there is one element which we cannot fail to notice; this is the protection and support which the study of philosophy now seems to have come to need in several other directions. Think of the numerous publications in the field of the positive sciences,[21] as well as edifying religious works and vague literature of other kinds, which reveal to their readers the contempt for philosophy I have already mentioned, in that, although the thought in them is immature to the last degree and philosophy is entirely alien to them, they treat it as something over and done with. More than this, they expressly rail against it and pronounce its content, namely the speculative knowledge of God, nature, and mind, the knowledge of truth, to be a foolish and even sinful presumptuousness, while reason, and again reason, and reason repeated *ad infinitum* is arraigned, disparaged, and condemned. At the very least such writings reveal to us that, to a majority of those engaged in activities supposedly scientific, the claims of the concept are an embarrassment which none the less they cannot escape. I venture to say that anyone with such phenomena before him may very well begin to think that, if they alone are considered, tradition is now neither worthy of respect nor sufficient to secure for the study of philosophy either tolerance or existence as a public institution.* The arrogant declamations current in our time against philosophy present the singular spectacle, on the one hand of deriving their justification from the superficiality to which that study has been degraded, and, on the other, of being themselves rooted in this element against which they turn so ungratefully. For by pronouncing the knowledge of truth a wild-goose chase, this self-styled philosophizing has reduced all thoughts and all topics to the same level, just as the despotism of the Roman Empire abolished the distinction between free men and slaves, virtue and vice, honour and dishonour, learning and ignorance. The result of this levelling process is that the concepts of what is true, the laws of ethics, likewise become nothing more than opinions and subjective convictions. The maxims of the worst of criminals, since they too are convictions, are put on the same level of value as those laws; and at the same time any object, however sorry, however accidental, any material however insipid, is put on the same level of value as what constitutes the interest of all thinking men and the bonds of the ethical world.

It is therefore to be taken as a piece of *luck* for philosophic science—though in actual fact, as I have said,[23] it is the *necessity* of the thing—that this philosophizing which like an exercise in scholasticism might have continued to spin its web in seclusion, has now been put into closer touch and so into open variance with actuality, in which the principles of rights and duties are a serious matter, and which lives in the light of its consciousness of these.

* I came across a similar view in a letter of Joh. von Müller (*Werke*,[22] Part vii, p. 57). In talking of the state of Rome in 1803 when the city was under French control, he says: 'Asked how the public educational institutions were faring, a professor replied *On les tolère comme les bordels.*' The so-called 'Doctrine of Reason', logic namely, we can indeed still hear recommended, perhaps with the conviction that it is such a dry and profitless science that nobody will busy himself with it, or that if here and there a man does take it up, he will thereby acquire mere empty formulae, unproductive and innocuous, and that therefore in either case the recommendation will do no harm, even if it does no good.

It is just this placing of philosophy in the actual world which
meets with misunderstandings, and so I revert to what I have said
before,[24] namely that, since philosophy is the exploration of the
rational, it is for that very reason the apprehension of the present
and the actual, not the erection of a beyond, supposed to exist, God
knows where, or rather which exists, and we can perfectly well say
where, namely in the error of a one-sided, empty, ratiocination. In
the course of this book,[25] I have remarked that even Plato's *Republic*, which passes proverbially as an empty ideal, is in essence
nothing but an interpretation of the nature of Greek ethical life.
Plato was conscious that there was breaking into that life in his own
time a deeper principle which could appear in it directly only as a
longing still unsatisfied, and so only as something corruptive. To
combat it, he needs must have sought aid from that very longing
itself. But this aid had to come from on High and all that Plato
could do was to seek it in the first place in a particular external form
of that same Greek ethical life. By that means he thought to master
this corruptive invader, and thereby he did fatal injury to the
deeper impulse which underlay it, namely free infinite personality.
Still, his genius is proved by the fact that the principle on which
the distinctive character of his Idea of the state turns is precisely
the pivot on which the impending world revolution turned at that
time.[26]

What is rational is actual and what is actual is rational.[27] On this
conviction the plain man like the philosopher takes his stand, and
from it philosophy starts in its study of the universe of mind as well
as the universe of nature. If reflection, feeling, or whatever form
subjective consciousness may take, looks upon the present as something vacuous and looks beyond it with the eyes of superior wisdom,
it finds itself in a vacuum, and because it is actual only in the
present, it is itself mere vacuity. If on the other hand the Idea
passes for 'only an Idea', for something represented in an opinion,
philosophy rejects such a view and shows that nothing is actual
except the Idea. Once that is granted, the great thing is to apprehend in the show of the temporal and transient the substance which
is immanent and the eternal which is present. For since rationality
(which is synonymous with the Idea) enters upon external existence simultaneously with its actualization,[28] it emerges with an
infinite wealth of forms, shapes, and appearances. Around its heart
it throws a motley covering with which consciousness is at home to
begin with, a covering which the concept has first to penetrate

before it can find the inward pulse and feel it still beating in the out-ward appearances. But the infinite variety of circumstance which is developed in this externality by the light of the essence glinting in it—this endless material and its organization—this is not the subject matter of philosophy. To touch this at all would be to meddle with things to which philosophy is unsuited; on such topics it may save itself the trouble of giving good advice. Plato[29] might have omitted his recommendation to nurses to keep on the move with infants and to rock them continually in their arms. And Fichte[30] too need not have carried what has been called the 'con-struction' of his passport regulations to such a pitch of perfection as to require suspects not merely to sign their passports but to have their likenesses painted on them. Along such tracks all trace of philosophy is lost, and such super-erudition it can the more readily disclaim since its attitude to this infinite multitude of topics should of course be most liberal. In adopting this attitude, philosophic science shows itself to be poles apart from the hatred with which the folly of superior wisdom regards a vast number of affairs and institutions, a hatred in which pettiness takes the greatest delight because only by venting it does it attain a feeling of its self-hood.

This book, then, containing as it does the science of the state, is to be nothing other than the endeavour to apprehend and portray the state as something inherently rational. As a work of philo-sophy, it must be poles apart from an attempt to construct a state as it ought to be. The instruction which it may contain cannot consist in teaching the state what it ought to be; it can only show how the state, the ethical universe, is to be understood.

> Ἰδοὺ Ῥόδος ἰδοὺ καὶ τὸ πήδημα.
> *Hic* Rhodus, *hic* saltus.[31]

To comprehend what is, this is the task of philosophy, because what is, is reason. Whatever happens, every individual is a child of his time; so philosophy too is its own time apprehended in thoughts.[32] It is just as absurd to fancy that a philosophy can transcend its contemporary world as it is to fancy that an individual can overleap his own age, jump over Rhodes. If his theory really goes beyond the world as it is and builds an ideal one as it ought to be, that world exists indeed, but only in his opinions, an unsub-stantial element where anything you please may, in fancy, be built.

With hardly an alteration, the proverb just quoted would run:

> Here is the rose, dance thou here.[33]

What lies between reason as self-conscious mind and reason as an actual world before our eyes, what separates the former from the latter and prevents it from finding satisfaction in the latter, is the fetter of some abstraction or other which has not been liberated [and so transformed] into the concept. To recognize reason as the rose in the cross of the present[34] and thereby to enjoy the present, this is the rational insight which reconciles us to the actual, the reconciliation which philosophy affords to those in whom there has once arisen an inner voice bidding them to comprehend, not only to dwell in what is substantive while still retaining subjective freedom, but also to possess subjective freedom while standing not in anything particular and accidental but in what exists absolutely.[35]

It is this too which constitutes the more concrete meaning of what was described above[36] rather abstractly as the unity of form and content; for form in its most concrete signification is reason as speculative knowing, and content is reason as the substantial essence of actuality, whether ethical or natural. The known identity of these two is the philosophical Idea. It is a sheer obstinacy, the obstinacy which does honour to mankind, to refuse to recognize in conviction anything not ratified by thought. This obstinacy is the characteristic of our epoch, besides being the principle peculiar to Protestantism. What Luther[37] initiated as faith in feeling and in the witness of the spirit, is precisely what spirit, since become more mature, has striven to apprehend in the concept in order to free and so to find itself in the world as it exists to-day. The saying[38] has become famous that 'a half-philosophy leads away from God'—and it is the same half-philosophy that locates knowledge in an 'approximation' to truth[39]—'while true philosophy leads to God'; and the same is true of philosophy and the state. Just as reason is not content with an approximation which, as something 'neither cold nor hot', it will 'spue out of its mouth',[40] so it is just as little content with the cold despair which submits to the view that in this earthly life things are truly bad or at best only tolerable, though here they cannot be improved and that this is the only reflection which can keep us at peace with the world. There is less chill in the peace with the world which knowledge supplies.

One word more about giving instruction as to what the world ought to be. Philosophy in any case always comes on the scene too late to give it. As the thought of the world, it appears only when actuality is already there cut and dried after its process of formation has been completed. The teaching of the concept, which is also history's inescapable lesson, is that it is only when actuality is mature that the ideal first appears over against the real and that the ideal apprehends this same real world in its substance and builds it up for itself into the shape of an intellectual realm. When philosophy paints its grey in grey,[41] then has a shape of life grown old. By philosophy's grey in grey it cannot be rejuvenated but only understood. The owl of Minerva spreads its wings only with the falling of the dusk.

But it is time to close this preface. After all, as a preface, its only business has been to make some external and subjective remarks about the standpoint of the book it introduces. If a topic is to be discussed philosophically, it spurns any but a scientific and objective treatment, and so too if criticisms of the author take any form other than a scientific discussion of the thing itself, they can count only as a personal epilogue and as capricious assertion, and he must treat them with indifference.

BERLIN, *June 25th*, 1820.

INTRODUCTION

[Concept of the Philosophy of Right, of the Will, Freedom, and Right.¹]

1. The subject-matter of the philosophical science of right is the Idea of right, i.e. the concept of right together with the actualization of that concept.

Philosophy has to do with Ideas, and therefore not with what are commonly dubbed 'mere concepts'. On the contrary, it exposes such concepts as one-sided and false, while showing at the same time that it is the concept alone (not the mere abstract category of the understanding which we often hear called by the name) which has actuality, and further that it gives this actuality to itself. All else, apart from this actuality established through the working of the concept itself, is ephemeral existence, external contingency, opinion, unsubstantial appearance, falsity, illusion, and so forth. The shapes which the concept assumes in the course of its actualization are indispensable for the knowledge of the concept itself. They are the second essential moment of the Idea, in distinction from the first, i.e. from its form, from its mode of being as concept alone.² [A.]

2. The science of right is a section of philosophy. Consequently, its task is to develop the Idea—the Idea being the rational factor in any object of study—out of the concept, or, what is the same thing, to look on at the proper immanent development of the thing itself. As a section, it has a definite starting-point, i.e. the result and the truth of what has preceded, and it is what has preceded which constitutes the so-called 'proof' of the starting-point. Hence the concept of right, so far as its coming to be is concerned, falls outside the science of right; it is to be taken up here as given and its deduction is presupposed.³

According to the abstract, non-philosophical, method of the sciences, the first thing sought and demanded is a definition, or at any rate this demand is made for the sake of preserving the external form of scientific procedure. (But the science of positive law at least cannot be very intimately concerned with definitions since it begins in the first place by stating what is legal, i.e. what the particular legal provisions are, and for this reason the warning has been given: *omnis definitio in jure civili periculosa.*⁴ In fact, the more disconnected and inherently contradictory are the provisions giving determinate character to a right, the less are any definitions in its field possible, for definitions should be stated in universal terms, while to use these immediately exposes in all its nakedness what contradicts them—the wrong in this instance. Thus in Roman law, for example, there could be no definition of 'man', since 'slave' could not be brought under it—the very status of slave indeed is an outrage on the conception of man; it would appear just as hazardous to attempt a definition of 'property' and 'proprietor' in many cases.) But the deduction of the definition is derived, it may be, from etymology, or especially by abstraction from particular cases, so that it is based on human feelings and ideas. The correctness of the definition is then made to lie in its correspondence with current ideas. This method neglects what is all-essential for science—i.e. in respect of content, the absolute necessity of the thing (right, in this instance), and, in respect of form, the nature of the concept.

The truth is that in philosophical knowledge the necessity of a concept is the principal thing; and the process of its production as a result is its proof and deduction. Then, once its content has been shown in this way to be necessary on its own account, the second step is to look round for what corresponds to it in our ideas and language. But this concept as it actually is in its truth not only may be different from our common idea of it, but in fact must be different from it in form and outline. If, however, the common idea of it is not false in content also, the concept may be exhibited as implied in it and as essentially present in it. In other words, the common idea may be raised to assume the form of the concept. But the common idea is so far from being the standard or criterion of the concept (which is necessary and true on its own account) that it must rather derive its truth from the latter, adjust itself to it, and recognize its own nature by its aid.

But while the above-mentioned abstract way of knowing with its formal definitions, syllogisms, proofs, and the like, is more or less a thing of the past, still it is a poor substitute which a different artifice has provided, namely to adopt and uphold Ideas in general (and in particular the Idea of right and its further specifications) as immediate 'facts of consciousness'[5] and to make into the source of right our natural or our worked up feelings and the inspirations of our own hearts. This method may be the handiest of all, but it is also the most unphilosophical—not to mention here other aspects of such an outlook, which has a direct bearing on action and not simply on knowledge.[6] While the old method, abstract as it is, does at least insist on the *form* of the concept in its definition and the *form* of necessary knowledge in its demonstration, the artifice of feeling and immediate awareness elevates into a guiding principle the subjectivity, contingency, and arbitrariness of sapience. What constitutes scientific procedure in philosophy is expounded in philosophical logic and is here presupposed.[7] [A.]

3. Right is positive[8] in general (*a*) when it has the *form* of being valid in a particular state, and this legal authority is the guiding principle for the knowledge of right in this positive form, i.e. for the science of positive law. (*b*) Right in this positive form acquires a positive element in its *content*

(α) through the particular national character of a people, its stage of historical development, and the whole complex of relations connected with the necessities of nature;[9]

(β) because a system of positive law must necessarily involve the application of the universal concept to particular, externally given, characteristics of objects and cases.[10] This application lies outside speculative thought and the development of the concept, and is the subsumption by the Understanding [of the particular under the universal];

(γ) through the finally detailed provisions requisite for actually pronouncing judgement in court.[11]

If inclination, caprice, and the sentiments of the heart are set up in opposition to positive right and the laws, philosophy at least cannot recognize authorities of that sort.—That force and tyranny may be an element in law is accidental to law and has nothing to do with its nature. Later on in this book, in Paragraphs 211–14, it will be shown at what point right must become positive. The details to be expounded there are being mentioned here only to indicate the limits of the philosophical study of law and to obviate at once any possible supposition, let alone demand, that the outcome of its systematic development should be a code of positive law, i.e. a code like the one an actual state requires.

Natural law, or law from the philosophical point of view, is distinct from positive law; but to pervert their difference into an opposition and a contradiction would be a gross misunderstanding. The relation between them is much more like that between Institutes and Pandects.[12]

As for the historical element in positive law, mentioned above in Paragraph 3, Montesquieu[13] proclaimed the true historical view, the genuinely philosophical position, namely that legislation both in general and in its particular provisions is to be treated not as something isolated and abstract but rather as a subordinate moment in a whole, interconnected with all the other features which make up the character of a nation and an epoch. It is in being so connected that the various laws acquire their true meaning and therewith their justification. To consider particular laws as they appear and develop in time is a purely historical task. Like acquaintance with what can be logically deduced from a comparison of these laws with previously existing legal principles, this task is appreciated and rewarded in its own sphere and has no relation whatever to the philosophical study of the subject—unless of course the derivation of particular laws from historical events is confused with their derivation from the concept, and the historical explanation and justifica-

tion is stretched to become an absolutely valid justification. This difference, which is very important and should be firmly adhered to, is also
very obvious. A particular law may be shown to be wholly grounded in
and consistent with the circumstances and with existing legally established
institutions, and yet it may be wrong and irrational in its essential
character, like a number of provisions in Roman private law which followed quite logically from such institutions as Roman matrimony and
Roman *patria potestas*.[14] But even if particular laws *are* both right and
reasonable, still it is one thing to *prove* that they have that character—
which cannot be truly done except by means of the concept—and quite
another to describe their appearance in history or the circumstances, contingencies, needs, and events which brought about their enactment.
That kind of exposition and (pragmatic)[15] knowledge, based on proximate or remote historical causes, is frequently called 'explanation' or
preferably 'comprehension'[16] by those who think that to expound
history in this way is the only thing, or rather the essential thing, the
only important thing, to be done in order to comprehend law or an
established institution; whereas what is really essential, the concept of
the thing, they have not discussed at all. From the same point of view,
reference is commonly made[17] also to the Roman or the German 'concepts' of law, i.e. concepts of law as they might be defined in this or that
legal code, whereas what is meant is not concepts but only general legal
principles, propositions of the Understanding, maxims, positive laws,
and the like.

By dint of obscuring the difference between the historical and the
philosophical study of law, it becomes possible to shift the point of view
and slip over from the problem of the true justification of a thing to a
justification by appeal to circumstances, to deductions from presupposed
conditions which in themselves may have no higher validity, and so
forth. To generalize, by this means the relative is put in place of the
absolute and the external appearance in place of the true nature of the
thing. When those who try to justify things on historical grounds confound an origin in external circumstances with one in the concept, they
unconsciously achieve the very opposite of what they intend. Once the
origination of an institution has been shown to be wholly to the purpose
and necessary in the circumstances of the time, the demands of history
have been fulfilled. But if this is supposed to pass for a general justification of the thing itself, it turns out to be the opposite, because, since
those circumstances are no longer present, the institution so far from
being justified has by their disappearance lost its meaning and its right.
Suppose, for example, that we accept as a vindication of the monasteries
their service in cultivating wildernesses and populating them, in keeping
learning alive by transcribing manuscripts and giving instruction, &c.,
and suppose further that this service has been deemed to be the ground
and the purpose of their continued existence, then what really follows

from considering this past service is that, since circumstances have now entirely altered, the monasteries are at least in this respect superfluous and inappropriate.

Now that the historical meaning of coming to be—the historical method of portraying it and making it comprehensible—is at home in a different sphere from the philosophical survey of the concept of the thing and of a thing's coming to be too,[18] philosophy and history are able to that extent to preserve an attitude of mutual indifference. But they are not always at peace in this way, even in scientific circles, and so I quote something, relevant to their contact, which appears in Herr Hugo's *Lehrbuch der Geschichte des römischen Rechts*,[19] and which will at the same time cast further light on the affectation[20] that they are opposed. Herr Hugo says* that 'Cicero praises the Twelve Tables with a side-glance at the philosophers . . . but the philosopher Favorinus treats them exactly as many a great philosopher since his day has treated positive law'. In the same context Herr Hugo makes the final retort to a treatment of the subject like Favorinus' when he gives as the reason for it that 'Favorinus understood the Twelve Tables just as little as these philosophers have understood positive law'.[21]

The correction of the philosopher Favorinus by the jurist Sextus Caecilius in Aulus Gellius† is primarily an expression of the permanent and true principle for justifying what is purely positive in its intrinsic worth. *Non . . . ignoras*, Caecilius happily retorts to Favorinus, *legum opportunitates et medelas pro temporum moribus et pro rerum publicarum generibus, ac pro utilitatum praesentium rationibus, proque vitiorum, quibus medendum est, fervoribus, mutari ac flecti, neque uno statu consistere, quin, ut facies coeli et maris, ita rerum atque fortunae tempestatibus varientur. Quid salubrius visum est rogatione illa Stolonis . . ., quid utilius plebiscito Voconio . . .? Quid tam necessarium existimatum est . . . quam Lex Licinia . . .? Omnia tamen haec obliterata et operta sunt civitatis opulentia.*[22] These laws are positive in so far as they have their meaning and appropriateness in contemporary conditions, and therefore their sole value is historical and they are of a transitory nature. The wisdom of what legislators and administrators did in their day or settled to meet the needs of the hour is a separate matter and one properly to be assessed by history. History's recognition of it will be all the deeper the more its assessment is supported by a philosophical outlook.

Of Caecilius's further arguments in justification of the Twelve Tables against Favorinus, however, I will give an example, because he introduces in them the eternally deceptive method and argumentation of the Understanding, I mean the production of a good reason for a bad thing and the supposition that the bad thing has thereby been justified. Caecilius is discussing the horrible law that gave a creditor the right after a fixed period of time to kill his debtor or sell him into slavery, or, if there

---

* 5th edn., § 53.   † *Noctes Atticae*, xx. 1.

were several creditors, to cut pieces off their debtor and divide him up amongst themselves; and there was even a further proviso that if one of them cut off too much or too little, no action was for that reason to lie against him—a clause which would have benefited Shakespeare's Shylock in the *Merchant of Venice* and of which he would most gratefully have availed himself. For this law Caecilius adduces the good reason that it rendered trust and credit all the more secure and that because of its horrible character there was never to have been any question of its application. In his thoughtlessness not only does the reflection escape him that if the law could never have been applied, then the aim of securing trust and credit by it was frustrated, but he even goes on directly afterwards to give an example of how the law concerning false witness was made ineffective owing to its immoderate penalties.

There is no knowing, however, what Herr Hugo means when he says that Favorinus did not understand the law. Any schoolboy is perfectly capable of understanding it, and Shylock would have understood better than anyone else the clause, cited above, which would have been so advantageous to him. By 'understand' Herr Hugo must have meant only that level of understanding which in the case of such a law is content if it can find a good reason for it.

Still, another misunderstanding of which Favorinus was convicted by Caecilius in the same context is one to which a philosopher may surely confess without exactly blushing; I mean the failure to understand that *jumentum* (which 'as distinct from *arcera*' is, according to the law, the only conveyance to be provided for a sick man who has to appear in court) is to be interpreted to mean not only a horse but also a carriage or wagon. From this legal proviso Caecilius was able to derive a further proof of the excellence and precision of the old laws by pointing out that, in fixing the terms of a summons to a sick man to appear in court, they even carried precision so far as to distinguish not only between a horse and a wagon, but even between one wagon and another, between one covered in and 'upholstered',[23] according to Caecilius' interpretation, and one not so comfortable. Here we would have the choice between the severity of the original law and the triviality of such distinctions, but to describe such things, and still more their learned interpretation, as 'trivial' would be one of the worst of insults to erudition of this kind and others!

But in the same *Lehrbuch* Herr Hugo goes on to speak of rationality in connexion with Roman law, and what has struck me in his remarks is the following. In his treatment of the 'period from the origin of the state to the Twelve Tables' he says* that (in Rome) 'men had many wants and were compelled to work and hence needed the assistance of draught and pack animals, such as we are familiar with ourselves; that in Roman territory hills and valleys alternated and that the city was built on a hill'

* §§ 38–9 [ibid. in 7th edn.].

and so forth—disquisitions which were perhaps intended to carry out Montesquieu's ideas, but in which one will hardly find that his spirit has been caught. Then he goes on to say* that 'the legal position was still very far from satisfying the highest demands of reason'. That is quite right, Roman law in respect of the family, slavery, &c., fails even to satisfy reason's most modest demands. But in dealing with later periods of Roman history, Herr Hugo forgets to tell us whether in any of them, and if so in which, Roman law did 'satisfy the highest demands of reason'. However, of the classical jurists in the period of the 'highest maturity of Roman law as a science', Herr Hugo writes:† 'It has long since been observed that the classical jurists were educated through philosophy', yet 'few know' (though more know now, thanks to the numerous editions of Herr Hugo's *Lehrbuch*) 'that no class of writers is so well entitled as these same Roman jurists to be compared with mathematicians in respect of the rigorous logic of their deductive reasoning or with the new founder of metaphysics in respect of their quite strikingly distinctive method of developing their concepts—a contention supported by the curious fact that nowhere are there to be found so many trichotomies as there are in the classical jurists and in Kant'. Logical deduction, a method commended by Leibniz,[24] is certainly an essential characteristic of the study of positive law, as of mathematics and any other science of the Understanding, but this deductive method of the Understanding has nothing whatever to do with the satisfaction of the demands of reason or with philosophical science. But apart from that it is the *il*logicality of the Roman jurists and praetors that must be regarded as one of their chief virtues, for by dint of being illogical they evaded unjust and detestable laws, though in the process they found themselves compelled *callide*[25] to devise empty verbal distinctions (e.g. to call *bonorum possessio* what was nevertheless *hereditas*) and downright foolish subterfuges (and folly also is illogicality) in order to preserve the letter of the Twelve Tables (e.g. by the *fictio*, ὑπόκρισις, that a *filia*[26] was a *filius*).‡ It is ludicrous though to see the classical jurists compared with Kant because of a few trichotomous divisions, especially those cited as examples[27] in the fifth note to Herr Hugo's paragraph, and to see that kind of thing called 'development of concepts'.

4. The basis of right is, in general, mind; its precise place and point of origin is the will. The will is free, so that freedom is both the substance of right and its goal, while the system of right is the realm of freedom made actual, the world of mind brought forth out of itself like a second nature.[28]

---

* § 40 [ibid. in 7th edn.]. † § 289 [§ 314 in 7th edn.].

‡ J. G. Heineccius: *Antiquitatum Romanarum jurisprudentiam illustrantium Syntagma* [Basel, 1752], lib. i, tit. ii, § 24.

In considering the freedom of the will, we may recall the old method of cognition. The procedure was to presuppose the idea of the will and to attempt to establish a definition of the will by deriving it from that idea; then the so-called 'proof' of the will's freedom was extracted, in the manner of the old empirical psychology, from the various feelings and phenomena of the ordinary consciousness, such as remorse, guilt, and the like, by maintaining that they were to be explained only in the light of a will that was free. But it is more convenient of course to arrive at the same point by taking the short cut of supposing that freedom is given as a 'fact of consciousness' and that we must simply *believe* in it!

The proof that the will is free and the proof of the nature of the will and freedom can be established (as has already been pointed out in Paragraph 2) only as a link in the whole chain [of philosophy]. The fundamental premisses of this proof are that mind to start with is intelligence, that the phases through which it passes in its development from feeling, through representative thinking, to thinking proper, are the road along which it produces itself as will, and that will, as practical mind in general, is the truth of intelligence, the stage next above it. These premisses I have expounded in my *Encyclopaedia of the Philosophical Sciences** and I hope by and by to be able to elaborate them still further.[29] There is all the more need for me by so doing to make my contribution to what I hope is the deeper knowledge of the nature of mind in that, as I have said in the *Encyclopaedia*,† scarcely any philosophical science is so neglected and so ill off as the theory of mind, usually called 'psychology'. The moments in the concept of the will which are dealt with in this and the following Paragraphs of the Introduction result from the premisses to which I have just referred, but in addition anyone may find help towards forming an idea of them by calling on his own self-consciousness. In the first place, anyone can discover in himself ability to abstract from everything whatever, and in the same way to determine himself, to posit any content in himself by his own effort; and similarly the other specific characteristics of the will are exemplified for him in his own consciousness. [A.]

5. The will contains (α) the element of pure indeterminacy or that pure reflection of the ego into itself which involves the dissipation of every restriction and every content either immediately presented by nature, by needs, desires, and impulses, or given and determined by any means whatever. This is the unrestricted infinity of absolute abstraction or universality, the pure thought of oneself.

Those who regard thinking as one special faculty, distinct from the will as another special faculty, and who even proceed to contend that

---

* Heidelberg, 1817, §§ 363–99 [3rd edn. §§ 440–82].
† [1st edn.] Remark to § 367 [3rd edn. § 444 and cf. § 378].

thinking is prejudicial to the will, especially the good will, reveal at the very outset their complete ignorance of the nature of the will—a remark we shall have to make rather often when dealing with this same subject.

In Paragraph 5, it is only one side of the will which is described, namely this unrestricted possibility of abstraction from every determinate state of mind which I may find in myself or which I may have set up in myself, my flight from every content as from a restriction. When the will's self-determination consists in this alone, or when representative thinking regards this side by itself as freedom and clings fast to it, then we have negative freedom, or freedom as the Understanding conceives it. This is the freedom of the void which rises to a passion and takes shape in the world; while still remaining theoretical, it takes shape in religion as the Hindu fanaticism of pure contemplation, but when it turns to actual practice, it takes shape in religion and politics alike as the fanaticism of destruction—the destruction of the whole subsisting social order—as the elimination of individuals who are objects of suspicion to any social order, and the annihilation of any organization which tries to rise anew from the ruins.[30] Only in destroying something does this negative will possess the feeling of itself as existent. Of course it imagines that it is willing some positive state of affairs, such as universal equality or universal religious life, but in fact it does not will that this shall be positively actualized, and for this reason: such actuality leads at once to some sort of order, to a particularization of organizations and individuals alike; while it is precisely out of the annihilation of particularity and objective characterization that the self-consciousness of this negative freedom proceeds. Consequently, what negative freedom intends to will can never be anything in itself but an abstract idea, and giving effect to this idea can only be the fury of destruction. [A.]

6. (β) At the same time, the ego is also the transition from undifferentiated indeterminacy to the differentiation, determination, and positing of a determinacy as a content and object. Now further, this content may either be given by nature or engendered by the concept of mind. Through this positing of itself as something determinate, the ego steps in principle into determinate existence. This is the absolute moment,[31] the finitude or particularization of the ego.

This second moment—determination—is negativity and cancellation like the first, i.e. it cancels the abstract negativity of the first. Since it is the general rule that the particular is contained in the universal, it follows that this second moment is already contained in the first and is simply an explicit positing of what the first already was implicitly. The first moment, I mean—because by itself it is only the first—is not true infinity or concrete universality, not the concept, but only something determinate, one-sided; i.e., being abstraction from all determinacy, it is itself not without determinacy; and to be something abstract and one-sided constitutes its determinacy, its defectiveness, and its finitude.

The determination and differentiation of the two moments which have been mentioned is to be found in the philosophies of Fichte, Kant, and others; only, in Fichte—to confine ourselves to his exposition—the ego, as that which is without limitation, is taken (in the first proposition[32] of his *Science of Knowledge*) purely and simply as something positive and so as the universality and identity of the Understanding. The result is that this abstract ego by itself is supposed to be the whole truth, and therefore the restriction—the negative in general, whether as a given external barrier or as an activity of the ego itself—appears (in the second proposition)[33] as an addition merely.

To apprehend the negativity immanent in the universal or self-identical, e.g. in the ego, was the next step which speculative philosophy had to take—a step of whose necessity they have no inkling who hold to the dualism of infinite and finite and do not even grasp it in that immanence and abstraction in which Fichte did.[34] [A.]

7. (γ) The will is the unity of both these moments. It is particularity reflected into itself and so brought back to universality, i.e. it is individuality. It is the *self*-determination of the ego, which means that at one and the same time the ego posits itself as its own negative, i.e. as restricted and determinate, and yet remains by itself, i.e. in its self-identity and universality. It determines itself and yet at the same time binds itself together with itself. The ego determines itself in so far as it is the relating of negativity to itself.[35] As this self-relation, it is indifferent to this determinacy; it knows it as something which is its own, something which is only ideal,[36] a mere possibility by which it is not constrained and in which it is confined only because it has put itself in it.—This is the freedom of the will and it constitutes the concept or substantiality of the will, its weight, so to speak, just as weight constitutes the substantiality of a body.

Every self-consciousness knows itself (i) as universal, as the potentiality of abstracting from everything determinate, and (ii) as particular, with a determinate object, content, and aim. Still, both these moments are only abstractions; what is concrete and true (and everything true is concrete) is the universality which has the particular as its opposite, but the particular which by its reflection into itself has been equalized with the universal. This unity is individuality, not individuality in its immediacy as a unit, our first idea of individuality, but individuality in accordance with its concept;* indeed, individuality in this sense is just precisely the

* *Enc.*, [1st edn.] §§ 112–14 [3rd edn. §§ 163–5].

concept itself. The first two moments—(i) that the will can abstract from everything, and (ii) that it is also determined in some specific way either by itself or by something else—are readily admitted and grasped because, taken independently, they are false and moments of the Understanding. But the third moment, which is true and speculative (and everything true must be thought speculatively if it is to be comprehended) is the one into which the Understanding declines to advance, for it is precisely the concept which it persists in calling the inconceivable. It is the task of logic as purely speculative philosophy to prove and explain further this innermost secret of speculation, of infinity as negativity relating itself to itself, this ultimate spring of all activity, life, and consciousness. Here attention can only be drawn to the fact that if you say 'the will is universal, the will determines itself', the words you use to describe the will presuppose it to be a subject or substratum from the start.[37] But the will is not something complete and universal prior to its determining itself and prior to its superseding and idealizing this determination. The will is not a will until it is this self-mediating activity, this return into itself. [A.]

8. The more detailed process of particularization (see Paragraph 6) constitutes the difference between the forms of the will: (*a*) If the will's determinate character lies in the abstract opposition of its subjectivity to the objectivity of external immediate existence, then this is the formal will of mere self-consciousness which finds an external world confronting it. As individuality returning in its determinacy into itself, it is the process of translating the subjective purpose into objectivity through the use of its own activity and some external means. Once mind has developed its potentialities to actuality (*wie er an und für sich ist*), its determinate character is true and simply its own.* At that stage, the relation of consciousness constitutes only the *appearance* of the will,[38] an aspect which is not separately considered any further here. [A.]

9. (*b*) In so far as the specific determinations of the will are its own or, in general, its particularization reflected into itself, they are its content. This content, as content of the will, is, in accordance with the form of will described in (*a*), its purpose,[39] either its inward or subjective purpose when the will merely images its object, or else its purpose actualized and achieved by means of its activity of translating its subjective purpose into objectivity.

10. This content, or the will's determination on something specific, is in the first place immediate. Consequently the will is

---

* *Enc.*, [1st edn.] § 363 [3rd edn. § 440].

then free only *in* itself or *for* an external observer, or, to speak generally, it is the will in its concept. It is not until it has itself as its object[40] that the will is for *itself* what it is in itself.[41]

Finitude consists therefore in this, that what something is *in* itself or in accordance with its concept is one phenomenon or exists in one way, while what it is *for* itself is a different phenomenon or exists in another way; so, for example, *in* itself the abstract reciprocal externality characteristic of nature is space, but *for* itself it is time.[42] In this connexion, two things are to be noticed: (i) The true is the Idea and the Idea alone, and hence if you take an object or a category only as it is in itself or in its concept, you have not yet grasped it in its truth. (ii) A thing which is in itself or as concept is also existent in some way and its existence in such a way is a shape proper to the thing itself (as space is in the example just given). The gulf present in the sphere of the finite between 'in-itself-ness' and 'for-itself-ness' constitutes at the same time that sphere's mere existential or phenomenal character. (Examples of this—the natural will and then formal rights, &c.—will be forthcoming directly.)[43]

The Understanding goes no further than the purely implicit character of a thing and consequently calls the freedom which accords with this implicit character a 'potency', because if freedom is only implicit it is indeed mere potentiality. But the Understanding looks upon this implicit character as absolute and perennial; and it takes the relation of freedom to what it wills, or in general to the object in which it is realized, as merely a matter of its application to a given material, not belonging to the essence of freedom itself. Thus it has to do with the abstract only, not with its Idea and its truth. [A.]

11. The will which is but implicitly free is the immediate or natural will. The specific characteristics of the difference which the self-determining concept[44] sets up within the will appear in the natural will as an immediately existing content, i.e. as the impulses, desires, inclinations, whereby the will finds itself determined in the course of nature. This content, together with the specific differences developed within it, arises from the rationality of the will and so is implicitly rational; but, poured out in this way into the mould of immediacy, it still lacks the form of rationality. It is true that this content has for me the general character of being mine; but this form is still different from the content, and hence the will is still a will finite in character.

Empirical psychology details and describes these impulses and inclinations, and the needs arising from them, as it finds them, or presumes it finds them, in experience, and it proceeds in the usual way to classify this given material. Consideration is given below[45] to the objective element in these impulses, both to its true character stripped of the form of irrationality which it possesses as impulse and also to the manner in which at the same time it is shaped externally. [A.]

12. The whole of this content, as we light upon it in its immediacy in the will, is there only as a medley and multiplicity of impulses, each of which is merely 'my desire' but exists alongside other desires which are likewise all 'mine', and each of which is at the same time something universal and indeterminate, aimed at all kinds of objects and satiable in all kinds of ways. When, in this twofold indeterminacy,[46] the will gives itself the form of individuality (see Paragraph 7), this constitutes the resolution of the will, and it is only in so far as it resolves that the will is an actual will at all.

To resolve on something is to cancel the state of indeterminacy in which one content is prima facie just as much of a possibility as any other. As an alternative to *etwas beschliessen* (to resolve on something) the German language also contains the expression *sich entschliessen*.[47] This expresses the fact that the indeterminate character of the will itself, as itself neutral yet infinitely prolific, the original seed of all determinate existence, contains its determinations and aims within itself and simply brings them forth out of itself.

13. By resolving, the will posits itself as the will of a specific individual and as a will separating itself off against another individual. But apart from this finitude as consciousness (see Paragraph 8), the immediate will is on account of the difference between its form and its content (see Paragraph 11) a will only in form. The decision which belongs to it as such is only abstract and its content is not yet the content and product of its freedom.

In so far as intelligence thinks,[48] its object and content remains something universal, while its own behaviour consists of a universal activity. In the will, 'the universal' also means in essence 'mine', 'individuality'; and in the immediate will—the will which is will in form only —it means abstract individuality, individuality not yet filled with its free universality. Hence it is in the will that the intrinsic finitude of intelligence has its beginning; and it is only by raising itself to become thought again,[49] and endowing its aims with immanent universality, that the will cancels the difference of form and content and makes itself the objective, infinite, will. Thus they[50] understand little of the nature of thinking and willing who suppose that while, in willing as such, man is infinite, in thinking, he, or even reason itself, is restricted. In so far as thinking and willing are still distinguished, the opposite is rather the truth, and will is thinking reason resolving itself to finitude. [A.]

14. The finite will as, in respect of its form, though only its form, the self-reflecting, independent, and infinite ego (see Paragraph 5), stands over its content, i.e. its various impulses, and also over the further separate ways in which these are actualized and satisfied. At the same time, since it is infinite in form only, it is tied to this content (see Paragraphs 6 and 11) as to the specific determinations of its nature and its external actuality; though since it is indeterminate, it is not tied to this or that specific content. From the point of view of the ego reflected into itself, this content is only a possible one, i.e. it may be mine or it may not; and the ego similarly is the possibility of determining myself to this or to something else, of *choosing* between these specific determinations, which at this point I regard as external to me.

15. At this stage, the freedom of the will is arbitrariness (*Willkür*) and this involves two factors: (*a*) free reflection, abstracting from everything, and (*b*) dependence on a content and material given either from within or from without. Because this content, implicitly necessary as purpose,[51] is at the same time qualified in the face of free reflection as possible, it follows that arbitrariness is contingency manifesting itself as will.[52]

The idea which people most commonly have of freedom is that it is arbitrariness—the mean, chosen by abstract reflection, between the will wholly determined by natural impulses, and the will free absolutely. If we hear it said that the definition of freedom is ability to do what we please, such an idea can only be taken to reveal an utter immaturity of thought, for it contains not even an inkling of the absolutely free will, of right, ethical life, and so forth. Reflection, the formal universality and unity of self-consciousness, is the will's abstract certainty of its freedom, but it is not yet the truth of freedom, because it has not yet got *itself* as its content and aim, and consequently the subjective side is still other than the objective; the content of this self-determination, therefore, also remains purely and simply finite. Instead of being the will in its truth, arbitrariness is more like the will as contradiction.

In the controversy carried on especially at the time of Wolff's metaphysic[53] as to whether the will were really free or whether the conviction of its freedom were only a delusion, it was arbitrariness which was in view. In opposition to the certitude of this abstract self-determination, determinism has rightly pointed to the content which, as something met with, is not contained in that certitude and so comes to it from outside, although 'outside' in this case means impulses, ideas, or, in general, consciousness so filled in one way or another that its content is not intrinsic to its self-determining activity as such. Since, then, arbitrariness has

immanent in it only the formal element in willing, i.e. free self-determination, while the other element is something given to it, we may
readily allow that, if it is arbitrariness which is supposed to be freedom,
it may indeed be called an illusion. In every philosophy of reflection,
like Kant's, and Kant's deprived of all its depth by Fries, freedom is
nothing else but this empty self-activity. [A.]

16. What the will has decided to choose (see Paragraph 14) it
can equally easily renounce (see Paragraph 5). But its ability to go
beyond any other choice which it may substitute, and so on *ad
infinitum*, never enables it to get beyond its own finitude, because
the content of every such choice is something other than the form
of the will and therefore something finite, while the opposite of
determinacy, namely indeterminacy, i.e. indecision or abstraction
from any content, is only the other, equally one-sided, moment of
the will.[54]

17. The contradiction which the arbitrary will is (see Paragraph
15), comes into appearance as a dialectic of impulses and inclinations; each of them is in the way of every other—the satisfaction of
one is unavoidably subordinated or sacrificed to the satisfaction of
another, and so on. An impulse is simply a uni-directional urge
and thus has no measuring-rod in itself, and so this determination
of its subordination or sacrifice is the contingent decision of the
arbitrary will which, in deciding, may proceed either by using intelligence to calculate which impulse will give most satisfaction, or
else in accordance with any other optional consideration.   [A.]

18. In connexion with the *judgement* of impulses, this dialectic
appears in the following form: (*a*) As immanent and so positive,
the determinations of the immediate will are good; thus man is
said to be by nature good. (*b*) But, in so far as these determinations
are natural and thus are in general opposed to freedom and the
concept of mind, and hence negative, they must be uprooted, and
so man is said to be by nature evil.—At this point a decision in
favour of either thesis depends equally on subjective arbitrariness.
[A.]

19. In the demand for the *purification*[55] of impulses there lies
the general notion that they should be freed both from their form
as immediate and natural determinations, and also from the subjectivity and contingency of their content, and so brought back to
their substantial essence. The truth behind this vague demand is

that the impulses should become the rational system of the will's volitions. To grasp them like that, proceeding out of the concept of the will, is the content of the philosophical science of right.

The content of this science through every single one of its moments, e.g. right, property, morality, family, state, and so forth, may be expounded in the form: man has by nature the impulse towards right, also the impulse to property and morality, also the impulse of love between the sexes, the impulse to sociability, &c. This form is to be found in empirical psychology. But if in its stead the greater dignity of a philosophical dress is desired, then according to what, as was remarked before,[56] has passed in recent times, and still passes, for philosophy, this dress may be had cheap by the simple device of saying that man discovers within himself as a 'fact of his consciousness' that right, property, the state, &c., are objects of his volition. Later in the text,[57] this same subject-matter, which appears here in the shape of impulses, will come on the scene in another form, i.e. in the shape of duties.

20. When reflection is brought to bear on impulses, they are imaged, estimated, compared with one another, with their means of satisfaction and their consequences, &c., and with a sum of satisfaction (i.e. with happiness). In this way reflection invests this material with abstract universality and in this external manner purifies it from its crudity and barbarity. This growth of the universality of thought is the absolute value in education[58] (compare Paragraph 187). [A.]

21. The truth, however, of this abstract universality, which is indeterminate in itself and finds its determinacy in the material mentioned in Paragraph 20, is self-determining universality, the will, freedom. In having universality, or itself *qua* infinite form,[59] for its object, content, and aim, the will is free not only *in* itself but *for* itself also; it is the Idea in its truth.

(i) When the will's self-consciousness takes the form of desire and impulse, this consciousness is sense-consciousness, just as sensation in general denotes externality and therefore the condition in which self-consciousness is self-external.[60] (ii) When the will is reflective, it contains two elements—this sense-consciousness and the universality of thought. (iii) When the will's potentialities have become fully explicit, then it has for its object the will itself as such, and so the will in its sheer universality—a universality which is what it is simply because it has absorbed in itself the immediacy of instinctive desire and the particularity which is produced by reflection and with which such desire *eo ipso* becomes imbued. But this process of absorption in or elevation to universality is what is called the activity of thought. The self-consciousness which purifies its object, content, and aim, and raises them to this universality effects this as thinking getting its own way in the will. Here is the point at which it becomes clear that it is only as thinking intelligence that the will is genuinely a will and free. The slave does not know his essence, his infinity, his freedom; he does not know himself as human in essence;[61] and he lacks this knowledge of himself because he does not think himself. This self-consciousness which apprehends itself through thinking as essentially human, and thereby frees itself from the contingent and the false, is the principle of right, morality, and all ethical life. Philosophic utterances about right, morality, and ethical life from those who would banish thought and have recourse instead to feeling, enthusiasm, the heart and the breast, are expressive of the utterly contemptible position into which thought and philosophic science have fallen, because what this amounts to is that even philosophic science itself, plunged in self-despair and extreme exhaustion, is taking as its principle barbarity and absence of thought, and would do its best to rob mankind of all truth, worth, and dignity. [A.]

22. It is the will whose potentialities have become fully explicit which is truly infinite, because its object is itself and so is not in its eyes an 'other' or a barrier; on the contrary, in its object this will has simply turned backward into itself. Further this will is not mere potentiality, capacity, potency (*potentia*), but the infinite in actuality (*infinitum actu*), since the concept's existence or its objective externality is inwardness itself.[62]

Thus, if anyone speaks simply of the 'free will' as such, without specifically referring to the will which is free absolutely, he is speaking only of the capacity for freedom, or of the natural and finite will (see Paragraph 11), and not by any means therefore of the free will, despite his intention and the words he uses.

Since the Understanding takes the infinite only as something negative and so as something 'beyond', it supposes that it is doing all the more honour to the infinite, the more it pushes it into the distance away from itself and removes it from itself as something alien. In the free will, the truly infinite becomes actual and present; the free will itself is this Idea whose nature it is to be present here and now. [A.]

23. Only in freedom of this kind is the will by itself without qualification, because then it is related to nothing except itself and so is released from every tie of dependence on anything else. The will is then true, or rather truth itself, because its self-determination consists in a correspondence between what it is in its existence (i.e. what it is as objective to itself) and its concept; or in other words, the pure concept of the will has the intuition of itself for its goal and its reality.

24. The will is then universal, because all restriction and all particular individuality have been absorbed within it. These lie only in the difference between the concept and its content or object, or, to put it otherwise, in the difference between its implicit character and its subjective awareness of itself, or between its universality and its exclusive individuality, the individuality which resolves.

The various types of universality develop in logic.* In connexion with this word 'universality', what strikes representative thinking first is the idea of abstract and external universality; but in connexion with absolute universality—and the universality here in question is of this character—we have to think neither of the universality of reflection, i.e. 'all-ness' or the universal as a common characteristic, nor of the abstract universality which stands outside and over against the individual, the abstract identity of the Understanding (see Remark to Paragraph 6). It is the universality concrete in character and so explicitly universal which is the substance of self-consciousness, its immanent generic essence, or its immanent Idea. This—the concept of the free will—is the universal which overlaps its object, penetrates its particular determination through and through and therein remains identical with itself.[63] The absolutely universal is definable as what is called the 'rational', and it can be apprehended only in this speculative way.

25. The subjective, in relation to the will in general, means the will's self-conscious side, its individuality (see Paragraph 7) in distinction from its implicit concept. The subjectivity of the will means therefore

(α) the pure form of the will, the absolute unity of self-consciousness with itself (a unity in which self-consciousness, as $I = I$, is purely and simply inward and abstractly self-dependent), the pure certainty, as distinguished from the truth, of individuality;

(β) the particular will as the arbitrary will and the contingent content of optional aims;

(γ) in general, the one-sided form of the will (see Paragraph 8) for which the thing willed, whatever its content, is but a content belonging to self-consciousness and an aim unfulfilled.

26. (α) The will is purely and simply objective in so far as it has itself for its determination and so is in correspondence with its concept and genuinely a will;

* *Enc.*, [1st edn.] §§ 118–26 [3rd edn. §§ 169–78].

(β) but the objective will, being without the infinite form of self-consciousness, is the will absorbed in its object or condition, whatever the content of these may be; it is the will of the child, the ethical will,[64] also the will of the slave, the superstitious man, &c.;

(γ) objectivity, finally, is the one-sided form opposed to the subjective volition, and hence it is the immediacy of existence as external reality; the will first becomes objective to itself in this sense through the fulfilment of its aims.

These logical categories—subjectivity and objectivity—have been set forth in detail here primarily with a view to pointing out expressly in relation to them, since they are often used in the sequel, that they, like other distinctions and opposed categories of reflection, pass over into their opposites as a result of their finitude and their dialectical character. In other cases of opposition between two categories, each opposite retains a hard and fast meaning for representative thinking and the Understanding, because the identity of the opposites is still only something inward. In the will, on the other hand, these opposed aspects are supposed to be at one and the same time abstractions and yet determinations of the *will*, which can be known only as something concrete, and they lead automatically to their identity and to the confusion of their meanings—a confusion into which the Understanding slips quite unconsciously. Thus, for example, the will as inward freedom is subjectivity itself; subjectivity therefore is the concept of the will and so its objectivity. But it is its subjectivity, contrasted with objectivity, which is finitude, and yet, because of this very contrast, the will is not by itself but is entangled with its object, and so its finitude consists quite as much in the fact that it is not subjective—and so on. Hence the meaning to be attributed in what follows to 'subjective' or 'objective' in respect of the will must each time appear from the context, which supplies the data for inferring their position in relation to the will as a whole. [A.]

27. The absolute goal, or, if you like, the absolute impulse, of free mind (see Paragraph 21) is to make its freedom its object, i.e. to make freedom objective as much in the sense that freedom shall be the rational system of mind, as in the sense that this system shall be the world of immediate actuality (see Paragraph 26). In making freedom its object, mind's purpose is to be explicitly, as Idea, what the will is implicitly. The definition of the concept of the will in abstraction from the Idea of the will is 'the free will which wills the free will'.[65]

28. The will's activity consists in annulling the contradiction between subjectivity and objectivity and giving its aims an objective instead of a subjective character, while at the same time remaining by itself even in objectivity. Outside the formal mode of willing (i.e. consciousness, see Paragraph 8) where objectivity is present only as immediate actuality, this activity is in essence the development of the substantive content of the Idea (see Paragraph 21)—a development through which the concept determines the Idea, itself at first abstract, until it becomes a systematized whole. This whole, as what is substantive, is independent of the opposition between a merely subjective aim and its realization and is the same in both despite their difference in form.

29. An existent of any sort embodying the free will, this is what right is. Right therefore is by definition freedom as Idea.

The crucial point in both the Kantian and the generally accepted definition of right (see the Introduction to Kant's *Philosophy of Law*)[66] is the '*restriction* which makes it possible for my freedom or self-will to co-exist with the self-will of each and all according to a universal law'. On the one hand, this definition contains only a negative category, restriction, while on the other hand the positive factor—the universal law or the so-called 'law of reason', the correspondence of the self-will of one individual with that of another—is tantamount to the principle of contradiction and the familiar notion of abstract identity. The definition of right which I have quoted involves that way of looking at the matter, especially popular since Rousseau,[67] according to which what is fundamental, substantive, and primary is supposed to be the will of a single person in his own private self-will, not the absolute or rational will, and mind as a particular individual, not mind as it is in its truth. Once this principle is adopted, of course the rational can come on the scene only as a restriction on the type of freedom which this principle involves, and so also not as something immanently rational but only as an external abstract universal. This view is devoid of any speculative thinking and is repudiated by the philosophic concept. And the phenomena which it has produced both in men's heads and in the world[68] are of a frightfulness parallel only to the superficiality of the thoughts on which they are based.

30. It is only because right is the embodiment of the absolute concept or of self-conscious freedom that it is something sacrosanct. But the exclusively formal character of right (and duty also, as we shall see)[69] arises at a distinct stage in the development of the concept of freedom. By contrast with the right which is comparatively formal (i.e. abstract) and so comparatively restricted, a higher right belongs to the sphere and stage of mind in which mind has determined and actualized within itself the further moments contained in its Idea;[70] and it belongs to this sphere as the sphere which is concreter, intrinsically richer, and more genuinely universal.

Every stage in the development of the Idea of freedom has its own special right, since it is the embodiment of freedom in one of its proper specific forms. When there is said to be a clash between the moral or the ethical and the right, the right in question is only the elementary, formal, right of abstract personality. Morality, ethical life, the interest of the state, each of these is a right of a special character because each of them is a specific form and embodiment of freedom. They can come into collision with each other only in so far as they are all on the same footing as rights. If mind's moral attitude were not also a right, or freedom in one of its forms, it could not possibly come into collision with the right of personality or with any other right, because any right whatever has inherent in it the concept of freedom, i.e. the highest category of mind, in contrast with which any other thing is without substance. Yet at the same time collision involves another moment, namely the fact that it is restrictive, and so if two rights collide one is subordinated to the other. It is only the right of the world-mind which is absolute without qualification.

31. The method whereby, in philosophic science, the concept develops itself out of itself is expounded in logic and is here likewise presupposed.[71] Its development is a purely immanent progress, the engendering of its determinations. Its advance is not effected by the assertion that various things exist and then by the application of the universal to extraneous material of that sort culled from elsewhere.

The concept's moving principle, which alike engenders and dissolves the particularizations of the universal, I call 'dialectic', though I do not mean that dialectic which takes an object, proposition, &c., given to feeling or, in general, to immediate consciousness, and explains it away, confuses it, pursues it this way and that, and has as its sole task the deduction of the contrary of that with which it starts—a negative type of dialectic commonly appearing even in Plato. Dialectic of this kind may regard as its final result either the contrary of the idea with which it begins, or, if it is as incisive as the scepticism of the ancients, the contradictory of this idea, or again, it may be feeble enough to be content with an 'approximation' to the truth, a modern half-measure.[72] The loftier dialectic of the concept consists not simply in producing the determination as a contrary and a restriction, but in producing and seizing upon the positive content and outcome of the determination, because it is this which makes it solely a development and an immanent progress. Moreover, this dialectic is not an activity of subjective thinking applied to some matter externally, but is rather the matter's very soul putting forth its branches and fruit organically. This development of the Idea is the proper activity of its rationality, and thinking, as something subjective, merely looks on at it without for its part adding to it any ingredient of its own. To consider a thing rationally means not to bring reason to bear on the object from the outside and so to tamper with it, but to find that the object is rational on its own account; here it is mind in its freedom, the culmination of self-conscious reason, which gives itself actuality and engenders itself as an existing world. The sole task of philosophic science is to bring into consciousness this proper work of the reason of the thing itself.

32. The determinations of the concept in the course of its development are from one point of view themselves concepts, but from another they take the form of existents, since the concept is in essence Idea. The series of concepts which this development yields is therefore at the same time a series of shapes of experience, and philosophic science must treat them accordingly.

In a more speculative sense, a concept's determinacy and its mode of existence are one and the same thing. But it is to be noticed that the moments, whose result is a further determined form of the concept, precede it in the philosophical development of the Idea as determinations of the concept, but they do not go in advance of it in the temporal development as shapes of experience. Thus, for instance, the Idea determined as the family, presupposes the determinations of the concept from which the family will later on in this work be shown to result. But the explicit existence of these inner presuppositions as shapes of experience also, e.g. as the right of property, contract, morality, and so forth, is the other aspect of the development, and it is only in a higher and more complete civilization that the development has gone so far as to endow its moments with this appropriately shaped existence.[73] [A.]

Division of the Subject

33. In correspondence with the stages in the development of the Idea of the absolutely free will, the will is

A. immediate; its concept therefore is abstract, namely personality, and its embodiment is an immediate external thing—the sphere of *Abstract* or *Formal Right*;

B. reflected from its external embodiment into itself—it is then characterized as subjective individuality in opposition to the universal. The universal here is characterized as something inward, the good, and also as something outward, a world presented to the will; both these sides of the Idea are here mediated only by each other. This is the Idea in its division or in its existence as particular; and here we have the right of the subjective will in relation to the right of the world and the right of the Idea, though only the Idea implicit—the sphere of *Morality*;

C. the unity and truth of both these abstract moments—the Idea of the good not only apprehended in thought but so realized both in the will reflected into itself and in the external world that freedom exists as substance, as actuality and necessity, no less than as subjective will; this is the Idea in its absolutely universal existence—*Ethical Life*.

But on the same principle the ethical substance is

(*a*) natural mind, the *Family*;

(*b*) in its division and appearance, *Civil Society*;

(*c*) the *State* as freedom, freedom universal and objective even in the free self-subsistence of the particular will. This actual and organic mind (α) of a single nation (β) reveals and actualizes itself through the inter-relation of the particular national minds until (γ) in the process of world-history it reveals and actualizes itself as the universal world-mind whose right is supreme.

The fact that when a thing or a content is posited first of all in accordance with its concept or as it is implicitly, it then has the form of immediacy or pure being, is the doctrine of speculative logic, here presupposed; the concept which confronts itself in the form of the concept is a different thing and no longer something immediate.

The principle which determines the division of the subject is likewise here presupposed.[74] The division may also be looked upon as a pre-declaration in historical form of the parts of the book, since the various stages must engender themselves out of the subject-matter itself as moments in the development of the Idea. A philosophical division is far from being an external one, i.e. it is not an external classification of a given material in accordance with one or more borrowed bases of division, but, on the contrary, is the immanent self-differentiation of the concept.

'Morality' and 'ethical life',[75] which perhaps usually pass current as synonyms, are taken here in essentially different senses. Yet even commonplace thinking seems to be distinguishing them; Kant generally prefers to use the word 'morality' and, since the principles of action in his philosophy are always limited to this conception, they make the standpoint of ethical life completely impossible, in fact they explicitly nullify and spurn it. But even if 'moral' and 'ethical' meant the same thing by derivation, that would in no way hinder them, once they had become different words, from being used for different conceptions. [A.]

FIRST PART
ABSTRACT RIGHT

34. The absolutely free will, at the stage when its concept is abstract, has the determinate character of immediacy. Accordingly this stage is its negative actuality, an actuality contrasted with the real world, only an abstractly self-related actuality—the inherently single will of a subject. Pursuant to the moment of the particularity of the will, it has in addition a content consisting of determinate aims and, as exclusive individuality, it has this content at the same time as an external world directly confronting it.[1] [A.]

35. The universality of this consciously free will is abstract universality, the self-conscious but otherwise contentless and simple relation of itself to itself in its individuality, and from this point of view the subject is a person. Personality implies that as *this* person: (i) I am completely determined on every side (in my inner caprice, impulse, and desire, as well as by immediate external facts) and so finite, yet (ii) none the less I am simply and solely self-relation, and therefore in finitude I know myself as something infinite, universal, and free.

Personality begins not with the subject's mere general consciousness of himself as an ego concretely determined in some way or other, but rather with his consciousness of himself as a completely abstract ego in which every concrete restriction and value is negated and without validity. In personality, therefore, knowledge is knowledge of oneself as an object, but an object raised by thinking to the level of simple infinity and so an object purely self-identical.[2] Individuals and nations have no personality until they have achieved this pure thought and knowledge of themselves. Mind fully explicit differs from the phenomenal mind in this, that at the same level at which the latter is only self-consciousness— a consciousness of self but only one pursuant to the natural will and its still external oppositions*—the former has itself, as the abstract and free ego, for its object and aim, and so is personality.[3] [A.]

36. (1) Personality essentially involves the capacity for rights and constitutes the concept and the basis (itself abstract) of the system of abstract and therefore formal right. Hence the imperative of right is: 'Be a person and respect others as persons.'

* See *Phenomenology* (Bamberg and Würzburg, 1807), pp. 101 ff. [Eng. tr. pp. 218 ff.], and *Enc.* [1st edn.], § 344 [3rd edn. § 424].

37. (2) The particularity of the will is a moment in the consciousness of the will as a whole (see Paragraph 34), but it is not yet contained in abstract personality as such. Therefore, it is present at this point, but as still sundered from personality, from the character of freedom, present as desire, need, impulse, casual whim, and so forth. In formal right, therefore, there is no question of particular interests, of my advantage or my welfare, any more than there is of the particular motive behind my volition, of insight and intention.[4] [A.]

38. In relation to action in the concrete and to moral and ethical ties, abstract right is, in contrast with the further content which these involve, only a possibility, and to have a right is therefore to have only a permission or a warrant. The unconditional commands of abstract right are restricted, once again because of its abstractness, to the negative: 'Do not infringe personality and what personality entails.' The result is that there are only prohibitions in the sphere of right, and the positive form of any command in this sphere is based in the last resort, if we examine its ultimate content, on prohibition.

39. (3) As *immediate* individuality, a person in making decisions is related to a world of nature directly confronting him, and thus the personality of the will stands over against this world as something subjective. For personality, however, as inherently infinite and universal, the restriction of being only subjective is a contradiction and a nullity. Personality is that which struggles to lift itself above this restriction and to give itself reality, or in other words to claim that external world as its own.

40. Right is in the first place the immediate embodiment which freedom gives itself in an immediate way, i.e. (a) possession, which is *property*-ownership. Freedom is here the freedom of the abstract will in general or, *eo ipso*, the freedom of a single person related only to himself. (b) A person by distinguishing himself from himself relates himself to another person,[5] and it is only as owners that these two persons really exist for each other. Their implicit identity is realized through the transference of property from one to the other in conformity with a common will and without detriment to the rights of either. This is *contract*. (c) The will which is differentiated not in the sense of (b) as being contrasted with another person, but in the sense of (a) as related to itself, is as a particular will at variance with and opposed to itself as an absolute will. This opposition is wrongdoing and *crime*.

The classification[6] of the system of rights into *jus ad personam* and *jus ad rem* on the one hand, and *jus ad actiones* on the other, like the many other similar classifications, has as its primary aim the imposition of an external order on the mass of unorganized material confronting the classifier. The striking thing about this classification is the confusion in it due to the disorderly intermixture of rights which presuppose substantial ties, e.g. those of family and political life, and rights which only concern abstract personality as such. This confusion is exemplified in the classification of rights (adopted by Kant and since favoured by others) into *jus reale*, *jus personale*, and *jus realiter personale*.[7]

To develop the perversity and lack of speculative thought in the classification of rights into *jus ad personam* and *jus ad rem*, which lies at the root of Roman law (*jus ad actiones* concerns the administration of justice and is of a different order altogether), would take us too far afield.[8] Here this much at least is clear : it is personality alone which can confer a right to things and therefore *jus ad personam* in its essence is *jus ad rem*, *rem* being taken here in its general sense as anything external to my freedom, including even my body and my life. In this sense, *jus ad rem* is the right of personality as such. But from the point of view of what is called *jus ad personam* in Roman law, a man is reckoned a person only when he is treated as possessing a certain status.* Hence in Roman law, even personality itself is only a certain standing or status contrasted with slavery. The so-called Roman law of 'personal' rights, then, is concerned with family relationships, though it excludes the right over slaves (and 'slaves' almost includes children too) as well as the status (called *capitis diminutio*) of having lost one's rights.[9] (In Kant, by the way, family relationships are the *jura realiter personalia*.[10]) The Roman *jus ad personam* is therefore not the right of the person as person but at most the right of a person in his particular capacity. (Later on in this book,[11] it will be shown that the substantial basis of family relationships is rather the sacrifice of personality.) Now it must be obvious that it is perverse to treat the right of a specific person in his particular capacity before the universal right of personality as such.

Kant's *jura personalia*[12] are the rights issuing from a contract whereby I undertake to give something or to perform something—the *jus ad rem* conferred by an *obligatio* in Roman law. To be sure, it is only a person who is required to execute the covenants of a contract, just as it is also only a person who acquires the right to their execution. But a right of this sort cannot for this reason be called a 'personal' right; rights of whatever sort belong to a person alone. Objectively considered, a right arising from a contract is never a right over a person, but only a right

* J. G. Heineccius: *Elementa juris civilis* [Bonn, 1763], § lxxv.

over something external to a person or something which he can alienate, always a right over a thing.

SUB-SECTION I

PROPERTY

41. A person must translate his freedom into an external sphere in order to exist as Idea. Personality is the first, still wholly abstract, determination of the absolute and infinite will, and therefore this sphere distinct from the person, the sphere capable of embodying his freedom, is likewise determined as what is immediately different and separable from him. [A.]

42. What is immediately different from free mind is that which, both for mind and in itself, is the external pure and simple, a thing, something not free, not personal, without rights.

'Thing', like 'the objective', has two opposed meanings. If we say 'that's the thing' or 'the thing is what matters, not the person', 'thing' means what is substantive. On the other hand, when 'thing' is contrasted with 'person' as such, not with the particular subject, it means the opposite of what is substantive, i.e. that whose determinate character lies in its pure externality. From the point of view of free mind, which must, of course, be distinguished from mere consciousness, the external is external absolutely, and it is for this reason that the determinate character assigned to nature by the concept is inherent externality.[13] [A.]

43. As the concept in its *immediacy*, and so as in essence a unit, a person has a *natural* existence partly within himself and partly of such a kind that he is related to it as to an external world.—It is only these things[14] in their immediacy as things, not what they are capable of becoming through the mediation of the will, i.e. things with determinate characteristics, which are in question here where the topic under discussion is personality, itself at this point still in its most elementary immediacy.

Mental aptitudes, erudition, artistic skill, even things ecclesiastical (like sermons, masses, prayers, consecration of votive objects), inventions, and so forth, become subjects of a contract, brought on to a parity, through being bought and sold, with things recognized as things. It may be asked whether the artist, scholar, &c., is from the legal point of view in possession of his art, erudition, ability to preach a sermon, sing a mass, &c., that is, whether such attainments are 'things'. We may hesitate to call such abilities, attainments, aptitudes, &c., 'things', for while possession of these may be the subject of business dealings and contracts, as if they were things, there is also something inward and mental about it, and for this reason the Understanding may be in perplexity about how to describe such possession in legal terms, because its field of vision is as limited to the dilemma that this is 'either a thing or not a thing' as to the dilemma 'either finite or infinite'. Attainments, erudition, talents, and so forth, are, of course, owned by free mind and are something internal and not external to it, but even so, by expressing them it may embody them in something external and alienate them (see below),[15] and in this way they are put into the category of 'things'. Therefore they are not immediate at the start but only acquire this character through the mediation of mind which reduces its inner possessions to immediacy and externality.

It was an unjustifiable and unethical proviso of Roman law that children were from their father's point of view 'things'. Hence he was legally the owner of his children, although, of course, he still also stood to them in the ethical relation of love (though this relation must have been much weakened by the injustice of his legal position). Here, then, the two qualities 'being a thing' and 'not being a thing' were united, though quite wrongly.

In the sphere of abstract right, we are concerned only with the person as person, and therefore with the particular (which is indispensable if the person's freedom is to have scope and reality) only in so far as it is something separable from the person and immediately different from him, no matter whether this separability constitutes the essential nature of the particular, or whether the particular receives it only through the mediation of the subjective will. Hence in this sphere we are concerned with mental aptitudes, erudition, &c., only in so far as they are possessions in a legal sense; we have not to treat here the possession of our body and mind which we can achieve through education, study, habit, &c., and which exists as an *inward* property of mind. But it is not until we come to deal with alienation[16] that we need begin to speak of the *transition* of such mental property into the external world where it falls under the category of property in the legal sense.

44. A person has as his substantive end the right of putting his will into any and every thing and thereby making it his, because it has no such end in itself and derives its destiny and soul from his will. This is the absolute right of appropriation which man has over all 'things'.

The so-called 'philosophy' which attributes reality in the sense of self-subsistence and genuine independent self-enclosed existence to unmediated single things, to the non-personal, is directly contradicted by the free will's attitude to these things. The same is true of the other philosophy which assures us that mind cannot apprehend the truth or know the nature of the thing-in-itself.[17] While so-called 'external' things have a show of self-subsistence for consciousness, intuition, and representative thinking, the free will idealizes that type of actuality and so is its truth.[18] [A.]

45. To have power over a thing *ab extra* constitutes possession. The particular aspect of the matter, the fact that I make something my own as a result of my natural need, impulse, and caprice, is the particular interest satisfied by possession. But I as free will am an object to myself in what I possess and thereby also for the first time am an actual will, and this is the aspect which constitutes the category of *property*, the true and right factor in possession.

If emphasis is placed on my needs, then the possession of property appears as a means to their satisfaction, but the true position is that, from the standpoint of freedom, property is the first embodiment of freedom and so is in itself a substantive end.

46. Since my will, as the will of a person, and so as a single will, becomes objective to me in property, property acquires the character of private property; and common property of such a nature that it may be owned by separate persons acquires the character of an inherently dissoluble partnership in which the retention of my share is explicitly a matter of my arbitrary preference.

The nature of the elements[19] makes it impossible for the use of them to become so particularized as to be the private possession of anyone.

In the Roman agrarian laws[20] there was a clash between public and private ownership of land. The latter is the more rational and therefore had to be given preference even at the expense of other rights.

One factor in family testamentary trusts[21] contravenes the right of personality and so the right of private property. But the specific characteristics pertaining to private property may have to be subordinated to a higher sphere of right (e.g. to a society or the state), as happens, for instance, when private property is put into the hands of a so-called 'artificial' person[22] and into mortmain. Still, such exceptions to private property cannot be grounded in chance, in private caprice, or private advantage, but only in the rational organism of the state.

The general principle that underlies Plato's ideal state violates the right of personality by forbidding the holding of private property.[23] The idea of a pious or friendly and even a compulsory brotherhood of men holding their goods in common and rejecting the principle of private property may readily present itself to the disposition which mistakes the true nature of the freedom of mind and right and fails to apprehend it in its determinate moments. As for the moral or religious view behind this idea, when Epicurus's friends proposed to form such an association holding goods in common, he forbade them, precisely on the ground that their proposal betrayed distrust and that those who distrusted each other were not friends.* [A.]

47. As a person, I am myself an *immediate* individual; if we give further precision to this expression, it means in the first instance that I am alive in this bodily organism which is my external existence, universal in content and undivided, the real pre-condition of every further determined mode of existence.[24] But, all the same, as person, I possess my life and my body, like other things, only in so far as my will is in them.

The fact that, considered as existing not as the concept explicit but only as the concept in its immediacy, I am alive and have a bodily organism, depends on the concept of life and on the concept of mind as soul—on moments which are taken over here from the Philosophy of Nature† and from Anthropology.‡

I possess the members of my body, my life, only so long as I will to possess them. An animal cannot maim or destroy itself, but a man can. [A.]

48. In so far as the body is an immediate existent, it is not in conformity with mind. If it is to be the willing organ and soul-endowed instrument[25] of mind, it must first be taken into possession by mind (see Paragraph 57). But from the point of view of others, I am in essence a free entity in my body while my possession of it is still immediate.

It is only because I am alive as a free entity in my body that this living existent ought not to be misused by being made a beast of burden. While I am alive, my soul (the concept and, to use a higher term, the free entity) and my body are not separated; my body is the embodiment of my freedom and it is with my body that I feel. It is therefore only abstract sophistical reasoning which can so distinguish body and soul as to hold that the 'thing-in-itself', the soul, is not touched or attacked if the body is maltreated and the existent embodiment of personality is subjected to the power of another. I can withdraw into myself out of my bodily existence and make my body something external to myself; particular feelings I can regard as something outside me and

* Diogenes Laertius, x. 6.

† *Enc.* [1st edn.], §§ 259 ff. Cf. §§ 161, 164, 298. [3rd edn. §§ 336 ff. Cf. §§ 213, 216, 376].

‡ *Enc.* [1st edn.], § 318 [3rd edn. §§ 388 ff.].

in chains I can still be free. But this is *my* will; so far as *others* are concerned, I am in my body. To be free from the point of view of others[26] is identical with being free in my determinate existence.* If another does violence to my body, he does violence to me.

If my body is touched or suffers violence, then, because I feel, I am touched myself actually, here and now. This creates the distinction between personal injury and damage to my external property, for in such property my will is not actually present in this direct fashion.

49. In relation to external things, the rational aspect is that I possess property, but the particular aspect comprises subjective aims, needs, arbitrariness, abilities, external circumstances, and so forth (see Paragraph 45). On these mere possession as such depends, but this particular aspect has in this sphere of abstract personality not yet been established as identical with freedom. What and how much I possess, therefore, is a matter of indifference so far as rights are concerned.

If at this stage we may speak of more persons than one, although no such distinction has yet been made, then we may say that in respect of their personality persons are equal. But this is an empty tautology, for the person, as something abstract, has not yet been particularized or established as distinct in some specific way.

'Equality' is the abstract identity of the Understanding; reflective thought and all kinds of intellectual mediocrity stumble on it at once when they are confronted by the relation of unity to a difference.[27] At this point, equality could only be the equality of abstract persons as such, and therefore the whole field of possession, this terrain of inequality, falls outside it.

The demand sometimes made[28] for an equal division of land, and other available resources too, is an intellectualism all the more empty and superficial in that at the heart of particular differences there lies not only the external contingency of nature but also the whole compass of mind, endlessly particularized and differentiated, and the rationality of mind developed into an organism.[29]

We may not speak of the injustice of nature in the unequal distribution of possessions and resources, since nature is not free and therefore is neither just nor unjust. That everyone ought to have subsistence enough for his needs is a moral wish and thus vaguely expressed is well enough meant, but like anything that is only well meant it lacks objectivity. On the other hand, subsistence is not the same as possession and belongs to another sphere, i.e. to civil society.[30] [A.]

---

* See my *Science of Logic* [1st edn.], vol. i, pp. 49 ff. [Eng. tr. vol. i, pp. 127–35, but this is a translation of the second edition, in which the passage in question was much altered, as Lasson points out].

50. The principle that a thing belongs to the person who happens to be the first in time to take it into his possession is immediately self-explanatory and superfluous, because a second person cannot take into his possession what is already the property of another.[31] [A.]

51. Since property is the *embodiment* of personality, my inward idea and will that something is to be mine is not enough to make it my property; to secure this end occupancy is requisite. The embodiment which my willing thereby attains involves its recognizability by others.—The fact that a thing of which I can take possession is a *res nullius* is (see Paragraph 50) a self-explanatory negative condition of occupancy, or rather it has a bearing on the anticipated relation to others.[32] [A.]

52. Occupancy makes the matter of the thing my property, since matter in itself does not belong to itself.

Matter offers resistance to me—and matter is nothing except the resistance it offers to me—that is, it presents itself to my mind as something abstractly independent only when my mind is taken abstractly as sensation.[33] (Sense-perception perversely takes mind as sensation for the concrete and mind as reason for the abstract.) In relation to the will and property, however, this independence of matter has no truth. Occupancy, as an external activity whereby we actualize our universal right of appropriating natural objects, comes to be conditioned by physical strength, cunning, dexterity, the means of one kind or another whereby we take physical possession of things. Owing to the qualitative differences between natural objects, mastery and occupancy of these has an infinite variety of meanings and involves a restriction and contingency that is just as infinite. Apart from that, a 'kind' of thing, or an element as such, is not the correlative object of an individual person. Before it can become such and be appropriated, it must first be individualized into single parts, into a breath of air or a drink of water. In the fact that it is impossible to take possession of an external 'kind' of thing as such, or of an element, it is not the external physical impossibility which must be looked on as ultimate, but the fact that a person, as will, is characterized as individual, while as person he is at the same time *immediate* individuality; hence as person he is related to the external world as to single things (see Remark to Paragraph 13 and Paragraph 43).

Thus the mastery and external possession of things becomes, in ways that again are infinite, more or less indeterminate and incomplete. Yet matter is never without an essential form of its own and only because it has one is it anything. The more I appropriate this form, the more do I enter into actual possession of the thing. The consumption of food is an out and out alteration of its qualitative character, the character on the strength of which it was what it was before it was eaten. The training of my body in dexterity, like the training of my mind, is likewise a more or less complete occupancy and penetration of it. It is my mind which of all things I can make most completely my own. Yet this actual occupancy is different from property as such because property is complete as the work of the free will alone.[34] In face of the free will, the thing retains no property in itself even though there still remains in possession, as an external relation to an object, something external. The empty abstraction of a matter without properties which, when a thing is my property, is supposed to remain outside me and the property of the thing, is one which thought must master. [A.]

53. Property has its modifications determined in the course of the will's relation to the thing. This relation is
   (A) *taking possession* of the thing directly (here it is in the thing *qua* something positive that the will has its embodiment);
   (B) *use* (the thing is negative in contrast with the will and so it is in the thing as something to be negated that the will has its embodiment);
   (C) *alienation*, the reflection of the will back from the thing into itself.

These three are respectively the positive, negative, and infinite judgements[35] of the will on the thing.

A. *Taking Possession*

54. We take possession of a thing (α) by directly grasping it physically, (β) by forming it, and (γ) by merely marking it as ours. [A.]

55. (α) From the point of view of sensation, to grasp a thing physically is the most complete of these modes, because then I am directly present in this possession, and therefore my will is recognizable in it. But at bottom this mode is only subjective, temporary, and seriously restricted in scope, as well as by the qualitative nature of the things grasped.—As a result of the connexion which I may effect between something and things which have already become my property in other ways, or into which something may otherwise be accidentally brought, the scope of this method is somewhat enlarged, and the same result is produced by other means also.

Mechanical forces, weapons, tools, extend the range of my power. Connexions between my property and something else may be regarded as making it more easily possible for me than for another owner, or sometimes possible for me alone, to take possession of something or to make use of it. Instances of such connexions are that my land may be on the seashore, or on a river bank; or my estate may march with hunting country or pasture or land useful for some other purpose; stone or other mineral deposits may be under my fields; there may be treasure in or under my ground, and so on. The same is true of connexions made by chance and subsequent to possession, like some of what are called 'natural accessions',[36] such as alluvial deposits, &c., and jetsam. (*Fetura* is an accession to my wealth too, but the connexion here is an organic one, it is not a case of a thing being added *ab extra* to another thing already in my possession; and therefore *fetura* is of a type quite different from the other accessions.) Alternatively, the addition to my property may be looked upon[37] as a non-self-subsistent accident of the thing to which it has been added. In every case, however, these are *external* conjunctions whose bond of connexion is neither life nor the concept. It devolves, therefore, on the Understanding to adduce and weigh their pros and cons, and on positive legislation to make decisions about them in accordance with the extent to which the relation between the things conjoined has or has not any essentiality. [A.]

56. (β) When I impose a form on something, the thing's determinate character as mine acquires an independent externality and ceases to be restricted to my presence here and now and to the direct presence of my awareness and will.

To impose a form on a thing is the mode of taking possession most in conformity with the Idea to this extent, that it implies a union of subject and object, although it varies endlessly with the qualitative character of the objects and the variety of subjective aims.

Under this head there also falls the formation of the organic. What I do to the organic does not remain external to it but is assimilated by it. Examples are the tilling of the soil, the cultivation of plants, the taming and feeding of animals, the preservation of game, as well as contrivances for utilizing raw materials or the forces of nature and processes for making one material produce effects on another, and so forth. [A.]

57. Man, pursuant to his *immediate* existence within himself, is something natural, external to his concept. It is only through the development of his own body and mind, essentially through his self-consciousness's apprehension of itself as free, that he takes possession of himself and becomes his own property and no one else's. This taking possession of oneself, looked at from the opposite point of view, is the translation into actuality of what one is according to one's concept, i.e. a potentiality, capacity, potency. In that translation one's self-consciousness for the first time becomes established as one's own, as one's object also and distinct from self-consciousness pure and simple, and thereby capable of taking the form of a 'thing' (compare Remark to Paragraph 43).

The alleged justification of slavery (by reference to all its proximate beginnings through physical force, capture in war, saving and preservation of life, upkeep, education, philanthropy, the slave's own acquiescence, and so forth), as well as the justification of a slave-ownership as simple lordship in general, and all historical views of the justice of slavery and lordship, depend on regarding man as a natural entity pure and simple, as an existent not in conformity with its concept (an existent also to which arbitrariness is appropriate). The argument for the absolute injustice of slavery, on the other hand, adheres to the concept of man as mind, as something inherently free. This view is one-sided in regarding man as free by nature, or in other words it takes the concept as such in its immediacy, not the Idea, as the truth. This antinomy rests, like all others, on the abstract thinking which asserts both the moments of an Idea in separation from one another and clings to each of them in its independence and so in its inadequacy to the Idea and in its falsity. Free mind consists precisely (see Paragraph 21) in its being no longer implicit or as concept alone, but in its transcending this formal stage of its being, and *eo ipso* its immediate natural existence, until the existence which it gives to itself is one which is solely its own and free. The side of the antinomy which asserts the concept of freedom therefore has the merit of implying the absolute starting-point, though only the starting-point, for the discovery of truth, while the other side goes no further than existence without the concept and therefore excludes the outlook of rationality and right altogether. The position of the free will, with which right and the science of right begin, is already in advance of the false position at which man, as a natural entity and only the concept implicit, is for that reason capable of being enslaved. This false, comparatively primitive, phenomenon of slavery is one which befalls mind when mind is only at the level of consciousness. The dialectic of the concept and of the purely immediate consciousness of freedom brings about at that point the fight for recognition and the relationship of master and slave.* But that objective mind, the content of the right, should no longer be apprehended in its subjective concept alone, and consequently that man's absolute unfitness for slavery should no longer be apprehended as a mere 'ought to be', is something which does not come home to our minds until we recognize that the Idea of freedom is genuinely actual only as the state. [A.]

* See *Phenomenology* [1st edn.], pp. 115 ff. [Eng. tr. pp. 229 ff.], and *Enc.* [1st edn.], §§ 352 ff. [3rd edn. §§ 430 ff.].

58. (γ) The mode of taking possession which in itself is not actual but is only *representative* of my will is to mark the thing, and the meaning of the mark is supposed to be that I have put my will into the thing. In its objective scope and its meaning, this mode of taking possession is very indeterminate. [A.]

B. *Use of the Thing*

59. By being taken into possession, the thing acquires the predicate 'mine' and my will is related to it positively. Within this identity, the thing is equally established as something negative,[38] and my will in this situation is a particular will, i.e. need, inclination, and so forth. Yet my need, as the particular aspect of a single will, is the positive element which finds satisfaction, and the thing, as something negative in itself, exists only for my need and is at its service.—The use of the thing is my need being externally realized through the change, destruction, and consumption of the thing. The thing thereby stands revealed as naturally self-less and so fulfils its destiny.[39]

The fact that property is realized and actualized only in use floats before the minds of those who look upon property as derelict and a *res nullius* if it is not being put to any use, and who excuse its unlawful occupancy on the ground that it has not been used by its owner. But the owner's will, in accordance with which a thing is his, is the primary substantive basis of property; use is a further modification of property, secondary to that universal basis, and is only its manifestation and particular mode. [A.]

60. To use a thing by grasping it directly is in itself to take possession of a *single* thing here and now. But if my use of it is grounded on a persistent need, and if I make repeated use of a product which continually renews itself, restricting my use if necessary to safeguard that renewal, then these and other circumstances transform the direct single grasp of the thing into a mark, intended to signify that I am taking it into my possession in a universal way, and thereby taking possession of the elemental or organic basis of such products, or of anything else that conditions them.[40]

61. Since the substance of the thing which is my property is, if we take the thing by itself, its externality, i.e. its non-substantiality[41] —in contrast with me it is not an end in itself (see Paragraph 42)— and since in my use or employment of it this externality is realized, it follows that my full use or employment of a thing is the thing in its entirety, so that if I have the full use of the thing I am its owner. Over and above the entirety of its use, there is nothing left of the thing which could be the property of another. [A.]

62. My merely partial or temporary use of a thing, like my partial or temporary possession of it (a possession which itself is simply the partial or temporary possibility of using it) is therefore to be distinguished from ownership of the thing itself. If the whole and entire use of a thing were mine, while the abstract ownership was supposed to be someone else's, then the thing as mine would be penetrated through and through by my will (see Paragraphs 52 and 61), and at the same time there would remain in the thing something impenetrable by me, namely the will, the empty will, of another. As a positive will, I would be at one and the same time objective and not objective to myself in the thing—an absolute contradiction. Ownership therefore is in essence free and complete.

To distinguish between the right to the whole and entire use of a thing and ownership in the abstract is the work of the empty Understanding for which the Idea—i.e. in this instance the unity of (a) ownership (or even the person's will as such) and (b) its realization—is not the truth, but for which these two moments in their separation from one another pass as something which is true. This distinction, then, as a relation in the world of fact, is that of an overlord to nothing, and this might be called an 'insanity of personality' (if we may mean by 'insanity' not merely the presence of a direct contradiction between a man's purely subjective ideas and the actual facts of his life), because 'mine' as applied to a single object would have to mean the direct presence in it of both my single exclusive will and also the single exclusive will of someone else.

In the *Institutes** we read : '*ususfructus est jus alienis rebus utendifruendi salva rerum substantia. . . . Ne tamen in universum inutiles essent proprietates, semper abscedente usufructu, placuit certis modis extingui usumfructum et ad proprietatem reverti.*'⁴² *Placuit!* As if it were in the first instance a whim or a fiat to make this proviso and thereby give some sense to that empty distinction! A *proprietas* SEMPER *abscedente usufructu* would not merely be *inutilis*, it would be no *proprietas* at all.

To examine other distinctions in property itself, e.g. between *res mancipi* and *nec mancipi*, *dominium quiritarium* and *bonitarium*,⁴³ &c., is inappropriate here since they have no bearing on any of the modifications of property determined by the concept and are merely tit-bits

* [Of Justinian,] ii. 4.

culled from the history of the right of property. The empty distinction discussed above, however, is in a way contained in the relations of *dominium directum* and *dominium utile*,[44] in the *contractus emphyteuticus*, in the further relations involved in estates in fee with the ground rents and other rents, dues, villeinage, &c., entailed in their sundry modifications, in cases where such burdens are irredeemable. But from another point of view, these relations preclude that distinction. They preclude it in so far as burdens are entailed in *dominium utile*, with the result that *dominium directum* becomes at the same time a *dominium utile*. Were there nothing in these two relationships except that distinction in its rigid abstraction, then in them we would not have two overlords (*domini*) in the strict sense, but an owner on the one hand and an overlord who was the overlord of nothing on the other. But on the score of the burdens imposed there are two owners standing in relation to each other. Although their relation is not that of being common owners of a property, still the transition from it to common ownership is very easy—a transition which has already begun in *dominium directum* when the yield of the property is calculated and looked upon as the essential thing, while that incalculable factor in the overlordship of a property, the factor which has perhaps been regarded as the honourable thing about property, is subordinated to the *utile* which here is the rational factor.[45]

It is about a millennium and a half since the freedom of personality began through the spread of Christianity to blossom and gain recognition as a universal principle from a part, though still a small part, of the human race. But it was only yesterday, we might say, that the principle of the freedom of property became recognized in some places.[46] This example from history may serve to rebuke the impatience of opinion and to show the length of time that mind requires for progress in its self-consciousness.

63. A thing in use is a single thing determined quantitatively and qualitatively and related to a specific need. But its specific utility, being quantitatively determinate, is at the same time comparable with [the specific utility of] other things of like utility. Similarly, the specific need which it satisfies is at the same time need in general and thus is comparable on its particular side with other needs, while the thing in virtue of the same considerations is comparable with things meeting other needs. This, the thing's universality, whose simple determinate character arises from the particularity of the thing, so that it is *eo ipso* abstracted from the thing's specific quality, is the thing's *value*, wherein its genuine substantiality becomes determinate and an object of consciousness.[47] As full owner of the thing, I am *eo ipso* owner of its value as well as of its use.

The distinctive character of the property of a feudal tenant is that he is supposed to be the owner of the use only, not of the value of the thing. [A.]

64. The form given to a possession and its mark are themselves externalities but for the subjective presence of the will which alone constitutes the meaning and value of externalities. This presence, however, which is use, employment, or some other mode in which the will expresses itself, is an event in time, and what is objective in time is the continuance of this expression of the will. Without this the thing becomes a *res nullius*, because it has been deprived of the actuality of the will and possession. Therefore I gain or lose possession of property through prescription.[48]

Prescription, therefore, has not been introduced into law solely from an external consideration running counter to right in the strict sense, i.e. with a view to truncating the disputes and confusions which old claims would introduce into the security of property. On the contrary, prescription rests at bottom on the specific character of property as 'real',[49] on the fact that the will to possess something must express itself.

Public memorials are national property, or, more precisely, like works of art in general so far as their enjoyment is concerned, they have life and count as ends in themselves so long as they enshrine the spirit of remembrance and honour. If they lose this spirit, they become in this respect *res nullius* in the eyes of a nation and the private possession of the first comer, like e.g. the Greek and Egyptian works of art in Turkey.

The right of private property which the family of an author has in his publications dies out for a similar reason; such publications become *res nullius* in the sense that like public memorials, though in an opposite way,[50] they become public property, and, by having their special handling of their topic copied, the private property of anyone.

Vacant land consecrated for a burial ground, or even to lie unused in perpetuity, embodies an empty absent arbitrary will. If such a will is infringed, nothing actual is infringed, and hence respect for it cannot be guaranteed.[51] [A.]

C. *Alienation of Property*

65. The reason I can alienate my property is that it is mine only in so far as I put my will into it. Hence I may abandon (*derelinquere*) as a *res nullius* anything that I have or yield it to the will of another and so into his possession, provided always that the thing in question is a thing external by nature. [A.]

66. Therefore those goods, or rather substantive characteristics, which constitute my own private personality and the universal essence of my self-consciousness are inalienable and my right to them is imprescriptible. Such characteristics are my personality as such, my universal freedom of will, my ethical life, my religion.

The fact that what mind is in accordance with its concept or implicitly it also should be explicitly and existentially (the fact that thus mind should be a person, be capable of holding property, should have an ethical life, a religion) is the Idea which is itself the concept of mind. As *causa sui*, i.e. as free causality, mind is that[52] *cuius natura non potest concipi nisi existens.**

It is just in this concept of mind as that which is what it is only through its own free causality and through its endless return into itself out of the natural immediacy of its existence, that there lies the possibility of a clash: i.e. what it is potentially it may not be actually (see Paragraph 57), and vice versa what it is actually (e.g. evil, in the case of the will) may be other than what it is potentially. Herein lies the possibility of the alienation of personality and its substantive being, whether this alienation occurs unconsciously or intentionally. Examples of the alienation of personality are slavery, serfdom, disqualification from holding property, encumbrances on property, and so forth. Alienation of intelligence and rationality, of morality, ethical life, and religion, is exemplified in superstition, in ceding to someone else full power and authority to fix and prescribe what actions are to be done (as when an individual binds himself expressly to steal or to murder, &c., or to a course of action that may involve crime), or what duties are binding on one's conscience or what religious truth is, &c.

The right to what is in essence inalienable is imprescriptible, since the act whereby I take possession of my personality, of my substantive essence, and make myself a responsible being, capable of possessing rights and with a moral and religious life, takes away from these characteristics of mine just that externality which alone made them capable of passing into the possession of someone else. When I have thus annulled their externality, I cannot lose them through lapse of time or from any other reason drawn from my prior consent or willingness to alienate them. This return of mine into myself, whereby I make myself existent as Idea, as a person with rights and moral principles, annuls the previous position and the wrong done to my concept and my reason by others and myself when the infinite embodiment of self-consciousness[53] has been treated as something external, and that with my consent. This return into myself makes clear the contradiction in supposing that I have given into another's possession my capacity for rights, my ethical life and religious feeling; for either I have given up what I myself did not possess, or I am giving up what, so soon as I possess it, exists in essence as mine alone and not as something external. [A.]

* Spinoza: *Ethics*, Part I, Definition i.

67. Single products of my particular physical and mental skill and of my power to act I can alienate to someone else[54] and I can give him the use of my abilities for a restricted period, because, on the strength of this restriction, my abilities acquire an external relation to the totality and universality of my being. By alienating the whole of my time, as crystallized in my work, and everything I produced, I would be making into another's property the substance of my being, my universal activity and actuality, my personality.

The relation here between myself and the exercise of my abilities is the same as that between the substance of a thing and its use (see Paragraph 61). It is only when use is restricted that a distinction between use and substance arises. So here, the use of my powers differs from my powers and therefore from myself, only in so far as it is quantitatively restricted. Force is the totality of its manifestations, substance of its accidents, the universal of its particulars. [A.]

68. What is peculiarly mine in a product of my mind may, owing to the method whereby it is expressed, turn at once into something external like a 'thing' which *eo ipso* may then be produced by other people. The result is that by taking possession of a thing of this kind, its new owner may make his own the thoughts communicated in it or the mechanical invention which it contains, and it is ability to do this which sometimes (i.e. in the case of books) constitutes the value of these things and the only purpose of possessing them. But besides this, the new owner at the same time comes into possession of the universal methods of so expressing himself and producing numerous other things of the same sort.

In the case of works of art, the form—the portrayal of thought in an external medium—is, regarded as a thing, so peculiarly the property of the individual artist that a copy of a work of art is essentially a product of the copyist's own mental and technical ability. In the case of a literary work, the form in virtue of which it is an external thing is of a mechanical kind, and the same is true of the invention of a machine; for in the first case the thought is presented not *en bloc*, as a statue is, but in a series of separable abstract symbols, while in the second case the thought has a mechanical content throughout. The ways and means of producing things of that mechanical kind as things are commonplace accomplishments.

But between the work of art at one extreme and the mere journeyman production at the other there are transitional stages which to a greater or less degree partake of the character of one or other of the extremes.

69. Since the owner of such a product, in owning a copy of it, is in possession of the entire use and value of that copy *qua* a single thing, he has complete and free ownership of that copy *qua* a *single* thing, even if the author of the book or the inventor of the machine remains the owner of the *universal* ways and means of multiplying such books and machines, &c. *Qua* universal ways and means of expression, he has not necessarily alienated them, but may reserve them to himself as means of expression which belong to him.

The substance of an author's or an inventor's right cannot in the first instance be found in the supposition that when he disposes of a single copy of his work, he arbitrarily makes it a condition that the power to produce facsimiles as things, a power which thereupon passes into another's possession, should not become the property of the other but should remain his own. The first question is whether such a separation between ownership of the thing and the power to produce facsimiles which is given with the thing is compatible with the concept of property, or whether it does not cancel the complete and free ownership (see Paragraph 62) on which there originally depends the option of the original producer of intellectual work to reserve to himself the power to reproduce, or to part with this power as a thing of value, or to attach no value to it at all and surrender it together with the single exemplar of his work. I reply that this power to reproduce has a special character, viz. it is that in virtue of which the thing is not merely a possession but a capital asset (see Paragraphs 170 ff.); the fact that it is such an asset depends on the particular external kind of way in which the thing is used, a way distinct and separable from the use to which the thing is directly destined (the asset[55] here is not, as has been said, an *accessio naturalis* like *fetura*). Since then this distinction falls into the sphere of that whose nature entails its divisibility, into the sphere of *external* use, the retention of part of a thing's [external] use and the alienation of another part is not the retention of a proprietorship without *utile*.

The purely negative, though the primary, means of advancing the sciences and arts is to guarantee scientists and artists against theft and to enable them to benefit from the protection of their property, just as it was the primary and most important means of advancing trade and industry to guarantee it against highway robbery.

Moreover, the purpose of a product of mind is that people other than its author should understand it and make it the possession of their ideas, memory, thinking, &c. Their mode of expression, whereby in turn they make what they have *learnt* (for 'learning' means more than 'learning things by heart', 'memorizing them'; the thoughts of others can be apprehended only by thinking, and this re-thinking the thoughts of others is learning too) into a 'thing' which they can alienate, very likely has some special form of its own in every case. The result is that they may regard as their own property the capital asset accruing from their learning and may claim for themselves the right to reproduce their learning in books of their own. Those engaged in the propagation of knowledge of all kinds, in particular those whose appointed task is teaching, have as their specific function and duty (above all in the case of the positive sciences, the doctrine of a church, the study of positive law, &c.) the repetition of well-established thoughts, taken up *ab extra* and all of them given expression already. The same is true of writings devised for teaching purposes and the spread and propagation of the sciences. Now to what extent does the new form which turns up when something is expressed again and again transform the available stock of knowledge, and in particular the thoughts of others who still retain *external* property in those intellectual productions of theirs, [56] into a private mental property of the individual reproducer and thereby give him or fail to give him the right to make them his *external* property as well? To what extent is such repetition of another's material in one's book a plagiarism? There is no precise principle of determination available to answer these questions, and therefore they cannot be finally settled either in principle or by positive legislation. Hence plagiarism would have to be a matter of honour and be held in check by honour.

Thus copyright legislation attains its end of securing the property rights of author and publisher only to a very restricted extent, though it does attain it within limits. [57] The ease with which we may deliberately change something in the form of what we are expounding or invent a trifling modification in a large body of knowledge or a comprehensive theory which is another's work, and even the impossibility of sticking to the author's words in expounding something we have learnt, all lead of themselves (quite apart from the particular purposes for which such repetitions are required) to an endless multiplicity of alterations which more or less superficially stamp someone else's property as our own. For instance, the hundreds and hundreds of compendia, selections, anthologies, &c., arithmetics, geometries, religious tracts, &c., show how every new idea in a review or annual or encyclopaedia, &c., can be forthwith repeated over and over again under the same or a different title, and yet may be claimed as something peculiarly the writer's own. The result of this may easily be that the profit promised to the author, or the projector of the original undertaking, by his work or his original idea becomes negligible or reduced for both parties or lost to all concerned.

But as for the effectiveness of honour in checking plagiarism, what has happened is that nowadays we scarcely hear the word 'plagiarism', nor are scholars accused of stealing each other's results. It may be that honour has been effective in abolishing plagiarism, or perhaps plagiarism has ceased to be dishonourable and feeling against it is a thing of the past; or possibly an ingenious and trivial idea, and a change in external form, is rated so highly as originality and a product of independent thinking that the thought of plagiarism becomes wholly insufferable.

70. The comprehensive sum of external activity, i.e. life, is not external to personality as that which itself is immediate and a *this*. The surrender or the sacrifice of life is not the existence of *this* personality but the very opposite. There is therefore no unqualified right to sacrifice one's life. To such a sacrifice nothing is entitled except an ethical Idea⁵⁸ as that in which *this* immediately single personality has vanished and to whose power it is actually subjected. Just as life as such is immediate, so death is its immediate negation and hence must come from without, either by natural causes, or else, in the service of the Idea, by the hand of a foreigner. [A.]

Transition from Property to Contract

71. Existence as determinate being is in essence being for another (see Remark to Paragraph 48). One aspect of property is that it is an existent as an external thing, and in this respect property exists for other external things and is connected with their necessity and contingency. But it is also an existent as an embodiment of the will, and from this point of view the 'other' for which it exists can only be the will of another person. This relation of will to will is the true and proper ground in which freedom is existent.—The sphere of contract is made up of this mediation whereby I hold property not merely by means of a thing and my subjective will, but by means of another person's will as well and so hold it in virtue of my participation in a common will.

Reason makes it just as necessary for men to enter into contractual relationships—gift, exchange, trade, &c.—as to possess property (see Remark to Paragraph 45). While all they are conscious of is that they are led to make contracts by need in general, by benevolence, advantage, &c., the fact remains that they are led to do this by reason implicit within them, i.e. by the Idea of the real existence of free personality, 'real' here meaning 'present in the will alone'.⁵⁹

Contract presupposes that the parties entering it recognize each other as persons and property owners. It is a relationship at the level of mind objective, and so contains and presupposes from the start the moment of recognition (compare Remarks to Paragraphs 35 and 57). [A.]

SUB-SECTION 2

CONTRACT

72. Contract brings into existence the property whose external side, its side as an existent, is no longer a mere 'thing' but contains the moment of a will (and consequently the will of a second person also). Contract is the process in which there is revealed and mediated the contradiction that I am and remain the independent owner of something from which I exclude the will of another only in so far as in identifying my will with the will of another I cease to be an owner.

73. I have power to alienate a property as an external thing (see Paragraph 65); but more than this, the concept compels me to alienate it *qua* property in order that thereby my will may become objective to me as determinately existent. In this situation, however, my will as alienated is at the same time another's will.[60] Consequently this situation wherein this compulsion of the concept is realized is the unity of different wills and so a unity in which both surrender their difference and their own special character. Yet this identity of their wills implies also (at this stage) that each will still is and remains *not* identical with the other but retains from its own point of view a special character of its own.

74. This contractual relationship, therefore, is the means whereby one identical will can persist within the absolute difference between independent property owners. It implies that each, in accordance with the common will of both, ceases to be an owner and yet is and remains one. It is the mediation of the will to give up a property, a single property, and the will to take up another, i.e. another belonging to someone else; and this mediation takes place when the two wills are associated in an identity in the sense that one of them comes to its decision only in the presence of the other.

75. The two contracting parties are related to each other as *immediate* self-subsistent persons. Therefore (α) contract arises from the arbitrary will. (β) The identical will which is brought into existence by the contract is only one *posited* by the parties, and so is only a will shared in common and not an absolutely universal will. (γ) The object about which a contract is made is a single external thing, since it is only things of that kind which the parties' purely arbitrary will has it in its power to alienate (see Paragraphs 65 ff.).

To subsume marriage under the concept of contract is thus quite impossible; this subsumption—though shameful is the only word for it—is propounded in Kant's *Philosophy of Law*.* It is equally far from the

* [§§ 24–7. Eng. tr. pp. 109–13.]

truth to ground the nature of the state on the contractual relation, whether the state is supposed to be a contract of all with all, or of all with the monarch and the government.

The intrusion of this contractual relation, and relationships concerning private property generally, into the relation between the individual and the state has been productive of the greatest confusion in both constitutional law and public life. Just as at one time[61] political rights and duties were considered and maintained to be an unqualified private property of particular individuals, something contrasted with the right of the monarch and the state, so also in more recent times the rights of the monarch and the state have been regarded as the subjects of a contract and as grounded in contract, as something embodying merely a common will and resulting from the arbitrariness of parties united into a state. However different these two points of view may be, they have this in common, that they have transferred the characteristics of private property into a sphere of a quite different and higher nature. (See below,[62] Ethical Life and the State.) [A.]

76. Contract is *formal* when the double consent whereby the common will is brought into existence is apportioned between the two contracting parties so that one of them has the negative moment—the alienation of a thing—and the other the positive moment—the appropriation of the thing. Such a contract is *gift*. But contract may be called *real* when each of the two contracting wills is the sum of these mediating moments and therefore in such a contract becomes a property owner and remains so. This is a contract of *exchange*. [A.]

77. Since in real contract each party retains the same property with which he enters the contract and which at the same time he surrenders, what thus remains identical throughout as the property implicit in the contract is distinct from the external things whose owners alter when the exchange is made. What remains identical is the value, in respect of which the subjects of the contract are equal to one another whatever the qualitative external differences of the things exchanged. Value is the universal in which the subjects of the contract participate (see Paragraph 63).

The legal provision that *laesio enormis*[63] annuls the obligation arising out of the making of a contract has its source, therefore, in the concept of contract, particularly in this moment of it, that the contracting party by alienating his property still remains a property owner and, more precisely, an owner of the quantitative equivalent of what he alienates. But a *laesio* is not merely *enormis* (as it is taken to be if it exceeds one-half of the value) but infinite, if someone has entered on a contract or made a stipulation of any sort for the alienation of inalienable goods (see Paragraph 66).

A stipulation, moreover, differs from a contract, first, in its *content*, because it signifies only some single part or moment of the whole contract, and secondly, because it is the *form* in which the contract is settled (a point on which more will be said later).[64] So far as its content is concerned, it comprises only the formal character of contract, i.e. the willingness of one party to give something and the willingness of the other to accept it; for this reason, the stipulation has been enumerated amongst so-called 'unilateral' contracts. The distinction between unilateral and bilateral contracts, and distinctions in Roman law[65] between other types of contract, are sometimes superficial juxtapositions made from an isolated and often external point of view such as that of the different types of contractual forms; or sometimes they confuse characteristics intrinsic to contract itself with others which only arise later in connexion with the administration of justice (*actiones*) and the legal processes giving effect to positive laws, and which are often derived from quite external circumstances and contravene the concept of right.

78. The distinction between property and possession, the substantive and external aspects of ownership (see Paragraph 45), appears in the sphere of contract as the distinction between a common will and its actualization, or between a covenant and its performance. Once made, a covenant taken by itself in distinction from its performance is something held before the mind, something therefore to which a particular determinate existence must be given in accordance with the appropriate mode of giving determinate existence to ideas by symbolizing them.* This is done, therefore, by expressing the stipulation in formalities such as gestures and other symbolic actions, particularly by declaring it with precision in language, the most worthy medium for the expression of our mental ideas.

The stipulation accordingly is the form given to the content of a contract, i.e. to what is agreed in it, and thereby this content, previously only an idea, attains its determinate existence. But the idea which we have of the content is itself only a form which the content takes; to have an idea of the content does not mean that the content is still something subjective, a desire or a wish for so and so. On the contrary, the content is the will's ultimate decision on such subjective wishes. [A.]

79. In contract it is the will, and therefore the substance of what is right in contract, that the stipulation enshrines. In contrast with this substance, the possession which is still being retained while

* *Enc.*, [1st edn.] §§ 379 ff. [3rd edn. §§ 458 ff.].

the contract remains unfulfilled is in itself only something external, dependent for its character as a possession on the will alone. By making the stipulation, I have given up a property and withdrawn my particular arbitrary will from it, and it has *eo ipso* become the property of another. If then I agree to stipulated terms, I am by rights at once bound to carry them out.

The difference between a mere promise and a contract lies in the fact that a promise is a statement that I will give or do or perform something in the *future*, and a promise still remains a subjective volition which because it is subjective I can still alter. A stipulation in a contract, on the other hand, is itself already the embodiment of the will's decision in the sense that by making the stipulation I have alienated my property, it has *now* ceased to be mine, and I already recognize it as the property of another. The distinction in Roman law between *pactum* and *contractus* is one of a false type.[66]

Fichte at one time[67] maintained that my obligation to keep a contract begins only when the other party starts fulfilling his side of it; his reason was that up to that point I am uncertain whether the other party's declarations are seriously meant. In that case it would follow that the obligation to keep a contract before it was carried out would only be a moral one, not an obligation by *rights*.—But the expression of the stipulation is not simply a declaration of a general character; it embodies a common will which has been brought into existence and which has superseded the arbitrary and alterable dispositions of the parties. The question therefore is not whether the other party *could* have had different private intentions when the contract was made or afterwards, but whether he had any *right* to have them. Even if the other party begins to fulfil his side of the contract, it is equally open to me to do wrong if I like. The nullity of Fichte's view is also shown by the fact that it would base contractual rights on the false infinite, i.e. on the progress *ad infinitum* involved in the infinite divisibility of time, things, action, &c.[68] The embodiment of the will in formal gestures or in explicit and precise language is already the complete embodiment of the will as an intelligent entity, and the performance of the covenant so embodied is only the mechanical consequence.

It is true that in positive law there are so-called 'real' contracts as distinguished from 'consensual' contracts, in the sense that the former are looked upon as fully valid only when the actual performance (*res, traditio rei*) of the undertaking supervenes upon willingness to perform it; but this has nothing to do with the thing at issue. For one thing, these 'real' contracts cover particular cases where it is only this delivery by the other party which puts me in a position to fulfil my side of the bargain, and where my obligation to do my part relates only to the thing after it has come into my hands, as happens for instance in loans, pawning, or deposits. (The same may also be the case in other contracts.) But this is a matter which concerns not the nature of the relation of the stipulation to performance but only the manner of performance.—For another thing, it is always open to the parties at their discretion to stipulate in any contract that the obligation of one party to perform his side shall not lie in the making of the contract itself as such, but shall arise only from the performance by the other party of his side.

80. The classification of contracts and an intelligent treatment of their various species once classified is not here to be derived from external circumstances but from distinctions lying in the very nature of contract. These distinctions are those between formal and real[69] contracts, between ownership and possession and use, between value and specific thing, and they yield contracts of the following sorts:*

A. *Gift.*

(1) Gift of a thing—gift properly so called.

(2) Loan of a thing—i.e. the gift of a portion of it or of restricted use and enjoyment of it; here the lender remains the owner of the thing (*mutuum* and *commodatum*[71] without interest). Here the thing lent is either a specific thing or else, even if it be such, it may none the less be looked on as universal, or it may be a thing which counts (like money) as a thing universal in itself.

(3) Gift of service of any sort, e.g. the mere safe-keeping of a property (*depositum*). The gift of a thing on the special condition that its recipient shall not become its owner until the date of the donor's death, i.e. the date at which he ceases in any case to be an owner of property, is testamentary disposition; this is not contained in the concept of contract but presupposes civil society and positive legislation.[72]

B. *Exchange.*

(1) Exchange as such:

(α) exchange of a thing pure and simple, i.e. exchange of one specific thing for another of the same kind.

(β) purchase or sale (*emtio, venditio*); exchange of a specific thing for one characterized as universal, one which

* The classification given here agrees on the whole with Kant's (*Philosophy of Law* [§ 31. Eng. tr. pp. 121 ff.]). One would have expected that the usual humdrum classification of contracts as real and consensual, nominate and innominate,[70] &c., would have been long since abandoned in favour of a rational classification.

counts as value alone and which lacks the other specifc character, utility—i.e. for money.

(2) Letting (*locatio, conductio*); alienation of the temporary use of a property in return for rent:

    (α) letting of a specific thing—letting strictly so called, or

    (β) letting of a universal thing, so that the lessor remains only the owner of this universal, or in other words of the value—loan (*mutuum*, or even *commodatum*, if interest is charged). The additional empirical characteristics of the thing (which may be, e.g., a flat, furniture, a house, *res fungibilis* or *non fungibilis*, &c.) entail (as in A. 2 above) other particular though unimportant subdivisions.

(3) Contract for wages (*locatio operae*)—alienation of my productive capacity or my services so far, that is, as these are alienable, the alienation being restricted in time or in some other way (see Paragraph 67).

Counsel's acceptance of a brief is akin to this, and so are other contracts whose fulfilment depends on character, good faith, or superior gifts, and where an incommensurability arises between the services rendered and a value in terms of cash. (In such cases the cash payment is called not 'wages' but 'honorarium'.)

C. *Completion of a contract* (*cautio*) *through giving a pledge.*

In the contracts whereby I part with the *use* of a thing, I am no longer in possession of the thing though I am still its owner, as for example when I let a house. Further, in gifts or contracts for exchange or purchase, I may have become the owner of a thing without as yet being in possession of it, and the same cleavage between ownership and possession arises in respect of the implementing of any undertaking which is not simply a cash or barter transaction. Now what the pledge effects is that in the one case I remain, and in the other case I am put, in actual possession of the value as that which is still or has already become my property, without in either case being in possession of the specific thing which I am renouncing or which is to be mine. The pledge is a specific thing but one which is my property only to the extent of the value of the property which I have renounced into another's possession or which is due to me; its specific character as a thing and any excess value it may have still belong to the person who gave the pledge. Giving a pledge, therefore, is not itself a contract but only a stipulation (see [Remark to] Paragraph 77), i.e. it is the moment which brings a contract to completion so far as the *possession* of the property is concerned. Mortgage and surety are particular forms of pledge. [A.]

81. In the bare relation of *immediate* persons to one another, their wills while implicitly identical, and in contract posited by them as common, are yet particular. Because they are *immediate* persons, it is a matter of chance whether or not their particular wills actually correspond with the implicit will, although it is only through the former that the latter has its real existence. If the particular will is explicitly at variance with the universal, it assumes a way of looking at things and a volition which are capricious and fortuitous and comes on the scene in opposition to the principle of rightness. This is *wrong*.

The transition to wrong is made by the logical higher necessity that the moments of the concept—here the principle of rightness or the will as universal, and right in its real existence, which is just the particularity of the will—should be posited as explicitly different, and this happens when the concept is realized abstractly. But this particularity of the will, taken by itself, is arbitrariness and contingency, and in contract I have surrendered these only as arbitrariness in the case of a single thing and not as the arbitrariness and contingency of the will itself. [A.]

SUB-SECTION 3

WRONG

82. In contract the principle of rightness is present as something posited, while its inner universality is there as something common in the arbitrariness and particular will of the parties. This *appearance* of right, in which right and its essential embodiment, the particular will, correspond immediately, i.e. fortuitously, proceeds in wrong to become a *show*,[73] an opposition between the principle of rightness and the particular will as that in which right becomes particularized. But the truth of this show is its nullity and the fact that right reasserts itself by negating this negation of itself. In this process the right is mediated by returning into itself out of the negation of itself; thereby it makes itself actual and valid, while at the start it was only implicit and something immediate. [A.]

83. When right is something particular and therefore manifold in contrast with its implicit universality and simplicity, it acquires the form of a show. (*a*) This show of right is implicit or immediate—non-malicious wrong or a civil offence; (*b*) right is made a show by the agent himself—fraud; (*c*) the agent makes it a nullity altogether—crime. [A.]

A. *Non-malicious Wrong*

84. Taking possession (see Paragraph 54) and contract—both in themselves and in their particular species—are in the first instance different expressions and consequences of my willing pure and simple; but since the will is the inherently universal, they are, through their recognition by others, grounds of title. Such grounds are external to one another and multiple, and this implies that different persons may have them in relation to one and the same thing. Each person may look upon the thing as his property on the strength of the particular ground on which he bases his title. It is in this way that one man's right may clash with another's.

85. This clash which arises when a thing has been claimed on some single ground, and which comprises the sphere of civil suits at law, entails the recognition of rightness as the universal and decisive factor, so that it is common ground that the thing in dispute should belong to the party who has the right to it. The suit is concerned only with the subsumption of the thing under the property of one or other of the parties—a straightforward negative judgement, where, in the predicate 'mine', only the particular is negated.[74]

86. The recognition of rightness by the parties is bound up with their opposed particular interest and point of view. In opposition to this show of rightness, yet within this show itself (see the preceding Paragraph), the principle of rightness arises as something kept in view and demanded by the parties. But at first it arises only as an 'ought-to-be' because the will is not yet present here as a will so freed from the immediacy of interest as, despite its particularity, to have the universal will for its aim; nor is it yet at this point characterized as a recognized actuality of such a sort that in face of it the parties would have to renounce their particular interest and point of view. [A.]

B. *Fraud*

87. The principle of rightness, when distinguished from the right as particular and as determinately existent, is characterized as something demanded, as the essential thing; yet in this situation it is still only something *demanded* and from that point of view something purely subjective, and so inessential—something merely showing there. Thus we have *fraud* when the universal is set aside by the particular will and reduced to something only showing in the situation, primarily in contract, when the universal will is reduced to a will which is common only from the outsider's point of view. [A.]

88. In contract I acquire a property for the sake of its particular characteristics, and at the same time my acquisition of it is governed by the inner universality which it possesses partly in respect of its value and partly because it has been the *property* of another. If the other likes, a false disguise may be given to the thing I acquire, so that the contract is right enough so far as it is an exchange, voluntary on both sides, of *this* thing in its immediacy and uniqueness, but still the aspect of implicit universality is lacking. (Here we have an infinite judgement expressed positively[75] or as a tautology.*)

89. Here again it is in the first instance only a demand that, in contrast with this acceptance of the thing simply as *this* thing and with the mere intentions and arbitrariness of the will, objectivity or universality should be recognizable as value and should prevail as right, and equally a demand only that the subjective arbitrary will, opposing itself to the right, should be superseded. [A.]

C. *Coercion and Crime*

90. In owning property I place my will in an external thing, and this implies that my will, just by being thus reflected in the object, may be seized in it and brought under compulsion. It may simply be forced in the thing unconditionally, or it may be constrained to sacrifice something or to do some action as a condition of retaining one or other of its possessions or embodiments—it may be coerced. [A.]

91. As a living thing man may be coerced, i.e. his body or anything else external about him may be brought under the power of others; but the free will cannot be coerced at all (see Paragraph 5), except in so far as it fails to withdraw itself out of the external object in which it is held fast, or rather out of its idea of that object (see Paragraph 7).[76] Only the will which allows itself to be coerced can in any way be coerced.

92. Since it is only in so far as the will has an existence in something determinate that it is Idea or actually free, and since the existent in which it has laid itself is freedom in being, it follows

---

* *Enc.* [1st edn.], § 121 [3rd edn. § 173].

that force or coercion is in its very conception directly self-destructive because it is an expression of a will which annuls the expression or determinate existence of a will. Hence force or coercion, taken abstractly, is wrong.

93. That coercion is in its conception self-destructive is exhibited in the world of reality by the fact that coercion is annulled by coercion;[77] coercion is thus shown to be not only right under certain conditions but necessary, i.e. as a second act of coercion which is the annulment of one that has preceded.

Breaking a contract by failing to carry out its stipulated terms, or neglect of duty rightly owed to family or state, or action in defiance of that duty, is the first act of coercion or at least force, in that it involves depriving another of his property or evading a service due to him.

Coercion by a schoolmaster, or coercion of savages and brutes, seems at first sight to be an initial act of coercion, not a second, following on one that has preceded. But the merely natural will is implicitly a force against the implicit Idea of freedom which must be protected against such an uncivilized will and be made to prevail in it. Either an ethical institution has already been established in family or government, and the natural will is a mere display of force against it; or else there is only a state of nature, a state of affairs where mere force prevails and against which the Idea establishes a right of Heroes.[78] [A.]

94. Abstract right is a right to coerce, because the wrong which transgresses it is an exercise of force against the existence of my freedom in an external thing. The maintenance of this existent against the exercise of force therefore itself takes the form of an external act and an exercise of force annulling the force originally brought against it.

To define abstract right, or right in the strict sense, at the very outset as a right in the name of which coercion may be used, means to fasten on it in a result which first comes on the scene by the indirect route of wrong. [A.]

95. The initial act of coercion as an exercise of force by the free agent, an exercise of force which infringes the existence of freedom in its concrete sense, infringes the right as right, is crime—a negatively infinite judgement[79] in its full sense,* whereby not only the particular (i.e. the subsumption under my will of a single thing —see Paragraph 85) is negated, but also the universality and infinity in the predicate 'mine' (i.e. my capacity for rights). Here the

---

* See my [*Science of*] *Logic* [1st edn.], vol. ii, p. 99 [Eng. tr. vol. 11, pp. 277-8].

negation does not come about with the co-operation of my thinking (as it does in fraud—see Paragraph 88) but in defiance of it. This is the sphere of criminal law.

Right, the infringement of which is crime, has so far only those formations which we have seen in the preceding Paragraphs; hence crime also, to begin with, has its more precise significance in relation to these specific rights. But the substance of these forms is the universal which remains the same throughout its further development and formation, and consequently its infringement, crime, also remains the same and accords with its concept. Thus the specific characteristic of crime [in general] to be noticed in the next Paragraph is characteristic also of the particular, more determinate, content in e.g. perjury, treason, forgery, coining, &c.

96. It is only the will existent in an object that can suffer injury. In becoming existent in something, however, the will enters the sphere of quantitative extension and qualitative characteristics, and hence varies accordingly. For this reason, it makes a difference to the objective aspect of crime whether the will so objectified and its specific quality is injured throughout its entire extent, and so in the infinity which is equivalent to its concept (as in murder, slavery, enforced religious observance, &c.), or whether it is injured only in a single part or in one of its qualitative characteristics, and if so, in which of these.

The Stoic view[80] that there is only one virtue and one vice, the laws of Draco which prescribe death as a punishment for every offence,[81] the crude formal code of Honour[82] which takes any insult as an offence against the infinity of personality, all have this in common, that they go no further than the abstract thought of the free will and personality and fail to apprehend it in the concrete and determinate existence which it must possess as Idea.

The distinction between robbery and theft is qualitative;[83] when I am robbed, personal violence is done to me and I am injured in my character as consciousness existing here and now and so as *this* infinite subject.

Many qualitative characteristics of crime, e.g. its danger to public safety,[84] have their basis in more concrete circumstances, although in the first instance they also are often fastened on by the indirect route as consequences instead of from the concept of the thing. For instance, the crime which taken by itself is the more dangerous in its immediate character is an injury of a more serious type in its range or its quality.

The subjective, moral, quality of crime rests on the higher distinction implied in the question of how far an event or fact pure and simple is an action, and concerns the subjective character of the action itself, on which see below.[85] [A.]

97. The infringement of right as right is something that happens and has positive existence in the external world, though inherently it is nothing at all. The manifestation of its nullity is the appearance, also in the external world, of the annihilation of the infringement. This is the right actualized, the necessity of the right mediating itself with itself by annulling what has infringed it. [A.]

98. In so far as the infringement of the right is only an injury to a possession or to something which exists externally, it is a *malum* or damage to some kind of property or asset. The annulling of the infringement, so far as the infringement is productive of damage, is the satisfaction given in a civil suit, i.e. compensation for the wrong done, so far as any such compensation can be found.

Apropos of such satisfaction, the universal character of the damage, i.e. its 'value', must here again take the place of its specific qualitative character in cases where the damage done amounts to destruction and is quite irreparable.

99. But the injury which has befallen the *implicit* will (and this means the implicit will of the *injuring* party as well as that of the injured and everyone else) has as little positive existence in this implicit will as such as it has in the mere state of affairs which it produces. In itself this implicit will (i.e. the right or law implicit) is rather that which has no external existence and which for that reason cannot be injured. Consequently, the injury from the point of view of the particular will of the injured party and of onlookers is only something negative. The sole positive existence which the injury possesses is that it is the particular will of the criminal.[86] Hence to injure [or penalize] this particular will as a will determinately existent is to annul the crime, which otherwise would have been held valid, and to restore the right.

The theory of punishment is one of the topics which have come off worst in the recent study of the positive science of law, because in this theory the Understanding is insufficient; the essence of the matter depends on the concept.

If crime and its annulment (which later[87] will acquire the specific character of punishment) are treated as if they were unqualified evils, it must, of course, seem quite unreasonable to will an evil merely because 'another evil is there already'.* To give punishment this superficial character of an evil is, amongst the various theories of punishment, the fundamental presupposition of those which regard it as a preventive, a deterrent, a threat, as reformative, &c., and what on these theories is supposed to result from punishment is characterized equally superficially as a good. But it is not merely a question of an evil or of this, that, or the other good; the precise point at issue is wrong and the righting of it. If you adopt that superficial attitude to punishment,[88] you brush aside the objective treatment of the righting of wrong, which is the primary and fundamental attitude in considering crime; and the natural consequence is that you take as essential the moral attitude, i.e. the subjective aspect of crime, intermingled with trivial psychological ideas of stimuli, impulses too strong for reason, and psychological factors coercing and working on our ideas (as if freedom were not equally capable of thrusting an idea aside and reducing it to something fortuitous!). The various considerations which are relevant to punishment as a phenomenon and to the bearing it has on the particular consciousness, and which concern its effects (deterrent, reformative, &c.) on the imagination, are an essential topic for examination in their place, especially in connexion with modes of punishment, but all these considerations presuppose as their foundation the fact that punishment is inherently and actually just. In discussing this matter the only important things are, first, that crime is to be annulled, not because it is the producing of an evil, but because it is an infringement of the right as right, and secondly, the question of what that positive existence is which crime possesses and which must be annulled; it is this existence which is the real evil to be removed, and the essential point is the question of where it lies. So long as the concepts here at issue are not clearly apprehended, confusion must continue to reign in the theory of punishment. [A.]

100. The injury [the penalty] which falls on the criminal is not merely *implicitly* just—as just, it is *eo ipso* his implicit will, an embodiment of his freedom, his right; on the contrary, it is also a right *established* within the criminal himself, i.e. in his objectively embodied will, in his action. The reason for this is that his action is the action of a rational being and this implies that it is something universal and that by doing it the criminal has laid down a law which he has explicitly recognized in his action and under which in consequence he should be brought as under his right.

As is well known, Beccaria[89] denied to the state the right of inflicting capital punishment. His reason was that it could not be presumed that

* [E. F.] Klein: *Grundsätze des peinlichen Rechts* [Halle, 1796], §§ 9 ff.

the readiness of individuals to allow themselves to be executed was included in the social contract, and that in fact the contrary would have to
be assumed. But the state is not a contract at all (see [Remark to]
Paragraph 75) nor is its fundamental essence the unconditional protection and guarantee of the life and property of members of the public as
individuals. On the contrary, it is that higher entity which even lays
claim to this very life and property and demands its sacrifice. Further,
what is involved in the action of the criminal is not only the concept of
crime, the rational aspect present in crime as such whether the individual wills it or not, the aspect which the state has to vindicate, but
also the abstract rationality of the individual's *volition*. Since that is so,
punishment is regarded as containing the criminal's right and hence by
being punished he is honoured as a rational being. He does not receive
this due of honour unless the concept and measure of his punishment
are derived from his own act. Still less does he receive it if he is treated
either as a harmful animal who has to be made harmless, or with a view
to deterring and reforming him.

Moreover, apart from these considerations, the form in which the
righting of wrong exists in the state, namely punishment, is not its only
form, nor is the state a pre-condition of the principle of righting
wrong. [A.]

101. The annulment of the crime is retribution in so far as (*a*)
retribution in *conception* is an 'injury of the injury', and (*b*) since as
existent a crime is something determinate in its scope both qualitatively and quantitatively, its negation as *existent* is similarly determinate. This identity rests on the concept, but it is not an equality
between the specific character of the crime and that of its negation;
on the contrary, the two injuries are equal only in respect of their
implicit character, i.e. in respect of their 'value'.

Empirical science requires that the definition of a class concept
(punishment in this case) shall be drawn from ideas universally present
to conscious psychological experience. This method would prove that
the universal feeling of nations and individuals about crime is and has
been that it deserves punishment, that as the criminal has done, so
should it be done to him. (There is no understanding how these
sciences, which find the source of their class concepts in ideas universally shared, come on other occasions to take for granted propositions
contradictory of like 'facts of consciousness' also styled 'universal'.)

But a point of great difficulty has been introduced into the idea of
retribution by the category of equality, though it is still true that the
justice of specific types or amounts of punishment is a further matter,
subsequent to the substance of the thing itself. Even if to determine
the later question of specific punishments we had to look round for

principles other than those determining the universal character of punishment, still the latter remains what it is. The only thing is that the concept itself must in general contain the *fundamental* principle for determining the particular too. But the determinate character given by the concept to punishment is just that necessary connexion between crime and punishment already mentioned; crime, as the will which is implicitly null, *eo ipso* contains its negation in itself and this negation is manifested as punishment. It is this inner identity whose reflection in the external world appears to the Understanding as 'equality'. The qualitative and quantitative characteristics of crime and its annulment fall, then, into the sphere of externality. In any case, no absolute determinacy is possible in this sphere (compare Paragraph 49); in the field of the finite, absolute determinacy remains only a demand, a demand which the Understanding has to meet by continually increasing delimitation—a fact of the greatest importance—but which continues *ad infinitum* and which allows only of perennially approximate satisfaction.

If we overlook this nature of the finite and then into the bargain refuse to go beyond abstract and specific equality, we are faced with the insuperable difficulty of fixing punishments (especially if psychology adduces in addition the strength of sensual impulses and consequentially either the greater strength of the evil will or the greater weakness, or the restricted freedom, of the will as such—we may choose which we please). Furthermore, it is easy enough from this point of view to exhibit the retributive character of punishment as an absurdity (theft for theft, robbery for robbery, an eye for an eye, a tooth for a tooth— and then you can go on to suppose that the criminal has only one eye or no teeth). But the concept has nothing to do with this absurdity, for which indeed the introduction of this specific equality is solely to blame. Value, as the inner equality of things which in their outward existence are specifically different from one another in every way, is a category which has appeared already in connexion with contracts (see Paragraph 77), and also in connexion with injuries that are the subject of civil suits (see Remark to Paragraph 98);[90] and by means of it our idea of a thing is raised above its immediate character to its universality. In crime, as that which is characterized at bottom by the infinite aspect[91] of the deed, the purely external specific character vanishes all the more obviously, and equality remains the fundamental regulator of the essential thing, to wit the deserts of the criminal, though not for the specific external form which the payment of those deserts may take. It is only in respect of that form that there is a plain inequality between theft and robbery on the one hand, and fines, imprisonment, &c., on the other. In respect of their 'value', however, i.e. in respect of their universal property of being injuries, they are comparable. Thus, as was said above, it is a matter for the Understanding to look for something approximately equal to their 'value' in this sense. If the implicit interconnexion of crime and its negation, and if also the thought of value and the comparability of crime and punishment in respect of their value are not apprehended, then it may become possible to see in a punishment proper only an 'arbitrary'* connexion of an evil with an unlawful action. [A.]

102. The annulling of crime in this sphere where right is immediate is principally revenge, which is just in its content in so far as it is retributive. But in its form it is an act of a subjective will which can place its infinity in every act of transgression and whose justification, therefore, is in all cases contingent, while to the other party too it appears as only particular. Hence revenge, because it is a positive action of a particular will, becomes a new transgression; as thus contradictory in character, it falls into an infinite progression and descends from one generation to another *ad infinitum.*

In cases where crimes are prosecuted and punished not as *crimina publica* but as *crimina privata* (e.g. in Jewish law and Roman law, theft and robbery; in English law to this day, certain crimes,[92] &c.) punishment is in principle, at least to some extent, revenge. There is a difference between private revenge and the revenge of heroes, knights-errant, &c., which is part of the founding of states. [A.]

103. The demand that this contradiction, which is present here in the manner in which wrong is annulled, be resolved like contradictions in the case of other types of wrong (see Paragraphs 86, 89), is the demand for a justice freed from subjective interest and a subjective form and no longer contingent on might, i.e. it is the demand for justice not as revenge but as punishment. Fundamentally, this implies the demand for a will which, though particular and subjective, yet wills the universal as such. But this concept of *Morality* is not simply something demanded; it has emerged in the course of this movement[93] itself.

Transition from Right to Morality

104. That is to say, crime, and justice in the form of revenge, display (i) the shape which the will's development takes when it has passed over into the distinction between the universal implicit will and the single will explicitly in opposition to the universal; and (ii) the fact that the universal will, returning into itself through superseding this opposition, has now itself become actual and explicit. In this way, the right, upheld in face of the explicitly

* Klein: op. cit., § 9.

independent single will, is and is recognized as actual on the score of its necessity. At the same time, however, this external formation which the will has here is *eo ipso* a step forward in the inner determination of the will by the concept. The will's immanent actualization in accordance with its concept is the process whereby it supersedes its implicit stage and the form of immediacy in which it begins and which is the shape it assumes in abstract right (see [Remark to] Paragraph 21); this means that it first puts itself in the opposition between the implicit universal will and the single explicitly independent will; and then, through the supersession of this opposition (through the negation of the negation), it determines itself in its *existence* as a will, so that it is a free will not only in itself but for itself also, i.e. it determines itself as self-related negativity. Its personality—and in abstract right the will is personality and no more—it now has for its object; the infinite subjectivity of freedom, a subjectivity become explicit in this way, is the principle of the *moral* standpoint.[94]

Let us look back more closely over the moments through which the concept of freedom develops itself from the will's determinate character as originally abstract to its character as self-related, and so at this point to its self-determination as subjectivity. In property this determinate character is the abstract one, 'mine', and is therefore found in an external thing. In contract, 'mine' is mediated by the wills of the parties and means only something common. In wrong the will of the sphere of right has its abstract character of implicit being or immediacy posited as contingency through the act of a single will, itself a contingent will. At the moral standpoint, the abstract determinacy of the will in the sphere of right has been so far overcome that this contingency itself is, as reflected in upon itself and self-identical, the inward infinite contingency of the will, i.e. its subjectivity. [A.]

SECOND PART

MORALITY

105. The standpoint of morality is the standpoint of the will which is infinite not merely in itself but for itself (see Paragraph 104). In contrast with the will's implicit being, with its immediacy and the determinate characteristics developed within it at that level, this reflection of the will into itself and its explicit awareness of its identity makes the person into the subject.

106. It is as subjectivity that the concept has now been determined, and since subjectivity is distinct from the concept as such, i.e. from the implicit principle of the will, and since furthermore it is at the same time the will of the subject as a single individual aware of himself (i.e. still has immediacy in him), it constitutes the determinate *existence* of the concept. In this way a higher ground has been assigned to freedom; the Idea's existential aspect, or its moment of reality, is now the subjectivity of the will. Only in the will as subjective can freedom or the implicit principle of the will be actual.[1]

The second sphere, Morality, therefore throughout portrays the real aspect of the concept of freedom, and the movement of this sphere is as follows: the will, which at the start is aware only of its independence and which before it is mediated is only implicitly identical with the universal will or the principle of the will, is raised beyond its [explicit] difference from the universal will, beyond this situation in which it sinks deeper and deeper into itself, and is established as explicitly identical with the principle of the will.[2] This process is accordingly the cultivation of the ground in which freedom is now set, i.e. subjectivity. What happens is that subjectivity, which is abstract at the start, i.e. distinct from the concept, becomes likened to it, and thereby the Idea acquires its genuine realization. The result is that the subjective will determines itself as objective too and so as truly concrete. [A.]

107. The self-determination of the will is at the same time a moment in the concept of the will, and subjectivity is not merely its existential aspect but its own determinate character (see Paragraph 104). The will aware of its freedom and determined as subjective is at the start concept alone, but itself has determinate existence in order to exist as Idea. The moral standpoint therefore takes shape as the right of the subjective will.³ In accordance with this right, the will recognizes something and is something, only in so far as the thing is its own and as the will is present to itself there as something subjective.

The same process through which the moral attitude develops (see the Remark to the preceding Paragraph) has from this point of view the form of being the development of the right of the subjective will, or of the mode of its existence. In this process the subjective will further determines what it recognizes as its own in its object (*Gegenstand*), so that this object becomes the will's own true concept, becomes objective (*objektiv*) as the expression of the will's own universality.⁴ [A.]

108. The subjective will, directly aware of itself, and distinguished from the principle of the will (see Remark to Paragraph 106), is therefore abstract, restricted, and formal. But not merely is subjectivity itself formal; in addition, as the infinite self-determination of the will, it constitutes the form of all willing. In this, its first appearance in the single will, this form has not yet been established as identical with the concept of the will, and therefore the moral point of view is that of relation, of ought-to-be, or demand. And since the self-difference of subjectivity involves at the same time the character of being opposed to objectivity as external fact, it follows that the point of view of consciousness comes on the scene here too (see Paragraph 8). The general point of view here is that of the will's self-difference, finitude, and appearance.⁵

The moral is not characterized primarily by its having already been opposed to the immoral, nor is right directly characterized by its opposition to wrong. The point is rather that the general characteristics of morality and immorality alike rest on the subjectivity of the will. [A.]

109. This form of all willing primarily involves in accordance with its general character (*a*) the opposition of subjectivity and objectivity, and (*b*) the activity (see Paragraph 8) related to this opposition. Now existence and specific determinacy are identical in the concept of the will (see Paragraph 104), and the will as subjective is itself this concept.⁶ Hence the moments of this activity consist more precisely in (*a*) distinguishing between objectivity and subjectivity and even ascribing independence to them both, and (*b*) establishing them as identical. In the will which is self-determining, (α) its specific determinacy is in the first place established in the will itself by itself as its inner particularization, as a content which it gives to itself. This is the first negation, and the formal limitation (*Grenze*) of this negation is that of being only something posited, something subjective. (β) As infinitely reflected into itself, this limitation exists for the will, and the will is the struggle to transcend this barrier (*Schranke*), i.e. it is the activity of translating this content in some way or other from subjectivity into objectivity, into an immediate existence. (γ) The simple identity of the will with itself in this opposition is the content which remains self-identical in both these opposites and indifferent to this formal distinction of opposition. In short, it is my aim [the purpose willed].[7]

110. But, at the standpoint of morality, where the will is aware of its freedom, of this identity of the will with itself (see Paragraph 105), this identity of content acquires the more particularized character appropriate to itself.

(*a*) The content as 'mine' has for me this character: by virtue of its identity in subject and object it enshrines for me my subjectivity, not merely as my inner purpose, but also inasmuch as it has acquired outward existence. [A.]

111. (*b*) Though the content does have in it something particular, whencesoever it may be derived, still it is the content of the will reflected into itself in its determinacy and thus of the self-identical and universal will; and therefore:

(α) the content is inwardly characterized as adequate to the principle of the will or as possessing the objectivity of the concept;

(β) since the subjective will, as aware of itself, is at the same time still formal (see Paragraph 108), the content's adequacy to the concept is still only something demanded, and hence this entails the possibility that the content may *not* be adequate to the concept.

112. (*c*) Since in carrying out my aims I retain my subjectivity (see Paragraph 110), during this process of objectifying them I simultaneously supersede the immediacy of this subjectivity as well as its character as this my individual subjectivity. But the external subjectivity which is thus identical with me is the will of others[8] (see Paragraph 73). The will's ground of existence is now subjectivity (see Paragraph 106) and the will of others is that existence which I give to my aim and which is at the same time to me an other. The achievement of my aim, therefore, implies this identity of my will with the will of others, it has a positive bearing on the will of others.

The objectivity of the aim achieved thus involves three meanings, or rather it has three moments present within it at once; it is:

(α) something existing externally and immediately (see **Paragraph** 109);

(β) adequate to the concept (see **Paragraph** 111);[9]

(γ) *universal* subjectivity.

The subjectivity which maintains itself in this objectivity consists:

(α) in the fact that the objective aim is mine, so that in it I maintain myself as *this* individual (see Paragraph 110);

(β) and (γ), in moments which coincide with the moments (β) and (γ) above.

At the standpoint of morality, subjectivity and objectivity are distinct from one another, or united only by their mutual contradiction; it is this fact more particularly which constitutes the finitude of this sphere or its character as mere appearance (see Paragraph 108), and the development of this standpoint is the development of these contradictions and their resolutions, resolutions, however, which within this field can be no more than relative. [A.]

113. The externalization of the subjective or moral will is action. Action implies the determinate characteristics here indicated:

(α) in its externality it must be known to me as *my* action;

(β) it must bear essentially on the concept as an 'ought' [see Paragraph 131];

(γ) it must have an essential bearing on the will of others.

It is not until we come to the externalization of the moral will that we come to action. The existence which the will gives to itself in the sphere of formal rights is existence in an immediate thing and is itself immediate; to start with, it neither has in itself any express bearing on the concept, which is at that point not yet contrasted with the subjective will and so is not distinguished from it, nor has it a positive bearing on the will of others; in the sphere of right, command in its fundamental character is only prohibition (see Paragraph 38). In contract and wrong, there is the beginning of a bearing on the will of others; but the correspondence established in contract between one will and another is grounded in arbitrariness, and the essential bearing which the will has there on the will of the other is, as a matter of rights, something negative, i.e. one party retains his property (the value of it) and allows the other to retain his. On the other hand, crime in its aspect as issuing from the subjective will, and the question of the mode of its existence in that will, come before us now for consideration for the first time.

The content of an action at law (*actio*), as something determined by legal enactment, is not imputable to me.[10] Consequently, such an action contains only some of the moments of a moral action proper, and contains them only incidentally. The aspect of an action in virtue of which it is properly moral is therefore distinct from its aspect as legal.

114. The right of the moral will involves three aspects:

(*a*) The abstract or formal right of action, the right that the content of the action as carried out in immediate existence, shall be in principle mine, that thus the action shall be the *Purpose* of the subjective will.

(*b*) The particular aspect of the action is its inner content (α) as I am aware of it in its general character; my awareness of this general character constitutes the worth of the action and the reason I think good to do it—in short my *Intention*. (β) Its content is my special aim, the aim of my particular, merely individual, existence, i.e. *Welfare*.

(*c*) This content (as something which is inward and which yet at the same time is raised to its universality as to absolute objectivity) is the absolute end of the will, the *Good*—with the opposition in the sphere of reflection, of *subjective* universality, which is now wickedness and now conscience.[11] [A.]

SUB-SECTION I

PURPOSE AND RESPONSIBILITY

115. The finitude of the subjective will in the immediacy of acting consists directly in this, that its action *presupposes* an external object with a complex environment. The deed sets up an alteration in this state of affairs confronting the will, and my will has responsibility[12] in general for its deed in so far as the abstract predicate 'mine' belongs to the state of affairs so altered.

An event, a situation which has been produced, is a concrete external actuality which because of its concreteness has in it an indeterminable multiplicity of factors. Any and every single element which appears as the condition, ground, or cause of one such factor, and so has contributed its share to the event in question, may be looked upon as responsible for the event, or at least as sharing the responsibility for it. Hence, in the case of a complex event (e.g. the French Revolution) it is open to the abstract Understanding to choose which of an endless number of factors it will maintain to be responsible for it. [A.]

116. It is, of course, not my own doing if damage is caused to others by things whose owner I am and which as external objects stand and are effective in manifold connexions with other things (as may also be the case with my self as a bodily mechanism or as a living thing). This damage, however, is to some extent chargeable to me because the things that cause it are in principle mine, although it is true that they are subject to my control, vigilance, &c., only to an extent varying with their special character.

117. The freely acting will, in directing its aim on the state of affairs confronting it, has an idea of the attendant circumstances. But because the will is finite, since this state of affairs is presupposed, the objective phenomenon is contingent so far as the will is concerned, and may contain something other than what the will's idea of it contains. The will's right, however, is to recognize as its action, and to accept responsibility for, only those presuppositions of the deed of which it was conscious in its aim and those aspects of the deed which were contained in its purpose. The deed can be imputed to me only if my will is responsible for it—this is the right to know. [A.]

118. Further, action is translated into external fact, and external fact has connexions in the field of external necessity through which it develops itself in all directions. Hence action has a multitude of consequences. These consequences are the outward form whose inner soul is the aim of the action, and thus they are the consequences *of the action*, they belong to the action. At the same time, however, the action, as the aim posited in the external world, has become the prey of external forces which attach to it something totally different from what it is explicitly and drive it on into alien and distant consequences. Thus the will has the right to repudiate the imputation of all consequences except the first, since it alone was purposed.

To determine which results are accidental and which necessary is impossible, because the necessity implicit in the finite comes into determinate existence as an external necessity, as a relation of single things to one another, things which as self-subsistent are conjoined in indifference to one another and externally. The maxim: 'Ignore the consequences of actions' and the other: 'Judge actions by their consequences and make these the criterion of right and good' are both alike maxims of the abstract Understanding. The consequences, as the shape proper to the action and immanent within it, exhibit nothing but its nature and are simply the action itself; therefore the action can neither disavow nor ignore them. On the other hand, however, among the consequences there is also comprised something interposed from without and introduced by chance, and this is quite unrelated to the nature of the action itself.

The development in the external world of the contradiction involved in the *necessity* of the *finite* is just the conversion of necessity into contingency and vice versa. From this point of view, therefore, acting means surrendering oneself to this law.[13] It is because of this that it is to the advantage of the criminal if his action has comparatively few bad consequences (while a good action must be content to have had no consequences or very few), and that the fully developed consequences of a crime are counted as part of the crime.

The self-consciousness of heroes (like that of Oedipus and others in Greek tragedy) had not advanced out of its primitive simplicity either to reflection on the distinction between act and action, between the external event and the purpose and knowledge of the circumstances, or to the subdivision of consequences. On the contrary, they accepted responsibility for the whole compass of the deed. [A.]

SUB-SECTION 2

INTENTION AND WELFARE

119. An action as an external event is a complex of connected parts which may be regarded as divided into units *ad infinitum*, and the action may be treated as having touched in the first instance only one of these units. The truth of the single, however, is the universal; and what explicitly gives action its specific character is not an isolated content limited to an external unit, but a universal content, comprising in itself the complex of connected parts. Purpose, as issuing from a thinker, comprises more than the mere unit; essentially it comprises that universal side of the action, i.e. the intention.

Etymologically, *Absicht* (intention) implies abstraction, either the form of universality or the extraction of a particular aspect of the concrete thing.[14] The endeavour to justify an action by the intention behind it involves the isolation of one or other of its single aspects which is alleged to be the essence of the action on its subjective side.

To judge an action as an external deed without yet determining its rightness or wrongness is simply to bestow on it a universal predicate, i.e. to describe it as burning, killing, &c.

The discrete character of the external world shows what the nature of that world is, namely a chain of external relations. Actuality is touched in the first instance only at a single point (arson, for instance, *directly* concerns only a tiny section of the firewood, i.e. is describable in a proposition, not a judgement),[15] but the universal nature of this point entails its expansion. In a living thing, the single part is there in its immediacy not as a mere part, but as an organ in which the universal is really present as the universal; hence in murder, it is not a piece of flesh, as something isolated, which is injured, but life itself which is injured in that piece of flesh. It is subjective reflection, ignorant of the logical nature of the single and the universal, which indulges *ad libitum* in the subdivision of single parts and consequences; and yet it is the nature of the finite deed itself to contain such separable contingencies.— The device of *dolus indirectus*[16] has its basis in these considerations. [A.]

120. The right of intention is that the universal quality of the action shall not merely be implicit but shall be known by the agent, and so shall have lain from the start in his subjective will. Vice versa, what may be called the right of the objectivity of action is the right of the action to evince itself as known and willed by the subject as a *thinker*.

This right to insight of this kind entails the complete, or almost complete, irresponsibility of children, imbeciles, lunatics, &c., for their actions.—But just as actions on their external side as events include accidental consequences, so there is involved in the subjective agent an indeterminacy whose degree depends on the strength and force of his self-consciousness and circumspection. This indeterminacy, however, may not be taken into account except in connexion with childhood or imbecility, lunacy, &c., since it is only such well marked states of mind that nullify the trait of thought and freedom of will, and permit us to treat the agent as devoid of the dignity of being a thinker and a will.

121. The universal quality of the action is the manifold content of the action as such, reduced to the simple form of universality. But the subject, an entity reflected into himself and so particular in correlation with the particularity of his object, has in his end his own particular content, and this content is the soul of the action and determines its character. The fact that this moment of the particularity of the agent is contained and realized in the action constitutes subjective freedom in its more concrete sense, the right of the subject to find his satisfaction in the action. [A.]

122. It is on the strength of this particular aspect that the action has subjective worth or interest for me. In contrast with this *end*— the content of the intention—the direct character of the action in its further content is reduced to a *means*. In so far as such an end is something finite, it may in its turn be reduced to a means to some further intention and so on *ad infinitum.*

123. For the content of these ends nothing is available at this point except (α) pure activity itself, i.e. the activity present owing to the fact that the subject puts himself into whatever he is to look upon and promote as his end. Men are willing to be *active* in pursuit of what interests them, or should interest them, as something which is their own. (β) A more determinate content, however, the still abstract and formal freedom of subjectivity possesses only in its natural subjective embodiment, i.e. in needs, inclinations, passions, opinions, fancies, &c. The satisfaction of these is welfare or happiness, both in general and in its particular species— the ends of the whole sphere of finitude.

Here—the standpoint of relation (see Paragraph 108), when the subject is characterized by his self-difference and so counts as a particular—is the place where the content of the natural will (see Paragraph 11) comes on the scene. But the will here is not as it is in its immediacy; on the contrary, this content now belongs to a will reflected into itself and so is elevated to become a universal end, the end of welfare or happiness;* this happens at the level of the thinking which does not yet apprehend the will in its freedom but reflects on its content as on one natural and given—the level, for example, of the time of Croesus and Solon.[17] [A.]

124. Since the subjective satisfaction of the individual himself (including the recognition which he receives by way of honour and fame) is also part and parcel of the achievement of ends of absolute worth, it follows that the demand that such an end alone shall appear as willed and attained, like the view that, in willing, objective and subjective ends are mutually exclusive, is an empty dogmatism of the abstract Understanding. And this dogmatism is more than empty, it is pernicious if it passes into the assertion that because subjective satisfaction is present, as it always is when any task is brought to completion, it is what the agent intended in essence to secure and that the objective end was in his eyes only a means to that.—What the subject is, is the series of his actions. If these are a series of worthless productions, then the subjectivity of his willing is just as worthless. But if the series of his deeds is of a substantive nature, then the same is true also of the individual's inner will.

* *Enc.* [1st edn.], §§ 395 ff. [3rd edn. §§ 478 ff.].

The right of the subject's particularity, his right to be satisfied, or in other words the right of subjective freedom, is the pivot and centre of the difference between antiquity and modern times. This right in its infinity is given expression in Christianity and it has become the universal effective principle of a new form of civilization. Amongst the primary shapes which this right assumes are love, romanticism, the quest for the eternal salvation of the individual, &c.; next come moral convictions and conscience; and, finally, the other forms, some of which come into prominence in what follows as the principle of civil society and as moments in the constitution of the state, while others appear in the course of history, particularly the history of art, science, and philosophy.[18]

Now this principle of particularity is, to be sure, one moment of the antithesis, and in the first place at least it is just as much identical with the universal as distinct from it. Abstract reflection, however, fixes this moment in its distinction from and opposition to the universal and so produces a view of morality as nothing but a bitter, unending, struggle against self-satisfaction, as the command: 'Do with abhorrence what duty enjoins.'[19]

It is just this type of ratiocination which adduces that familiar psychological view of history which understands how to belittle and disparage all great deeds and great men by transforming into the main intention and operative motive of actions the inclinations and passions which likewise found their satisfaction from the achievement of something substantive, the fame and honour, &c., consequential on such actions, in a word their particular aspect, the aspect which it has decreed in advance to be something in itself pernicious. Such ratiocination assures us that, while great actions and the efficiency which has subsisted through a series of them have produced greatness in the world and have had as their consequences for the individual agent power, honour, and fame, still what belongs to the individual is not the greatness itself but what has accrued to him from it, this purely particular and external result; because this result is a consequence, it is therefore supposed to have been the agent's end and even his sole end. Reflection of this sort stops short at the subjective side of great men, since it itself stands on purely subjective ground, and consequently it overlooks what is substantive in this emptiness of its own making. This is the view of those valet psychologists 'for whom there are no heroes, not because there are no heroes, but because these psychologists are only valets'.* [A.]

125. The subjective element of the will, with its particular content—welfare, is reflected into itself and infinite and so stands related to the universal element, to the principle of the will. This

---

* *Phenomenology* [1st edn.], p. 616 [Eng. tr. p. 673].

moment of universality, posited first of all within this particular content itself, is the welfare of others also, or, specified completely, though quite emptily, the welfare of all.[20] The welfare of many other unspecified particulars is thus also an essential end and right of subjectivity. But since the absolutely universal, in distinction from such a particular content, has not so far been further determined than as 'the right', it follows that these ends of particularity, differing as they do from the universal, may be in conformity with it, but they also may not.

126. My particularity, however, like that of others, is only a right at all in so far as I am a free entity. Therefore it may not make claims for itself in contradiction to this its substantive basis, and an intention to secure my welfare or that of others (and it is particularly in this latter case that such an intention is called 'moral') cannot justify an action which is wrong.

It is one of the most prominent of the corrupt maxims of our time to enter a plea for the so-called 'moral' intention behind wrong actions and to imagine bad men with well-meaning hearts, i.e. hearts willing their own welfare and perhaps that of others also. This doctrine is rooted in the 'benevolence' (*guten Herzens*) of the pre-Kantian philosophers[21] and constitutes, e.g., the quintessence of well-known touching dramatic productions;[22] but to-day it has been resuscitated in a more extravagant form, and inner enthusiasm and the heart, i.e. the form of particularity as such, have been made the criterion of right, rationality, and excellence. The result is that crime and the thoughts that lead to it, be they fancies however trite and empty, or opinions however wild, are to be regarded as right, rational, and excellent, simply because they issue from men's hearts and enthusiasms. (See the Remark to Paragraph 140, where more details are given.)

Incidentally, however, attention must be paid to the point of view from which right and welfare are being treated here. We are considering right as abstract right and welfare as the particular welfare of the single agent. The so-called 'general good', the welfare of the state, i.e. the right of mind actual and concrete, is quite a different sphere, a sphere in which abstract right is a subordinate moment like particular welfare and the happiness of the individual. As was remarked above,[23] it is one of the commonest blunders of abstract thinking to make private rights and private welfare count as *absolute* in opposition to the universality of the state. [A.]

127. The particularity of the interests of the natural will, taken in their entirety as a single whole, is personal existence or life. In

extreme danger and in conflict with the rightful property of someone else, this life may claim (as a right, not a mercy) a right of distress, because in such a situation there is on the one hand an infinite
injury to a man's existence and the consequent loss of rights
altogether, and on the other hand only an injury to a single restricted embodiment of freedom, and this implies a recognition
both of right as such and also of the injured man's capacity for
rights, because the injury affects only *this* property of his.

The right of distress is the basis of *beneficium competentiae*[24] whereby
a debtor is allowed to retain of his tools, farming implements, clothes,
or, in short, of his resources, i.e. of his creditor's property, so much as is
regarded as indispensable if he is to continue to support life—to support
it, of course, on his own social level. [A.]

128. This distress reveals the finitude and therefore the contingency of both right and welfare,[25] of right as the abstract embodiment of freedom without embodying the particular person,
and of welfare as the sphere of the particular will without the universality of right. In this way they are *established* as one-sided and
ideal, the character which in *conception* they already possessed.
Right has already (see Paragraph 106) determined its embodiment
as the particular will; and subjectivity, in its particularity as a comprehensive whole, is itself the *embodiment* of freedom (see Paragraph 127), while as the infinite relation of the will to itself, it is
implicitly the *universal* element in freedom. The two moments
present in right and subjectivity, thus integrated and attaining their
truth, their identity, though in the first instance still remaining
relative to one another, are (*a*) the good (as the concrete, absolutely
determinate, universal), and (*b*) conscience (as infinite subjectivity
inwardly conscious and inwardly determining its content).

GOOD AND CONSCIENCE

129. The good is the Idea as the unity of the concept of the will
with the particular will. In this unity, abstract right, welfare, the
subjectivity of knowing and the contingency of external fact, have
their independent self-subsistence superseded, though at the same
time they are still contained and retained within it in their essence.
The good is thus freedom realized, the absolute end and aim of the
world. [A.]

130. In this Idea, welfare has no independent validity as the embodiment of a single particular will but only as universal welfare and essentially as universal in principle, i.e. as according with freedom. Welfare without right is not a good. Similarly, right without welfare is not the good; *fiat justitia* should not be followed by *pereat mundus*. Consequently, since the good must of necessity be actualized through the particular will and is at the same time its substance, it has absolute right in contrast with the abstract right of property and the particular aims of welfare. If either of these moments becomes distinguished from the good, it has validity only in so far as it accords with the good and is subordinated to it.

131. For the subjective will, the good and the good alone is the essential, and the subjective will has value and dignity only in so far as its insight and intention accord with the good. Inasmuch as the good is at this point still only this *abstract* Idea of good, the subjective will has not yet been caught up into it and established as according with it. Consequently, it stands in a *relation* to the good, and the relation is that the good *ought* to be substantive for it, i.e. it ought to make the good its aim and realize it completely, while the good on its side has in the subjective will its only means of stepping into actuality. [A.]

132. The right of the subjective will is that whatever it is to recognize as valid shall be seen by it as good, and that an action, as its aim entering upon external objectivity, shall be imputed to it as right or wrong, good or evil, legal or illegal, in accordance with its *knowledge* of the worth which the action has in this objectivity.

The good is in principle the essence of the will in its substantiality and universality, i.e. of the will in its truth, and therefore it exists simply and solely in thinking and by means of thinking. Hence assertions such as 'man cannot know the truth but has to do only with phenomena', or 'thinking injures the good will' are dogmas depriving mind not only of intellectual but also of all ethical worth and dignity.

The right of giving recognition only to what my insight sees as rational is the highest right of the subject, although owing to its subjective character it remains a formal right; against it the right which reason *qua* the objective possesses over the subject remains firmly established.

On account of its formal character, insight is capable equally of being true and of being mere opinion and error. The individual's acquisition of this right of insight is, on the principles of the sphere which is still moral only, part and parcel of his particular

subjective education. I may demand from myself, and regard it as one
of my subjective rights, that my insight into an obligation shall be based
on good reasons, that I shall be convinced of the obligation and even
that I shall apprehend it from its concept and fundamental nature.
But whatever I may claim for the satisfaction of my conviction about
the character of an action as good, permitted, or forbidden, and so about
its imputability in respect of this character, this in no way detracts from
the right of objectivity.

This right of insight into the good is distinct from the right of insight
in respect of action as such (see Paragraph 117);[26] the form of the right
of objectivity which corresponds to the latter is this, that since action is
an alteration which is to take place in an actual world and so will have
recognition in it, it must in general accord with what has validity there.
Whoever wills to act in this world of actuality has *eo ipso* submitted
himself to its laws and recognized the right of objectivity.

Similarly, in the state as the objectivity of the concept of reason,
legal responsibility cannot be tied down to what an individual may hold
to be or not to be in accordance with his reason, or to his subjective
insight into what is right or wrong, good or evil, or to the demands
which he makes for the satisfaction of his conviction. In this objective
field, the right of insight is valid as insight into the legal or illegal, *qua*
into what is recognized as right, and it is restricted to its elementary
meaning, i.e. to knowledge in the sense of acquaintance with what is
legal and to that extent obligatory. By means of the publicity of the
laws and the universality of manners,[27] the state removes from the right
of insight its formal aspect and the contingency which it still retains for
the subject at the level of morality. The subject's right to know action
in its specific character as good or evil, legal or illegal, has the result
of diminishing or cancelling in this respect too[28] the responsibility of
children, imbeciles, and lunatics, although it is impossible to delimit
precisely either childhood, imbecility, &c., or their degree of irresponsibility. But to turn momentary blindness, the goad of passion, in-
toxication, or, in a word, what is called the strength of sensual impulse
(excluding impulses which are the basis of the right of distress—see
Paragraph 127)[29] into *reasons* when the imputation, specific character,
and culpability of a crime are in question, and to look upon such circumstances as if they took away the criminal's guilt, again means
(compare Paragraph 100 and the Remark to Paragraph 120)[30] failing to
treat the criminal in accordance with the right and honour due to him
as a man; for the nature of man consists precisely in the fact that he is
essentially something universal, not a being whose knowledge is an
abstractly momentary and piecemeal affair.

Just as what the incendiary really sets on fire is not the isolated
square inch of wooden surface to which he applies his torch, but the
universal in that square inch, e.g. the house as a whole, so, as subject,

he is neither the single existent of this moment of time nor this isolated hot feeling of revenge. If he were, he would be an animal which would have to be knocked on the head as dangerous and unsafe because of its liability to fits of madness.

The claim is made that the criminal in the moment of his action must have had a 'clear idea' of the wrong and its culpability before it can be imputed to him as a crime. At first sight, this claim seems to preserve the right of his subjectivity, but the truth is that it deprives him of his indwelling nature as intelligent, a nature whose effective presence is not confined to the 'clear ideas' of Wolff's psychology,[31] and only in cases of lunacy is it so deranged as to be divorced from the knowing and doing of isolated things.

The sphere in which these extenuating circumstances come into consideration as grounds for the mitigation of punishment is a sphere other than that of rights, the sphere of pardon.[32]

133. The particular subject is related to the good as to the essence of his will, and hence his will's obligation arises directly in this relation.[33] Since particularity is distinct from the good and falls within the subjective will, the good is characterized to begin with only as the universal abstract essentiality of the will, i.e. as duty. Since duty is thus abstract and universal in character, it should be done for duty's sake. [A.]

134. Because every action explicitly calls for a particular content and a specific end, while duty as an abstraction entails nothing of the kind, the question arises: what is my duty? As an answer nothing is so far available except: (a) to do the right, and (b) to strive after welfare, one's own welfare, and welfare in universal terms, the welfare of others (see Paragraph 119).[34] [A.]

135. These specific duties, however, are not contained in the definition of duty itself; but since both of them are conditioned and restricted, they *eo ipso* bring about the transition to the higher sphere of the unconditioned, the sphere of duty. Duty itself in the moral self-consciousness is the essence or the universality of that consciousness, the way in which it is inwardly related to itself alone; all that is left to it, therefore, is abstract universality, and for its determinate character it has identity without content, or the abstractly positive, the indeterminate.

However essential it is to give prominence to the pure unconditioned self-determination of the will as the root of duty, and to the way in which knowledge of the will, thanks to Kant's philosophy, has won its firm foundation and starting-point for the first time owing to the thought of its infinite autonomy, still to adhere to the exclusively moral position, without making the transition to the conception of ethics, is to reduce this gain to an empty formalism, and the science of morals to the preaching of duty for duty's sake. From this point of view, no immanent doctrine of duties is possible; of course, material may be brought in from outside and particular duties may be arrived at accordingly, but if the definition of duty is taken to be the absence of contradiction, formal correspondence with itself—which is nothing but abstract indeterminacy stabilized—then no transition is possible to the specification of particular duties nor, if some such particular content for acting comes under consideration, is there any criterion in that principle for deciding whether it is or is not a duty. On the contrary, by this means any wrong or immoral line of conduct may be justified.

Kant's further formulation,[35] the possibility of visualizing an action as a *universal* maxim, does lead to the more concrete visualization of a situation, but in itself it contains no principle beyond abstract identity and the 'absence of contradiction' already mentioned.

The absence of property contains in itself just as little contradiction as the non-existence of this or that nation, family, &c., or the death of the whole human race. But if it is already established on other grounds and presupposed that property and human life are to exist and be respected, then indeed it is a contradiction to commit theft or murder; a contradiction must be a contradiction of something, i.e. of some content presupposed from the start as a fixed principle. It is to a principle of that kind alone, therefore, that an action can be related either by correspondence or contradiction. But if duty is to be willed simply for duty's sake and not for the sake of some content, it is only a formal identity whose nature it is to exclude all content and specification.

The further antinomies and configurations of this never-ending ought-to-be, in which the exclusively moral way of thinking—thinking in terms of *relation*—just wanders to and fro without being able to resolve them and get beyond the ought-to-be, I have developed in my *Phenomenology of Mind.** [A.]

136. Because of the abstract characterization of the good, the other moment of the Idea—particularity in general—falls within subjectivity. Subjectivity in its universality reflected into itself is the subject's absolute inward certainty (*Gewißheit*) of himself, that which establishes the particular and is the determining and decisive element in him, his conscience (*Gewissen*).[36] [A.]

137. True conscience is the disposition to will what is absolutely good. It therefore[37] has fixed principles and it is aware of these as

* [1st edn.] pp. 550 ff. [Eng. tr. pp. 615 ff.]. Cf. *Enc.* [1st edn.], §§ 420 ff. [3rd edn. §§ 507 ff.].

its explicitly objective determinants and duties. In distinction from this its content (i.e. truth), conscience is only the formal side of the activity of the will, which as *this* will has no special content of its own.[38] But the objective system of these principles and duties, and the union of subjective knowing with this system, is not present until we come to the standpoint of ethical life. Here at the abstract standpoint of morality, conscience lacks this objective content and so its explicit character is that of infinite abstract self-certainty, which at the same time is for this very reason the self-certainty of *this* subject.

Conscience is the expression of the absolute title of subjective self-consciousness to know in itself and from within itself what is right and obligatory, to give recognition only to what it thus knows as good, and at the same time to maintain that whatever in this way it knows and wills is in truth right and obligatory. Conscience as this unity of sub-jective knowing with what is absolute is a sanctuary which it would be sacrilege to violate. But whether the conscience of a specific individual corresponds with this Idea of conscience, or whether what it takes or declares to be good is actually so, is ascertainable only from the content of the good it seeks to realize. What is right and obligatory is the absolutely rational element in the will's volitions and therefore it is not in essence the *particular* property of an individual, and its form is not that of feeling or any other private (i.e. sensuous) type of knowing, but essentially that of universals determined by thought, i.e. the form of laws and principles. Conscience is therefore subject to the judgement of its truth or falsity, and when it appeals only to itself for a decision, it is directly at variance with what it wishes to be, namely the rule for a mode of conduct which is rational, absolutely valid, and universal. For this reason, the state cannot give recognition to conscience in its private form as subjective knowing, any more than science can grant validity to subjective opinion, dogmatism, and the appeal to a subjective opinion. In true conscience, its elements are not different, but they may become so, and it is the determining element, the subjectivity of willing and knowing, which can sever itself from the true content of conscience, establish its own independence, and reduce that content to a form and a show. The ambiguity in connexion with conscience lies therefore in this: it is presupposed to mean the *identity* of subjective knowing and willing with the true good, and so is claimed and recog-nized to be something sacrosanct; and yet at the same time, as the mere subjective reflection of self-consciousness into itself, it still claims for itself the title due, solely on the strength of its absolutely valid rational *content*, to that identity alone.

At the level of morality, distinguished as it is in this book from the

level of ethics, it is only formal conscience that is to be found. True
conscience has been mentioned only to indicate its distinction from the
other and to obviate the possible misunderstanding that here, where it
is only formal conscience that is under consideration, the argument is
about true conscience. The latter is part of the ethical disposition
which comes before us for the first time in the following section.[39]—
The religious conscience, however, does not belong to this sphere at
all. [A.]

138. This subjectivity, *qua* abstract self-determination and pure
certainty of oneself alone, as readily evaporates into itself the whole
determinate character of right, duty, and existence, as it remains
both the power to judge, to determine from within itself alone,
what is good in respect of any content, and also the power to which
the good, at first only an ideal and an ought-to-be, owes its
actuality.

The self-consciousness which has attained this absolute reflection into
itself knows itself in this reflection to be the kind of consciousness
which is and should be beyond the reach of every existent and given
specific determination. As one of the commoner features of history
(e.g. in Socrates,[40] the Stoics, and others), the tendency to look deeper
into oneself and to know and determine from within oneself what is
right and good appears in ages when what is recognized as right and
good in contemporary manners cannot satisfy the will of better men.
When the existing world of freedom has become faithless to the will of
better men, that will fails to find itself in the duties there recognized and
must try to find in the ideal world of the inner life alone the harmony
which actuality has lost. Once self-consciousness has grasped and
secured its formal right in this way, everything depends on the character
of the content which it gives to itself. [A.]

139. Once self-consciousness has reduced all otherwise valid
duties to emptiness and itself to the sheer inwardness of the will, it
has become the potentiality of either making the absolutely universal its principle, or equally well of elevating above the universal
the self-will of private particularity, taking that as its principle and
realizing it through its actions, i.e. it has become potentially evil.

To have a conscience, if conscience is only formal subjectivity, is
simply to be on the verge of slipping into evil; in independent self-
certainty, with its independence of knowledge and decision, both
morality and evil have their common root.

The origin of evil in general is to be found in the mystery of freedom
(i.e. in the speculative aspect of freedom), the mystery whereby freedom

of necessity arises out of the natural level of the will and is something inward in comparison with that level.[41] It is this natural level of the will which comes into existence as a self-contradiction, as incompatible with itself in this opposition, and so it is just this particularity of the will which later makes itself evil. That is to say, particularity is always duality; here it is the opposition of the natural level and the inwardness of the will. In this opposition, the latter is only a relative and abstract subjectivity which can draw its content only from the determinate content of the natural will, from desire, impulse, inclination, &c. Now it is said of these desires, impulses, &c., that they may be either good or evil. But since the will here makes into a determinant of its content both these impulses in this contingent character which they possess as natural, and also, therefore, the form which it has at this point, the form of particularity itself, it follows that it is set in opposition to the universal as inner objectivity, to the good, which comes on the scene as the opposite extreme to immediate objectivity, the natural pure and simple, as soon as the will is reflected into itself and consciousness is a *knowing* consciousness. It is in this opposition that this inwardness of the will is evil. Man is therefore evil by a conjunction between his natural or undeveloped character and his reflection into himself; and therefore evil belongs neither to nature as such by itself—unless nature were supposed to be the natural character of the will which rests in its particular content—nor to introverted reflection by itself, i.e. cognition in general, unless this were to maintain itself in that opposition to the universal.

With this facet of evil, its necessity, there is inevitably combined the fact that this same evil is condemned to be that which of necessity ought not to be, i.e. the fact that evil ought to be annulled. It is not that there ought never to be a diremption of any sort in the will—on the contrary, it is just this level of diremption which distinguishes man from the unreasoning animal; the point is that the will should not rest at that level and cling to the particular as if that and not the universal were the essential thing; it should overcome the diremption as a nullity. Further, as to this necessity of evil, it is subjectivity, as infinite self-reflection, which is present in and confronted by this opposition of universal and particular; if it rests in this opposition, i.e. if it is evil, then it is *eo ipso* independent, regarding itself as isolated, and is itself this self-will.[42] Therefore if the individual subject as such does evil, the evil is purely and simply his own responsibility. [A.]

140. In every end of a self-conscious subject, there is a *positive* aspect (see Paragraph 135) necessarily present because the end is what is purposed in an actual concrete action. This aspect he knows how to elicit and emphasize, and he may then proceed to regard it as a duty or a fine intention. By so interpreting it, he is enabled to pass off his action as good in the eyes both of himself and others, despite the fact that, owing to his reflective character and his knowledge of the universal aspect of the will, he is aware of the contrast between this aspect and the essentially *negative* content of his action. To impose in this way on others is hypocrisy; while to impose on oneself is a stage beyond hypocrisy, a stage at which subjectivity claims to be absolute.[43]

This final, most abstruse, form of evil, whereby evil is perverted into good and good into evil, and consciousness, in being aware of its power to effect this perversion, is also made aware of itself as absolute, is the highwater mark of subjectivity at the level of morality; it is the form into which evil has blossomed in our present epoch, a result due to philosophy, i.e. to a shallowness of thought which has twisted a profound concept into this shape and usurped the name of philosophy, just as it has arrogated to evil the name of good.

In this Remark I will indicate briefly the chief forms of this subjectivity which have become current.

(*a*) In hypocrisy the following moments are contained: (α) knowledge of the true universal, whether knowledge in the form merely of a feeling for right and duty, or of a deeper cognition and apprehension of them; (β) volition of the particular which conflicts with this universal; (γ) conscious comparison of both moments (α) and (β), so that the conscious subject is aware in willing that his particular volition is evil in character.

These points are descriptive of acting with a bad conscience; hypocrisy proper involves something more.

At one time great importance was attached to the question whether an action was evil only in so far as it was done with a bad conscience, i.e. with explicit knowledge of the three moments just specified. The inference from an affirmative answer is admirably drawn by Pascal: *Ils seront tous damnés ces demi-pécheurs, qui ont quelque amour pour la vertu. Mais pour ces franc-pécheurs, pécheurs endurcis, pécheurs sans mélange, pleins et achevés, l'enfer ne les tient pas; ils ont trompé le diable à force de s'y abandonner.**

* *Lettres provinciales*, iv. In the same context, Pascal also quotes Christ's intercession on the Cross for his enemies: 'Father, forgive them, for they know not what they do'—a superfluous prayer if the fact that they did not know what they did made their action innocent and so took away the need of forgiveness. Pascal quotes there too Aristotle's distinction (*Nic. Eth.* 1110 b 24)[44] between the man who acts οὐκ εἰδώς and the one who acts ἀγνοῶν; in the former type of ignorance, his action is not freely willed (here the ignorance depends on external circumstances, see above, Paragraph 117) and his action is not imputable to him. But of the latter Aristotle says: 'Every wicked man is ignorant of what he ought to do and what he ought to refrain from doing; and it is this kind of failure (ἁμαρτία) which makes men unjust and in general bad. . . . An ignorant choice' between good and evil 'is the cause not of the action's being involuntary' (of being non-imputable) 'but only of its being wicked'. Aristotle evidently had a deeper in-

The subjective right of self-consciousness to know whether an action is truly good or evil in character must not be thought of as so colliding with the absolute right of the objectivity of this character that the two rights are represented as separable, indifferent to one another, and related only accidentally. It was such a conception of their relation that lay in particular at the root of the old questions about efficacious grace.[45] On its formal side, evil is most peculiarly the individual's own, since (a) it is precisely his subjectivity establishing itself purely and simply for itself, and for that reason it is purely and simply the individual's own responsibility (see Paragraph 139 and the Remark thereto); (b) on his objective side man accords with his concept inasmuch as he is mind, in a word a rational entity, and has in his own nature as such the character of self-knowing universality. Therefore it means failing to treat him with the respect due to his concept if his good side is divorced from him, so that the character of his evil action as evil is divorced from him too and is not imputed to him as evil. How determinate is the consciousness of these moments in distinction from one another, or to what extent it has developed or failed to develop in clarity so as to become a recognition of them, and to what degree an evil action has been done with a conscience more or less downright evil—all these questions are the more trivial aspect of the matter, the aspect mainly concerned with the empirical.

(b) Evil and doing evil with a bad conscience, however, is not quite hypocrisy. Into hypocrisy there enters in addition the formal character of falsity, first the falsity of holding up evil as good in the eyes of others, of setting oneself up to all appearance as good, conscientious, pious, and so on—conduct which in these circumstances is only a trick to deceive others. Secondly, however, the bad man may find in his good conduct on other occasions, or in his piety, or, in a word, in good reasons, a justification in his own eyes for the evil he does, because he can use these reasons to pervert its apparent character from evil into good. His ability to do this depends on the subjectivity which, as abstract negativity, knows that all determinations are subordinate to itself and issue from its own will.

(c) In this perversion of evil into good we may prima facie include the form of subjectivism known as Probabilism.[46] Its guiding principle is that an action is permissible, and may be done with an easy conscience, provided that the agent can hunt out any single good reason for it, be it only the authority of a single theologian, and even if other theologians are known by the agent to dissent ever so widely from that authority. Even in this idea there is still present the correct apprehension that authority and a reason based on authority gives probability

sight into the connexion between knowing and willing than has become common in a superficial philosophy which teaches that the opposite of knowledge, the heart and enthusiasm, are the true principles of ethical action.

only, although this is supposed to be enough to produce an easy conscience; it is granted in Probabilism that a good reason is inevitably of
such a character that there may exist along with it different reasons at
least as good. Even here we must recognize a vestige of objectivity in
the admission that it is a reason which should be the determining
factor. But since the discrimination between good and evil is made to
depend on all those good reasons, including theological authorities too,
despite the fact that they are so numerous and contradictory, the
implication is that it is not this objectivity of the thing, but subjectivity,
which has the last word. This means that caprice and self-will are
made the arbiters of good and evil, and the result is that ethics as well
as religious feeling is undermined. But the fact that it is private subjectivity to which the decision falls is one which Probabilism does not
openly avow as its principle; on the contrary, as has already been
stated, it gives out that it is some reason or other which is decisive,
and Probabilism is to that extent still a form of hypocrisy.

(d) In the stages of subjectivism, the next in ascending order is the
view that the goodness of the will consists in its willing the good;[47] this
willing of the abstract good is supposed to suffice, in fact to be the sole
requisite, to make its action good. As the willing of something determinate, action has a content, but good in the abstract determines
nothing, and hence it devolves on particular subjectivity to give this
content its character and constituents. Just as in Probabilism anyone who is not himself a learned *Révérend Père* may have the subsumption of a determinate content under the universal predicate 'good'
effected for him by the sole[48] authority of one such theologian, so here
every subject, without any further qualification, is invested with this
honour of giving a content to good in the abstract, or in other words
subsuming a content under a universal. This content is only one of the
many elements in an action as a concrete whole, and the others may
perhaps entail its description as 'criminal' and 'bad'. That determinate
content which I, as subject, give to the good, however, is the good
known to me in the action, i.e. it is my good intention (see Paragraph
114).[49] Thus there arises a contradiction between descriptions: according to one the action is good, according to the other it is criminal.
Hence also there seems to arise, in connexion with a concrete action,
the question whether in such circumstances the intention behind it is
actually good. It may generally be the case that the good is what is
actually intended; but this in fact must always be the case if it is held
that good in the abstract is the subject's determining motive. Where
wrong is done through an action which is well intentioned but in other
respects criminal and bad, the wrong so done must, of course, also be
good, and the important question would seem to be: which of these
sides of the action is really the essential one? This objective question,
however, is here out of place, or rather it is the subjective consciousness

alone whose decision constitutes objectivity at this point. Besides, 'essential' and 'good' mean the same thing; one is just as much an abstraction as the other. Good is that which is essential in respect of the will; and the essential in this respect should be precisely this, that my action be characterized as good in my eyes. But the subsumption under the good of any content one pleases is the direct and explicit result of the fact that this abstract good is totally devoid of content and so is simply reduced to meaning anything positive, i.e. to something which is valid from some single point of view and which in its immediate character may even be valid as an essential end, as for example to do good to the poor, to take thought for myself, my life, my family, and so forth. Further, just as the good is the abstract, so the bad too must be without content and derive its specification from my subjectivity; and it is in this way also that there arises the moral end of hating and uprooting the bad, the nature of the bad being left unspecified.

Theft, cowardice, murder, and so forth, as actions, i.e. as achievements of a subjective will, have the immediate character of being satisfactions of such a will and therefore of being something positive. In order to make the action a good one, it is only a question of recognizing this positive aspect of the action as my intention, and this then becomes the essential aspect in virtue of which the action is made good, simply because I recognize it as the good in my intention. Theft in order to do good to the poor, theft or flight from battle for the sake of fulfilling one's duty to care for one's life or one's family (a poor family perhaps into the bargain), murder out of hate or revenge (i.e. in order to satisfy one's sense of one's own rights or of right in general, or one's sense of another's wickedness, of wrong done by him to oneself or to others or to the world or the nation at large, by extirpating this wicked individual who is wickedness incarnate, and thereby contributing at least one's quota to the project of uprooting the bad)—all these actions are made well intentioned and therefore good by this method of taking account of the positive aspect of their content. Only the bare minimum of intelligence is required to discover in any action, as those learned theologians can, a positive side and so a good reason for it and a good intention behind it. Hence it has been said that in the strict sense there are no wicked men, since no one wills evil for the sake of evil, i.e. no one wills a pure negative as such. On the contrary, everyone always wills something positive, and therefore, on the view we are considering, something good. In this abstract good the distinction between good and evil has vanished together with all concrete duties; for this reason, simply to will the good and to have a good intention in acting is more like evil than good, because the good willed is only this abstract form of good and therefore to make it concrete devolves on the arbitrary will of the subject.

To this context there also belongs the notorious maxim: 'The end justifies the means.' In itself and prima facie this expression is trivial and pointless. Quite so, one may retort in terms equally general, a just end of course justifies the means, while an unjust end does not. The phrase:[50] 'If the end is right, so is the means' is a tautology, since the means is precisely that which is nothing in itself but is for the sake of something else, and therein, i.e. in the end, has its purpose and worth—provided of course it be truly a means.

But when someone says that the end justifies the means, his purport is not confined to this bare tautology; he understands by the words something more specific, namely that to use as means to a good end something which in itself is simply not a means at all, to violate something in itself sacrosanct, in short to commit a crime as a means to a good end, is permissible and even one's bounden duty. (i) There floats before the minds of those who say that the end justifies the means a vague consciousness of the dialectic of the aforesaid 'positive' element in isolated legal or ethical principles, or of such equally vague general maxims as: 'Thou shalt not kill', or 'Thou shalt take thought for thy welfare and the welfare of thy family'. Executioners and soldiers have not merely the right but the duty to kill men, though there it has been precisely laid down what kind of men and what circumstances make the killing permissible and obligatory. So also my welfare and the welfare of my family must be subordinated to higher ends and so reduced to means to their attainment. (ii) And yet what bears the mark of crime is not a general maxim of that kind, left vague and still subject to a dialectic; on the contrary, its specific character is already objectively fixed. Now what is set up against such a determinate crime, what is supposed to have deprived the crime of its criminal nature, is the justifying end, and this is simply subjective opinion about what is good and better. What happens here is the same as what happens when the will stops at willing good in the abstract, i.e. the absolute and valid determinate character assigned to good and evil, right and wrong, is entirely swept away and the determination of them is ascribed instead to the individual's feeling, imagination, and caprice.

(e)[51] Subjective opinion is at last expressly given out as the measuring-rod of right and duty and it is supposed that the conviction which holds something to be right is to decide the ethical character of an action. Since the good we will to do is here still without content, the principle of conviction only adds the information that the subsumption of an action under the category of good is purely a personal matter. If this be so, the very pretence of an ethical objectivity has totally disappeared. A doctrine like this is directly connected with the self-styled philosophy, often mentioned already, which denies that the truth is knowable—and the truth of mind qua will, the rationality of mind in its self-actualizing process, is the laws of ethics. Asserting, as such philosophizing does, that the knowledge of the true is an empty vanity, transcending the territory of science (which is supposed to be mere appearance), it must in the matter of action at once find its principle also in the apparent; thereby ethics is reduced to the special theory of life held by the individual and to his private conviction. The degradation into which philosophy has thus sunk appears doubtless at a first glance to be only an affair of supreme indifference, an occurrence confined to the trivial field of academic futilities; but the view necessarily makes itself a home in ethics, an essential part of philosophy; and it is then that the true meaning of these theories makes its first appearance in and is apprehended by the world of actuality.

The result of the dissemination of the view that subjective conviction, and it alone, decides the ethical character of an action is that the charge of hypocrisy, once so frequent, is now rarely heard; you can only qualify wickedness as hypocrisy on the assumption that certain actions are inherently and actually misdeeds, vices, and crimes, and that the defaulter is necessarily aware of them as such, because he is aware of and recognizes the principles and outward acts of piety and honesty even in the pretence to which he misapplies them. In other words, it was generally assumed as regards evil that it is a duty to know the good and to be aware of its distinction from evil. In any case, however, it was an absolute injunction which forbade the commission of vicious and criminal actions and which insisted on such actions being imputed to the agent, so far as he was a man and not a beast. But if a good heart, a good intention, a subjective conviction are set forth as the sources from which conduct derives its worth, then there is no longer any hypocrisy or immorality at all; for whatever a man does, he can always justify by the reflection on it of good intentions and motives, and by the influence of that conviction it is good.* Thus there is no longer anything absolutely vicious or criminal; and instead of the above-mentioned[53] frank and free, hardened and unperturbed sinner, we have the man who is conscious of being fully justified by intention and conviction. My good intention in my action and my conviction of its goodness make it good. We speak of judging and estimating an *action*; but on this principle it is only the intention and conviction of the agent, his faith, by which he ought to be judged. Not, however, his

---

* 'That he feels completely *convinced* I have not the least doubt. But how many men are led by such feelings of conviction into the worst of misdeeds! Besides, if everything may be excused on this ground, then that terminates the rational judgement of good and wicked, honourable and shameful, resolutions. Lunacy in that case would have equal rights with reason; or in other words reason would have no rights whatever, its judgement would cease to have any validity. Its voice would be a minus quantity; truth would be the possession of the man with no doubts! I tremble at the results of such toleration, for it would be exclusively to the advantage of unreason.' (F. H. Jacobi to Count Holmer, on Count Stolberg's change of faith, Eutin, August 5th, 1800. *Brennus*, Berlin, August 1802.)[52]

faith in the sense in which Christ requires faith in objective truth, so
that on one who has a false faith, i.e. a conviction bad in its content,
the judgement to be pronounced must be a condemnation, i.e. one in
conformity with this content. On the contrary, faith here means
fidelity to conviction, and the question to be asked about action is:
'Has the agent in his acting kept true to his conviction?' Fidelity to
formal subjective conviction is thus made the sole measuring-rod of
duty.

This principle, under which conviction is expressly made something
subjective, cannot but thrust upon us the thought of possible error,
with the further implied presupposition of an absolute law. But the
law is no agent; it is only the actual human being who acts. And, on
the aforesaid principle, the only question, in estimating the worth of
human actions, is how far he has taken up the law into his conviction.
But if on this theory it is not actions which are to be judged, i.e. measured
generally, by that law, it is impossible to see what the law is for and
what end it is to serve. Such a law is degraded to a mere external
letter, in fact to an empty word, if it is only my conviction which makes
it a law and invests it with obligatory force.

Such a law may claim its authority from God or the state. It may
even have behind it the authority of tens of centuries during which it
was the bond which gave men, with all their deeds and destiny, coherence
and subsistence. And these are authorities which enshrine the convictions of countless individuals. Now if I set against these the authority
of my single conviction—for as my subjective conviction its sole
validity is authority—that at first seems a piece of monstrous self-
conceit, but in virtue of the principle that subjective conviction is to
be the measuring-rod, it is pronounced not to be self-conceit at all.

Even if reason and conscience—which shallow science and bad
sophistry can never altogether expel—admit with a noble illogicality
that error is possible, still by describing crime, and evil generally, as
only an error, we minimize the fault. To err is human—who has not
been mistaken on one point or another, whether he had fresh or pickled
cabbage for dinner yesterday, and about innumerable other things of
more or less importance? But the difference between importance and
triviality vanishes if everything turns on the subjectivity of conviction
and on persistence in it. The said noble illogicality which admits the
possibility of error is inevitable then in the nature of the case, but when
it comes round to say that a wrong conviction is only an error, it only
falls into a further illogicality, the illogicality of dishonesty. At one
moment conviction is made the basis of ethics and of man's supreme
value, and is thus pronounced the supreme and the sacrosanct; at
another, all we have to do with is error, and my conviction is something
trivial and casual, in fact something strictly external, which may turn
out this way or that. Really, my being convinced *is* something supremely

trivial if I cannot *know* the truth; for then it is a matter of indifference how I think, and all that is left to my thinking is that empty good, the abstraction to which the Understanding reduces the good.

One other point. It follows further, on this principle of justification by conviction, that logic requires me, in dealing with the way others act against my action, to admit that they are quite in the right—so far at any rate as they maintain with faith and conviction that my action is criminal. On such logic, not merely do I gain nothing, I am even deposed from the post of liberty and honour into a situation of slavery and dishonour. Justice, which in the abstract is mine as well as theirs, I feel only as a foreign subjective conviction, and when it is executed on me, I fancy myself to be treated only by an external force.

(*f*) Finally, the supreme form in which this subjectivism is completely comprised and expressed is the phenomenon which has been called by a name borrowed from Plato—'Irony'. The name alone, however, is taken from Plato; he used it to describe a way of speaking which Socrates employed in conversation when defending the Idea of truth and justice against the conceit of the Sophists and the uneducated.[54] What he treated ironically, however, was only their type of mind, not the Idea itself. Irony is only a manner of talking against *people*. Except as directed against persons, the essential movement of thought is dialectic, and Plato was so far from regarding the dialectical in itself, still less irony, as the last word in thought and a substitute for the Idea, that he terminated the flux and reflux of thinking, let alone of a subjective opinion, and submerged[55] it in the substantiality of the Idea.*

---

* My colleague, the late Professor Solger,[56] adopted the word 'irony' which Friedrich von Schlegel brought into use at a comparatively early period of his literary career and enhanced to equivalence with the said principle of subjectivity knowing itself as supreme. But Solger's finer mind was above such an exaggeration; he had philosophic insight and so seized upon, emphasized, and retained only that part of Schlegel's view which was dialectic in the strict sense, i.e. dialectic as the pulsating drive of speculative inquiry. His last publication, a solid piece of work, a thorough *Kritik über die Vorlesungen des Herrn August Wilhelm von Schlegel über dramatische Kunst und Literatur* (Wiener Jahrbuch. vol. vii, pp. 90 ff.), I find somewhat obscure, however, and I cannot agree with the argument which he develops. 'True irony', he says (p. 92), 'arises from the view that so long as man lives in this present world, it is only in this world that he can fulfil his "appointed task" no matter how elevated a sense we give to this expression. Any hope we may have of transcending finite ends is foolish and empty conceit. Even the highest is existent for our conduct only in a shape that is limited and finite.' Rightly understood, this is Platonic doctrine, and a true remark in rejection of what he has referred to earlier, the empty striving towards the (abstract) infinite. But to say that the highest is existent in a limited and finite shape, like the ethical order (and that order is in essence actual life and action), is very different from saying that the highest thing is a *finite* end. The outward shape, the form of finitude, in no way deprives the content of ethical life of its substantiality and the infinity inherent within it. Solger continues: 'And just for this reason the highest is in *us* as negligible as the lowest and perishes of

The culminating form of this subjectivity which conceives itself as the final court of appeal—our topic here—can be nothing except what was implicitly present already in its preceding forms, namely subjectivity knowing itself as the arbiter and judge of truth, right, and duty. It consists then in this, that it knows the objective ethical principles, but fails in self-forgetfulness and self-renunciation to immerse itself in their seriousness and to base action upon them. Although related to them, it holds itself aloof from them and knows itself as that which wills and decides thus, although it may equally well will and decide otherwise. You actually accept a law, it says, and respect it as absolute. So do I, but I go further than you, because I am beyond this law and can make it to suit myself. It is not the thing that is excellent, but I who am so; as the master of law and thing alike, I simply play with them as with my caprice; my consciously ironical attitude lets the highest perish and I merely hug myself at the thought. This type of subjectivism not merely substitutes a void for the whole content of

necessity with us and our nugatory thoughts and feelings. The highest is truly existent in God alone, and as it perishes in us it is transfigured into something divine, a divinity in which we would have had no share but for its immediate presence revealed in the very disappearance of our actuality; now the mood to which this process directly comes home in human affairs is tragic irony.' The arbitrary name 'irony' would be of no importance, but there is an obscurity here when it is said that it is 'the highest' which perishes with our nothingness and that it is in the disappearance of our actuality that the divine is first revealed; e.g. again (ibid., p. 91): 'We see heroes beginning to wonder whether they have erred in the noblest and finest elements of their feelings and sentiments, not only in regard to their successful issue, but also to their source and their worth; indeed, what elevates us is the destruction of the best itself.' (The *just* destruction of utter scoundrels and criminals who flaunt their villainy—the hero of a modern tragedy, *Die Schuld*,[57] is one—has an interest for criminal law, but none at all for art proper which is what is in question here.) The *tragic* destruction of figures whose ethical life is on the highest plane can interest and elevate us and reconcile us to its occurrence only in so far as they come on the scene in opposition to one another together with equally justified but different ethical powers which have come into collision through misfortune, because the result is that then these figures acquire guilt through their opposition to an ethical law. Out of this situation there arises the right and wrong of both parties and therefore the true ethical Idea, which, purified and in triumph over this one-sidedness, is thereby reconciled in *us*. Accordingly, it is not the highest in us which perishes; we are elevated not by the destruction of the best but by the triumph of the true. This it is which constitutes the true, purely ethical, interest of ancient tragedy (in romantic tragedy the character of the interest undergoes a certain modification).[58] All this I have worked out in detail in my *Phenomenology of Mind* (1st edn., pp. 404 ff. Cf. pp. 683 ff. [Eng. tr. pp. 484 ff. Cf. pp. 736 ff.]). But the ethical Idea is actual and present in the world of social institutions without the misfortune of tragic clashes and the destruction of individuals overcome by this misfortune. And this Idea's (the highest's) revelation of itself in its actuality as anything but a nullity is what the external embodiment of ethical life, the state, purposes and effects, and what the ethical self-consciousness possesses, intuits, and knows in the state and what the thinking mind comprehends there.

ethics, right, duties, and laws—and so is evil, in fact evil through and through and universally—but in addition its form is a subjective void, i.e. it knows itself as this contentless void and in this knowledge knows itself as absolute.

In my *Phenomenology of Mind*,* I have shown how this absolute self-complacency fails to rest in a solitary worship of itself but builds up a sort of community whose bond and substance is, e.g., the 'mutual asseveration of conscientiousness and good intentions, the enjoyment of this mutual purity', but is above all 'the refreshment derived from the glory of this self-knowledge and self-expression, from the glory of fostering and cherishing this experience'. I have shown also how what has been called[59] a 'beautiful soul'—that still nobler type of subjectivism which empties the objective of all content and so fades away until it loses all actuality—is a variation of subjectivism like other forms of the same phenomenon akin to the series of them here considered. What is said here may be compared with the entire section (C), 'Conscience', in the *Phenomenology*, especially the part dealing with the transition to a higher stage—a stage, however, there different in character.[60] [A.]

Transition from Morality to Ethical Life

141. For the good as the substantial universal of freedom, but as something still abstract, there are therefore required determinate characteristics of some sort and the principle for determining them, though a principle identical with the good itself. For conscience similarly, as the purely abstract principle of determination, it is required that its decisions shall be universal and objective. If good and conscience are each kept abstract and thereby elevated to independent totalities, then both become the indeterminate which ought to be determined.—But the integration of these two relative totalities into an absolute identity has already been implicitly achieved in that this very subjectivity of pure self-certainty, aware in its vacuity of its gradual evaporation, is identical with the abstract universality of the good. The identity of the good with the subjective will, an identity which therefore is concrete and the truth of them both, is Ethical Life.

The details of such a transition of the concept are made intelligible in logic. Here, however, it need only be said that it is the nature of the restricted and the finite (i.e. here the abstract good which only ought to be [but is not], and the equally abstract subjectivity which only *ought* to be good [but is not]) to have its opposite implicit within it, the good

* [1st edn.] pp. 605 ff. [Eng. tr. pp. 663 ff.].

its actuality, and subjectivity (the moment in which ethical life is actual) the good; but since they are one-sided they are not yet posited in accordance with their implicit nature. They become so posited in their negation. That is to say, in their one-sidedness, when each is bent on declining to have in it what is in it implicitly—when the good is without subjectivity and a determinate character, and the determining principle, subjectivity, is without what is implicit within it—and when both build themselves into independent totalities, they are annulled and thereby reduced to moments, to moments of the concept which becomes manifest as their unity and, having acquired reality precisely through this positing of its moments, is now present as Idea—as the concept which has matured its determinations to reality and at the same time is present in their identity as their implicit essence.

The embodiment of freedom which was (α) first of all immediate as right, is (β) characterized in the reflection of self-consciousness as good. (γ) The third stage, originating here, in its transition from (β) to ethical life, as the truth of good and subjectivity, is therefore the truth both of subjectivity and right. Ethical life is a subjective disposition, but one imbued with what is inherently right. The fact that this Idea is the truth of the concept of freedom is something which, in philosophy, must be proved, not presupposed, not adopted from feeling or elsewhere. This demonstration is contained only in the fact that right and the moral self-consciousness both display in themselves their regression to this Idea as their outcome.[61] Those who hope to be able to dispense with proof and demonstration in philosophy show thereby that they are still far from knowing the first thing about what philosophy is. On other topics argue they may, but in philosophy they have no right to join in the argument if they wish to argue without the concept. [A.]

THIRD PART

ETHICAL LIFE

142. Ethical life is the Idea of freedom in that on the one hand it is the good become alive—the good endowed in self-conscious-ness with knowing and willing and actualized by self-conscious action—while on the other hand self-consciousness has in the ethical realm its absolute foundation and the end which actuates its effort.[1] Thus ethical life is the concept of freedom developed into the existing world and the nature of self-consciousness.

143. Since this unity of the concept of the will with its embodi-ment—i.e. the particular will—is knowing, consciousness of the distinction between these two moments of the Idea is present, but present in such a way that now each of these moments is in its own eyes the totality of the Idea and has that totality as its foundation and content.[2]

144. (α) The objective ethical order, which comes on the scene in place of good in the abstract, is substance made concrete by sub-jectivity as infinite form.[3] Hence it posits within itself distinctions whose specific character is thereby determined by the concept,[4] and which endow the ethical order with a stable content indepen-dently necessary and subsistent in exaltation above subjective opinion and caprice. These distinctions are absolutely valid laws and institutions. [A.]

145. It is the fact that the ethical order is the system of these specific determinations of the Idea which constitutes its ration-ality. Hence the ethical order is freedom or the absolute will as what is objective, a circle of necessity whose moments are the ethical powers which regulate the life of individuals. To these powers individuals are related as accidents to substance, and it is in individuals that these powers are represented, have the shape of appearance, and become actualized.[5] [A.]

146. (β) The substantial order, in the self-consciousness which it has thus actually attained in individuals, knows itself and so is an object of knowledge. This ethical substance and its laws and powers are on the one hand an object over against the subject, and from his point of view they *are*—'are' in the highest sense of self-subsistent being. This is an absolute authority and power infinitely more firmly established than the being of nature.[6]

The sun, the moon, mountains, rivers, and the natural objects of all kinds by which we are surrounded, *are*. For consciousness they have the authority not only of mere being but also of possessing a particular nature which it accepts and to which it adjusts itself in dealing with them, using them, or in being otherwise concerned with them. The authority of ethical laws is infinitely higher, because natural objects conceal rationality under the cloak of contingency and exhibit it only in their utterly external and disconnected way.

147. On the other hand, they are not something alien to the subject. On the contrary, his spirit bears witness to them as to its own essence, the essence in which he has a feeling of his selfhood, and in which he lives as in his own element which is not distinguished from himself. The subject is thus directly linked to the ethical order by a relation which is more like an identity than even the relation of faith or trust.

Faith and trust emerge along with reflection; they presuppose the power of forming ideas and making distinctions. For example, it is one thing to be a pagan, a different thing to believe in a pagan religion. This relation or rather this absence of relation, this identity in which the ethical order is the actual living soul of self-consciousness, can no doubt pass over into a relation of faith and conviction and into a relation produced by means of further reflection, i.e. into an *insight* due to reasoning starting perhaps from some particular purposes interests, and considerations, from fear or hope, or from historical conditions. But adequate *knowledge* of this identity depends on thinking in terms of the concept.

148. As substantive in character, these laws and institutions are duties binding on the will of the individual, because as subjective, as inherently undetermined, or determined as particular, he distinguishes himself from them and hence stands related to them as to the substance of his own being.

The 'doctrine of duties' in moral philosophy (I mean the objective doctrine, not that which is supposed to be contained in the empty principle of moral subjectivity, because that principle determines nothing— see Paragraph 134) is therefore comprised in the systematic development of the circle of ethical necessity[7] which follows in this Third Part. The difference between the exposition in this book and the form of a 'doctrine of duties'[8] lies solely in the fact that, in what follows, the specific types of ethical life turn up as necessary relationships; there the exposition ends, without being supplemented in each case by the addition that 'therefore men have a duty to conform to this institution'.

A 'doctrine of duties' which is other than a philosophical science takes its material from existing relationships and shows its connexion with the moralist's personal notions or with principles and thoughts, purposes, impulses, feelings, &c., that are forthcoming everywhere; and as reasons for accepting each duty in turn, it may tack on its further consequences in their bearing on the other ethical relationships or on welfare and opinion. But an immanent and logical 'doctrine of duties' can be nothing except the serial exposition of the relationships which are necessitated by the Idea of freedom and are therefore actual in their entirety, to wit in the state.

149. The bond of duty can appear as a restriction only on indeterminate subjectivity or abstract freedom, and on the impulses either of the natural will or of the moral will which determines its indeterminate good arbitrarily. The truth is, however, that in duty the individual finds his liberation; first, liberation from dependence on mere natural impulse and from the depression which as a particular subject he cannot escape in his moral reflections on what ought to be and what might be; secondly, liberation from the indeterminate subjectivity which, never reaching reality or the objective determinacy of action, remains self-enclosed and devoid of actuality. In duty the individual acquires his substantive freedom. [A.]

150. Virtue is the ethical order reflected in the individual character so far as that character is determined by its natural endowment. When virtue displays itself solely as the individual's simple conformity with the duties of the station to which he belongs, it is rectitude.[9]

In an *ethical* community, it is easy to say what man must do, what are the duties he has to fulfil in order to be virtuous: he has simply to follow the well-known and explicit rules of his own situation. Rectitude is the general character which may be demanded of him by law or custom. But from the standpoint of *morality*, rectitude often seems to be something comparatively inferior, something beyond which still higher demands must be made on oneself and others, because the craving to be something special is not satisfied with what is absolute and universal; it finds consciousness of peculiarity only in what is exceptional.

The various facets of rectitude may equally well be called virtues, since they are also properties of the individual, although not specially of him in contrast with others. Talk about virtue, however, readily borders on empty rhetoric, because it is only about something abstract and indeterminate; and furthermore, argumentative and expository talk of the sort is addressed to the individual as to a being of caprice and subjective inclination. In an existing ethical order in which a complete system of ethical relations has been developed and actualized, virtue in the strict sense of the word is in place and actually appears only in exceptional circumstances or when one obligation clashes with another. The clash, however, must be a genuine one, because moral reflection can manufacture clashes of all sorts to suit its purpose and give itself a consciousness of being something special and having made sacrifices. It is for this reason that the phenomenon of virtue proper is commoner when societies and communities are uncivilized, since in those circumstances ethical conditions and their actualization are more a matter of private choice or the natural genius of an exceptional individual. For instance, it was especially to Hercules that the ancients ascribed virtue.[10] In the states of antiquity, ethical life had not grown into this free system of an objective order self-subsistently developed, and consequently it was by the personal genius of individuals that this defect had to be made good. It follows that if a 'doctrine of virtues' is not a mere 'doctrine of duties', and if therefore it embraces the particular facet of character, the facet grounded in natural endowment, it will be a natural history of mind.[11]

Since virtues are ethical principles applied to the particular, and since in this their subjective aspect they are something indeterminate, there turns up here for determining them the quantitative principle of more or less. The result is that consideration of them introduces their corresponding defects or vices, as in Aristotle, who defined each particular virtue as strictly a mean between an excess and a deficiency.[12]

The content which assumes the form of duties and then virtues is the same as that which also has the form of impulses (see Remark to Paragraph 19). Impulses have the same basic content as duties and virtues, but in impulses this content still belongs to the immediate will and to instinctive feeling; it has not been developed to the point of becoming ethical. Consequently, impulses have in common with the content of duties and virtues only the abstract object on which they are directed, an object indeterminate in itself, and so devoid of anything to discriminate them as good or evil.[13] Or in other words, impulses, considered abstractly in their positive aspect alone, are good, while, considered abstractly in their negative aspect alone, they are evil (see Paragraph 18). [A.]

151. But when individuals are simply identified with the actual order, ethical life (*das Sittliche*) appears as their general mode of conduct, i.e. as custom[14] (*Sitte*), while the habitual practice of ethical living appears as a second nature which, put in the place of the initial, purely natural will, is the soul of custom permeating it through and through, the significance and the actuality of its existence. It is mind living and present as a world, and the substance of mind thus exists now for the first time as mind. [A.]

152. In this way the ethical substantial order has attained its right, and its right its validity. That is to say, the self-will of the individual has vanished together with his private conscience which had claimed independence and opposed itself to the ethical substance. For, when his character is ethical, he recognizes as the end which moves him to act the universal which is itself unmoved but is disclosed in its specific determinations as rationality actualized. He knows that his own dignity and the whole stability of his particular ends are grounded in this same universal, and it is therein that he actually attains these. Subjectivity is itself the absolute form and existent actuality of the substantial order, and the distinction between subject on the one hand and substance on the other, as the object, end, and controlling power of the subject, is the same as, and has vanished directly along with, the distinction between them in form.

Subjectivity is the ground wherein the concept of freedom is realized (see Paragraph 106). At the level of morality, subjectivity is still distinct from freedom, the concept of subjectivity; but at the level of ethical life it is the realization of the concept in a way adequate to the concept itself.

153. The right of individuals to be subjectively destined to freedom is fulfilled when they belong to an actual ethical order, because their conviction of their freedom finds its truth in such an objective order, and it is in an ethical order that they are actually in possession of their own essence or their own inner universality (see Paragraph 147).

When a father inquired about the best method of educating his son in ethical conduct, a Pythagorean replied: 'Make him a citizen of a state with good laws.' (The phrase has also been attributed to others.[15]) [A.]

154. The right of individuals to their *particular* satisfaction is also contained in the ethical substantial order, since particularity is the outward appearance of the ethical order—a mode in which that order is existent.[16]

155. Hence in this identity of the universal will with the particular will, right and duty coalesce, and by being in the ethical order a man has rights in so far as he has duties, and duties in so far as he has rights. In the sphere of abstract right, I have the right and another has the corresponding duty. In the moral sphere, the right of my private judgement and will, as well as of my happiness, has not, but only ought to have, coalesced with duties and become objective. [A.]

156. The ethical substance, as containing independent self-consciousness united with its concept, is the actual mind of a family and a nation. [A.]

157. The concept of this Idea has being only as mind, as something knowing itself and actual, because it is the objectification of itself, the movement running through the form of its moments.[17] It is therefore

(A) ethical mind in its natural or immediate phase—the *Family*. This substantiality loses its unity, passes over into division, and into the phase of relation, i.e. into

(B) *Civil Society*—an association of members as self-subsistent individuals in a universality which, because of their self-subsistence, is only abstract. Their association is brought about by their needs, by the legal system—the means to security of person and property—and by an external organization for attaining their particular and common interests. This external state

(C) is brought back[18] to and welded into unity in the *Constitution of the State* which is the end and actuality of both the substantial universal order and the public life devoted thereto.

SUB-SECTION I

THE FAMILY

158. The family, as the immediate substantiality of mind, is specifically characterized by love, which is mind's feeling of its own unity. Hence in a family, one's frame of mind is to have self-consciousness of one's individuality within this unity as the absolute essence of oneself, with the result that one is in it not as an independent person but as a member. [A.]

159. The right which the individual enjoys on the strength of the family unity and which is in the first place simply the individual's life within this unity, takes on the *form* of right (as the abstract moment of determinate individuality) only when the family begins to dissolve. At that point those who should be family-members both in their inclination and in actuality begin to be self-subsistent persons, and whereas they formerly constituted one specific moment within the whole, they now receive their share separately and so only in an external fashion by way of money, food, educational expenses, and the like. [A.]

160. The family is completed in these three phases:

(a) *Marriage*, the form assumed by the concept of the family in its immediate phase;

(b) *Family Property and Capital* (the external embodiment of the concept) and attention to these;

(c) *The Education of Children and the Dissolution of the Family.*

A. *Marriage*

161. Marriage, as the immediate type of ethical relationship, contains first, the moment of physical life; and since marriage is a *substantial* tie, the life involved in it is life in its totality, i.e. as the actuality of the race and its life-process.* But, secondly, in self-consciousness the natural sexual union—a union purely inward or implicit and for that very reason *existent* as purely external—is changed into a union on the level of mind, into self-conscious love.[19] [A.]

162. On the subjective side, marriage may have a more obvious source in the particular inclination of the two persons who are entering upon the marriage tie, or in the foresight and contrivance of the parents, and so forth. But its objective source lies in the free consent of the persons, especially in their consent to make themselves one person, to renounce their natural and individual personality to this unity of one with the other. From this point of view, their union is a self-restriction, but in fact it is their liberation, because in it they attain their substantive self-consciousness.

Our objectively appointed end and so our ethical duty is to enter the married state. The external origin of any *particular* marriage is in the nature of the case contingent, and it depends principally on the extent to which reflective thought has been developed. At one extreme, the first step is that the marriage is arranged by the contrivance of benevolent parents; the appointed end of the parties is a union of mutual love, and their inclination to marry arises from the fact that each grows acquainted with the other from the first as a destined partner. At the other extreme, it is the inclination of the parties which comes first,

* Cf. *Enc.* [1st edn.], §§ 167 ff. and §§ 288 ff. [3rd edn. §§ 220 ff. and §§ 366 ff.].

appearing in them as *these* two infinitely particularized individuals. The more ethical way to matrimony may be taken to be the former extreme or any way at all whereby the decision to marry comes first and the inclination to do so follows, so that in the actual wedding both decision and inclination coalesce. In the latter extreme, it is the uniqueness of the infinitely particularized which makes good its claims in accordance with the subjective principle of the modern world (see Remark to Paragraph 124).

But those works of modern art, dramatic and other, in which the love of the sexes is the main interest, are pervaded by a chill despite the heat of passion they portray, for they associate the passion with accident throughout and represent the entire dramatic interest as if it rested solely on the characters as *these individuals*; what rests on them may indeed be of infinite importance to *them*, but is of none whatever in itself.[20] [A.]

163. The ethical aspect of marriage consists in the parties' consciousness of this unity as their substantive aim, and so in their love, trust, and common sharing of their entire existence as individuals. When the parties are in this frame of mind and their union is actual, their physical passion sinks to the level of a physical moment, destined to vanish in its very satisfaction. On the other hand, the spiritual bond of union secures its rights as the substance of marriage and thus rises, inherently indissoluble, to a plane above the contingency of passion and the transience of particular caprice.

It was noted above (in Paragraph 75) that marriage, so far as its essential basis is concerned, is not a contractual relation. On the contrary, though marriage begins in contract, it is precisely a contract to transcend the standpoint of contract, the standpoint from which persons are regarded in their individuality as self-subsistent units. The identification of personalities, whereby the family becomes one person and its members become its accidents (though substance is in essence the relation of accidents to itself*), is the ethical mind. Taken by itself and stripped of the manifold externals of which it is possessed owing to its embodiment in *these* individuals and the interests of the phenomenal realm, interests limited in time and numerous other ways, this mind emerges in a shape for representative thinking and has been revered as *Penates*, &c.; and in general it is in this mind that the religious character of marriage and the family, or *pietas*,[21] is grounded. It is a further abstraction still to separate the divine, or the substantive, from its body, and then to stamp it, together with the feeling and consciousness of mental unity, as what is falsely called 'Platonic' love. This separation is in keeping with the monastic doctrine which characterizes the moment of physical life as purely negative and which, precisely by thus separating

---

* See *Enc.* [1st edn.], § 98 [3rd edn. § 150].

the physical from the mental, endows the former by itself with infinite importance. [A.]

164. Mere agreement to the stipulated terms of a contract in itself involves the genuine transfer of the property in question (see Paragraph 79). Similarly, the solemn declaration by the parties of their consent to enter the ethical bond of marriage, and its corresponding recognition and confirmation by their family and community,* constitutes the formal completion and actuality of marriage. The knot is tied and made ethical only after this ceremony, whereby through the use of signs, i.e. of language (the most mental embodiment of mind—see Paragraph 78), the substantial thing in the marriage is brought completely into being. As a result, the sensuous moment, the one proper to physical life, is put into its ethical place as something only consequential and accidental, belonging to the external embodiment of the ethical bond, which indeed can subsist exclusively in reciprocal love and support.

If with a view to framing or criticizing legal enactments, the question is asked: what should be regarded as the chief end of marriage?, the question may be taken to mean: which single facet of marriage in its actuality is to be regarded as the most essential one? No one facet by itself, however, makes up the whole range of its implicit and explicit content, i.e. of its ethical character, and one or other of its facets may be lacking in an existing marriage without detriment to the essence of marriage itself.

It is in the actual conclusion of a marriage, i.e. in the wedding, that the essence of the tie is expressed and established beyond dispute as something ethical, raised above the contingency of feeling and private inclination. If this ceremony is taken as an external formality, a mere so-called 'civil requirement', it is thereby stripped of all significance except perhaps that of serving the purpose of edification and attesting the civil relation of the parties. It is reduced indeed to a mere *fiat* of a civil or ecclesiastical authority. As such it appears as something not merely indifferent to the true nature of marriage, but actually alien to it. The heart is constrained by the law to attach a value to the formal ceremony and the latter is looked upon merely as a condition which must precede the complete mutual surrender of the parties to one another. As such it appears to bring disunion into their loving disposition and, like an alien intruder, to thwart the inwardness of their union. Such a doctrine pretentiously claims to afford the highest conception of the freedom, inwardness, and perfection of love; but in fact it is a travesty of the

---

* The fact that the church comes in in this connexion is a further point, but not one for discussion here.[22]

ethical aspect of love, the higher aspect which restrains purely sensual impulse and puts it in the background. Such restraint is already present at the instinctive level in shame, and it rises to chastity and modesty as consciousness becomes more specifically intelligent. In particular, the view just criticized casts aside marriage's specifically ethical character, which consists in this, that the consciousness of the parties is crystallized out of its physical and subjective mode and lifted to the thought of what is substantive; instead of continually reserving to itself the contingency and caprice of bodily desire, it removes the marriage bond from the province of this caprice, surrenders to the substantive, and swears allegiance to the *Penates*; the physical moment it subordinates until it becomes something wholly conditioned by the true and ethical character of the marriage relation and by the recognition of the bond as an ethical one. It is effrontery and its buttress, the Understanding, which cannot apprehend the speculative character of the substantial tie; nevertheless, with this speculative character there correspond both ethical purity of heart and the legislation of Christian peoples. [A.]

165. The difference in the physical characteristics of the two sexes has a rational basis and consequently acquires an intellectual and ethical significance. This significance is determined by the difference into which the ethical substantiality, as the concept, internally sunders itself in order that its vitality may become a concrete unity consequent upon this difference.[23]

166. Thus one sex is mind in its self-diremption into explicit personal self-subsistence and the knowledge and volition of free universality, i.e. the self-consciousness of conceptual thought and the volition of the objective final end. The other sex is mind maintaining itself in unity as knowledge and volition of the substantive, but knowledge and volition in the form of concrete individuality and feeling. In relation to externality, the former is powerful and active, the latter passive and subjective. It follows that man has his actual substantive life in the state, in learning, and so forth, as well as in labour and struggle with the external world and with himself so that it is only out of his diremption that he fights his way to self-subsistent unity with himself. In the family he has a tranquil intuition of this unity, and there he lives a subjective ethical life on the plane of feeling. Woman, on the other hand, has her substantive destiny in the family, and to be imbued with family piety is her ethical frame of mind.

For this reason, family piety is expounded in Sophocles' *Antigone*—one of the most sublime presentations of this virtue—as principally the

law of woman, and as the law of a substantiality at once subjective and on
the plane of feeling, the law of the inward life, a life which has not yet
attained its full actualization; as the law of the ancient gods, 'the gods
of the underworld'; as 'an everlasting law, and no man knows at what
time it was first put forth'.²⁴ This law is there displayed as a law opposed
to public law, to the law of the land. This is the supreme opposition in
ethics and therefore in tragedy; and it is individualized in the same play
in the opposing natures of man and woman.* [A.]

167. In essence marriage is monogamy because it is personality
—immediate exclusive individuality—which enters into this tie
and surrenders itself to it; and hence the tie's truth and inwardness
(i.e. the subjective form of its substantiality) proceeds only from
the mutual, whole-hearted, surrender of this personality. Personality attains its right of being conscious of itself in another only in
so far as the other is in this identical relationship as a person, i.e. as
an atomic individual.

Marriage, and especially monogamy, is one of the absolute principles
on which the ethical life of a community depends. Hence marriage
comes to be recorded as one of the moments in the founding of states
by gods or heroes.

168. Further, marriage results from the free surrender by both
sexes of their personality—a personality in every possible way
unique in each of the parties. Consequently, it ought not to be
entered by two people identical in stock who are already acquainted
and perfectly known to one another; for individuals in the same
circle of relationship have no special personality of their own in
contrast with that of others in the same circle. On the contrary,
the parties should be drawn from separate families and their personalities should be different in origin. Since the very conception
of marriage is that it is a freely undertaken ethical transaction, not
a tie directly grounded in the physical organism and its desires, it
follows that the marriage of blood-relations runs counter to this
conception and so also to genuine natural feeling.

Marriage itself is sometimes said to be grounded not in natural rights
but simply in instinctive sexual impulses; or again it is treated as a
contract with an arbitrary basis. External arguments in support of
monogamy have been drawn from physical considerations such as the
number of men and women. Dark feelings of repulsion are advanced
as the sole ground for prohibiting consanguineous marriage. The basis

---

* Cf. *Phenomenology* [1st edn.], pp. 383 ff., 417 ff. [Eng. tr. pp. 466 ff.,
495 ff.].

of all these views is the fashionable idea of a state of nature and a natural origin for rights, and the lack of the concept of rationality and freedom. [A.]

169. The family, as person, has its real external existence in property; and it is only when this property takes the form of capital[25] that it becomes the embodiment of the substantial personality of the family.

B. *The Family Capital*

170. It is not merely property which a family possesses; as a universal and enduring person, it requires possessions specifically determined as permanent and secure, i.e. it requires capital. The arbitrariness of a single owner's particular needs is one moment in property taken abstractly; but this moment, together with the selfishness of desire, is here transformed into something ethical, into labour and care for a common possession.

In the sagas of the founding of states, or at least of a social and orderly life, the introduction of permanent property is linked with the introduction of marriage. The nature of this capital, however, and the proper means of its consolidation will appear in the section on civil society.[26]

171. The family as a legal entity in relation to others must be represented by the husband as its head. Further, it is his prerogative to go out and work for its living, to attend to its needs, and to control and administer its capital. This capital is common property so that, while no member of the family has property of his own, each has his right in the common stock. This right, however, may come into collision with the head of the family's right of administration owing to the fact that the ethical temper of the family is still only at the level of immediacy (see Paragraph 158) and so is exposed to partition and contingency.

172. A marriage brings into being a new family which is self-subsistent and independent of the clans or 'houses' from which its members have been drawn. The tie between these and the new family has a natural basis—consanguinity, but the new family is based on love of an ethical type. Thus an individual's property too has an essential connexion with his conjugal relationship and only a comparatively remote one with his relation to his clan or 'house'.

The significance of marriage settlements which impose a restriction on the couple's common ownership of their goods, of arrangements to secure continued legal assistance for the woman, and so forth, lies in their being provisions in case of the dissolution of the marriage, either naturally by death, or by divorce, &c. They are also safeguards for securing that in such an eventuality the different members of the family shall secure their share of the common stock. [A.]

C. The Education of Children and the Dissolution of the Family

173. In substance marriage is a unity, though only a unity of inwardness or disposition; in outward existence, however, the unity is sundered in the two parties. It is only in the children that the unity itself exists externally, objectively, and explicitly as a unity, because the parents love the children as their love, as the embodiment of their own substance. From the physical point of view, the presupposition—persons immediately existent (as parents)—here becomes a result,[27] a process which runs away into the infinite series of generations, each producing the next and presupposing the one before. This is the mode in which the single mind of the *Penates* reveals its existence in the finite sphere of nature as a race. [A.]

174. Children have the right to maintenance and education at the expense of the family's common capital. The right of the parents to the service as service of their children is based upon and is restricted by the common task of looking after the family generally. Similarly, the right of the parents over the wishes of their children is determined by the object in view—discipline and education. The punishment of children does not aim at justice as such; the aim is more subjective and moral in character, i.e. to deter them from exercising a freedom still in the toils of nature and to lift the universal into their consciousness and will. [A.]

175. Children are potentially free and their life directly embodies nothing save potential freedom. Consequently they are not things and cannot be the property either of their parents or others. In respect of his relation to the family, the child's education has the positive aim of instilling ethical principles into him in the form of an immediate feeling for which differences are not yet explicit, so that thus equipped with the foundation of an ethical life, his heart may live its early years in love, trust, and obedience. In respect of the same relation, this education has the negative aim of raising children out of the instinctive, physical, level on which they are originally, to self-subsistence and freedom of personality and so to the level on which they have power to leave the natural unity of the family.

One of the blackest marks against Roman legislation is the law whereby children were treated by their fathers as slaves. This gangrene of the ethical order at the tenderest point of its innermost life is one of the most important clues for understanding the place of the Romans in the history of the world and their tendency towards legal formalism.[28]

The necessity for education is present in children as their own feeling of dissatisfaction with themselves as they are, as the desire to belong to the adult world whose superiority they divine, as the longing to grow up. The play theory of education[29] assumes that what is childish is itself already something of inherent worth and presents it as such to the children; in their eyes it lowers serious pursuits, and education itself, to a form of childishness for which the children themselves have scant respect. The advocates of this method represent the child, in the immaturity in which he feels himself to be, as really mature and they struggle to make him satisfied with himself as he is. But they corrupt and distort his genuine and proper need for something better, and create in him a blind indifference to the substantial ties of the intellectual world, a contempt of his elders because they have thus posed before him, a child, in a contemptible and childish fashion, and finally a vanity and conceit which feeds on the notion of its own superiority. [A.]

176. Marriage is but the ethical Idea in its *immediacy* and so has its objective actuality only in the inwardness of subjective feeling and disposition. In this fact is rooted the fundamental contingency of marriage in the world of existence. There can be no compulsion on people to marry; and, on the other hand, there is no merely legal or positive bond which can hold the parties together once their dispositions and actions have become hostile and contrary. A third[30] ethical authority, however, is called for to maintain the right of marriage—an ethical substantiality—against the mere whims of hostile disposition or the accident of a purely passing mood, and so forth. Such an authority distinguishes these from the total estrangement of the two parties and may not grant divorce until it is satisfied that the estrangement is total. [A.]

177. The ethical dissolution of the family consists in this, that once the children have been educated to freedom of personality, and have come of age, they become recognized as persons in the eyes of the law and as capable of holding free property of their own and founding families of their own, the sons as heads of new families, the daughters as wives. They now have their substantive destiny in the new family; the old family on the other hand falls into the background as merely their ultimate basis and origin, while *a fortiori* the clan is an abstraction, devoid of rights.

178. The natural dissolution of the family by the death of the parents, particularly the father, has inheritance as its consequence so far as the family capital is concerned. The essence of inheritance is the transfer to private ownership of property which is in principle common. When comparatively remote degrees of kinship are in question, and when persons and families are so dispersed in civil society that they have begun to gain self-subsistence, this transfer becomes the less hard and fast as the sense of family unity fades away and as every marriage becomes the surrender of previous family relationships and the founding of a new self-subsistent family.

It has been suggested[31] that the basis of inheritance lies in the fact that, by a man's death, his property becomes wealth without an owner, and as such falls to the first person who takes possession of it, because of course it is the relatives who are normally nearest a man's death-bed and so they are generally the first to take possession. Hence it is supposed that this customary occurrence is made a rule by positive legislation in the interests of orderliness. This ingenious idea disregards the nature of family relationship.

179. The result of this disintegration of the family is that a man may at will either squander his capital altogether, mainly in accordance with his private caprices, opinions, and ends, or else look upon a circle of friends and acquaintances, &c., as if they were his family and make a will embodying a declaration to that effect, with the result that they become his legal heirs.

The ethical justification of freedom to dispose of one's property by will to a circle of friends would depend on the formation of such a circle;[32] but there goes to its formation so much accident, arbitrariness, and shrewd self-seeking, &c.—especially since testamentary hopes have a bearing on readiness to enter it—that the ethical moment in it is only something very vague. Further, the recognition of a man's competence to bequeath his property arbitrarily is much more likely to be an occasion for breach of ethical obligations and for mean exertions and equally mean subservience; and it also provides opportunity and justification for the folly, caprice, and malice of attaching to professed benefactions and gifts vain, tyrannical, and vexatious conditions operative after the testator's death and so in any case after his property ceases to be his.

180. The principle that the members of the family grow up to be self-subsistent persons in the eyes of the law (see Paragraph 177) lets into the circle of the family something of the same arbitrariness and discrimination among the natural heirs, though its exercise there must be restricted to a minimum in order to prevent injury to the basic family relationship.

The mere downright arbitrariness of the deceased cannot be made the principle underlying the right to make a will, especially if it runs counter to the substantive right of the family. For after all no respect would be forthcoming for his wishes after his death, if not from the family's love and veneration for its deceased fellow-member. Such arbitrariness by itself contains nothing worthy of higher respect than the right of the family as such—on the contrary.

The other ground for the validity of testamentary disposition would consist simply in its arbitrary recognition by others.[33] But such an argument may prima facie be admitted only when family ties, to which testamentary disposition is intrinsic, become remoter and more ineffective. If they are actually present, however, without being effective, the situation is unethical; and to give extended validity to arbitrary dispositions at the expense of family ties *eo ipso* weakens the ethical character of the latter.

To make the father's arbitrary will within the family the main principle of inheritance was part of the harsh and unethical legal system of Rome to which reference has been made already. That system even gave a father power to sell his son, and if the son was manumitted by a third party, he came under his father's *potestas* once more. Not until he was manumitted a third time was he actually and finally free. The son never attained his majority *de jure* nor did he become a person in law; the only property he could hold was booty won in war (*peculium castrense*). If he passed out of his father's *potestas* after being thrice sold and manumitted, he did not inherit along with those who had continued in bondage to the head of the family, unless the will specifically so provided.[34] Similarly, a wife* remained attached to her family of origin rather than to the new family which by her marriage she had helped to found, and which was now properly her own, and she was therefore precluded from inheriting any share of the goods of what was properly her own family, for neither wife nor mother shared in the distribution of an estate.

Later, with the growing feeling for rationality, the unethical provisions of laws such as these and others were evaded in the course of their administration, for example with the help of the expression *bonorum*

---

* i.e. a *matrona*, not a wife who *in manum convenit, in mancipio est*, and whose marriage was a slavery to her husband.[35]

*possessio** instead of *hereditas*, and through the fiction of nicknaming a
filia a *filius*. This was referred to above (see Remark to Paragraph 3)
as the sad necessity to which the judge was reduced in the face of bad
laws—the necessity of smuggling reason into them on the sly, or at
least into some of their consequences. Connected with this were the
terrible instability of the chief political institutions and a riot of legislation to stem the outbreak of resulting evils.

From Roman history and the writings of Lucian and others,[37] we are
sufficiently familiar with the unethical consequences of giving the head
of a Roman family the right to name whom he pleased as his heir.

Marriage is ethical life at the level of immediacy; in the very nature of
the case, therefore, it must be a mixture of a substantial tie with natural
contingency and inner arbitrariness. Now when by the slave-status of
children, by legal provisions such as those mentioned above as well as
others consequential upon them, and in addition by the ease of Roman
divorce, pride of place is given to arbitrariness instead of to the right of
the substantial (so that even Cicero—and what fine writing about the
Honestum and *Decorum* there is in his *De Officiis* and in all sorts of other
places!—even Cicero divorced his wife as a business speculation in order
to pay his debts with his new wife's dowry), then a legal road is paved to
the corruption of manners, or rather the laws themselves necessitate
such corruption.

The institution of heirs-at-law with a view to preserving the family and
its *splendor* by means of *fideicommissa* and *substitutiones*[38] (in order to
favour sons by excluding daughters from inheriting, or to favour the
eldest son by excluding the other children) is an infringement of the
principle of the freedom of property (see Paragraph 62), like the admission of any other inequality in the treatment of heirs. And besides, such
an institution depends on an arbitrariness which in and by itself has no
right to recognition, or more precisely on the thought of wishing to
preserve intact not so much *this* family but rather *this* clan or 'house'.
Yet it is not this clan or 'house', but the family proper which is the Idea
and which therefore possesses the right to recognition, and both the
ethical disposition and family trees are much more likely to be preserved
by freedom of property and equality of inheritance than by the reverse
of these.

Institutions of this kind, like the Roman, wholly ignore the right due
to marriage, because by a marriage the foundation of a unique actual
family is *eo ipso* completed (see Paragraph 172), and because what is
called, in contrast with the new family, the family in the wide sense, i.e.
the *stirps* or *gens*, becomes only an abstraction (see Paragraph 177)
growing less and less actual the further it recedes into the background

---

* The fact that there is a further distinction between this and *possessio bonorum* is a piece of the erudition which constitutes the juristic expert.[36]

as one generation succeeds another. Love, the ethical moment in
marriage, is by its very nature a feeling for actual living individuals, not
for an abstraction. This abstraction of the Understanding [the *gens*]
appears in history as the principle underlying the contribution of the
Roman Empire to world history (see Paragraph 357).[39] In the higher
sphere of the state, a right of primogeniture arises together with estates
rigidly entailed; it arises, however, not arbitrarily but as the inevitable
outcome of the Idea of the state. On this point see below, Paragraph
306. [A.]

Transition of the Family into Civil Society

181. The family disintegrates (both essentially, through the
working of the principle of personality, and also in the course of
nature) into a plurality of families, each of which conducts itself
as in principle a self-subsistent concrete person and therefore as
externally related to its neighbours. In other words, the moments
bound together in the unity of the family, since the family is the
ethical Idea still in its concept, must be released from the concept
to self-subsistent objective reality. This is the stage of difference.
This gives us, to use abstract language in the first place, the determination of particularity which is related to universality but in
such a way that universality is its basic principle, though still only
an inward principle; for that reason, the universal merely shows in
the particular as its form.[40] Hence this relation of reflection prima
facie portrays the disappearance of ethical life or, since this life
as the essence necessarily shows itself,* this relation constitutes
the world of ethical appearance—civil society.

The expansion of the family, as its transition into a new principle, is
in the external world sometimes its peaceful expansion until it becomes
a people, i.e. a nation, which thus has a common natural origin, or sometimes the federation of scattered groups of families under the influence
of an overlord's power or as a result of a voluntary association produced
by the tie of needs and the reciprocity of their satisfaction. [A.]

SUB-SECTION 2

CIVIL SOCIETY

182. The concrete person,[41] who is himself the object of his
particular aims, is, as a totality of wants and a mixture of caprice
and physical necessity, one principle of civil society. But the particular person is essentially so related to other particular persons

---

* Cf. *Enc.* [1st edn.], §§ 64 ff., §§ 81 ff. [3rd edn. §§ 115 ff., §§ 131 ff.].

that each establishes himself and finds satisfaction by means of the others, and at the same time purely and simply by means of the form of universality, the second principle here. [A.]

183. In the course of the actual attainment of selfish ends—an attainment conditioned in this way by universality—there is formed a system of complete interdependence, wherein the livelihood, happiness, and legal status of one man is interwoven with the livelihood, happiness, and rights of all. On this system, individual happiness, &c., depend, and only in this connected system are they actualized and secured. This system may be prima facie regarded as the external state,[42] the state based on need, the state as the Understanding envisages it.

184. The Idea in this its stage of division imparts to each of its moments a characteristic embodiment; to particularity it gives the right to develop and launch forth in all directions; and to universality the right to prove itself not only the ground and necessary form of particularity, but also the authority standing over it and its final end. It is the system of the ethical order, split into its extremes and lost, which constitutes the Idea's abstract moment, its moment of reality. Here the Idea is present only as a relative totality[43] and as the inner necessity behind this outward appearance. [A.]

185. Particularity by itself, given free rein in every direction to satisfy its needs, accidental caprices, and subjective desires, destroys itself and its substantive concept in this process of gratification. At the same time, the satisfaction of need, necessary and accidental alike, is accidental because it breeds new desires without end, is in thoroughgoing dependence on caprice and external accident, and is held in check by the power of universality. In these contrasts and their complexity, civil society affords a spectacle of extravagance and want as well as of the physical and ethical degeneration common to them both.

The development of particularity to self-subsistence (compare Remark to Paragraph 124) is the moment which appeared in the ancient world as an invasion of ethical corruption and as the ultimate cause of that world's downfall. Some of these ancient states were built on the patriarchal and religious principle, others on the principle of an ethical order which was more explicitly intellectual, though still comparatively simple; in either case they rested on primitive unsophisticated intuition. Hence they could not withstand the disruption of this state of mind when self-consciousness was infinitely reflected into itself; when this reflection began to emerge, they succumbed to it, first in spirit and then in substance, because the simple principle underlying them lacked the truly infinite power to be found only in that unity which allows both sides of the antithesis[44] of reason to develop themselves separately in all their strength and which has so overcome the antithesis that it maintains itself in it and integrates it in itself.

In his *Republic*, Plato displays the substance of ethical life in its ideal beauty[45] and truth; but he could only cope with the principle of self-subsistent particularity, which in his day had forced its way into Greek ethical life, by setting up in opposition to it his purely substantial state. He absolutely excluded it from his state, even in its very beginnings in private property (see Remark to Paragraph 46) and the family, as well as in its more mature form as the subjective will, the choice of a social position, and so forth. It is this defect which is responsible both for the misunderstanding of the deep and substantial truth of Plato's state and also for the usual view of it as a dream of abstract thinking, as what is often called a 'mere ideal'. The principle of the self-subsistent inherently infinite personality of the individual, the principle of subjective freedom, is denied its right in the purely substantial form which Plato gave to mind in its actuality. This principle dawned in an inward form in the Christian religion and in an external form (and therefore in one linked with abstract universality) in the Roman world. It is historically subsequent to the Greek world, and the philosophic reflection which descends to its depth is likewise subsequent to the substantial Idea of Greek philosophy. [A.]

186. But in developing itself independently to totality, the principle of particularity passes over into universality, and only there does it attain its truth and the right to which its positive actuality is entitled. This unity is not the identity which the ethical order requires, because at this level, that of division (see Paragraph 184), both principles are self-subsistent. It follows that this unity is present here not as freedom but as necessity, since it is by compulsion that the particular rises to the form of universality and seeks and gains its stability in that form.

187. Individuals in their capacity as burghers[46] in this state are private persons whose end is their own interest. This end is *mediated* through the universal which thus *appears* as a *means* to its realization. Consequently, individuals can attain their ends only in so far as they themselves determine their knowing, willing, and acting in a universal way and make themselves links in this chain of social connexions. In these circumstances, the interest of the Idea—an interest of which these members of civil society are as such unconscious—lies in the process whereby their singularity and their natural condition are raised, as a result of the necessities imposed by nature as well as of arbitrary needs, to formal freedom and formal universality of knowing and willing—the process whereby their particularity is educated up to subjectivity.

The idea that the state of nature is one of innocence and that there is a simplicity of manners in uncivilized (*ungebildeter*) peoples, implies treating education (*Bildung*) as something purely external, the ally of corruption. Similarly, the feeling that needs, their satisfaction, the pleasures and comforts of private life, and so forth, are absolute ends, implies treating education as a mere means to these ends. Both these views display lack of acquaintance with the nature of mind and the end of reason. Mind attains its actuality only by creating a dualism within itself, by submitting itself to physical needs and the chain of these external necessities, and so imposing on itself this barrier and this finitude, and finally by maturing (*bildet*) itself inwardly even when under this barrier until it overcomes it and attains its objective reality in the finite. The end of reason, therefore, is neither the manners of an unsophisticated state of nature, nor, as particularity develops, the pleasure for pleasure's sake which education procures. On the contrary, its end is to banish natural simplicity, whether the passivity which is the absence of the self, or the crude type of knowing and willing, i.e. immediacy and singularity, in which mind is absorbed. It aims in the first instance at securing for this, its external condition, the rationality of which it is capable, i.e. the form of universality or the Understanding (*Verständigkeit*). By this means alone does mind become at home with itself within this pure externality. There, then, mind's freedom is existent and mind becomes objective to itself in this element which is implicitly inimical to mind's appointed end, freedom; it has to do there only with what it has itself produced and stamped with its seal. It is in this way then that the form of universality comes explicitly into existence in thought, and this form is the only worthy element for the existence of the Idea. The final purpose of education, therefore, is liberation and the struggle for a higher liberation still; education is the absolute transition from an ethical substantiality which is immediate and natural to the one which is intellectual and so both infinitely subjective and lofty enough to have attained universality of form. In the individual subject, this liberation is the hard struggle against pure subjectivity of demeanour, against the immediacy of desire, against the empty subjectivity of feeling and the caprice of inclination. The disfavour showered on education is due in part to its being this hard struggle; but it is through this educational struggle that the subjective will itself

attains objectivity within, an objectivity in which alone it is for its part
capable and worthy of being the actuality of the Idea.

Moreover, this form of universality—the Understanding, to which
particularity has worked its way and developed itself, brings it about at
the same time that particularity becomes individuality genuinely
existent in its own eyes. And since it is from this particularity that the
universal derives the content which fills it as well as its character as
infinite self-determination, particularity itself is present in ethical life
as infinitely independent free subjectivity. This is the position which
reveals education as a moment immanent in the Absolute and which
makes plain its infinite value. [A.]

188. Civil society contains three moments:

(A) The mediation of need and one man's satisfaction through
his work and the satisfaction of the needs of all others—the
System of Needs.

(B) The actuality of the universal principle of freedom therein
contained—the protection of property through the *Administration of Justice.*

(C) Provision against contingencies still lurking in systems (A)
and (B), and care for particular interests as a common
interest, by means of the *Police* and the *Corporation.*

A. *The System of Needs*

189. Particularity is in the first instance characterized in general
by its contrast with the universal principle of the will and thus is
subjective need (see Paragraph 59).[47] This attains its objectivity,
i.e. its satisfaction, by means of (x) external things, which at this
stage are likewise the property and product of the needs and wills
of others, and (β) work and effort, the middle term between the
subjective and the objective. The aim here is the satisfaction of
subjective particularity, but the universal asserts itself in the bearing which this satisfaction has on the needs of others and their free
arbitrary wills. The show of rationality thus produced in this
sphere of finitude is the Understanding, and this is the aspect
which is of most importance in considering this sphere and which
itself constitutes the reconciling element within it.

Political economy is the science which starts from this view of needs
and labour but then has the task of explaining mass-relationships and
mass-movements in their complexity and their qualitative and quantitative character. This is one of the sciences which have arisen out of the
conditions of the modern world. Its development affords the interesting

spectacle (as in Smith, Say, and Ricardo[48]) of thought working upon the endless mass of details which confront it at the outset and extracting therefrom the simple principles of the thing, the Understanding effective in the thing and directing it. It is to find reconciliation here to discover in the sphere of needs this show of rationality lying in the thing and effective there; but if we look at it from the opposite point of view, this is the field in which the Understanding with its subjective aims and moral fancies vents its discontent and moral frustration. [A.]

(a) The Kind of Need and Satisfaction [typical of civil society]

190. An animal's needs and its ways and means of satisfying them are both alike restricted in scope. Though man is subject to this restriction too, yet at the same time he evinces his transcendence of it and his universality, first by the multiplication of needs and means of satisfying them, and secondly by the differentiation and division of concrete need into single parts and aspects which in turn become different needs, particularized and so more abstract.

In [abstract] right, what we had before us was the person; in the sphere of morality, the subject; in the family, the family-member; in civil society as a whole, the burgher or *bourgeois*. Here at the standpoint of needs (compare Remark to Paragraph 123) what we have before us is the composite idea which we call *man*. Thus this is the first time, and indeed properly the only time, to speak of *man* in this sense.[49] [A.]

191. Similarly, the means to particularized needs and all the various ways of satisfying these are themselves divided and multiplied and so in turn become proximate ends and abstract needs. This multiplication goes on *ad infinitum*; taken as a whole, it is refinement, i.e. a discrimination between these multiplied needs, and judgement on the suitability of means to their ends. [A.]

192. Needs and means, as things existent *realiter*, become something which has being for others by whose needs and work satisfaction for all alike is conditioned. When needs and means become abstract in quality (see Paragraph 191), abstraction is also a character of the reciprocal relation of individuals to one another.[50] This abstract character, universality, is the character of being recognized and is the moment which makes concrete, i.e. social, the isolated and abstract needs and their ways and means of satisfaction. [A.]

193. This social moment thus becomes a particular end-determinant for means in themselves and their acquisition, as well as for the manner in which needs are satisfied. Further, it directly involves the demand for equality of satisfaction with others. The need for this equality and for emulation, which is the equalizing of oneself with others, as well as the other need also present here, the need of the particular to assert itself in some distinctive way, become themselves a fruitful source of the multiplication of needs and their expansion.

194. Since in social needs, as the conjunction of immediate or natural needs with mental needs arising from ideas, it is needs of the latter type which because of their universality make themselves preponderant, this social moment has in it the aspect of liberation, i.e. the strict natural necessity of need is obscured and man is concerned with his own opinion, indeed with an opinion which is universal, and with a necessity of his own making alone, instead of with an external necessity, an inner contingency, and mere caprice.

The idea has been advanced that in respect of his needs man lived in freedom in the so-called 'state of nature' when his needs were supposed to be confined to what are known as the simple necessities of nature, and when he required for their satisfaction only the means which the acci- dents of nature directly assured to him. This view takes no account of the moment of liberation intrinsic to work, on which see the following Paragraphs. And apart from this, it is false, because to be confined to mere physical needs as such and their direct satisfaction would simply be the condition in which the mental is plunged in the natural and so would be one of savagery and unfreedom, while freedom itself is to be found only in the reflection of mind into itself, in mind's distinction from nature, and in the reflex of mind in nature.

195. This liberation is abstract since the particularity of the ends remains their basic content. When social conditions tend to multiply and subdivide needs, means, and enjoyments indefinitely —a process which, like the distinction between natural and refined[51] needs, has no qualitative limits—this is luxury. In this same pro- cess, however, dependence and want increase *ad infinitum*, and the material to meet these is permanently barred to the needy man because it consists of external objects with the special character of being property, the embodiment of the free will of others, and hence from his point of view its recalcitrance is absolute.[52] [A.]

(b) The Kind of Work [typical of civil society]

196. The means of acquiring and preparing the particularized means appropriate to our similarly particularized needs is work.

Through work the raw material directly supplied by nature is specifically adapted to these numerous ends by all sorts of different processes. Now this formative change confers value on means and gives them their utility, and hence man in what he consumes is mainly concerned with the products of men. It is the products of human effort which man consumes. [A.]

197. The multiplicity of objects and situations which excite interest is the stage on which theoretical education develops. This education consists in possessing not simply a multiplicity of ideas and facts, but also a flexibility and rapidity of mind, ability to pass from one idea to another, to grasp complex and general relations, and so on. It is the education of the understanding in every way, and so also the building up of language. Practical education, acquired through working, consists first in the automatically recurrent need for something to do and the habit of simply being busy; next, in the strict adaptation of one's activity according not only to the nature of the material worked on, but also, and especially, to the pleasure of other workers; and finally, in a habit, produced by this discipline, of objective activity and universally recognized aptitudes. [A.]

198. The universal and objective element in work, on the other hand, lies in the abstracting process which effects the subdivision of needs and means and thereby *eo ipso* subdivides production and brings about the division of labour. By this division, the work of the individual becomes less complex, and consequently his skill at his section of the job increases, like his output. At the same time, this abstraction of one man's skill and means of production from another's completes and makes necessary everywhere the dependence of men on one another and their reciprocal relation in the satisfaction of their other needs. Further, the abstraction of one man's production from another's makes work more and more mechanical, until finally man is able to step aside and install machines in his place.

(c) Capital [and class-divisions][53]

199. When men are thus dependent on one another and reciprocally related to one another in their work and the satisfaction of their needs, subjective self-seeking turns into a contribution to the satisfaction of the needs of everyone else. That is to say, by a dialectical advance,[54] subjective self-seeking turns into the mediation of the particular through the universal, with the result that each man in earning, producing, and enjoying on his own account is *eo ipso* producing and earning for the enjoyment of everyone else. The compulsion which brings this about is rooted in the complex interdependence of each on all, and it now presents itself to each as the universal permanent capital (see Paragraph 170) which gives each the opportunity, by the exercise of his education and skill, to draw a share from it and so be assured of his livelihood, while what he thus earns by means of his work maintains and increases the general capital.

200. A particular man's resources, or in other words his opportunity of sharing in the general resources, are conditioned, however, partly by his own unearned principal (his capital), and partly by his skill; this in turn is itself dependent not only on his capital, but also on accidental circumstances whose multiplicity introduces differences in the development of natural, bodily, and mental characteristics, which were already in themselves dissimilar. In this sphere of particularity, these differences are conspicuous in every direction and on every level, and, together with the arbitrariness and accident which this sphere contains as well, they have as their inevitable consequence disparities of individual resources and ability.

The objective right of the particularity of mind is contained in the Idea. Men are made unequal by nature, where inequality is in its element, and in civil society the right of particularity is so far from annulling this natural inequality that it produces it out of mind and raises it to an inequality of skill and resources, and even to one of moral and intellectual attainment. To oppose to this right a demand for equality is a folly of the Understanding which takes as real and rational its abstract equality and its 'ought-to-be'.

This sphere of particularity, which fancies itself the universal, is still only relatively identical with the universal, and consequently it still retains in itself the particularity of nature, i.e. arbitrariness, or in other words the relics of the state of nature. Further, it is reason, immanent in the restless system of human needs, which articulates it into an organic whole with different members (see the following Paragraph).

201. The infinitely complex, criss-cross, movements of reciprocal production and exchange, and the equally infinite multiplicity of means therein employed, become crystallized, owing to the universality inherent in their content, and distinguished into general groups. As a result, the entire complex is built up into particular systems of needs, means, and types of work relative to these needs, modes of satisfaction and of theoretical and practical education, i.e. into systems, to one or other of which individuals are assigned—in other words, into class-divisions.   [A.]

202. The classes are specifically determined in accordance with the concept as (*a*) the *substantial* or immediate [or agricultural] class; (*b*) the reflecting or *formal* [or business] class; and finally, (*c*) the *universal* class [the class of civil servants].[55]

203. (*a*) The substantial [or agricultural] class has its capital in the natural products of the soil which it cultivates—soil which is capable of exclusively private ownership and which demands formation in an objective way and not mere haphazard exploitation. In face of the connexion of [agricultural] work and its fruits with separate and fixed times of the year, and the dependence of harvests on the variability of natural processes, the aim of need in this class turns into provision for the future; but owing to the conditions here, the agricultural mode of subsistence remains one which owes comparatively little to reflection and independence of will, and this mode of life is in general such that this class has the substantial disposition of an ethical life which is immediate, resting on family relationship and trust.

The real beginning and original foundation of states has been rightly ascribed to the introduction of agriculture along with marriage, because the principle of agriculture brings with it the formation of the land and consequentially exclusively private property (compare Remark to Paragraph 170); the nomadic life of savages, who seek their livelihood from place to place, it brings back to the tranquillity of private rights and the assured satisfaction of their needs. Along with these changes, sexual love is restricted to marriage, and this bond in turn grows into an enduring league, inherently universal, while needs expand into care for a family, and personal possessions into family goods. Security, consolidation, lasting satisfaction of needs, and so forth—things which are the most obvious recommendations of marriage and agriculture—are nothing but forms of universality, modes in which rationality, the final end and aim, asserts itself in these spheres.

In this matter, nothing is of more interest than the ingenious and learned explanations which my distinguished friend, Herr Creuzer,[56] has given* of the agrarian festivals, images, and sanctuaries of the ancients. He shows that it was because the ancients themselves had

---

* Notably in the fourth volume of his *Mythologie und Symbolik*.

become conscious of the divine origin of agriculture and other institutions associated with it that they held them in such religious veneration.

In course of time, the character of this class as 'substantial' undergoes modifications through the working of the civil law, in particular the administration of justice, as well as through the working of education, instruction, and religion. These modifications, which occur in the other classes also, do not affect the substantial content of the class but only its form and the development of its power of reflection. [A.]

204. (*b*) The business class has for its task the adaptation of raw materials, and for its means of livelihood it is thrown back on its work, on reflection and intelligence, and essentially on the mediation of one man's needs and work with those of others. For what this class produces and enjoys, it has mainly itself, its own industry, to thank. The task of this class is subdivided into

(α) work to satisfy single needs in a comparatively concrete way and to supply single orders—craftsmanship;

(β) work of a more abstract kind, mass-production to satisfy single needs, but needs in more universal demand—manufacture;

(γ) the business of exchange, whereby separate utilities are exchanged the one for the other, principally through the use of the universal medium of exchange, money, which actualizes the abstract value of all commodities—trade. [A.]

205. (*c*) The universal class [the class of civil servants] has for its task the universal interests of the community. It must therefore be relieved from direct labour to supply its needs, either by having private means or by receiving an allowance from the state which claims its industry, with the result that private interest finds its satisfaction in its work for the universal.

206. It is in accordance with the concept that class-organization, as particularity become objective to itself, is split in this way into its general divisions. But the question of the particular class to which an individual is to belong is one on which natural capacity, birth, and other circumstances have their influence, though the essential and final determining factors are subjective opinion and the individual's arbitrary will, which win in this sphere their right, their merit, and their dignity. Hence what happens here by inner necessity occurs at the same time by the mediation of the arbitrary will, and to the conscious subject it has the shape of being the work of his own will.

In this respect too there is a conspicuous difference, in relation to the principle of particularity and the subject's arbitrary will, between the political life of the east and the west, and also between that of the ancient and the modern world. In the former, the division of the whole into classes came about objectively of itself, because it is inherently rational; but the principle of subjective particularity was at the same time denied its rights, in that, for example, the allotment of individuals to classes was left to the ruling class, as in Plato's *Republic*,* or to the accident of birth, as in the Indian caste-system. Thus subjective particularity was not incorporated into the organization of society as a whole; it was not reconciled in the whole, and therefore—since as an essential moment it emerges there in any event—it shows itself there as something hostile, as a corruption of the social order (see Remark to Paragraph 185). Either it overthrows society, as happened in the Greek states and in the Roman Republic; or else, should society preserve itself in being as a force or as a religious authority, for instance, it appears as inner corruption and complete degeneration, as was the case to some extent in Sparta and is now altogether the case in India.

But when subjective particularity is upheld by the objective order in conformity with it and is at the same time allowed its rights, then it becomes the animating principle of the entire civil society, of the development alike of mental activity, merit, and dignity. The recognition and the right that what is brought about by reason of necessity in civil society and the state shall at the same time be effected by the mediation of the arbitrary will is the more precise definition of what is primarily meant by freedom in common parlance (see Paragraph 121).

207. A man actualizes himself only in becoming something definite, i.e. something specifically particularized; this means restricting himself exclusively to one of the particular spheres of need. In this class-system, the ethical frame of mind therefore is rectitude and *esprit de corps*, i.e. the disposition to make oneself a member of one of the moments of civil society by one's own act, through one's energy, industry, and skill, to maintain oneself in this position, and to fend for oneself only through this process of mediating oneself with the universal, while in this way gaining recognition both in one's own eyes and in the eyes of others. Morality has its proper place in this sphere where the paramount thing is reflection on one's doings, and the quest of happiness and private wants, and where the contingency in satisfying these makes into a duty even a single and contingent act of assistance.

At first (i.e. especially in youth) a man chafes at the idea of resolving

* Book iii [415 *a–d*].

on a particular social position, and looks upon this as a restriction on his universal character and as a necessity imposed on him purely *ab extra*. This is because his thinking is still of that abstract kind which refuses to move beyond the universal and so never reaches the actual. It does not realize that if the concept is to be determinate, it must first of all advance into the distinction between the concept and its real existence and thereby into determinacy and particularity (see Paragraph 7). It is only thus that the concept can win actuality and ethical objectivity. [A.]

208. As the private particularity of knowing and willing, the principle of this system of needs contains absolute universality, the universality of freedom, only abstractly and therefore as the right of property. At this point, however, this right is no longer merely implicit but has attained its recognized actuality as the protection of property through the administration of justice.

B. *The Administration of Justice*

209. The relatedness arising from the reciprocal bearing on one another of needs and work to satisfy these is first of all reflected into itself as infinite personality, as abstract right.[57] But it is this very sphere of relatedness—a sphere of education—which gives abstract right the determinate existence of being something universally recognized, known, and willed, and having a validity and an objective actuality mediated by this known and willed character.

It is part of education, of thinking as the consciousness of the single in the form of universality, that the ego comes to be apprehended as a universal person in which all are identical. A man counts as a man in virtue of his manhood alone, not because he is a Jew, Catholic, Protestant, German, Italian, &c. This is an assertion which thinking ratifies and to be conscious of it is of infinite importance. It is defective only when it is crystallized, e.g. as a cosmopolitanism in opposition to the concrete life of the state. [A.]

210. The objective actuality of the right consists, first, in its existence for consciousness, in its being known in some way or other; secondly, in its possessing the power which the actual possesses, in its being valid, and so also in its becoming known as universally valid.

(*a*) Right as Law

211. The principle of rightness becomes the law (*Gesetz*) when, in its objective existence, it is posited (*gesetzt*), i.e. when thinking makes it determinate for consciousness and makes it known as what is right and valid; and in acquiring this determinate character, the right becomes positive law in general.

To posit something as universal, i.e. to bring it before consciousness as universal, is, I need hardly say, to think (compare Remarks to Paragraphs 13 and 21). Thereby its content is reduced to its simplest form and so is given its final determinacy. In becoming law, what is right acquires for the first time not only the form proper to its universality, but also its true determinacy. Hence making a law is not to be represented as merely the expression of a rule of behaviour valid for everyone, though that is one moment in legislation; the more important moment, the inner essence of the matter, is knowledge of the content of the law in its determinate universality.

Since it is only animals which have their law as instinct, while it is man alone who has law as custom, even systems of customary law⁵⁸ contain the moment of being thoughts and being known. Their difference from positive law consists solely in this, that they are known only in a subjective and accidental way, with the result that in themselves they are less determinate and the universality of thought is less clear in them. (And apart from this, knowledge of a system of law either in general or in its details, is the accidental possession of a few.) The supposition that it is customary law, on the strength of its character as custom, which possesses the privilege of having become part of life is a delusion, since the valid laws of a nation do not cease to be its customs by being written and codified—and besides, it is as a rule precisely those versed in the deadest of topics and the deadest of thoughts who talk nowadays of 'life' and of 'becoming part of life'. When a nation begins to acquire even a little culture, its customary law must soon come to be collected and put together. Such a collection is a legal code, but one which, as a mere collection, is markedly formless, indeterminate, and fragmentary. The main difference between it and a code properly so-called is that in the latter the principles of jurisprudence in their universality, and so in their determinacy, have been apprehended in terms of thought and expressed. English national law or municipal law⁵⁹ is contained, as is well known, in statutes (written laws) and in so-called 'unwritten' laws. This unwritten law, however, is as good as written, and knowledge of it may, and indeed must, be acquired simply by reading the numerous quartos which it fills. The monstrous confusion, however, which prevails both in English law and its administration is graphically portrayed by those acquainted with the matter.⁶⁰ In particular, they comment on the fact that, since this unwritten law is contained in court verdicts and judgements, the judges are continually legislators. The authority of precedent is binding on them, since their predecessors have done nothing but give expression to the unwritten law; and yet they are just as much exempt from its authority, because they are themselves repositories of the unwritten law and so have the right to criticize previous judgements and pronounce whether they accorded with the unwritten law or not.

A similar confusion might have arisen in the legal system of the later Roman Empire owing to the different but authoritative judgements of all the famous jurists. An Emperor[61] met the situation, however, by a sensible expedient when, by what was called the Law of Citations, he set up a kind of College of the jurists who were longest deceased. There was a President, and the majority vote was accepted.*

No greater insult[62] could be offered to a civilized people or to its lawyers than to deny them ability to codify their law; for such ability cannot be that of constructing a legal system with a novel content, but only that of apprehending, i.e. grasping in thought, the content of existing laws in its determinate universality and then applying them to particular cases. [A.]

212. It is only because of this identity between its implicit and its posited character that positive law has obligatory force in virtue of its rightness. In being posited in positive law, the right acquires determinate existence. Into such existence there may enter the contingency of self-will and other particular circumstances and hence there may be a discrepancy between the content of the law and the principle of rightness.

In positive law, therefore, it is the legal which is the source of our knowledge of what is right, or, more exactly, of our legal rights (*Rechtens*). Thus the science of positive law is to that extent an historical science with authority as its guiding principle. Anything over and above this historical study is matter for the Understanding and concerns the collection of laws, their classification on external principles, deductions from them, their application to fresh details, &c. When the Understanding meddles with the nature of the thing itself, its theories, e.g. of criminal law, show what its deductive argumentation can concoct.

The science of positive law has not only the right, but even the inescapable duty, to study given laws, to deduce from its positive data their progress in history, their applications and subdivisions, down to the last detail, and to exhibit their implications. On the other hand, if, after all these deductions have been proved, the further question about the rationality of a specific law is still raised, the question may seem perverse to those who are busied with these pursuits, but their astonishment at it should at least stop short of dismay.

With this Remark, compare what was said in the Remark to Paragraph 3 about 'understanding' the law.

* Hugo: *Lehrbuch der Geschichte des römischen Rechts,* § 354 [§ 385 in the 7th edn.].

213. Right becomes determinate in the first place when it has the form of being posited as positive law; it also becomes determinate in content by being applied both to the material of civil society (i.e. to the endlessly growing complexity and subdivision of social ties and the different species of property and contract within the society) and also to ethical ties based on the heart, on love and trust, though only in so far as these involve abstract right as one of their aspects (see Paragraph 159). Morality and moral commands concern the will on its most private, subjective, and particular side, and so cannot be a matter for positive legislation. Further material for the determinate content of law is provided by the rights and duties which have their source in the administration of justice itself, in the state, and so forth. [A.]

214. But apart from being applied to particular instances, right by being embodied in positive law becomes applicable to the single case. Hence it enters the sphere where quantity, not the concept, is the principle of determination. This is the sphere of the quantitative as such, of the quantitative as that which determines the relative value in exchange of *qualia*. In this sphere, the concept merely lays down a general limit, within which vacillation is still allowed. This vacillation must be terminated, however, in the interest of getting something done, and for this reason there is a place within that limit for contingent and arbitrary decisions.

The purely positive side of law lies chiefly in this focusing of the universal not merely on a particular instance, but on an isolated case, i.e. in its *direct* application. Reason cannot determine, nor can the concept provide any principle whose application could decide whether justice requires for an offence (i) a corporal punishment of forty lashes or thirty-nine, or (ii) a fine of five dollars or four dollars ninety-three, four, &c., cents, or (iii) imprisonment of a year or three hundred and sixty-four, three, &c., days, or a year and one, two, or three days. And yet injustice is done at once if there is one lash too many, or one dollar or one cent, one week in prison or one day, too many or too few.

Reason itself requires us to recognize that contingency, contradiction, and show have a sphere and a right of their own, restricted though it be, and it is irrational to strive to resolve and rectify contradictions within that sphere. Here the only interest present is that something be actually done, that the matter be settled and decided somehow, no matter how (within a certain limit). This decision pertains to abstract subjectivity, to formal self-certainty, which may decide either by simply holding to its power (within that limit) of settling the matter by merely terminating deliberation and thereby dismissing it out of hand, or else by adopting some reason for decision such as keeping to round numbers or always adopting, say thirty-nine.[63]

It is true that the law does not settle these ultimate decisions required by actual life; it leaves them instead to the judge's discretion, merely limiting him by a maximum and minimum. But this does not affect the point at issue, because the maximum and minimum are themselves in every instance only round numbers once more. To fix them, therefore, does not exempt the judge from making a finite, purely positive, decision, since on the contrary such a decision is still left to him by the necessities of the case. [A.]

(b) Law determinately existent

215. If laws are to have a binding force, it follows that, in view of the right of self-consciousness (see Paragraph 132 and the Remark thereto) they must be made universally known.

To hang the laws so high that no citizen could read them (as Dionysius[64] the Tyrant did) is injustice of one and the same kind as to bury them in row upon row of learned tomes, collections of dissenting judgements and opinions, records of customs, &c., and in a dead language too, so that knowledge of the law of the land is accessible only to those who have made it their professional study. Rulers who have given a national law to their peoples in the form of a well-arranged and clear-cut legal code— or even a mere formless collection of laws, like Justinian's[65]—have been the greatest benefactors of their peoples and have received thanks and praise for their beneficence. But the truth is that their work was at the same time a great act of justice. [A.]

216. For a public legal code, simple general laws are required, and yet the nature of the *finite* material to which law is applied leads to the further determining of general laws *ad infinitum*. On the one hand, the law ought to be a comprehensive whole, closed and complete; and yet, on the other hand, the need for further determinations is continual. But since this antinomy arises only when universal principles, which remain fixed and unchanged, are applied to particular types of case, the right to a complete legal code remains unimpaired, like the right that these simple general principles should be capable of being laid down and understood apart and in distinction from their application to such particular types.

A fruitful source of complexity in legislation is the gradual intrusion of reason, of what is inherently and actually right, into primitive institutions which have something wrong at their roots and so are purely historical survivals. This occurred in Roman law, as was remarked above (see Remark to Paragraph 180), in medieval feudal law, &c. It is essential to notice, however, that the very nature of the finite material to which law is applied necessarily entails an infinite progress in the application to it of principles universal in themselves and inherently and actually rational.

It is misunderstanding which has given rise alike to the demand—a morbid craving of German scholars chiefly—that a legal code should be something absolutely complete, incapable of any fresh determination in detail, and also to the argument that because a code is incapable of such completion, therefore we ought not to produce something 'incomplete', i.e. we ought not to produce a code at all. The misunderstanding rests in both cases on a misconception of the nature of a finite subject-matter like private law, whose so-called 'completeness' is a perennial approximation to completeness, on a misconception of the difference[66] between the universal of reason and the universal of the Understanding, and also on the application of the latter to the material of finitude and atomicity which goes on for ever.—*Le plus grand ennemi du Bien, c'est le Meilleur*[67] is the utterance of true common sense[68] against the common sense of idle argumentation and abstract reflection. [A.]

217. The principle of rightness passes over in civil society into law. My individual right, whose embodiment has hitherto been immediate and abstract, now similarly becomes embodied in the existent will and knowledge of everyone, in the sense that it becomes recognized. Hence property acquisitions and transfers must now be undertaken and concluded only in the form which that embodiment gives to them. In civil society, property rests on contract and on the formalities which make ownership capable of proof and valid in law.

Original, i.e. direct, titles and means of acquisition (see Paragraphs 54 ff.) are simply discarded in civil society and appear only as isolated accidents or as subordinated factors of property transactions. It is either feeling, refusing to move beyond the subjective, or reflection, clinging to its abstract essences, which casts formalities aside, while the dry-as-dust Understanding may for its part cling to formalities instead of the real thing and multiply them indefinitely.

Apart from this, however, the march of mental development is the long and hard struggle to free a content from its sensuous and immediate form, endow it with its appropriate form of thought, and thereby give it simple and adequate expression. It is because this is the case that when the development of law is just beginning, ceremonies and formalities are more circumstantial and count rather as the thing itself than as its symbol. Thus even in Roman law, a number of forms and especially phrases were retained from old-fashioned ceremonial usages, instead of being replaced by intelligible forms and phrases adequately expressing them.[69] [A.]

218. Since property and personality have legal recognition and validity in civil society, wrongdoing now becomes an infringement, not merely of what is subjectively infinite, but of the universal thing which is existent with inherent stability and strength. Hence a new attitude arises: the action is seen as a danger to society and thereby the magnitude of the wrongdoing is increased.[70] On the other hand, however, the fact that society has become strong and sure of itself diminishes the external importance of the injury and so leads to a mitigation of its punishment.

The fact that an injury to one member of society is an injury to all others does not alter the conception of wrongdoing, but it does alter it in respect of its outward existence as an injury done, an injury which now affects the mind and consciousness of civil society as a whole, not merely the external embodiment of the person directly injured. In heroic times, as we see in the tragedy of the ancients,[71] the citizens did not feel themselves injured by wrongs which members of the royal houses did to one another.

Implicitly, crime is an infinite[72] injury; but as an existent fact it must be measured in quantity and quality (see Paragraph 96), and since its field of existence here has the essential character of affecting an idea and consciousness of the validity of the laws, its danger to civil society is a determinant of the magnitude of a crime, or even *one* of its qualitative characteristics.

Now this quality or magnitude varies with the state of civil society; and this is the justification for sometimes attaching the penalty of death to a theft of a few pence or a turnip, and at other times a light penalty to a theft of a hundred or more times that amount.[73] If we consider its danger to society, this seems at first sight to aggravate the crime; but in fact it is just this which has been the prime cause of the mitigation of its punishment. A penal code, then, is primarily the child of its age and the state of civil society at the time. [A.]

(c) The Court of Justice

219. By taking the form of law, right steps into a determinate mode of being. It is then something on its own account, and in contrast with particular willing and opining of the right, it is self-subsistent and has to vindicate itself as something universal. This is achieved by recognizing it and making it actual in a particular case without the subjective feeling of private interest; and this is the business of a public authority—the court of justice.

The historical origin of the judge and his court may have had the form of a patriarch's gift to his people or of force or free choice; but this makes no difference to the concept of the thing. To regard the introduction of a legal system as no more than an optional act of grace or favour on the part of monarchs and governments (as Herr von Haller[74] does in his *Restauration der Staatswissenschaft*) is a piece of the mere thoughtlessness which has no inkling of the point at issue in a discussion of law and the state. The point is that legal and political institutions are rational in principle and therefore absolutely necessary, and the question of the form in which they arose or were introduced is entirely irrelevant to a consideration of their rational basis.

At the other extreme from Herr von Haller's point of view is the barbarous notion that the administration of justice is now, as it was in the days when might was right, an improper exercise of force, a suppression of freedom, and a despotism. The administration of justice must be regarded as the fulfilment of a duty by the public authority, no less than as the exercise of a right; and so far as it is a right, it does not depend upon an optional delegation to one authority by the individual members of society.

220. When the right against crime has the form of revenge (see Paragraph 102), it is only right implicit, not right in the form of right, i.e. no *act* of revenge is justified. Instead of the injured party, the injured *universal* now comes on the scene, and this has its proper actuality in the court of law. It takes over the pursuit and the avenging of crime, and this pursuit consequently ceases to be the subjective and contingent retribution of revenge and is transformed into the genuine reconciliation of right with itself, i.e. into punishment. Objectively, this is the reconciliation of the law with itself; by the annulment of the crime, the law is restored and its authority is thereby actualized. Subjectively, it is the reconciliation of the criminal with himself, i.e. with the law known by him as his own and as valid for him and his protection; when this law is executed upon him, he himself finds in this process the satisfaction of justice and nothing save his own act.

221. A member of civil society has the right *in judicio stare*[75] and, correspondingly, the duty of acknowledging the jurisdiction of the court and accepting its decision as final when his own rights are in dispute. [A.]

222. In court the specific character which rightness acquires is that it must be demonstrable. When parties go to law, they are put in the position of having to make good their evidence and their

claims and to make the judge acquainted with the facts. These
steps in a legal process are themselves rights, and their course must
therefore be fixed by law. They also constitute an essential part of
jurisprudence. [A.]

223. These steps in a legal process are subdivided continually
within no fixed limits into more and more actions, each being
distinct in itself and a right. Hence a legal process, in itself in any
case a means, now begins to be something external to its end and
contrasted with it. This long course of formalities is a right of the
parties at law and they have the right to traverse it from beginning
to end. Still, it may be turned into an evil, and even an instrument
of wrong, and for this reason it is by law made the duty of the
parties to submit themselves to the simple process of arbitration
(before a tribunal of arbitrators)[76] and to the attempt to reconcile
their differences out of court, in order that they—and right itself,
as the substance of the thing and so the thing really at issue—may
be protected against legal processes and their misuse.

Equity involves a departure from formal rights owing to moral or
other considerations and is concerned primarily with the content of the
lawsuit. A court of equity, however, comes to mean a court which
decides in a single case without insisting on the formalities of a legal
process or, in particular, on the objective evidence which the letter of
the law may require. Further, it decides on the merits of the single case
as a unique one, not with a view to disposing of it in such a way as to
create a binding legal precedent for the future.

224. Amongst the rights of the subjective consciousness are not
only the publication of the laws (see Paragraph 215) but also the
possibility of ascertaining the actualization of the law in a particular case (the course of the proceedings, the legal argument, &c.)
—i.e. the publicity of judicial proceedings. The reason for this is
that a trial is implicitly an event of universal validity, and although
the particular content of the action affects the interests of the
parties alone, its universal content, i.e. the right at issue and the
judgement thereon, affects the interests of everybody.

If the members of the bench deliberate amongst themselves about the
judgement which they are to deliver, such deliberations express opinions
and views still personal and so naturally are not public. [A.]

225. By the judgement of the court, the law is applied to a
single case, and the work of judgement has two distinct aspects:
first, ascertainment of the nature of the case as a unique, single,

occurrence (e.g. whether a contract, &c., &c., has been made, whether a trespass has been committed, and if so by whom) and, in criminal cases, reflection to determine the essential, criminal, character of the deed (see Remark to Paragraph 119); secondly, the subsumption of the case under the law that right must be restored. Punishment in criminal cases is a conception falling under this law. Decisions on these two different aspects are given by different functionaries.[77]

In the Roman judicial system, this distinction of functions appeared in that the Praetor pronounced judgement on the assumption that the facts were so and so, and then appointed a special *judex* to inquire into the facts.[78]

In English law, it is left to the insight or option of the prosecutor to determine the precise character of a criminal act (e.g. whether it is murder or manslaughter) and the court is powerless to alter the indictment if it finds the prosecutor's choice wrong.[79]

226. First, the conduct of the entire process of inquiry, secondly, the detailed stages of the action between the parties (these stages themselves being rights—see Paragraph 222), and then also the second of the aspects of the work of judgement mentioned in the previous Paragraph, are all a task which properly belongs to the judge at law. He is the organ of the law, and the case must be prepared for him in such a way as to make possible its subsumption under some principle; that is to say, it must be stripped of its apparent, empirical, character and exalted into a recognized fact of a general type.

227. The first aspect of the work of judgement, i.e. the knowledge of the facts of the case as a unique, single, occurrence, and the description of its general character, involves in itself no pronouncement on points of law. This is knowledge attainable by any educated man. In settling the character of an action, the subjective moment, i.e. the agent's insight and intention (see the Second Part[80]), is the essential thing; and apart from this, the proof depends not on objects of reason or abstractions of the Understanding, but only on single details and circumstances, objects of sensuous intuition and subjective certainty, and therefore does not contain in itself any absolute, objective, probative factor. It follows that judgement on the facts lies in the last resort with subjective conviction and conscience (*animi sententia*[81]), while the proof, resting as it does on the statements and affidavits of others, receives its final though purely subjective verification from the oath.

In this matter it is of the first importance to fix our eyes on the type of proof here in question and to distinguish it from knowledge and proof of another sort. To establish by proof a rational category, like the concept of right itself, means to apprehend its necessity, and so demands a method other than that requisite for the proof of a geometrical theorem. Further, in this latter case, the figure is determined by the Understanding and made abstract in advance according to a rule. But in the case of something empirical in content, like a fact, the material of knowledge is a given sensuous intuition and subjective sense-certainty, and statements and affidavits about such material. It is then a question of drawing conclusions and putting two and two together out of depositions of that kind, attestations and other details, &c. The objective truth which emerges from material of this kind and the method appropriate to it leads, when attempts are made to determine it rigidly and objectively, to half-proofs and then, by further sincere deductions from these—deductions which at the same time involve formal illogicality—to extraordinary punishments.[82] But such objective truth means something quite different from the truth of a rational category or a proposition whose content the Understanding has determined for itself abstractly in advance. To show that, since the strictly legal character of a court covers competence to ascertain this sort of truth about empirical events, it thereby properly qualifies a court for this task and so gives it an inherent exclusive right to perform it and lays on it the necessity of performing it—that is the best approach to settling the question of how far decisions on points of fact, as well as on points of law, should be ascribed to courts as strictly juristic bodies. [A.]

228. When judgement is pronounced—so far as the function of judgement is the subsumption under the law of the case whose nature has been settled—the right due to the parties on the score of their self-consciousness is preserved in relation to the *law* because the law is known and so is the law of the parties themselves, and in relation to the *subsumption*, because the trial is public. But when a verdict is given on the particular, subjective, and external facts of the case (knowledge of which falls under the first of the aspects described in Paragraph 225), this right is satisfied by the confidence which the parties feel in the subjectivity of those who give the verdict. This confidence is based primarily on the similarity between them and the parties in respect of their particularity, i.e. their social position, &c.

The right of self-consciousness, the moment of subjective freedom, may be regarded as the fundamental thing to keep before us in considering the necessity for publicity in legal proceedings and for the so-called jury-courts, and this in the last resort is the essence of whatever may be advanced in favour of these institutions on the score of their utility. Other points of view and reasoning about their several advantages and disadvantages may give rise to an argumentative exchange, but reasoning of this kind, like all deductive reasoning, is either secondary and inconclusive, or else drawn from other and perhaps higher spheres than that of advantage. It may be the case that if the administration of justice were entirely in the hands of professional lawyers, and there were no lay institutions like juries, it would in theory be managed just as well, if not better. It may be so, but even if this possibility rises by general consent to probability, or even certainty, it still does not matter, for on the other side there is always the right of self-consciousness, insisting on its claims and dissatisfied if laymen play no part.

Owing to the character of the entire body of the laws, knowledge both of what is right and also of the course of legal proceedings may become, together with the capacity to prosecute an action at law, the property of a class which makes itself an exclusive clique by the use of a terminology like a foreign tongue to those whose rights are at issue. If this happens, the members of civil society, who depend for their livelihood on their industry, on their own knowledge and will, are kept strangers to the law, not only to those parts of it affecting their most personal and intimate affairs, but also to its substantive and rational basis, the right itself, and the result is that they become the wards, or even in a sense the bondsmen, of the legal profession. They may indeed have the right to appear in court in person and to 'stand' there (*in judicio stare*), but their bodily presence is a trifle if their minds are not to be there also, if they are not to follow the proceedings with their own knowledge, and if the justice they receive remains in their eyes a doom pronounced *ab extra*.

229. In civil society, the Idea is lost in particularity and has fallen asunder with the separation of inward and outward. In the administration of justice, however, civil society returns to its concept, to the unity of the implicit universal with the subjective particular, although here the latter is only that present in single cases and the universality in question is that of *abstract* right. The actualization of this unity through its extension to the whole ambit of particularity is (i) the specific function of the Police, though the unification which it effects is only relative; (ii) it is the Corporation which actualizes the unity completely, though only in a whole which, while concrete, is restricted.[83] [A.]

C. *The Police and the Corporation*

230. In the system of needs, the livelihood and welfare of every single person is a possibility whose actual attainment is just as much conditioned by his caprices and particular endowment as by the objective system of needs. Through the administration of justice, offences against property or personality are annulled. But the right actually present in the particular requires, first, that accidental hindrances to one aim or another be removed, and undisturbed safety of person and property be attained; and secondly, that the securing of every single person's livelihood and welfare be treated and actualized as a right, i.e. that particular welfare as such be so treated.

(a) Police [or the public authority]

231. Inasmuch as it is still the particular will which governs the choice of this or that end, the universal authority by which security is ensured remains in the first instance, (a) restricted to the sphere of contingencies, and (b) an external organization.

232. Crime is contingency as subjective willing of evil, and this is what the universal authority must prevent or bring to justice. But, crime apart, the subjective willing which is permissible in actions lawful *per se* and in the private use of property, also comes into external relation with other single persons, as well as with public institutions, other than law-courts, established for realizing a common end. This universal aspect makes private actions a matter of contingency which escapes the agent's control and which either does or may injure others and wrong them.

233. There is here only a possibility of injury; but the actual non-occurrence of injury is at this stage not just another contingency. The point is that the actions of individuals may always be wrongful, and this is the ultimate reason for police control and penal justice.

234. The relations between external existents fall into the infinite of the Understanding; there is, therefore, no inherent line of distinction between what is and what is not injurious, even where crime is concerned, or between what is and what is not suspicious, or between what is to be forbidden or subjected to supervision and what is to be exempt from prohibition, from surveillance and suspicion, from inquiry and the demand to render an account of itself. These details are determined by custom, the spirit of the rest of the constitution, contemporary conditions, the crisis of the hour, and so forth. [A.]

235. In the indefinite multiplication and interconnexion of day-to-day needs, (*a*) the acquisition and exchange of the means to their satisfaction—a satisfaction which everyone confidently expects to be possible of attainment without hindrance, and (*b*) the endeavours made and the transactions carried out in order to shorten the process of attainment as much as possible, give rise to factors which are a common interest, and when one man occupies himself with these his work is at the same time done for all. The situation is productive too of contrivances and organizations[84] which may be of use to the community as a whole. These universal activities and organizations of general utility call for the oversight and care of the public authority.

236. The differing interests of producers and consumers may come into collision with each other; and although a fair balance between them on the whole may be brought about automatically, still their adjustment also requires a control which stands above both and is consciously undertaken. The right to the exercise of such control in a single case (e.g. in the fixing of the prices of the commonest necessaries of life) depends on the fact that, by being publicly exposed for sale,[85] goods in absolutely universal daily demand are offered not so much to an individual as such but rather to a universal purchaser, the public; and thus both the defence of the public's right not to be defrauded, and also the management of goods inspection, may lie, as a common concern, with a public authority. But public care and direction are most of all necessary in the case of the larger branches of industry, because these are dependent on conditions abroad and on combinations of distant circumstances which cannot be grasped as a whole by the individuals tied to these industries for their living.

At the other extreme to freedom of trade and commerce in civil society is public organization to provide for everything and determine everyone's labour—take for example in ancient times the labour on the pyramids and the other huge monuments in Egypt and Asia which were constructed for public ends, and the worker's task was not mediated through his private choice and particular interest. This interest invokes freedom of trade and commerce against control from above; but the more blindly it sinks into self-seeking aims, the more it requires such control to bring it back to the universal. Control is also necessary to diminish the danger of upheavals arising from clashing interests and to abbreviate the period in which their tension should be eased through the working of a necessity of which they themselves know nothing. [A.]

237. Now while the possibility of sharing in the general wealth is open to individuals and is assured to them by the public authority, still it is subject to contingencies on the subjective side (quite apart from the fact that this assurance must remain incomplete), and the more it presupposes skill, health, capital, and so forth as its conditions, the more is it so subject.

238. Originally the family is the substantive whole whose function it is to provide for the individual on his particular side by giving him either the means and the skill necessary to enable him to earn his living out of the resources of society, or else subsistence and maintenance in the event of his suffering a disability. But civil society tears the individual from his family ties, estranges the members of the family from one another, and recognizes them as self-subsistent persons. Further, for the paternal soil and the external inorganic resources of nature from which the individual formerly derived his livelihood, it substitutes its own soil and subjects the permanent existence of even the entire family to dependence on itself and to contingency. Thus the individual becomes a son of civil society which has as many claims upon him as he has rights against it. [A.]

239. In its character as a universal family, civil society has the right and duty of superintending and influencing education, inasmuch as education bears upon the child's capacity to become a member of society. Society's right here is paramount over the arbitrary and contingent preferences of parents, particularly in cases where education is to be completed not by the parents but by others. To the same end, society must provide public educational facilities so far as is practicable. [A.]

240. Similarly, society has the right and duty of acting as trustee to those whose extravagance destroys the security of their own subsistence or their families'. It must substitute for extravagance the pursuit of the ends of society and the individuals concerned. [A.]

241. Not only caprice, however, but also contingencies, physical conditions, and factors grounded in external circumstances (see Paragraph 200) may reduce men to poverty. The poor still have the needs common to civil society, and yet since society has withdrawn from them the natural means of acquisition (see Paragraph 217) and broken the bond of the family—in the wider sense of the clan (see Paragraph 181)—their poverty leaves them more or less deprived of all the advantages of society, of the opportunity of acquiring skill or education of any kind, as well as of the administration of justice, the public health services, and often even of the consolations of religion, and so forth. The public authority takes the place of the family where the poor are concerned in respect not only of their immediate want but also of laziness of disposition, malignity, and the other vices which arise out of their plight and their sense of wrong.

242. Poverty and, in general, the distress of every kind to which every individual is exposed from the start in the cycle of his natural life has a subjective side which demands similarly subjective aid, arising both from the special circumstances of a particular case and also from love and sympathy. This is the place where morality finds plenty to do despite all public organization. Subjective aid, however, both in itself and in its operation, is dependent on contingency and consequently society struggles to make it less necessary, by discovering the general causes of penury and general means of its relief, and by organizing relief accordingly.

Casual almsgiving and casual endowments, e.g. for the burning of lamps before holy images, &c., are supplemented by public almshouses, hospitals, street-lighting,[86] and so forth. There is still quite enough left over and above these things for charity to do on its own account. A false view is implied both when charity insists on having this poor relief reserved solely to private sympathy and the accidental occurrence of knowledge and a charitable disposition, and also when it feels injured or mortified by universal regulations and ordinances which are *obligatory*. Public social conditions are on the contrary to be regarded as all the more perfect the less (in comparison with what is arranged publicly) is left for an individual to do by himself as his private inclination directs.

243. When civil society is in a state of unimpeded activity, it is engaged in expanding internally[87] in population and industry. The amassing of wealth is intensified by generalizing (a) the linkage of men by their needs, and (b) the methods of preparing and distributing the means to satisfy these needs, because it is from this double process of generalization that the largest profits are derived. That is one side of the picture. The other side is the subdivision and restriction of particular jobs. This results in the dependence

and distress of the class tied to work of that sort, and these again entail inability to feel and enjoy the broader freedoms and especially the intellectual benefits of civil society.

244. When the standard of living of a large mass of people falls below a certain subsistence level—a level regulated automatically as the one necessary for a member of the society—and when there is a consequent loss of the sense of right and wrong, of honesty and the self-respect which makes a man insist on maintaining himself by his own work and effort, the result is the creation of a rabble[88] of paupers. At the same time this brings with it, at the other end of the social scale, conditions which greatly facilitate the concentration of disproportionate wealth in a few hands. [A.]

245. When the masses begin to decline into poverty, (a) the burden of maintaining them at their ordinary standard of living might be directly laid on the wealthier classes, or they might receive the means of livelihood directly from other public sources of wealth (e.g. from the endowments of rich hospitals, monasteries, and other foundations). In either case, however, the needy would receive subsistence directly, not by means of their work, and this would violate the principle of civil society and the feeling of individual independence and self-respect in its individual members. (b) As an alternative, they might be given subsistence indirectly through being given work, i.e. the opportunity to work. In this event the volume of production would be increased, but the evil consists precisely in an excess of production and in the lack of a proportionate number of consumers who are themselves also producers, and thus it is simply intensified by both of the methods (a) and (b) by which it is sought to alleviate it. It hence becomes apparent that despite an excess of wealth civil society is not rich enough, i.e. its own resources are insufficient to check excessive poverty and the creation of a penurious rabble.

In the example of England we may study these phenomena on a large scale and also in particular the results of poor-rates, immense foundations, unlimited private beneficence, and above all the abolition of the Guild Corporations. In Britain, particularly in Scotland, the most direct measure against poverty and especially against the loss of shame and self-respect—the subjective bases of society—as well as against laziness and extravagance, &c., the begetters of the rabble, has turned out to be to leave the poor to their fate and instruct them to beg in the streets.[89]

246. This inner dialectic of civil society thus drives it—or at any rate drives a specific civil society—to push beyond its own limits and seek markets, and so its necessary means of subsistence, in other lands which are either deficient in the goods it has over-produced, or else generally backward in industry, &c.

247. The principle of family life is dependence on the soil, on land, *terra firma*. Similarly, the natural element for industry, animating its outward movement, is the sea. Since the passion for gain involves risk, industry though bent on gain yet lifts itself above it; instead of remaining rooted to the soil and the limited circle of civil life with its pleasures and desires, it embraces the element of flux, danger, and destruction. Further, the sea is the greatest means of communication,[90] and trade by sea creates commercial connexions between distant countries and so relations involving contractual rights. At the same time, commerce of this kind is the most potent instrument of culture, and through it trade acquires its significance in the history of the world.

Rivers are not natural boundaries of separation, which is what they have been accounted to be in modern times. On the contrary, it is truer to say that they, and the sea likewise, link men together. Horace is wrong when he says:

> *deus abscidit*
> *prudens Oceano dissociabili*
> *terras.**

The proof of this lies not merely in the fact that the basins of rivers are inhabited by a single clan or tribe, but also, for example, in the ancient bonds between Greece, Ionia, and Magna Graecia, between Brittany and Britain, between Denmark and Norway, Sweden, Finland, Livonia, &c., bonds, further, which are especially striking in contrast with the comparatively slight intercourse between the inhabitants of the littoral and those of the hinterland. To realize what an instrument of culture lies in the link with the sea, consider countries where industry flourishes and contrast their relation to the sea with that of countries which have eschewed sea-faring and which, like Egypt and India, have become stagnant and sunk in the most frightful and scandalous superstition. Notice also how all great progressive peoples press onward to the sea.

248. This far-flung connecting link affords the means for the colonizing activity—sporadic or systematic—to which the mature civil society is driven and by which it supplies to a part of its

---

* *Odes*, I. iii [ll. 21–3, 'God of set purpose has sundered the lands by the estranging sea'].

population a return to life on the family basis in a new land and so also supplies itself with a new demand and field for its industry. [A.]

249. While the public authority must also undertake the higher directive function of providing for the interests which lead beyond the borders of its society (see Paragraph 246), its primary purpose is to actualize and maintain the universal contained within the particularity of civil society, and its control takes the form of an external system and organization for the protection and security of particular ends and interests *en masse*, inasmuch as these interests subsist only in this universal. This universal is immanent in the interests of particularity itself and, in accordance with the Idea, particularity makes it the end and object of its own willing and activity. In this way ethical principles circle back and appear in civil society as a factor immanent in it; this constitutes the specific character of the Corporation.

(b) The Corporation

250. In virtue of the substantiality of its natural and family life, the agricultural class has directly within itself the concrete universal in which it lives. The class of civil servants is universal in character and so has the universal explicitly as its ground and as the aim of its activity. The class between them, the business class, is essentially concentrated on the particular, and hence it is to it that Corporations are specially appropriate.

251. The labour organization of civil society is split, in accordance with the nature of its particulars, into different branches. The implicit likeness of such particulars to one another becomes really existent in an association, as something common to its members.[91] Hence a selfish purpose, directed towards its particular self-interest, apprehends and evinces itself at the same time as universal; and a member of civil society is in virtue of his own particular skill a member of a Corporation, whose universal purpose is thus wholly concrete[92] and no wider in scope than the purpose involved in business, its proper task and interest.

252. In accordance with this definition of its functions, a Corporation has the right, under the surveillance of the public authority, (a) to look after its own interests within its own sphere, (b) to co-opt members, qualified objectively by the requisite skill and rectitude, to a number fixed by the general structure of society, (c) to protect its members against particular contingencies, (d) to provide the education requisite to fit others to become members. In short, its right is to come on the scene like a second family for its members, while civil society can only be an indeterminate sort of family because it comprises everyone and so is farther removed from individuals and their special exigencies.

The Corporation member is to be distinguished from a day labourer or from a man who is prepared to undertake casual employment on a single occasion. The former who is, or will become, master of his craft, is a member of the association not for casual gain on single occasions but for the whole range, the universality, of his personal livelihood.

Privileges, in the sense of the rights of a branch of civil society organized into a Corporation, are distinct in meaning from privileges proper in the etymological sense.[93] The latter are casual exceptions to universal rules; the former, however, are only the crystallization, as regulations, of characteristics inherent in an essential branch of society itself owing to its nature as particular.

253. In the Corporation, the family has its stable basis in the sense that its livelihood is assured there, conditionally upon capability, i.e. it has a stable capital (see Paragraph 170). In addition, this nexus of capability and livelihood is a *recognized* fact, with the result that the Corporation member needs no external marks beyond his own membership as evidence of his skill and his regular income and subsistence, i.e. as evidence that he is a somebody.[94] It is also recognized that he belongs to a whole which is itself an organ of the entire society, and that he is actively concerned in promoting the comparatively disinterested end of this whole. Thus he commands the respect due to one in his social position.

The institution of Corporations corresponds, on account of its assurance of capital, to the introduction of agriculture and private property in another sphere (see Remark to Paragraph 203).

When complaints are made about the luxury of the business classes and their passion for extravagance—which have as their concomitant the creation of a rabble of paupers (see Paragraph 244)—we must not forget that besides its other causes (e.g. increasing mechanization of labour) this phenomenon has an ethical ground, as was indicated above.[95] Unless he is a member of an authorized Corporation (and it is only by being authorized that an association becomes a Corporation), an individual is without rank or dignity, his isolation reduces his business to mere self-seeking, and his livelihood and satisfaction become insecure. Consequently, he has to try to gain recognition for himself by giving external proofs of success in his business, and to these proofs no limits can be set. He cannot live in the manner of his class, for no class really exists for him, since in civil society it is only something common to particular persons which really exists, i.e. something legally constituted and recognized. Hence he cannot achieve for himself a way of life proper to his class and less idiosyncratic.

Within the Corporation the help which poverty receives loses its accidental character and the humiliation wrongfully associated with it. The wealthy perform their duties to their fellow associates and thus riches cease to inspire either pride or envy, pride in their owners, envy in others. In these conditions rectitude obtains its proper recognition and respect.

254. The so-called 'natural' right of exercising one's skill and thereby earning what there is to be earned is restricted within the Corporation only in so far as it is therein made rational instead of natural. That is to say, it becomes freed from personal opinion and contingency, saved from endangering either the individual work-man or others, recognized, guaranteed, and at the same time elevated to conscious effort for a common end.

255. As the family was the first, so the Corporation is the second ethical root of the state, the one planted in civil society. The former contains the moments of subjective particularity and objective universality in a substantial unity. But these moments are sundered in civil society to begin with; on the one side there is the particularity of need and satisfaction, reflected into itself, and on the other side the universality of abstract rights. In the Corporation these moments are united in an inward fashion, so that in this union particular welfare is present as a right and is actualized.

The sanctity of marriage and the dignity of Corporation membership are the two fixed points[96] round which the unorganized atoms of civil society revolve. [A.]

256. The end of the Corporation is restricted and finite, while the public authority was an external organization involving a separation and a merely relative identity of controller and controlled. The end of the former and the externality and relative identity of the latter find their truth in the absolutely universal end and its absolute actuality. Hence the sphere of civil society passes over into the state.

The town is the seat of the civil life of business. There reflection arises, turns in upon itself, and pursues its atomizing task;[97] each man maintains himself in and through his relation to others who, like himself, are persons possessed of rights. The country, on the other hand, is the seat of an ethical life resting on nature and the family. Town and country thus constitute the two moments, still ideal[98] moments, whose true ground is the state, although it is from them that the state springs.

The philosophic proof of the concept of the state is this development of ethical life from its immediate phase through civil society, the phase of division, to the state, which then reveals itself as the true ground of these phases. A proof in philosophic science can only be a development of this kind.

Since the state appears as a result in the advance of the philosophic concept through displaying itself as the true ground [of the earlier phases], that show of mediation is now cancelled and the state has become directly present before us. Actually, therefore, the state as such is not so much the result as the beginning. It is within the state that the family is first developed into civil society, and it is the Idea of the state itself which disrupts itself into these two moments. Through the development of civil society, the substance of ethical life acquires its infinite form, which contains in itself these two moments: (1) infinite differentiation down to the inward experience of independent self-consciousness, and (2) the form of universality involved in education, the form of thought whereby mind is objective and actual to itself as an organic totality in laws and institutions which are its will in terms of thought.

SUB-SECTION 3

THE STATE

257. The state is the actuality of the ethical Idea. It is ethical mind *qua* the substantial will manifest and revealed to itself, knowing and thinking itself, accomplishing what it knows and in so far as it knows it. The state exists immediately in custom, mediately in individual self-consciousness, knowledge, and activity, while self-consciousness in virtue of its sentiment towards the state finds in the state, as its essence and the end and product of its activity, its substantive freedom.

The *Penates* are inward gods, gods of the underworld; the mind of a nation[1] (Athene for instance) is the divine, knowing and willing itself. Family piety is feeling, ethical behaviour directed by feeling; political virtue is the willing of the absolute end in terms of thought.

258. The state is absolutely rational inasmuch as it is the actuality of the substantial will which it possesses in the particular self-consciousness once that consciousness has been raised to consciousness of its universality. This substantial unity is an absolute unmoved end in itself, in which freedom comes into its supreme right. On the other hand this final end has supreme right against the individual, whose supreme duty is to be a member of the state.

If the state is confused with civil society, and if its specific end is laid down as the security and protection of property and personal freedom, then the interest of the individuals as such becomes the ultimate end of their association, and it follows that membership of the state is something optional. But the state's relation to the individual is quite different from this. Since the state is mind objectified, it is only as one of its members that the individual himself has objectivity, genuine individuality, and an ethical life. Unification pure and simple is the true content and aim of the individual, and the individual's destiny is the living of a universal life. His further particular satisfaction, activity, and mode of conduct have this substantive and universally valid life as their starting point and their result.

Rationality, taken generally and in the abstract, consists in the thorough-going unity of the universal and the single. Rationality, concrete in the state, consists (a) so far as its content is concerned, in the unity of objective freedom (i.e. freedom of the universal or substantial will) and subjective freedom (i.e. freedom of everyone in his knowing and in his volition of particular ends); and consequently, (b) so far as its form is concerned, in self-determining action on laws and principles which are thoughts and so universal. This Idea is the absolutely eternal and necessary being of mind.[2]

But if we ask what is or has been the historical origin of the state in general, still more if we ask about the origin of any particular state, of its rights and institutions, or again if we inquire whether the state originally arose out of patriarchal conditions or out of fear or trust, or out of Corporations, &c., or finally if we ask in what light the basis of the state's rights has been conceived and consciously established, whether this basis has been supposed to be positive divine right, or contract, custom, &c.—all these questions are no concern of the Idea of the state. We are here dealing exclusively with the philosophic science of the state, and from that point of view all these things are mere appearance and therefore matters for history. So far as the authority of any existing state has anything to do with reasons, these reasons are culled from the forms of the law authoritative within it.

The philosophical treatment of these topics is concerned only with their inward side, with the thought of their concept. The merit of Rousseau's[3] contribution to the search for this concept is that, by adducing the will as the principle of the state, he is adducing a principle which has thought both for its form and its content, a principle indeed which is thinking itself, not a principle, like gregarious instinct, for instance, or divine authority, which has thought as its form only. Unfortunately, however, as Fichte[4] did later, he takes the will only in a determinate form as the individual will, and he regards the universal will not as the absolutely rational element in the will, but only as a 'general' will which proceeds out of this individual will as out of a conscious will. The result is that he reduces the union of individuals in the state to a contract and therefore to something based on their arbitrary wills, their opinion, and their capriciously given express consent; and abstract reasoning proceeds to draw the logical inferences which destroy the absolutely divine principle of the state, together with its majesty and absolute authority. For this reason, when these abstract conclusions came into power, they afforded for the first time in human history the prodigious spectacle of the overthrow of the constitution of a great actual state and its complete reconstruction *ab initio* on the basis of pure thought alone, after the destruction of all existing and given material. The will of its re-founders was to give it what they alleged was a purely rational basis, but it was only abstractions that were being used; the Idea was lacking; and the experiment ended in the maximum of frightfulness and terror.[5]

Confronted with the claims made for the individual will, we must remember the fundamental conception that the objective will is rationality implicit or in conception, whether it be recognized or not by individuals, whether their whims be deliberately for it or not. We must remember that its opposite, i.e. knowing and willing, or subjective freedom (the *only* thing contained in the principle of the individual will) comprises only one moment, and therefore a one-sided moment, of the Idea of the rational will, i.e. of the will which is rational solely because what it is implicitly, that it also is explicitly.

The opposite to thinking of the state as something to be known and apprehended as explicitly rational is taking external appearances—i.e. contingencies such as distress, need for protection, force, riches, &c.— not as moments in the state's historical development, but as its substance. Here again what constitutes the guiding thread of discovery is the individual in isolation—not, however, even so much as the *thought* of this individuality, but instead only empirical individuals, with attention focused on their accidental characteristics, their strength and weakness, riches and poverty, &c. This ingenious idea of ignoring the absolute infinity and rationality in the state and excluding thought from apprehension of its inward nature has assuredly never been put forward in such an unadulterated form as in Herr von Haller's *Restauration der Staatswissenschaft*.[6] I say 'unadulterated', because in all other attempts to grasp the essence of the state, no matter on what one-sided or superficial principles, this very intention of comprehending the state rationally has brought with it thoughts, i.e. universal determinations. Herr von Haller, however, with his eyes open, has not merely renounced the rational material of which the state consists, as well as the form of thought, but he has even gone on with passionate fervour to inveigh against the form and the material so set aside. Part of what Herr von Haller assures us is the 'wide-spread' effect of his principles, this *Restauration* undoubtedly owes to the fact that, in his exposition, he has deliberately dispensed with thought altogether, and has deliberately kept his whole book all of a piece with its lack of thought. For in this way he has eliminated the confusion and disorder which lessen the force of an exposition where the accidental is treated along with hints of the substantial, where the purely empirical and external are mixed with a reminiscence of the universal and rational, and where in the midst of wretched inanities the reader is now and again reminded of the loftier sphere of the infinite. For the same reason again his exposition is consistent. He takes as the essence of the state, not what is substantive but the sphere of accident, and consistency in dealing with a sphere of that kind amounts to the complete inconsistency of utter thoughtlessness which jogs along without looking behind, and is just as much at home now with the exact opposite of what it approved a moment ago.* [A.]

* I have described the book sufficiently to show that it is of an original kind. There might be something noble in the author's indignation by itself, since it was kindled by the false theories, mentioned above, emanating principally from Rousseau, and especially by the attempt to realize them in practice. But to save himself from these theories, Herr von Haller has gone to the other extreme by dispensing with thought altogether and consequently it cannot be said that there is anything of intrinsic value in his virulent hatred of all laws and legislation, of all expressly and legally determinate rights. The hatred of law, of right made determinate in law, is the shibboleth whereby fanaticism, flabby-mindedness, and the hypocrisy of good intentions are clearly and infallibly recognized for what they are, disguise themselves as they may.

Originality like Herr von Haller's is always a curious phenomenon, and for those of my readers who are not yet acquainted with his book I will quote a few specimen passages. This is how he lays down (vol. i, pp. 342 ff. [pp. 361 ff.]) his most important basic proposition: 'Just as, in the inorganic world, the greater dislodges the less and the mighty the weak . . . , so in the animal kingdom, and then amongst human beings, the same law appears in nobler' (often, too, surely in ignobler?) 'forms', and [p. 375] 'this, therefore, is the eternal, unalterable, ordinance of God, that the mightier rules, must rule, and will always rule'. It is clear enough from this, let alone from what follows, in what sense 'might' is taken here. It is not the might of justice and ethics, but only the irrational power of brute force. Herr von Haller then goes on (ibid., pp. 365 ff. [pp. 380 ff.]) to support this doctrine on various grounds, amongst them that 'nature with amazing wisdom has so ordered it that the mere sense of personal superiority irresistibly ennobles the character and encourages the development of just those virtues which are most necessary for dealing with subordinates'. He asks with a great elaboration of undergraduate rhetoric [ibid.] 'whether it is the strong or the weak in the kingdom of science who more misuse their trust and their authority in order to achieve their petty selfish ends and the ruin of the credulous; whether to be a past master in legal learning is not to be a pettifogger, a *leguleius*,[7] one who cheats the hopes of unsuspecting clients, who makes white black and black white, who misapplies the law and makes it a vehicle for wrongdoing, who brings to beggary those who need his assistance and rends them as the hungry vulture rends the innocent lamb', &c., &c. Herr von Haller forgets here that the point of this rhetoric is to support his proposition that the rule of the mightier is an everlasting ordinance of God; so presumably it is by the same ordinance that the vulture rends the innocent lamb, and that hence the mighty are quite right to treat their unsuspecting clients as the weak and to make use of knowledge of the law to empty their pockets. It would be too much, however, to ask that two thoughts should be put together where there is really not a single one.

It goes without saying that Herr von Haller is an enemy of codes of law. In his view, the laws of the land, are on the one hand, in principle 'unnecessary, because they spring self-explanatory from the laws of nature'. If men had remained satisfied with 'self-explanatory' as the basis of their thinking, then they would have been spared the endless labour devoted, since ever there were states, to legislation and legal codes, and which is still devoted thereto and to the study of positive law. 'On the other hand, laws are not exactly promulgated for private individuals, but as instructions to puisne judges, acquainting them with the will of the high court' [vol. ii, part i, chap. 32]. Apart from that, the provision of law-courts is (vol. i, p. 297 [pp. 309 ff.], vol. ii, part i, p. 254 [pp. 264–9] and all over the place) not a state duty, but a favour, help rendered by the authorities, and 'quite supererogatory'; it is not the most perfect method of guaranteeing men's rights; on the contrary, it is an insecure and uncertain method, 'the only one left to us by our modern lawyers. They have reft us of the other three methods, of just those which lead most swiftly and surely to the goal, those which, unlike law-courts, friendly nature has given to man for the safeguarding of his rightful freedom'. And these three methods are—what do you suppose?— '(1) Personal acceptance and inculcation of the law of nature; (2) Resistance to wrong; (3) Flight, when there is no other remedy'. Lawyers are unfriendly indeed, it appears, in comparison with the friendliness of nature! 'But' (vol. i, p. 292 [p. 305]) 'the natural, divine, law, given to everyone by nature the all-bountiful, is: Honour everyone as thine equal' (on the author's principles this should read 'Honour not the man who is thine equal, but the one who is mightier'); 'hurt no man who hurts thee not; demand from him nothing but what he owes' (but what does he owe?); 'nay more, love thy neighbour and serve him when thou canst'. The 'implanting of this law' is to make a legislator and a constitution superfluous. It would be curious to see how Herr von Haller makes it intelligible why legislators and constitutions have appeared in the world despite this 'implanting'.

In vol. iii, pp. 362 [361] ff., the author comes to the 'so-called national liberties', by which he means the laws and constitutions of nation states. Every legally constituted right is in this wide sense of the word a 'liberty'. Of these laws he says, *inter alia*, that 'their content is usually very insignificant, although in books a high value may be placed on documentary liberties of that kind'. When we then realize that the author is speaking here of the national liberties of the German Estates, of the English people (e.g. Magna Carta [p. 367] 'which is little read, and on account of its archaic phraseology still less understood', the Bill of Rights, and so forth), of the people of Hungary, &c., we are surprised to find that these possessions, formerly so highly prized, are only insignificant; and no less surprised to learn that it is only in books that these nations place a value on laws whose co-operation has entered into every coat that is worn and every crust that is eaten, and still enters into every day and hour of the lives of everyone.

To carry quotation further, Herr von Haller speaks particularly ill (vol. i, pp. 185 ff. [pp. 192–3]) of the Prussian General Legal Code, because of the 'incredible' influence on it of the errors of false philosophy (though in this instance at any rate the fault cannot be ascribed to Kant's philosophy, a topic on which Herr von Haller is at his angriest), especially where it speaks of the state, the resources

259. The Idea of the state

(a) has immediate actuality and is the individual state as a self-dependent organism—the *Constitution* or *Constitutional Law*;

(b) passes over into the relation of one state to other states—*International Law*;

(c) is the universal Idea as a genus and as an absolute power over individual states—the mind which gives itself its actuality in the process of *World-History*. [A.]

A. *Constitutional Law*

260. The state is the actuality of concrete freedom. But concrete freedom consists in this, that personal individuality and its particular interests not only achieve their complete development and gain explicit recognition for their right (as they do in the sphere of the family and civil society) but, for one thing, they also pass over of their own accord into the interest of the universal, and, for another thing, they know and will the universal; they even recognize it as their own substantive mind; they take it as their end and aim and are active in its pursuit. The result is that the universal does not prevail or achieve completion except along with particular interests and through the co-operation of particular knowing and

of the state, the end of the state, the head of the state, his duties, and those of civil servants, and so forth. Herr von Haller finds particularly mischievous [vol. i, pp. 198–9] 'the right of defraying the expenses of the state by levying taxes on the private wealth of individuals, on their businesses, on goods produced or consumed. Under those circumstances, neither the king himself (since the resources of the state belong to the state and are not the private property of the king), nor the Prussian citizens can call anything their own, neither their person nor their property; and all subjects are bondslaves to the law, since they may not withdraw themselves from the service of the state.'

In this welter of incredible crudity, what is perhaps most comical of all is the emotion with which Herr von Haller describes his unspeakable pleasure in his discoveries (vol. i, Preface [pp. xxv–xxvii])—'a joy such as only the friend of truth can feel when after honest search he has become confident that he has found as it were' (yes indeed! 'as it were' is right!) 'the voice of nature, the very word of God'. (The truth is that the word of God very clearly distinguishes its revelations from the voices of nature and unregenerate man.) 'The author could have sunk to the ground in open amazement, a stream of joyful tears burst from his eyes, and living religious feeling sprang up in him there and then.' Herr von Haller might have discovered by his 'religious feeling' that he should rather bewail his condition as the hardest chastisement of God. For the hardest thing which man can experience is to be so far excluded from thought and reason, from respect for the laws, and from knowing how infinitely important and divine it is that the duties of the state and the rights of the citizens, as well as the rights of the state and the duties of the citizens, should be defined by law—to be so far excluded from all this that absurdity can foist itself upon him as the word of God.

willing; and individuals likewise do not live as private persons for
their own ends alone, but in the very act of willing these they will
the universal in the light of the universal, and their activity is
consciously aimed at none but the universal end. The principle
of modern states has prodigious strength and depth because it
allows the principle of subjectivity to progress to its culmination
in the extreme of self-subsistent personal particularity, and yet at
the same time brings it back to the substantive unity and so maintains this unity in the principle of subjectivity itself. [A.]

261. In contrast with the spheres of private rights and private
welfare (the family and civil society), the state is from one point
of view an external necessity and their higher authority; its nature
is such that their laws and interests are subordinate to it and dependent on it. On the other hand, however, it is the end immanent
within them, and its strength lies in the unity of its own universal
end and aim with the particular interest of individuals, in the fact
that individuals have duties to the state in proportion as they have
rights against it (see Paragraph 155).

In the Remark to Paragraph 3 above, reference was made to the fact
that it was Montesquieu above all who, in his famous work *L'Esprit des
Lois*, kept in sight and tried to work out in detail both the thought of the
dependence of laws—in particular, laws concerning the rights of persons
—on the specific character of the state, and also the philosophic notion
of always treating the part in its relation to the whole.

Duty is primarily a relation to something which from my point of view
is substantive, absolutely universal. A right, on the other hand, is simply
the embodiment of this substance and thus is the particular aspect of it
and enshrines my particular freedom. Hence at abstract levels, right
and duty appear parcelled out on different sides or in different persons.
In the state, as something ethical, as the inter-penetration of the substantive and the particular, my obligation to what is substantive is at the
same time the embodiment of my particular freedom. This means that
in the state duty and right are united in one and the same relation. But
further, since none the less the distinct moments acquire in the state the
shape and reality peculiar to each, and since therefore the distinction
between right and duty enters here once again, it follows that while
implicitly, i.e. in form, identical, they at the same time differ in content.
In the spheres of personal rights and morality, the necessary bearing of
right and duty on one another falls short of actualization; and hence
there is at that point only an abstract similarity of content between them,
i.e. in those abstract spheres, what is one man's right ought also to be
another's, and what is one man's duty ought also to be another's. The

absolute identity of right and duty in the state is present in these spheres
not as a genuine identity but only as a similarity of content, because in
them this content is determined as quite general and is simply the
fundamental principle of both right and duty, i.e. the principle that men,
as persons, are free. Slaves, therefore, have no duties because they have
no rights, and vice versa. (Religious duties are not here in point.[8])

In the course of the inward development of the concrete Idea, however, its moments become distinguished and their specific determinacy
becomes at the same time a difference of content. In the family, the
content of a son's duties to his father differs from the content of his
rights against him; the content of the rights of a member of civil society
is not the same as the content of his duties to his prince and government.

This concept of the union of duty and right is a point of vital importance and in it the inner strength of states is contained.

Duty on its abstract side goes no farther than the persistent neglect
and proscription of a man's particular interest, on the ground that it is
the inessential, even the discreditable, moment in his life. Duty, taken
concretely as Idea, reveals the moment of particularity as itself essential
and so regards its satisfaction as indisputably necessary. In whatever
way an individual may fulfil his duty, he must at the same time find his
account therein and attain his personal interest and satisfaction. Out of
his position in the state, a right must accrue to him whereby public
affairs shall be his own particular affair. Particular interests should in
fact not be set aside or completely suppressed; instead, they should be
put in correspondence with the universal, and thereby both they and the
universal are upheld. The *isolated* individual, so far as his duties are
concerned, is in subjection; but as a member of *civil society* he finds in
fulfilling his duties to it protection of his person and property, regard for
his private welfare, the satisfaction of the depths of his being, the consciousness and feeling of himself as a member of the whole; and, in so
far as he completely fulfils his duties by performing tasks and services
for the *state*, he is upheld and preserved. Take duty abstractly, and the
universal's interest would consist simply in the completion as duties of
the tasks and services which it exacts. [A.]

262. The actual Idea is mind, which, sundering itself into the
two ideal spheres of its concept, family and civil society, enters
upon its finite phase, but it does so only in order to rise above its
ideality and become explicit as infinite actual mind. It is therefore
to these ideal spheres that the actual Idea assigns the material of
this its finite actuality, viz. human beings as a mass, in such a way
that the function assigned to any given individual is visibly mediated by circumstances, his caprice and his personal choice of his
station in life (see Paragraph 185 and the Remark thereto). [A.]

263. In these spheres in which its moments, particularity and individuality, have their immediate and reflected reality, mind is present as their objective universality glimmering in them as the power of reason in necessity (see Paragraph 184), i.e. as the institutions considered above. [A.]

264. Mind is the nature of human beings *en masse* and their nature is therefore twofold: (i) at one extreme, explicit individuality of consciousness and will, and (ii) at the other extreme, universality which knows and wills what is substantive. Hence they attain their right in both these respects only in so far as both their private personality and its substantive basis are actualized. Now in the family and civil society they acquire their right in the first of these respects directly and in the second indirectly, in that (i) they find their substantive self-consciousness in social institutions which are the universal implicit in their particular interests, and (ii) the Corporation supplies them with an occupation and an activity directed on a universal end.

265. These institutions are the components of the constitution (i.e. of rationality developed and actualized) in the sphere of particularity. They are, therefore, the firm foundation not only of the state but also of the citizen's trust in it and sentiment towards it. They are the pillars of public freedom since in them particular freedom is realized and rational, and therefore there is *implicitly* present even in them the union of freedom and necessity. [A.]

266. But mind is objective and actual to itself not merely as this necessity and as a realm of appearance, but also as the ideality and the heart of this necessity. Only in this way is this substantive universality *aware* of itself as its own object and end, with the result that the necessity appears to itself in the shape of freedom as well.

267. This necessity in ideality is the inner self-development of the Idea. As the substance of the individual subject, it is his political sentiment [patriotism]; in distinction therefrom, as the substance of the objective world, it is the organism of the state, i.e. it is the strictly political state[9] and its constitution. [A.]

268. The political sentiment, patriotism pure and simple, is assured conviction with truth as its basis—mere subjective assurance is not the outcome of truth but is only opinion—and a volition which has become habitual. In this sense it is simply a product of

the institutions subsisting in the state, since rationality is *actually* present in the state, while action in conformity with these institutions gives rationality its practical proof. This sentiment is, in general, trust (which may pass over into a greater or lesser degree of educated insight), or the consciousness that my interest, both substantive and particular, is contained and preserved in another's (i.e. in the state's) interest and end, i.e. in the other's relation to me as an individual. In this way, this very other is immediately not an other in my eyes, and in being conscious of this fact, I am free.

Patriotism is often understood to mean only a readiness for exceptional sacrifices and actions. Essentially, however, it is the sentiment which, in the relationships of our daily life and under ordinary conditions, habitually recognizes that the community is one's substantive groundwork and end. It is out of this consciousness, which during life's daily round stands the test in all circumstances, that there subsequently also arises the readiness for extraordinary exertions. But since men would often rather be magnanimous than law-abiding, they readily persuade themselves that they possess this exceptional patriotism in order to be sparing in the expression of a genuine patriotic sentiment or to excuse their lack of it. If again this genuine patriotism is looked upon as that which may begin of itself and arise from subjective ideas and thoughts, it is being confused with opinion, because so regarded patriotism is deprived of its true ground, objective reality. [A.]

269. The patriotic sentiment acquires its specifically determined content from the various members of the organism of the state. This organism is the development of the Idea to its differences and their objective actuality. Hence these different members are the various powers of the state with their functions and spheres of action, by means of which the universal continually engenders itself, and engenders itself in a necessary way because their specific character is fixed by the nature of the concept. Throughout this process the universal maintains its identity, since it is itself the presupposition of its own production. This organism is the constitution of the state. [A.]

270. (1) The abstract actuality or the substantiality of the state consists in the fact that its end is the universal interest as such and the conservation therein of particular interests since the universal interest is the substance of these. (2) But this substantiality of the state is also its *necessity*, since its substantiality is divided into the distinct spheres of its activity which correspond to the moments of its concept, and these spheres, owing to this substantiality, are thus actually fixed determinate characteristics of the state, i.e. its *powers*. (3) But this very substantiality of the state is mind knowing and willing itself after passing through the forming process of education.[10] The state, therefore, knows what it wills and knows it in its universality, i.e. as something thought. Hence it works and acts by reference to consciously adopted ends, known principles, and laws which are not merely implicit but are actually present to consciousness; and further, it acts with precise knowledge of existing conditions and circumstances, inasmuch as its actions have a bearing on these.

This is the place to allude to the relation of the state to religion, because it is often reiterated nowadays[11] that religion is the basis of the state, and because those who make this assertion even have the impertinence to suggest that, once it is made, political science has said its last word. No doctrine is more fitted to produce so much confusion, more fitted indeed to exalt confusion itself to be the constitution of the state and the proper form of knowledge.

In the first place, it may seem suspicious that religion is principally sought and recommended for times of public calamity, disorder, and oppression, and that people are referred to it as a solace in face of wrong or as a hope in compensation for loss. Then further, while the state is mind on earth (*der Geist der in der Welt steht*), religion may sometimes be looked upon as commanding downright indifference to earthly interests, the march of events, and current affairs, and so to turn men's attention to religion does not seem to be the way to exalt the interest and business of the state into the fundamental and serious aim of life. On the contrary, this suggestion seems to assert that politics is wholly a matter of caprice and indifference, either because this way of talking merely amounts to saying that it is only the aims of passion and lawless force, &c., which bear sway in the state, or because this recommendation of religion is supposed to be of self-sufficient validity, and religion is to claim to decide the law and administer it. While it might seem a bitter jest to stifle all animus against tyranny by asserting that the oppressed find their consolation in religion, it still must not be forgotten that religion may take a form leading to the harshest bondage in the fetters of superstition and man's degraded subservience to animals. (The Egyptians and the Hindus, for instance, revere animals as beings higher than themselves.) This phenomenon may at least make it evident that we ought not to speak of religion at all in general terms and that we really need a power to protect us from it in some of its forms and to espouse against them the rights of reason and self-consciousness.

The essence of the relation between religion and the state can be determined, however, only if we recall the concept of religion. The content of religion is absolute truth, and consequently the religious is the most sublime of all dispositions.[12] As intuition, feeling, representative knowledge, its task is concentrated upon God as the unrestricted principle and cause on which everything hangs. It thus involves the demand that everything else shall be seen in this light and depend on it for corroboration, justification, and verification. It is in being thus related to religion that state, laws, and duties all alike acquire for consciousness their supreme confirmation and their supreme obligatoriness, because even the state, laws, and duties are in their actuality something determinate which passes over into a higher sphere and so into that on which it is grounded.* It is for this reason that in religion there lies the place where man is always assured of finding a consciousness of the unchangeable, of the highest freedom and satisfaction, even within all the mutability of the world and despite the frustration of his aims and the loss of his interests and possessions.† Now if religion is in this way the groundwork which includes the ethical realm in general, and the state's fundamental nature—the divine will—in particular, it is at the same time only a groundwork; and it is at this point that state and religion begin to diverge. The state is the divine will, in the sense that it is mind present on earth, unfolding itself to be the actual shape and organization of a world. Those who insist on stopping at the form of *religion*, as opposed to the state, are acting like those logicians who think they are right if they continually stop at the essence and refuse to advance beyond that abstraction to existence, or like those moralists (see Remark to Paragraph 140) who will only good in the abstract and leave it to caprice to decide what is good. Religion is a relation to the Absolute, a relation which takes the form of feeling, representative thinking, faith; and, brought within its all-embracing circumference, everything becomes only accidental and transient. Now if, in relation to the state, we cling to this form of experience and make it the authority for the state and its essential determinant, the state must become a prey to weakness, insecurity, and disorder, because it is an organism in which firmly fixed distinct powers, laws, and institutions have been developed. In contrast with the form of religion, a form which draws a veil over everything

---

* See *Enc.* [1st edn.], § 453 [3rd edn. § 553].

† Religion, knowledge, and science have as their principle a form peculiar to each and different from that of the state. They therefore enter the state partly as *means*—means to education and [a higher] mentality—partly in so far as they are in essence *ends* in themselves, for the reason that they are embodied in existent institutions. In both these respects the principles of the state have, in their application, a bearing on them. A comprehensive, concrete treatise on the state would also have to deal with those spheres of life as well as with art and such things as mere geographical matters, and to consider their place in the state and their bearing on it. In this book, however, it is the principle of the state in its own special sphere which is being fully expounded in accordance with the Idea, and it is only in passing that reference can be made to the principles of religion, &c., and to the application of the right of the state to them.

determinate, and so comes to be purely subjective, the objective and universal element in the state, i.e. the laws, acquires a negative instead of a stable and authoritative character, and the result is the production of maxims of conduct like the following: 'To the righteous man no law is given; only be pious, and for the rest, practise what thou wilt; yield to thine own caprice and passion, and if thereby others suffer wrong, commend them to the consolations and hopes of religion, or better still, call them irreligious and condemn them to perdition.' This negative attitude, however, may not confine itself to an inner disposition and attitude of mind; it may turn instead to the outside world and assert its authority there, and then there is an outbreak of the religious fanaticism which, like fanaticism in politics, discards all government and legal order as barriers cramping the inner life of the heart and incompatible with its infinity, and at the same time proscribes private property, marriage, the ties and work involved in civil society, &c., &c., as degrading to love and the freedom of feeling. But since even then decisions must somehow be made for everyday life and practice, the same doctrine which we had before (see Remark to Paragraph 140, where we dealt generally with the subjectivity of the will which knows itself to be absolute) turns up again here, namely that subjective ideas, i.e. opinion and capricious inclination, are to do the deciding.

In contrast with the truth thus veiled behind subjective ideas and feelings, the genuine truth is the prodigious transfer of the inner into the outer, the building of reason into the real world, and this has been the task of the world during the whole course of its history. It is by working at this task that civilized man has actually given reason an embodiment in law and government and achieved consciousness of the fact. Those who 'seek guidance from the Lord' and are assured that the whole truth is directly present in their unschooled opinions, fail to apply themselves to the task of exalting their subjectivity to consciousness of the truth and to knowledge of duty and objective right. The only possible fruits of their attitude are folly, abomination, and the demolition of the whole ethical order, and these fruits must inevitably be reaped if the religious disposition holds firmly and exclusively to its intuitive form and so turns against the real world and the truth present in it in the form of the universal, i.e. of the laws. Still, there is no necessity for this disposition to turn outward and actualize itself in this way. With its negative standpoint, it is of course also open to it to remain something inward, to accommodate itself to government and law, and to acquiesce in these with sneers and idle longings, or with a sigh of resignation. It is not strength but weakness which has turned religious feeling nowadays into piety of a polemical kind, whether the polemic be connected with some genuine need or simply with unsatisfied vanity. Instead of subduing one's opinions by the labour of study, and subjecting one's will to discipline and so elevating it to free obedience, the line of least resistance is to renounce knowledge of objective truth. Along this line we may preserve a feeling of abject humility and so also of self-conceit, and claim to have ready to hand in godliness everything requisite for seeing into the heart of law and government, for passing sentence on them, and laying down what their character should and must be; and of course if we take this line, the source of our claims is a pious heart, and they are therefore infallible and unimpeachable, and the upshot is that since we make religion the basis of our intentions and assertions, they cannot be criticized on the score of their shallowness or their immorality.

But if religion be religion of a genuine kind, it does not run counter to the state in a negative or polemical way like the kind just described. It rather recognizes the state and upholds it, and furthermore it has a position and an external organization of its own. The practice of its worship consists in ritual and doctrinal instruction, and for this purpose possessions and property are required, as well as individuals dedicated to the service of the flock. There thus arises a relation between the state and the church. To determine this relation is a simple matter. In the nature of the case, the state discharges a duty by affording every assistance and protection to the church in the furtherance of its religious ends; and, in addition, since religion is an integrating factor in the state, implanting a sense of unity in the depths of men's minds, the state should even require all its citizens to belong to a church—a church is all that can be said, because since the content of a man's faith depends on his private ideas, the state cannot interfere with it. A state which is strong because its organization is mature may be all the more liberal in this matter; it may entirely overlook details of religious practice which affect it, and may even tolerate a sect (though, of course, all depends on its numbers) which on religious grounds declines to recognize even its direct duties to the state. The reason for the state's liberal attitude here is that it makes over the members of such sects to civil society and its laws, and is content if they fulfil their direct duties to the state passively, for instance by such means as commutation or the performance of a different service.*

* Quakers, Anabaptists, &c., may be said to be active members only of civil society, and they may be regarded as private persons standing in merely private relations to others. Even when this position has been allowed them, they have been exempted from taking the oath. They fulfil their direct duties to the state in a passive way; one of the most important of these duties, the defence of the state against its enemies, they refuse outright to fulfil, and their refusal may perhaps be admitted provided they perform some other service instead. To sects of this kind, the state's attitude is toleration in the strict sense of the word,[13] because since they decline to recognize their duty to the state, they may not claim the rights of citizenship. On one occasion when the abolition of the slave-trade[14] was being pressed with great vigour in the American Congress, a member from one of the Southern States made the striking retort: 'Give us our slaves, and you may keep your Quakers.' Only if the state is otherwise strong can it overlook and

But since the church owns property and carries on besides the practice of worship, and since therefore it must have people in its service, it forsakes the inner for the worldly life and therefore enters the domain of the state, and *eo ipso* comes under its laws. The oath and ethical ties generally, like the marriage bond, entail that inner permeation and elevation of *sentiment* which acquires its deepest confirmation through religion. But[15] since ethical ties are in essence ties within the actual *rational* order, the first thing is to affirm within that order the rights which it involves. Confirmation of these rights by the church is secondary and is only the inward, comparatively abstract, side of the matter.

As for the other ways in which an ecclesiastical communion gives expression to itself, so far as doctrine is concerned the inward preponderates over the outward to a greater extent than is the case with acts of worship and other lines of conduct connected with these, in which the legal side at least seems at once to be a matter for the state. (It is true, of course, that churches have managed to exempt their ministers and property from the power and jurisdiction of the state, and they have even arrogated to themselves jurisdiction over laymen as well in matters in which religion co-operates, such as divorce and the taking of the oath, &c.) Public control of actions of this kind is indeterminate in extent, but this is due to the nature of public control itself and obtains similarly in purely civil transactions (see Paragraph 234). When individuals, holding religious views in common, form themselves into a church, a Corporation, they fall under the general control and oversight of the higher state officials. Doctrine as such, however, has its domain in conscience and falls within the right of the subjective freedom of

suffer such anomalies, because it can then rely principally on the strength of custom and the inner rationality of its institutions to diminish and close the gap between the existence of anomalies and the full assertion of its own strict rights. Thus technically it may have been right to refuse a grant of even civil rights to the Jews on the ground that they should be regarded as belonging not merely to a religious sect but to a foreign race. But the fierce outcry raised against the Jews, from that point of view and others, ignores the fact that they are, above all, *men*; and manhood, so far from being a mere superficial, abstract quality (see Remark to Paragraph 209), is on the contrary itself the basis of the fact that what civil rights rouse in their possessors is the feeling of oneself as counting in civil society as a person with rights, and this feeling of self-hood, infinite and free from all restrictions, is the root from which the desired similarity in disposition and ways of thinking comes into being. To exclude the Jews from civil rights, on the other hand, would rather be to confirm the isolation with which they have been reproached—a result for which the state refusing them rights would be blamable and reproachable, because by so refusing, it would have misunderstood its own basic principle, its nature as an objective and powerful institution (compare the end of the Remark to Paragraph 268). The exclusion of the Jews from civil rights may be supposed to be a right of the highest kind and may be demanded on that ground; but experience has shown that so to exclude them is the silliest folly, and the way in which governments now treat them has proved itself to be both prudent and dignified.

self-consciousness, the sphere of the inner life, which as such is not the domain of the state. Yet the state, too, has a doctrine, since its organization and whatever rights and constitution are authoritative within it exist essentially in the form of thought as law. And since the state is not a mechanism but the rational life of self-conscious freedom, the system of the ethical world, it follows that an essential moment in the actual state is the mental attitude of the citizens, and so their consciousness of the *principles* which this attitude implies. On the other hand, the doctrine of the church is not purely and simply an inward concern of conscience. As doctrine it is rather the expression of something, in fact the expression of a subject-matter which is most closely linked, or even directly concerned, with ethical principles and the law of the land. Hence at this point the paths of church and state either coincide or diverge at right angles. The difference of their two domains may be pushed by the church into sheer antagonism since, by regarding itself as enshrining the content of religion—a content which is absolute—it may claim as its portion mind[16] in general and so the whole ethical sphere, and conceive the state as a mere mechanical scaffolding for the attainment of external, non-mental, ends. It may take itself to be the Kingdom of God, or at least as the road to it or its vestibule, while it regards the state as the kingdom of this world, i.e. of the transient and the finite. In a word, it may think that it is an end in itself, while the state is a mere means. These claims produce the demand, in connexion with doctrinal instruction, that the state should not only allow the church to do as it likes with complete freedom, but that it should pay unconditional respect to the church's doctrines as doctrines, whatever their character, because their determination is supposed to be the task of the church alone. The church bases this claim on the wide ground that the whole domain of mind (*Geist*) is its property. But science and all types of knowledge also have a footing in that domain and, like a church, they build themselves into a whole with a guiding principle of its own, and, with even better justification, may regard themselves as occupying the position which the church claims. Hence science also may in the same way demand to be independent of the state, which is then supposed to be a mere means with the task of providing for science as though science were an end in itself.

Further, for determining the relation between church and state, it makes no difference whether the leaders of congregations or individuals ordained to the service of the church feel impelled to withdraw from the state and lead a sort of secluded life of their own, so that only the other church members are subject to the state's control, or whether they remain within the state except in their capacity as ecclesiastics, a capacity which they take to be but one side of their life. The most striking thing about such a conception of the church's relation to the state is that it implies the idea that the state's specific function consists in protecting and securing everyone's life, property, and caprice, in so far as these do not encroach upon the life, property, and caprice of others.[17] The state from this point of view is treated simply as an organization to satisfy men's necessities. In this way the element of absolute truth, of mind in its higher development, is placed, as subjective religious feeling or theoretical science, beyond the reach of the state. The state, as the laity pure and simple, is confined to paying its respects to this element and so is entirely deprived of any strictly ethical character. Now it is, of course, a matter of history that in times and under conditions of barbarism, all higher forms of intellectual life had their seat only in the church, while the state was a mere mundane rule of force, caprice, and passion. At such times it was the abstract opposition of state and church which was the main underlying principle of history (see Paragraph 359).[18] But it is far too blind and shallow a proceeding to declare that this situation is the one which truly corresponds with the Idea. The development of this Idea has proved this rather to be the truth, that mind, as free and rational, is implicitly ethical, while the Idea in its truth is rationality actualized; and this it is which exists as the state. Further, this Idea has made it no less clearly evident that the ethical truth in it is present to conscious thought as a content worked up into the form of universality, i.e. as law—in short, that the state *knows* its aims, apprehends and gives practical proof of them with a clear-cut consciousness and in accordance with principles. Now, as I said earlier, religion has the truth as its universal subject-matter, but it possesses it only as a *given* content which has not been apprehended in its fundamental characteristics as a result of thinking and the use of concepts. Similarly, the relation of the individual to this subject-matter is an obligation grounded on authority, while the 'witness of his own spirit and heart', i.e. that wherein the moment of freedom resides, is faith and feeling. It is philosophic insight which sees that while church and state differ in form, they do not stand opposed in content, for truth and rationality are the content of both. Thus when the church begins to teach doctrines (though there are and have been some churches with a ritual only, and others in which ritual is the chief thing, while doctrine and a more educated consciousness are only secondary), and when these doctrines touch on objective principles, on thoughts of the ethical and the rational, then their expression *eo ipso* brings the church into the domain of the state. In contrast with the church's faith and authority in matters affecting ethical principles, rightness, laws, institutions, in contrast with the church's subjective conviction, the state is that which knows. Its principle is such that its content is in essence no longer clothed with the form of feeling and faith but is determinate thought.

If the content of absolute truth appears in the form of religion as a particular content, i.e. as the doctrines peculiar to the church as a religious community, then these doctrines remain out of the reach of the state (in Protestantism they are out of the reach of priests too because, as there is no laity there, so there is no priesthood to be an exclusive depository of church doctrine).[19] Since ethical principles and the organization of the state in general are drawn into the domain of religion and not only may, but also should, be established by reference thereto, this reference gives religious credentials to the state itself. On the other hand, however, the state retains the right and the form of self-conscious, objective, rationality, the right to make this form count and to maintain it against pretensions springing from truth in a subjective dress, no matter how such truth may girdle itself with certitude and authority.

The state is universal in form, a form whose essential principle is thought. This explains why it was in the state that freedom of thought and science had their origin. It was a church, on the other hand, which burnt Giordano Bruno, forced Galileo to recant on his knees his exposition of the Copernican view of the solar system, and so forth.* Science too, therefore, has its place on the side of the state since it has one element, its form, in common with the state, and its aim is knowledge,

---

* 'When Galileo published the discoveries' about the phases of Venus, &c., which he had made with the aid of the telescope, 'he showed that they incontestably proved the motion of the earth. But this idea of the motion of the earth was declared heretical by an assembly of Cardinals, and Galileo, its most famous advocate, was haled before the Inquisition and compelled to recant it, under pain of severe imprisonment. One of the strongest of passions is the love of truth in a man of genius.[20] . . . Convinced of the motion of the earth as a result of his own observations, Galileo meditated a long while on a new work in which he had resolved to develop all the proofs in its favour. But in order at the same time to escape from the persecution of which otherwise he would inevitably have been the victim, he hit upon the device of expounding them in the form of dialogues between three speakers. . . . It is obvious enough in them that the advantage lies with the advocate of the Copernican system; but since Galileo did not decide between the speakers, and gave as much weight as possible to the objections raised by the partisans of Ptolemy, he might well have expected to be left to enjoy undisturbed the peace to which his advanced age and his labours had entitled him. . . . In his seventieth year he was haled once more before the tribunal of the Inquisition. . . . He was imprisoned and required to recant his opinions a second time under threat of the penalty fixed for a relapse into heresy. . . . He was made to sign an abjuration in the following terms: "I, Galileo, appearing in person before the court in my seventieth year, kneeling, and with my eyes on the holy Gospels which I hold in my hands, abjure, damn, and execrate with my whole heart and true belief the absurd, false, and heretical doctrine of the motion of the earth. . . ." What a spectacle! An aged, venerable man, famous throughout a long life exclusively devoted to the study of nature, abjuring on his knees, against the witness of his own conscience, the truth which he had demonstrated so convincingly! By the judgement of the Inquisition he was condemned to perpetual imprisonment. A year later he was set at liberty through the intercession of the Grand Duke of Florence. . . . He died in 1642. . . . Europe mourned his loss. It had been enlightened by his labours and was exasperated by the judgement passed by a detested tribunal on a man of his greatness.' (Laplace: *Exposition du système du monde*, Book V, chap. 4.)

knowledge of objective truth and rationality in terms of thought. Such knowledge may, of course, fall from the heights of science into opinion and deductive argumentation, and, turning its attention to ethical matters and the organization of the state, set itself against their basic principles. And it may perhaps do this while making for this opining— as if it were reason and the right of subjective self-consciousness—the same pretentious claim as the church makes for its own sphere, the claim, namely, to be free from restraint in its opinions and convictions.

This principle of the subjectivity of knowing has been dealt with above (see Remark to Paragraph 140). It is here only necessary to add a note on the twofold attitude of the state to this opining. On the one hand, in so far as opining is mere opining, a purely subjective matter, it is without any genuine inherent force or power, plume itself as it may; and from this point of view the state may be as totally indifferent to it as the painter who sticks to the three primary colours on his palette is indifferent to the academic wisdom which tells him there are seven. On the other hand, however, when this opining of bad principles embodies itself in a general organization corrosive of the actual order, the state has to set its face against it and protect objective truth and the principles of ethical life (and it must do the same in face of the formulae of unconditioned subjectivity if these have proposed to take the starting point of science as their basis, and turn state educational institutions against the state by encouraging them to make against it claims as pretentious as those of a church); while, vice versa, in face of a church claiming unrestricted and unconditional authority, the state has in general to make good the formal right of self-consciousness to its own insight, its own conviction, and, in short, its own thought of what is to hold good as objective truth.

Mention may also be made of the 'unity of state and church'—a favourite topic of modern discussion and held up by some as the highest of ideals.[21] While state and church are essentially one in truth of principle and disposition, it is no less essential that, despite this unity, the distinction between their forms of consciousness should be externalized as a distinction between their special modes of existence. This often desired unity of church and state is found under oriental despotisms,[22] but an oriental despotism is not a state, or at any rate not the self-conscious form of state which is alone worthy of mind, the form which is organically developed and where there are rights and a free ethical life. Further, if the state is to come into existence as the self-*knowing* ethical actuality of mind, it is essential that its form should be distinct from that of authority and faith. But this distinction emerges only in so far as the church is subjected to inward divisions. It is only thereafter that the state, in contrast with the particular sects, has attained to universality of thought—its formal principle—and is bringing this universality into existence. (In order to understand this, it is necessary to know not only what universality is in itself, but also what its existence is.[23]) Hence so far from its being or its having been a misfortune for the state that the church is disunited, it is only as a result of that disunion that the state has been able to reach its appointed end as a self-consciously rational and ethical organization. Moreover, this disunion is the best piece of good fortune which could have befallen either the church or thought so far as the freedom and rationality of either is concerned.[24] [A.]

271. The constitution of the state is, in the first place, the organization of the state and the self-related process of its organic life, a process whereby it differentiates its moments within itself and develops them to self-subsistence. Secondly, the state is an individual, unique and exclusive, and therefore related to others. Thus it turns its differentiating activity outward and accordingly establishes within itself the ideality of its subsisting inward differentiations. [A.]

1. *The Constitution* (*on its internal side only*)

272. The constitution is rational[25] in so far as the state inwardly differentiates and determines its activity in accordance with the nature of the concept. The result of this is that each of these powers is in itself the totality of the constitution, because each contains the other moments and has them effective in itself, and because the moments, being expressions of the differentiation of the concept, simply abide in their ideality and constitute nothing but a single individual whole.

In our day there has come before the public an endless amount of babble about the constitution, as about reason itself, and the stalest babble of all has been produced in Germany, thanks to those[26] who have persuaded themselves that they have the best, or even the sole, understanding of what a constitution is. Elsewhere, particularly in governments, misunderstanding is supposed to reign. And these gentlemen are convinced that they have an unassailable justification for what they say because they claim that religion and piety are the basis of all this shallow thinking of theirs. It is no wonder that this babble has made reasonable men just as sick of the words 'reason', 'enlightenment', 'right', &c., as of the words 'constitution' and 'freedom', and a man might well be ashamed now to go on discussing the constitution of the state at all! However, we may at least hope that this surfeit will be effective in producing the general conviction that philosophical *knowledge* of such topics cannot arise from argumentation, deduction, calculations of purpose and utility, still less from the heart, love, and inspiration, but only from the concept. We may also hope that those[27] who hold that the divine is inconceivable and the knowledge of truth a wild-goose chase will feel themselves bound to refrain from taking part in the discussion. The products of their hearts and their inspirations are either undigested chatter or mere edification, and whatever the worth of these neither can pretend to notice from philosophy.

Amongst current ideas, mention may be made (in connexion with Paragraph 269) of the necessity for a division of powers within the state.[28] This point is of the highest importance and, if taken in its true sense, may rightly be regarded as the guarantee of public freedom. It is an idea, however, with which the very people who pretend to talk out of their inspiration and love neither have, nor desire to have, any acquaintance, since it is precisely there that the moment of rational determinacy lies. That is to say, the principle of the division of powers contains the essential moment of difference, of rationality *realized*. But when the abstract Understanding handles it, it reads into it the false doctrine of the absolute self-subsistence of each of the powers against the others, and then one-sidedly interprets their relation to each other as negative, as a mutual restriction. This view implies that the attitude adopted by each power to the others is hostile and apprehensive, as if the others were evils, and that their function is to oppose one another and as a result of this counterpoise to effect an equilibrium on the whole, but never a living unity. It is only the inner self-determination of the concept, not any other consideration, whether of purpose or advantage, that is the absolute source of the division of powers, and in virtue of this alone is the organization of the state something inherently rational and the image of eternal reason.

How the concept and then, more concretely, how the Idea, determine themselves inwardly and so posit their moments—universality, particularity, and individuality—in abstraction from one another, is discoverable from my logic, though not of course from the logic current elsewhere. To take the merely negative as a starting-point and to exalt to the first place the volition of evil and the mistrust of this volition, and then on the basis of this presupposition slyly to construct dikes whose efficiency simply necessitates corresponding dikes over against them,[29] is characteristic in thought of the negative Understanding and in sentiment of the outlook of the rabble (see Paragraph 244).

If the powers (e.g. what are called the 'Executive' and the 'Legislature') become self-subsistent, then as we have recently seen on a grand scale,[30] the destruction of the state is forthwith a *fait accompli*. Alternatively, if the state is maintained in essentials, it is strife which through the subjection by one power of the others, produces unity at least, however defective, and so secures the bare essential, the maintenance of the state. [A.]

273. The state as a political entity is thus cleft into three substantive divisions:

(*a*) the power to determine and establish the universal—the Legislature;

(*b*) the power to subsume single cases and the spheres of particularity under the universal—the Executive;

(*c*) the power of subjectivity, as the will with the power of ultimate decision—the Crown. In the crown, the different powers are bound into an individual unity which is thus at once the apex and basis of the whole, i.e. of constitutional monarchy.

The development of the state to constitutional monarchy is the achievement of the modern world, a world in which the substantial Idea has won the infinite form [of subjectivity—see Paragraph 144]. The history of this inner deepening of the world mind—or in other words this free maturation in course of which the Idea, realizing rationality in the external, releases its moments (and they are only its moments) from itself as totalities, and just for that reason still retains them in the ideal unity of the concept—the history of this genuine formation of ethical life is the content of the whole course of world-history.

The ancient division of constitutions into monarchy, aristocracy, and democracy, is based upon the notion of substantial, still undivided, unity, a unity which has not yet come to its inner differentiation (to a matured, internal organization) and which therefore has not yet attained depth or concrete rationality. From the standpoint of the ancient world, therefore, this division is the true and correct one, since for a unity of that still substantial type, a unity inwardly too immature to have attained its absolutely complete development, difference is essentially an external difference and appears at first as a difference in the number* of those in whom that substantial unity is supposed to be immanent.[32] These forms, which on this principle belong to different wholes, are given in limited monarchy the humbler position of moments in a whole. The monarch is a *single* person; the *few* come on the scene with the executive, and the *many* en masse with the legislative. But, as has been indicated,[33] purely quantitative distinctions like these are only superficial and do not afford the concept of the thing. Equally inadequate is the mass of contemporary talk about the democratic and aristocratic elements in monarchy, because when the elements specified in such talk are found in a monarchy there is no longer anything democratic or aristocratic about them. There are notions of constitutions in which the state is portrayed from top to bottom as an abstraction which is supposed to rule and command, and how many

* See *Enc.* [1st edn.], § 82[31] [3rd edn. § 132].

individuals are at the head of such a state, whether one or a few or all, is a question left undecided and regarded as a matter of indifference. [E.g.:] 'All these forms', says Fichte,[34] '. . . are justified, provided there be an ephorate' (a scheme devised by Fichte to be a counterpoise to the chief power in the state) 'and may . . . be the means of introducing universal rights into the state and maintaining them there.'* A view of this kind—and the device of the ephorate also—is begotten by the superficial conception of the state to which reference has just been made. It is true enough that in quite simple social conditions these differences of constitutional form have little or no meaning. For instance, in the course of his legislation Moses prescribed that, in the event of his people's desiring a king, its institutions should remain unchanged except for the new requirement that the king should not 'multiply horses to himself . . . nor wives . . . nor silver and gold'.† Besides, in a sense one may of course say that the Idea too is indifferent to these forms (including monarchy, but only when it is restricted in meaning by being defined as an *alternative* on a parity with aristocracy and democracy). But the Idea is indifferent to them, not in Fichte's but in the opposite sense, because every one of them is inadequate to it in its rational development (see Paragraph 272) and in none of them, taken singly, could the Idea attain its right and its actuality. Consequently, it is quite idle to inquire which of the three is most to be preferred. Such forms must be discussed historically or not at all.

Still, here again, as in so many other places, we must recognize the depth of Montesquieu's insight in his now famous treatment of the basic principles of these forms of government. To recognize the accuracy of his account, however, we must not misunderstand it. As is well known, he held that 'virtue'[35] was the principle of democracy [and rightly], since it is in fact the case that that type of constitution rests on sentiment, i.e. on the purely substantial form in which the rationality of the absolute will still exists in democracy. But Montesquieu goes on to say that in the seventeenth century England provided 'a fine spectacle of the way in which efforts to found a democracy were rendered ineffective by a lack of virtue in the leaders'. And again he adds 'when virtue vanishes from the republic, ambition enters hearts which are capable of it and greed masters everyone . . . so that the state becomes everyone's booty and its strength now consists only in the power of a few citizens and the licence of all alike'. These quotations call for the comment that in more mature social conditions and when the powers of particularity have developed and become free, a form of rational law other than the form of sentiment is required, because virtue in the heads of the state is not enough if the state as a whole is to gain the power to resist disruption and to bestow on the powers of particularity, now become mature, both

* *Science of Rights* [§ 16, sub-section 6, p. 248].
† Deut. xvii. 16 ff.

their positive and their negative rights. Similarly, we must remove the misunderstanding of supposing that because the sentiment of virtue is the substantial form of a democratic republic, it is evidently superfluous in monarchy or even absent from it altogether,[36] and, finally, we may not suppose that there is an opposition and an incompatibility between virtue and the legally determinate agency of a state whose organization is fully articulated.

The fact that 'moderation'[37] is cited as the principle of aristocracy implies the beginning at this point of a divorce between public authority and private interest. And yet at the same time these touch each other so directly that this constitution by its very nature stands on the verge of lapsing forthwith into tyranny or anarchy—the harshest of political conditions—and so into self-annihilation. See Roman history, for example.[38]

The fact that Montesquieu discerns 'honour'[39] as the principle of monarchy at once makes it clear that by 'monarchy' he understands, not the patriarchal or any ancient type, nor, on the other hand, the type organized into an objective constitution,[40] but only feudal monarchy, the type in which the relationships recognized in its constitutional law are crystallized into the rights of private property and the privileges of individuals and Corporations. In this type of constitution, political life rests on privileged persons and a great part of what must be done for the maintenance of the state is settled at their pleasure. The result is that their services are the objects not of duty but only of ideas and opinions. Thus it is not duty but only honour which holds the state together.

Another question readily presents itself here: 'Who is to frame the constitution?' This question seems clear, but closer inspection shows at once that it is meaningless, for it presupposes that there is no constitution there, but only an agglomeration of atomic individuals. How an agglomeration of individuals could acquire a constitution, whether automatically or by someone's aid, whether as a present or by force or by thought, it would have to be allowed to settle for itself, since with an agglomeration the concept has nothing to do. But if the question presupposes an already existent constitution, then it is not about framing, but only about altering the constitution, and the very presupposition of a constitution directly implies that its alteration may come about only by constitutional means. In any case, however, it is absolutely essential that the constitution should not be regarded as something made, even though it has come into being in time. It must be treated rather as something simply existent in and by itself, as divine therefore, and constant, and so as exalted above the sphere of things that are made. [A.]

274. Mind is actual only as that which it knows itself to be, and the state, as the mind of a nation, is both the law permeating all relationships within the state and also at the same time the manners and consciousness of its citizens. It follows, therefore, that the constitution of any given nation depends in general on the character and development of its self-consciousness.[41] In its self-consciousness its subjective freedom is rooted and so, therefore, is the actuality of its constitution.

The proposal to give a constitution—even one more or less rational in content—to a nation *a priori* would be a happy thought overlooking precisely that factor in a constitution which makes it more than an *ens rationis*. Hence every nation has the constitution appropriate to it and suitable for it. [A.]

(a) The Crown

275. The power of the crown contains in itself the three moments of the whole (see Paragraph 272), viz. (α) the *universality* of the constitution and the laws; (β) counsel, which refers the *particular* to the universal; and (γ) the moment of ultimate decision, as the *self-determination* to which everything else reverts and from which everything else derives the beginning of its actuality. This absolute self-determination constitutes the distinctive principle of the power of the crown as such, and with this principle our exposition is to begin. [A.]

276. (1) The fundamental characteristic of the state as a political entity is the substantial unity, i.e. the ideality, of its moments. (α) In this unity, the particular powers and their activities are dissolved and yet retained. They are retained, however, only in the sense that their authority is no independent one but only one of the order and breadth determined by the Idea of the whole; from its might they originate, and they are its flexible limbs while it is their single self. [A.]

277. (β) The particular activities and agencies of the state are its essential moments and therefore are proper to *it*. The individual functionaries and agents are attached to their office not on the strength of their immediate personality, but only on the strength of their universal and objective qualities. Hence it is in an external and contingent way that these offices are linked with particular persons, and therefore the functions and powers of the state cannot be private property. [A.]

278. These two points (α) and (β) constitute the sovereignty of the state. That is to say, sovereignty depends on the fact that the particular functions and powers of the state are not self-subsistent or firmly grounded either on their own account or in the particular will of the individual functionaries, but have their roots ultimately in the unity of the state as their single self.

This is the sovereignty of the state at home. Sovereignty has another side, i.e. sovereignty *vis-à-vis* foreign states, on which see below.[42]

In feudal times, the state was certainly sovereign *vis-à-vis* other states; at home however, not only was the monarch not sovereign at all, but the state itself was not sovereign either. For one thing, the particular functions and powers of the state and civil society were arranged (compare Remark to Paragraph 273) into independent Corporations and societies, so that the state as a whole was rather an aggregate than an organism; and, for another thing, office was the private property of individuals, and hence what they were to do in their public capacity was left to their own opinion and caprice.

The idealism which constitutes sovereignty is the same characteristic as that in accordance with which the so-called 'parts' of an animal organism are not parts but members, moments in an organic whole, whose isolation and independence spell disease.* The principle here is the same as that which came before us (see Paragraph 7) in the abstract concept of the will (see Remark to Paragraph 279) as self-related negativity, and therefore as the universality of the will determining itself to individuality and so cancelling all particularity and determinacy, as the absolute self-determining ground of all volition. To understand this, one must have mastered the whole conception of the substance and genuine subjectivity of the concept.

The fact that the sovereignty of the state is the ideality of all particular authorities within it gives rise to the easy and also very common misunderstanding that this ideality is only might and pure arbitrariness while 'sovereignty' is a synonym for 'despotism'. But despotism means any state of affairs where law has disappeared and where the particular will as such, whether of a monarch or a mob (ochlocracy), counts as law or rather takes the place of law; while it is precisely in legal, constitutional, government that sovereignty is to be found as the moment of ideality—the ideality of the particular spheres and functions. That is to say, sovereignty brings it about that each of these spheres is not something independent, self-subsistent in its aims and modes of working, something immersed solely in itself, but that instead, even in these aims and modes of working, each is determined by and dependent on the aim of the whole (the aim which has been denominated in general terms by the rather vague expression 'welfare of the state').

This ideality manifests itself in a twofold way:

(i) In times of peace, the particular spheres and functions pursue the path of satisfying their particular aims and minding their own busi-

* See *Enc.* [1st edn.], § 293 [3rd edn. § 371].

ness, and it is in part only by way of the unconscious necessity of the thing that their self-seeking is turned into a contribution to reciprocal support and to the support of the whole (see Paragraph 183). In part, however, it is by the direct influence of higher authority that they are not only continually brought back to the aims of the whole and restricted accordingly (see Paragraph 289), but are also constrained to perform direct services for the support of the whole.

(ii) In a situation of exigency, however, whether in home or foreign affairs, the organism of which these particular spheres are members fuses into the single concept of sovereignty. The sovereign is entrusted with the salvation of the state at the sacrifice of these particular authorities whose powers are valid at other times, and it is then that that ideality comes into its proper actuality (see Paragraph 321).

279. (2) Sovereignty, at first simply the universal *thought* of this ideality, comes into *existence* only as subjectivity sure of itself, as the will's abstract and to that extent ungrounded self-determination in which finality of decision is rooted. This is the strictly individual aspect of the state, and in virtue of this alone is the state *one*. The truth of subjectivity, however, is attained only in a subject, and the truth of personality only in a person; and in a constitution which has become mature as a realization of rationality, each of the three moments of the concept has its explicitly actual and separate formation. Hence this absolutely decisive moment of the whole is not individuality in general, but a single individual, the monarch.

The immanent development of a science, the derivation[43] of its entire content from the concept in its simplicity (a science otherwise derived, whatever its merit, does not deserve the name of a philosophical science) exhibits this peculiarity, that one and the same concept—the will in this instance—which begins by being abstract (because it is at the beginning), maintains its identity even while it consolidates its specific determinations, and that too solely by its own activity, and in this way gains a concrete content. Hence it is the basic moment of personality, abstract at the start in immediate rights, which has matured itself through its various forms of subjectivity, and now—at the stage of absolute rights, of the state, of the completely concrete objectivity of the will—has become the personality of the state, its certainty of itself. This last reabsorbs all particularity into its single self, cuts short the weighing of pros and cons between which it lets itself oscillate perpetually now this way and now that, and by saying 'I will' makes its decision and so inaugurates all activity and actuality.

Further, however, personality, like subjectivity in general, as infinitely self-related, has its truth (to be precise, its most elementary, immediate, truth) only in a person, in a subject existing 'for' himself, and what exists 'for' itself is just simply a unit. It is only as a person, the monarch, that the personality of the state is actual. Personality expresses the concept as such; but the person enshrines the actuality of the concept, and only when the concept is determined as person is it the Idea or truth. A so-called 'artificial person', be it a society, a community, or a family, however inherently concrete it may be, contains personality only abstractly, as one moment of itself. In an 'artificial person', personality has not achieved its true mode of existence. The state, however, is precisely this totality in which the moments of the concept have attained the actuality correspondent to their degree of truth. All these categories, both in themselves and in their external formations, have been discussed in the whole course of this treatise. They are repeated here, however, because while their existence in their particular external formations is readily granted, it does not follow at all that they are recognized and apprehended again when they appear in their true place, not isolated, but in their truth as moments of the Idea.

The conception of the monarch is therefore of all conceptions the hardest for ratiocination, i.e. for the method of reflection employed by the Understanding. This method refuses to move beyond isolated categories and hence here again knows only *raisonnement*, finite points of view, and deductive argumentation. Consequently it exhibits the dignity of the monarch as something deduced, not only in its form, but in its essence. The truth is, however, that to be something not deduced but purely self-originating is precisely the conception of monarchy. Akin, then, to this reasoning is the idea of treating the monarch's right as grounded in the authority of God, since it is in its divinity that its unconditional character is contained.[44] We are familiar, however, with the misunderstandings connected with this idea, and it is precisely this 'divine' element which it is the task of a philosophic treatment to comprehend.

We may speak of the 'sovereignty of the people' in the sense that any people whatever is self-subsistent *vis-à-vis* other peoples, and constitutes a state of its own, like the British people for instance. But the peoples of England, Scotland, or Ireland, or the peoples of Venice, Genoa, Ceylon, &c., are not sovereign peoples at all now that they have ceased to have rulers or supreme governments of their own.

We may also speak of sovereignty in home affairs residing in the people, provided that we are speaking generally about the whole state and meaning only what was shown above (see Paragraphs 277, 278), namely that it is to the state that sovereignty belongs.

The usual sense, however, in which men have recently[45] begun to speak of the 'sovereignty of the people' is that it is something opposed to the sovereignty existent in the monarch. So opposed to the sovereignty of the monarch, the sovereignty of the people is one of the confused notions based on the wild idea of the 'people'. Taken without its monarch and the articulation of the whole which is the indispensable and direct concomitant of monarchy, the people is a formless mass and no longer a state. It lacks every one of those determinate characteristics—sovereignty, government, judges, magistrates, class-divisions, &c.,—which are to be found only in a whole which is inwardly organized. By the very emergence into a people's life of moments of this kind which have a bearing on an organization, on political life, a people ceases to be that indeterminate abstraction which, when represented in a quite general way, is called the 'people'.

If by 'sovereignty of the people' is understood a republican form of government, or to speak more specifically (since under 'republic' are comprised all sorts of other mixed forms of government, which are purely empirical, let alone irrelevant in a philosophical treatise) a democratic form, then all that is needed in reply has been said already (in the Remark to Paragraph 273); and besides, such a notion cannot be further discussed in face of the Idea of the state in its full development.

If the 'people' is represented neither as a patriarchal clan, nor as living under the simple conditions which make democracy or aristocracy possible as forms of government (see Remark to Paragraph 273), nor as living under some other unorganized and haphazard conditions, but instead as an inwardly developed, genuinely organic, totality, then sovereignty is there as the personality of the whole, and this personality is there, in the real existence adequate to its concept, as the person of the monarch.

At the stage at which constitutions are divided, as above mentioned,[46] into democracy, aristocracy, and monarchy, the point of view taken is that of a still substantial unity, abiding in itself, without having yet embarked on its infinite differentiation and the plumbing of its own depths. At that stage, the moment of the final, self-determining, decision of the will does not come on the scene explicitly in its own proper actuality as an organic moment immanent in the state. None the less, even in those comparatively immature constitutional forms, there must always be individuals at the head. Leaders must either be available already, as they are in monarchies of that type, or, as happens in aristocracies, but more particularly in democracies, they may rise to the top, as statesmen or generals, by chance and in accordance with the particular needs of the hour. This must happen, since everything done and everything actual is inaugurated and brought to completion by the single decisive act of a leader. But comprised in a union of powers which remains undifferentiated, this subjectivity of decision is inevitably either contingent in its origin and appearance, or else is in one way or another subordinate to something else. Hence in such states, the power of the leaders was conditioned, and only in something beyond them could there be found a pure unambiguous decision, a *fatum*, determining affairs from without. As a moment of the Idea, this decision had to come into existence, though rooted in something outside the circle of human freedom with which the state is concerned. Herein lies the origin of the need for deriving the last word on great events and important affairs of state from oracles, a 'divine sign' (in the case of Socrates), the entrails of animals, the feeding and flight of birds, &c. It was when men had not yet plumbed the depths of self-consciousness or risen out of their undifferentiated unity of substance to their independence that they lacked strength to look within their own being for the final word.

In the 'divine sign' of Socrates[47] (compare Remark to Paragraph 138) we see the will which formerly had simply transferred itself beyond itself now beginning to apply itself to itself and so to recognize its own inward nature. This is the beginning of a self-knowing and so of a genuine freedom. This realized freedom of the Idea consists precisely in giving to each of the moments of rationality its own self-conscious actuality here and now. Hence it is this freedom which makes the ultimate self-determining certitude—the culmination of the concept of the will—the function of a single consciousness. This ultimate self-determination, however, can fall within the sphere of human freedom only in so far as it has the position of a pinnacle, explicitly distinct from, and raised above, all that is particular and conditional, for only so is it actual in a way adequate to its concept. [A.]

280. (3) This ultimate self in which the will of the state is concentrated is, when thus taken in abstraction, a single self and therefore is *immediate* individuality.[48] Hence its 'natural' character is implied in its very conception. The monarch, therefore, is essentially characterized as *this* individual, in abstraction from all his other characteristics, and *this* individual is raised to the dignity of monarchy in an immediate, natural, fashion, i.e. through his birth in the course of nature.

This transition of the concept of pure self-determination into the immediacy of being and so into the realm of nature is of a purely speculative character, and apprehension of it therefore belongs to logic. Moreover, this transition is on the whole same as that familiar to us in the nature of willing, and there the process is to translate something from subjectivity (i.e. some purpose held before the mind) into existence (see Paragraph 8). But the proper form of the Idea and of the transition here under consideration is the immediate conversion of the pure self-determination of the will (i.e. of the simple concept itself) into a single and natural existent without the mediation of a particular content (like a purpose in the case of action).

In the so-called 'ontological' proof of the existence of God, we have the same conversion of the absolute concept into existence. This conversion has constituted the depth of the Idea in the modern world, although recently it has been declared inconceivable,[49] with the result that knowledge of truth has been renounced, since truth is simply the unity of concept and existence (see Paragraph 23). Since the Understanding has no inner consciousness of this unity and refuses to move beyond the separation of these two moments of the truth, it may perhaps, so far as God is concerned, still permit a 'faith' in this unity. But since the idea of the monarch is regarded as being quite familiar to ordinary consciousness, the Understanding clings here all the more tenaciously to its separatism and the conclusions which its astute ratiocination deduces therefrom. As a result, it denies that the moment of ultimate decision in the state is linked implicitly and actually (i.e. in the rational concept) with the immediate birthright of the monarch. Consequently it infers, first, that this link is a matter of accident, and further—since it has claimed that the absolute diversity of these moments is the rational thing—that such a link is irrational, and then there follow the other deductions disruptive of the Idea of the state.[50] [A.]

281. Both moments in their undivided unity—(a) the will's ultimate ungrounded self, and (b) therefore its similarly ungrounded objective existence (existence being the category which is at home in nature)—constitute the Idea of something against which caprice is powerless,[51] the 'majesty' of the monarch. In this unity lies the actual unity of the state, and it is only through this, its inward and outward immediacy, that the unity of the state is saved from the risk of being drawn down into the sphere of particularity and its caprices, ends, and opinions, and saved too from the war of factions round the throne and from the enfeeblement and overthrow of the power of the state.

The rights of birth and inheritance constitute the basis of legitimacy, the basis of a right not purely positive but contained in the Idea.

If succession to the throne is rigidly determined, i.e. if it is hereditary, then faction is obviated at a demise of the crown; this is one aspect of hereditary succession and it has long been rightly stressed as a point in its favour. This aspect, however, is only consequential, and to make it the reason for hereditary succession is to drag down the majesty of the throne into the sphere of argumentation, to ignore its true character as ungrounded immediacy and ultimate inwardness, and to base it not on the Idea of the state immanent within it, but on something external to itself, on some extraneous notion such as the 'welfare of the state' or the 'welfare of the people'. Once it has been so based, its hereditary character may of course be deduced by the use of *medii termini*. But other *medii termini* are equally available, and so therefore are different conclusions, and it is only too well known what conclusions have in fact been drawn from this 'welfare of the people' (*salut du peuple*). Hence the majesty of the monarch is a topic for thoughtful treatment by philosophy alone, since every method of inquiry, other than the speculative method of the infinite Idea which is purely self-grounded, annuls the nature of majesty altogether.

An elective monarchy seems of course to be the most natural idea, i.e. the idea which superficial thinking finds handiest. Because it is the concerns and interests of his people for which a monarch has to provide, so the argument runs, it must be left to the people to entrust with its welfare whomsoever it pleases, and only with the grant of this trust does his right to rule arise. This view, like the notion of the monarch as the highest executive official in the state, or the notion of a contractual relation between him and his people, &c., &c., is grounded on the will interpreted as the whim, opinion, and caprice of the Many.[52] A will of this character counts as the first thing in civil society (as was pointed out long ago)[53] or rather it tries to count as the only thing there, but it is not the guiding principle of the family, still less of the state, and in short it stands opposed to the Idea of ethical life.

It is truer to say that elective monarchy is the worst of institutions, and its results suffice to reveal this to ratiocination. To ratiocination, however, these results have the appearance of something merely possible and probable, though they are in fact inherent in the very essence of this institution. In an elective monarchy, I mean, the nature of the relation between king and people implies that the ultimate decision is left with the particular will, and hence the constitution becomes a Compact of Election,[54] i.e. a surrender of the power of the state at the discretion of the particular will. The result of this is that the particular offices of state turn into private property, the sovereignty of the state is enfeebled and lost, and finally the state disintegrates within and is overthrown from without.[55] [A.]

282. The right to pardon criminals arises from the sovereignty of the monarch, since it is this alone which is empowered to actualize mind's power of making undone what has been done and wiping out a crime by forgiving and forgetting it.

The right of pardon is one of the highest recognitions of the majesty of mind. Moreover it is one of those cases where a category which belongs to a higher sphere is applied to or reflected in the sphere below.[56] Applications of higher categories to a lower sphere, however, concern the particular science which has to handle its subject-matter in all its empirical details (see [the second] footnote to the Remark to Paragraph 270). Another instance of the same kind of thing is the subsumption under the concept of crime (which came before us earlier—see Paragraphs 95–102) of injuries against the state in general, or against the sovereignty, majesty, and person of the prince. In fact these acquire the character of crime of the worst kind, requiring a special procedure, &c. [A.]

283. The second moment in the power of the crown is the moment of particularity, or the moment of a determinate content and its subsumption under the universal. When this acquires a special objective existence, it becomes the supreme council and the individuals who compose it. They bring before the monarch for his decision the content of current affairs of state or the legal provisions required to meet existing needs, together with their objective aspects, i.e. the grounds on which decision is to be based, the relative laws, circumstances, &c. The individuals who discharge these duties are in direct contact with the person of the monarch and therefore their choice and dismissal alike rest with his unrestricted caprice.

284. It is only for the *objective* side of decision, i.e. for knowledge of the problem and the attendant circumstances, and for the legal and other reasons which determine its solution, that men are answerable; in other words, it is these alone which are capable of objective proof. It is for this reason that these may fall within the province of a council which is distinct from the personal will of the monarch as such. Hence it is only councils or their individual members that are made answerable. The personal majesty of the monarch, on the other hand, as the final *subjectivity* of decision, is above all answerability for acts of government.

285. The third moment in the power of the crown concerns the absolute universality which subsists subjectively in the conscience of the monarch and objectively in the whole of the constitution and the laws. Hence the power of the crown presupposes the other moments in the state just as it is presupposed by each of them.

286. The *objective* guarantee of the power of the crown, of the hereditary right of succession to the throne, and so forth, consists in the fact that just as monarchy has its own actuality in distinction from that of the other rationally determined moments in the state, so these others explicitly possess the rights and duties appropriate to their own character. In the rational organism of the state, each member, by maintaining itself in its own position, *eo ipso* maintains the others in theirs.

One of the results of more recent history is the development of a monarchical constitution with succession to the throne firmly fixed on hereditary principles in accordance with primogeniture. With this development, monarchy has been brought back to the patriarchal principle in which it had its historical origin, but its determinate character is now higher, because the monarch is the absolute apex of an organically developed state. This historical result is of the utmost importance for public freedom and for rationality in the constitution, but, as was remarked above,[57] it is often grossly misunderstood despite the respect paid to it.

The history of despotisms, as of the now obsolete, purely feudal, monarchies, is a tale of the vicissitudes of revolt, monarchical tyranny, civil war, the ruin of princes of the blood and whole dynasties, and, consequentially, the general devastation and overthrow of the state in both its home and foreign concerns. This is all due to the fact that, in monarchies of that type, the division of the business of the state is purely mechanical, the various sections being merely handed over to pashas, vassals, &c. The difference between the departments is simply one of greater or lesser power instead of being one of form and specific character. Hence each department maintains itself and in doing so is productive only of itself and not of the others at the same time; each is independent and autonomous and completely incorporates in itself all the moments of the concept. When there is an *organic* relation subsisting between members, not parts, then each member by fulfilling the functions of its own sphere is *eo ipso* maintaining the others; what each fundamentally aims at and achieves in maintaining itself is the maintenance of the others.

The guarantees in question here for the maintenance of the succession to the throne or for the power of the crown generally, or for justice, public freedom, &c., are modes of securing these things by means of institutions. For *subjective* guarantees we may look to the affection of the people, to character, oaths of allegiance, power, and so forth, but, when the constitution is being discussed, it is only objective guarantees that are relevant. And such guarantees are institutions, i.e. mutually conditioning moments, organically interconnected. Hence public freedom in general and an hereditary monarchy guarantee each other; they stand or fall together of necessity, because public freedom means a rational constitution, while the hereditary character of the power of the crown is, as has been shown,[58] the moment lying in the concept of that power.

(b) The Executive

287. There is a distinction between the monarch's decisions and their execution and application, or in general between his decisions and the continued execution or maintenance of past decisions, existing laws, regulations, organizations for the securing of common ends, and so forth. This task of merely subsuming the particular under the universal is comprised in the executive power, which also includes the powers of the judiciary and the police. The latter have a more immediate bearing on the particular concerns of civil society and they make the universal interest authoritative over its particular aims.

288. Particular interests which are common to everyone fall within civil society and lie outside the absolutely universal interest of the state proper (see Paragraph 256). The administration of these is in the hands of Corporations (see Paragraph 251), commercial and professional as well as municipal, and their officials, directors, managers, and the like. It is the business of these officials to manage the private property and interests of these particular spheres and, from that point of view, their authority rests on the confidence of their commonalties and professional equals. On the other hand, however, these circles of particular interests must be subordinated to the higher interests of the state, and hence the filling of positions of responsibility in Corporations, &c., will generally be effected by a mixture of popular election by those interested with appointment and ratification by higher authority.

289. The maintenance of the state's universal interest, and of legality, in this sphere of particular rights, and the work of bringing these rights back to the universal, require to be superintended by holders of the executive power, by (a) the executive civil servants, and (b) the higher advisory officials (who are organized into committees). These converge in their supreme heads who are in direct contact with the monarch.

Just as civil society is the battlefield where everyone's individual private interest meets everyone else's, so here we have the struggle (a) of private interests against particular matters of common concern and (b) of both of these together against the organization of the state and its higher outlook. At the same time the corporation mind, engendered when the particular spheres gain their title to rights, is now inwardly converted into the mind of the state, since it finds in the state the means of maintaining its particular ends. This is the secret of the patriotism of the citizens in the sense that they know the state as their substance, because it is the state that maintains their particular spheres of interest together with the title, authority, and welfare of these. In the corporation mind the rooting of the particular in the universal is directly entailed, and for this reason it is in that mind that the depth and strength which the state possesses in sentiment is seated.

The administration of a Corporation's business by its own officials is frequently clumsy, because although they keep before their minds and are acquainted with its special interests and affairs, they have a far less complete appreciation of the connexion of those affairs with more remote conditions and the outlook of the state. In addition, other circumstances contribute to the same result, e.g. close private relationships and other factors putting officials on a footing of equality with those who should be their subordinates, the rather numerous ways in which officials lack independence, and so on. This sphere of private interests, however, may be regarded as the one left to the moment of formal freedom,[59] the one which affords a playground for personal knowledge, personal decisions and their execution, petty passions and conceits. This is all the more permissible, the more trivial, from the point of view of the more universal affairs of state, is the intrinsic worth of the business which in this way comes to ruin or is managed less well or more laboriously, &c. And further, it is all the more permissible, the more this laborious or foolish management of such trivial affairs stands in direct relation with the self-satisfaction and vanity derived therefrom.

290. Division of labour (see Paragraph 198) occurs in the business of the executive also. For this reason, the organization of officials has the abstract though difficult task of so arranging that (*a*) civil life shall be governed in a concrete manner from below where it is concrete, but that (*b*) none the less the business of government shall be divided into its abstract branches manned by special officials as different centres of administration, and further that (*c*) the operations of these various departments shall converge again when they are directed on civil life from above, in the same way as they converge into a general supervision in the supreme executive.[60] [A.]

291. The nature of the executive functions is that they are objective and that in their substance they have been explicitly fixed by previous decisions (see Paragraph 287); these functions have to be fulfilled and carried out by individuals. Between an individual and his office there is no immediate natural link. Hence individuals are not appointed to office on account of their birth or native personal gifts. The *objective* factor in their appointment is knowledge and proof of ability. Such proof guarantees that the state will get what it requires; and since it is the sole condition of appointment, it also guarantees to every citizen the chance of joining the class of civil servants.

292. Since the objective qualification for the civil service is not genius (as it is for work as an artist, for example), there is of necessity an indefinite plurality of eligible candidates whose relative excellence is not determinable with absolute precision. The selection of one of the candidates, his nomination to office, and the grant to him of full authority to transact public business—all this, as the linking of two things, a man and his office, which in relation to each other must always be fortuitous, is the *subjective* aspect of election to office, and it must lie with the crown as the power in the state which is sovereign and has the last word.

293. The particular public functions which the monarch entrusts to officials constitute one part of the objective aspect of the sovereignty residing in the crown. Their specific discrimination is therefore given in the nature of the thing. And while the actions of the officials are the fulfilment of their duty, their office is also a right exempt from contingency.

294. Once an individual has been appointed to his official position by the sovereign's act (see Paragraph 292), the tenure of his post is conditional on his fulfilling its duties. Such fulfilment is the very essence of his appointment, and it is only consequential that he finds in his office his livelihood and the assured satisfaction of his particular interests (see Paragraph 264), and further that his external circumstances and his official work are freed from other kinds of subjective dependence and influence.

The state does not count on optional, discretionary, services (e.g. on justice administered by knights errant). It is just because such services are optional and discretionary that the state cannot rely on them, for casual servants may fail for private reasons to fulfil their duties completely, or they may arbitrarily decide not to fulfil them at all but pursue their private ends instead. The opposite extreme to a knight errant, so far as the service of the state goes, would be an official who clung to his office purely and simply to make a living without any real sense of duty and so without any real right to go on holding it.

What the service of the state really requires is that men shall forgo the selfish and capricious satisfaction of their subjective ends; by this very sacrifice, they acquire the right to find their satisfaction in, but only in, the dutiful discharge of their public functions. In this fact, so far as public business is concerned, there lies the link between universal and particular interests which constitutes both the concept of the state and its inner stability (see Paragraph 260).

It follows that a man's tenure of his civil service post is not contractual (see Paragraph 75), although his appointment involves a consent and an undertaking on both sides. A civil servant is not appointed, like an agent, to perform a single casual act of service; on the contrary, he concentrates his main interests (not only his particular interests but his mental interests also) on his relation to his work. Similarly, the work imposed upon him and entrusted to him is not merely a particular thing, external in character; the value of such a thing is something inward and therefore distinct from its outward character, so that it is in no way impaired if what has been stipulated is not fulfilled (see Paragraph 77). The work of a civil servant, however, is as such a value in and for itself. Hence the wrong committed through its non-performance, or positive mis-performance (i.e. through an action contrary to official duty, and both of these are of that type), is an infringement of the universal content itself (i.e. is a negatively infinite judgement—see Paragraph 95) and so is a trespass or even a crime.

The assured satisfaction of particular needs removes the external compulsion which may tempt a man to seek ways and means of satisfying them at the expense of his official duties. Those who are entrusted with affairs of state find in its universal power the protection they need against another subjective phenomenon, namely the personal passions of the governed, whose private interests, &c., suffer injury as the interest of the state is made to prevail against them.

295. The security of the state and its subjects against the misuse of power by ministers and their officials lies directly in their hierarchical organization and their answerability; but it lies too in the authority given to societies and Corporations, because in itself this is a barrier against the intrusion of subjective caprice into the power entrusted to a civil servant, and it completes from below the state control which does not reach down as far as the conduct of individuals.

The conduct and culture of officials is the sphere where the laws and the government's decisions come into contact with individuals and are actually made good. Hence it is on the conduct of officials that there depend not only the contentment of citizens and their confidence in the government, but also the execution—or alternatively the distortion and frustration—of state projects; at any rate, this is the case in the sense that feeling and sentiment may easily rate the manner of execution as highly as the very content of the command to be executed, even though the content may in fact be the imposition of a tax. Owing to the direct and personal nature of this contact with individuals, control from above can attain its ends in this respect only to a rather incomplete extent. Moreover, its ends may also be hindered by interests common to officials who form a clique over against their inferiors on one side and their superiors on the other. In states whose institutions may perhaps be imperfectly developed in other respects also, the removal of hindrances like these requires and justifies the higher intervention of the sovereign (as for example of Frederick the Great in the notorious affair[61] of Arnold the miller).

296. But the fact that a dispassionate, upright, and polite demeanour becomes customary [in civil servants] is (i) partly a result of direct education in thought and ethical conduct. Such an education is a mental counterpoise to the mechanical and semi-mechanical activity involved in acquiring the so-called 'sciences' of matters connected with administration, in the requisite business training, in the actual work done, &c. (ii) The size of the state, however, is an important factor in producing this result, since it diminishes the stress of family and other personal ties, and also makes less potent and so less keen such passions as hatred, revenge, &c. In those who are busy with the important questions arising in a great state, these subjective interests automatically disappear, and the habit is generated of adopting universal interests, points of view, and activities.

297. Civil servants and the members of the executive constitute the greater part of the middle class, the class in which the consciousness of right and the developed intelligence of the mass of the people is found. The sovereign working on the middle class at the top, and Corporation-rights working on it at the bottom, are the institutions which effectually prevent it from acquiring the isolated position of an aristocracy and using its education and skill as means to an arbitrary tyranny.

At one time the administration of justice, which is concerned with the private interests of all members of the state, was in this way turned into an instrument of profit and tyranny, when the knowledge of the law was buried in pedantry and a foreign tongue, and knowledge of legal processes was similarly buried in involved formalities. [A.]

(c) The Legislature

298. The legislature is concerned (a) with the laws as such in so far as they require fresh and extended determination; and (b) with the content of home affairs affecting the entire state. The legislature is itself a part of the constitution which is presupposed by it and to that extent lies absolutely outside the sphere directly determined by it; none the less, the constitution becomes progressively more mature in the course of the further elaboration of the laws and the advancing character of the universal business of government. [A.]

299. Legislative business is more precisely determined, in relation to private individuals, under these two heads: (α) provision by the state for their well-being and happiness, and (β) the exaction of services from them. The former comprises the laws dealing with all sorts of private rights, the rights of communities, Corporations, and organizations affecting the entire state, and further it indirectly (see Paragraph 298) comprises the whole of the constitution. As for the services to be exacted, it is only if these are reduced to terms of money, the really existent and universal value of both things and services, that they can be fixed justly and at the same time in such a way that any particular tasks and services which an individual may perform come to be mediated through his own arbitrary will.

The proper object of universal legislation may be distinguished in a general way from the proper function of administrative officials or of some kind of state regulation, in that the content of the former is wholly universal, i.e. determinate laws, while it is what is particular in content which falls to the latter, together with ways and means of enforcing the law. This distinction, however, is not a hard and fast one, because a law, by being a law, is *ab initio* something more than a mere command in general terms (such as 'Thou shalt not kill'—compare Remark (*d*) to Paragraph 140). A law must in itself be something determinate, but the more determinate it is, the more readily are its terms capable of being carried out as they stand. At the same time, however, to give to laws such a fully detailed determinacy would give them empirical features subject inevitably to alteration in the course of their being actually carried out, and this would contravene their character as laws. The organic unity of the powers of the state itself implies that it is one single mind which both firmly establishes the universal and also brings it into its determinate actuality and carries it out.

In the state it may happen, to begin with,[62] that the numerous aptitudes, possessions, pursuits, and talents of its members, together with the infinitely varied richness of life intrinsic to these—all of which are at the same time linked with their owner's mentality—are not subject to direct levy by the state. It lays claim only to a single form of riches, namely money. (Services requisitioned for the defence of the state in war arise for the first time in connexion with the duty considered in the next subdivision of this book.) In fact, however, money is not one particular type of wealth amongst others, but the universal form of all types so far as they are expressed in an external embodiment and so can be taken as 'things'.[63] Only by being translated into terms of this extreme culmination of externality can services exacted by the state be fixed quantitatively and so justly and equitably.

In Plato's *Republic*, the Guardians are left to allot individuals to their particular classes and impose on them their particular tasks (compare Remark to Paragraph 185). Under the feudal monarchies the services required from vassals were equally indeterminate, but they had also to serve in their *particular* capacity, e.g. as judges. The same particular character pertains to tasks imposed in the East and in Egypt in connexion with colossal architectural undertakings, and so forth. In these circumstances the principle of subjective freedom is lacking, i.e. the principle that the individual's substantive activity—which in any case becomes something particular in content in services like those mentioned—shall be mediated through his particular volition. This is a right which can be secured only when the demand for service takes the form of a demand for something of universal value, and it is this right which has brought with it this conversion of the state's demands into demands for cash. [A.]

300. In the legislature as a whole the other powers are the first two moments which are effective, (i) the monarchy as that to which ultimate decisions belong; (ii) the executive as the advisory body since it is the moment possessed of (α) a concrete knowledge and oversight of the whole state in its numerous facets and the actual principles firmly established within it, and (β) a knowledge in particular of what the state's power needs. The last moment in the legislature is the Estates.[64] [A.]

301. The Estates have the function of bringing public affairs into existence not only implicitly, but also actually, i.e. of bringing into existence the moment of subjective formal freedom, the public consciousness as an empirical universal, of which the thoughts and opinions of the Many are particulars.

The phrase 'the Many' (οἱ πολλοί) denotes empirical universality more strictly than 'All', which is in current use. If it is said to be obvious that this 'all' prima facie excludes at least children, women, &c., then it is surely still more obvious that the quite definite word 'all' should not be used when something quite indefinite is meant.

Current opinion has put into general circulation such a host of perverse and false ideas and ways of speaking about 'People', 'Constitution', and 'Estates' that it would be a waste of energy to try to specify, expound, and correct them. The idea uppermost in men's minds when they speak about the necessity or the expediency of 'summoning the Estates' is generally something of this sort: (i) The deputies of the people, or even the people themselves, must know best what is in their best interest, and (ii) their will for its promotion is undoubtedly the most disinterested. So far as the first of these points is concerned, however, the truth is that if 'people' means a particular section of the citizens, then it means precisely that section which does *not* know what it wills. To know what one wills, and still more to know what the absolute will, Reason, wills, is the fruit of profound apprehension and insight, precisely the things which are *not* popular.

The Estates are a guarantee of the general welfare and public freedom. A little reflection will show that this guarantee does not lie in their particular power of insight, because the highest civil servants necessarily have a deeper and more comprehensive insight into the nature of the state's organization and requirements. They are also more habituated to the business of government and have greater skill in it, so that even without the Estates they are *able* to do what is best, just as they also continually *have* to do while the Estates are in session. No, the guarantee lies on the contrary (α) in the *additional* insight of the deputies, insight in the first place into the activity of such officials as are not immediately under the eye of the higher functionaries of state, and in particular into the more pressing and more specialized needs and deficiencies which are directly in their view; (β) in the fact that the anticipation of criticism from the Many, particularly of public criticism, has the effect of inducing officials to devote their best attention beforehand to their duties and the schemes under consideration, and to deal with these only in accordance with the purest motives. This same compulsion is effective also on the members of the Estates themselves.

As for the conspicuously good will for the general welfare which the Estates are supposed to possess, it has been pointed out already (in the Remark to Paragraph 272) that to regard the will of the executive as bad, or as less good [than that of the ruled] is a presupposition characteristic of the rabble or of the negative outlook generally. This presupposition might at once be answered on its own ground by the counter-charge that the Estates start from isolated individuals, from a private point of view, from particular interests, and so are inclined to devote their activities to these at the expense of the general interests, while *per contra* the other moments in the power of the state explicitly take up the standpoint of the state from the start and devote themselves to the universal end.

As for the general guarantee which is supposed to lie peculiarly in the Estates, each of the other political institutions shares with the Estates in being a guarantee of public welfare and rational freedom, and some of these institutions, as for instance the sovereignty of the monarch, hereditary succession to the throne, the judicial system, &c., guarantee these things far more effectively than the Estates can.

Hence the specific function which the concept assigns to the Estates is to be sought in the fact that in them the subjective moment in universal freedom—the private judgement and private will of the sphere called 'civil society' in this book—comes into existence integrally related to the state. This moment is a determination of the Idea once the Idea has developed to totality, a moment arising as a result of an inner necessity not to be confused with external necessities and expediencies. The proof of this follows, like all the rest of our account of the state, from adopting the philosophical point of view. [A.]

302. Regarded as a mediating organ, the Estates stand between the government in general on the one hand and the nation broken up into particulars (people and associations) on the other. Their function requires them to possess a political and administrative sense and temper, no less than a sense for the interests of individuals and particular groups. At the same time the significance of their position is that, in common with the organized executive, they are a middle term preventing both the extreme isolation of the power of the crown, which otherwise might seem a mere arbitrary tyranny, and also the isolation of the particular interests of persons, societies, and Corporations. Further, and more important, they prevent individuals from having the appearance of a mass or an aggregate and so from acquiring an unorganized opinion and volition and from crystallizing into a powerful *bloc* in opposition to the organized state.

It is one of the most important discoveries of logic that a specific moment which, by standing in an opposition, has the position of an extreme, ceases to be such and is a moment in an organic whole by being at the same time a mean. In connexion with our present topic it is all the more important to emphasize this aspect of the matter because of the popular, but most dangerous, prejudice which regards the Estates principally from the point of view of their opposition to the executive, as if that were their essential attitude. If the Estates become an organ in the whole by being taken up into the state, they evince themselves solely through their mediating function. In this way their opposition to the executive is reduced to a show. There may indeed be an appearance of opposition between them, but if they were opposed, not merely superficially, but actually and in substance, then the state would be in the throes of destruction. That the clash is not of this kind is evident in the nature of the thing, because the Estates have to deal, not with the essential elements in the organism of the state, but only with rather specialized and trifling matters, while the passion which even these arouse spends itself in party cravings in connexion with purely subjective interests such as appointments to the higher offices of state. [A.]

303. The universal class, or, more precisely, the class of civil servants, must, purely in virtue of its character as universal, have the universal as the end of its essential activity. In the Estates, as an element in the legislative power, the unofficial class acquires its political significance and efficacy; it appears, therefore, in the Estates neither as a mere indiscriminate multitude nor as an aggregate dispersed into its atoms, but as what it already is, namely a class subdivided into two, one sub-class [the agricultural class] being based on a tie of substance between its members, and the other [the business class] on particular needs and the work whereby these are met (see Paragraph 201 ff.). It is only in this way that there is a genuine link between the particular which is effective in the state and the universal.

This runs counter to another prevalent idea, the idea that since it is in the legislature that the unofficial class rises to the level of participating in matters of state, it must appear there in the form of individuals, whether individuals are to choose representatives for this purpose, or whether every single individual is to have a vote in the legislature himself. This atomistic and abstract point of view vanishes at the stage of the family, as well as that of civil society where the individual is in evidence only as a member of a general group. The state, however, is essentially an organization each of whose members is in itself a group of this kind, and hence no one of its moments should appear as an unorganized aggregate. The Many, as units—a congenial interpretation of 'people', are of course something connected, but they are connected only as an aggregate, a formless mass whose commotion and activity could therefore only be elementary, irrational, barbarous, and frightful. When we hear speakers on the constitution expatiating about the 'people'—this unorganized collection—we know from the start that we have nothing to expect but generalities and perverse declamations.

The circles of association in civil society are already communities. To picture these communities as once more breaking up into a mere conglomeration of individuals as soon as they enter the field of politics, i.e. the field of the highest concrete universality, is *eo ipso* to hold civil and political life apart from one another and as it were to hang the latter in the air, because its basis could then only be the abstract individuality of caprice and opinion, and hence it would be grounded on chance and not on what is absolutely stable and justified.

So-called 'theories' of this kind involve the idea that the classes (*Stände*) of civil society and the Estates (*Stände*), which are the 'classes' given a political significance, stand wide apart from each other. But the German language, by calling them both *Stände* has still maintained the unity which in any case they actually possessed in former times.

304. The Estates, as an element in political life, still retain in their own function the class distinctions already present in the lower spheres of civil life. The position of the classes is abstract to begin with, i.e. in contrast with the whole principle of monarchy or the crown, their position is that of an extreme—empirical universality. This extreme opposition implies the possibility, though no more, of harmonization, and the equally likely possibility of set hostility. This abstract position changes into a rational relation (into a syllogism, see Remark to Paragraph 302) only if the middle term between the opposites comes into existence. From the point of view of the crown, the executive already has this character (see Paragraph 300). So, from the point of view of the classes, one moment in them must be adapted to the task of existing as in essence the moment of mediation.

305. The principle of one of the classes of civil society is in itself capable of adaptation to this political position. The class in question is the one whose ethical life is natural, whose basis is family life, and, so far as its livelihood is concerned, the possession of land. Its particular members attain their position by birth, just as the monarch does, and, in common with him, they possess a will which rests on itself alone.[65]

306. This class is more particularly fitted for political position and significance in that its capital is independent alike of the state's capital, the uncertainty of business, the quest for profit, and any sort of fluctuation in possessions. It is likewise independent of favour, whether from the executive or the mob. It is even fortified against its own wilfulness, because those members of this class who are called to political life are not entitled, as other citizens are, either to dispose of their entire property at will, or to the assurance that it will pass to their children, whom they love equally, in similarly equal divisions. Hence their wealth becomes inalienable, entailed, and burdened by primogeniture. [A.]

307. The right of this section of the agricultural class is thus based in a way on the natural principle of the family. But this principle is at the same time reversed owing to hard sacrifices made for political ends, and thereby the activity of this class is essentially directed to those ends. As a consequence of this, this class is summoned and entitled to its political vocation by birth without the hazards of election. It therefore has the fixed, substantive position between the subjective wilfulness or contingency of both extremes; and while it mirrors in itself (see Paragraph 305) the moment of the monarchical power, it also shares in other respects

the needs and rights of the other extreme [i.e. civil society] and hence it becomes a support at once of the throne and society.

308. The second section of the Estates comprises the fluctuating element in civil society. This element can enter politics only through its deputies; the multiplicity of its members is an external reason for this, but the essential reason is the specific character of this element and its activity. Since these deputies are the deputies of civil society, it follows as a direct consequence that their appointment is made by the society as a society. That is to say, in making the appointment, society is not dispersed into atomic units, collected to perform only a single and temporary act, and kept together for a moment and no longer. On the contrary, it makes the appointment as a society, articulated into associations, communities, and Corporations, which although constituted already for other purposes, acquire in this way a connexion with politics. The existence of the Estates and their assembly finds a constitutional guarantee of its own in the fact that this class is entitled to send deputies at the summons of the crown, while members of the former class are entitled to present themselves in person in the Estates (see Paragraph 307).

To hold that every single person should share in deliberating and deciding on political matters of general concern on the ground that all individuals are members of the state, that its concerns are their concerns, and that it is their right that what is done should be done with their knowledge and volition, is tantamount to a proposal to put the democratic element without any rational form into the organism of the state, although it is only in virtue of the possession of such a form that the state is an organism at all. This idea comes readily to mind because it does not go beyond the abstraction of 'being a member of the state', and it is superficial thinking which clings to abstractions. The rational consideration of a topic, the consciousness of the Idea, is concrete, and to that extent coincides with a genuine practical sense. Such a sense is itself nothing but the sense of rationality or the Idea, though it is not to be confused with mere business routine or the horizon of a restricted sphere. The concrete state is the whole, articulated into its particular groups. The member of a state is a member of such a group, i.e. of a social class, and it is only as characterized in this objective way that he comes under consideration when we are dealing with the state. His mere character as universal implies that he is at one and the same time both a private person and also a thinking consciousness, a will which wills the universal. This consciousness and will, however, lose their emptiness and acquire a content and a living actuality only when they are filled with particularity, and particularity means determinacy as particular and a particular class-status; or, to put the matter otherwise, abstract individuality is a generic essence, but has its immanent universal actuality as the generic essence next higher in the scale.[66] Hence the single person attains his actual and living destiny for universality only when he becomes a member of a Corporation, a society, &c. (see Paragraph 251), and thereby it becomes open to him, on the strength of his skill, to enter any class for which he is qualified, the class of civil servants included.

Another presupposition of the idea that all should participate in the business of the state is that everyone is at home in this business—a ridiculous notion, however commonly we may hear it sponsored. Still, in public opinion (see Paragraph 316) a field is open to everyone where he can express his purely personal political opinions and make them count.

309. Since deputies are elected to deliberate and decide on *public* affairs, the point about their election is that it is a choice of individuals on the strength of confidence felt in them, i.e. a choice of such individuals as have a better understanding of these affairs than their electors have and such also as essentially vindicate the universal interest, not the particular interest of a society or a Corporation in preference to that interest. Hence their relation to their electors is not that of agents with a commission or specific instructions. A further bar to their being so is the fact that their assembly is meant to be a living body in which all members deliberate in common and reciprocally instruct and convince each other. [A.]

310. The guarantee that deputies will have the qualifications and disposition that accord with this end—since independent means attains its right in the first section of the Estates—is to be found so far as the second section is concerned—the section drawn from the fluctuating and changeable element in civil society— above all in the knowledge (of the organization and interests of the state and civil society), the temperament, and the skill which a deputy acquires as a result of the actual transaction of business in managerial or official positions, and then evinces in his actions. As a result, he also acquires and develops a managerial and political sense, tested by his experience, and this is a further guarantee of his suitability as a deputy.

Subjective opinion, naturally enough, finds superfluous and even perhaps offensive the demand for such guarantees, if the demand is made with reference to what is called the 'people'. The state, however, is characterized by objectivity, not by a subjective opinion and its self-confidence. Hence it can recognize in individuals only their objectively recognizable and tested character, and it must be all the more careful on this point in connexion with the second section of the Estates, since this section is rooted in interests and activities directed towards the particular, i.e. in the sphere where chance, mutability, and caprice enjoy their right of free play.

The external guarantee, a property qualification, is, if taken by itself, evidently just as one-sided in its externality as, at the other extreme, are purely subjective confidence and the opinion of the electorate. Both alike are abstractions in contrast with the concrete qualifications requisite for deliberation on affairs of state and comprised in the points indicated in Paragraph 302. This apart, however, a property qualification has a sphere, where it may work effectively, in the choice of the heads and other officers of the associations and societies, especially if many of these posts are honorary, and in direct reference to Estates business if the members draw no salary.

311. A further point about the election of deputies is that, since civil society is the electorate, the deputies should themselves be conversant with and participate in its special needs, difficulties, and particular interests. Owing to the nature of civil society, its deputies are the deputies of the various Corporations (see Paragraph 308), and this simple mode of appointment obviates any confusion due to conceiving the electorate abstractly and as an agglomeration of atoms. Hence the deputies *eo ipso* adopt the point of view of society, and their actual election is therefore either something wholly superfluous or else reduced to a trivial play of opinion and caprice.

It is obviously of advantage that the deputies should include representatives of each particular main branch of society (e.g. trade, manufactures, &c., &c.)—representatives who are thoroughly conversant with it and who themselves belong to it. The idea of free unrestricted election leaves this important consideration entirely at the mercy of chance. All such branches of society, however, have equal rights of representation. Deputies are sometimes regarded as 'representatives'; but they are representatives in an organic, rational sense only if they are representatives not of individuals or a conglomeration of them, but of one of the essential spheres of society and its large-scale interests. Hence representation cannot now be taken to mean simply the substitution of one man for another; the point is rather that the interest itself is actually present in its representative, while he himself is there to represent the objective element of his own being.

As for popular suffrage, it may be further remarked that especially in large states it leads inevitably to electoral indifference, since the casting of a single vote is of no significance where there is a multitude of electors. Even if a voting qualification is highly valued and esteemed by those who are entitled to it, they still do not enter the polling booth. Thus the result of an institution of this kind is more likely to be the opposite of what was intended; election actually falls into the power of a few, of a caucus, and so of the particular and contingent interest which is precisely what was to have been neutralized.

312. Each class in the Estates (see Paragraphs 305–8) contributes something peculiarly its own to the work of deliberation. Further, one moment in the class-element has in the sphere of politics the special function of mediation,[67] mediation between two existing things. Hence this moment must likewise acquire a separate existence of its own. For this reason the assembly of the Estates is divided into two houses.

313. This division, by providing chambers of the first and second instance, is a surer guarantee for ripeness of decision and it obviates the accidental character which a snap-division has and which a numerical majority may acquire. But the principal advantage of this arrangement is that there is less chance of the Estates being in direct opposition to the executive; or that, if the mediating element is at the same time on the side of the lower house, the weight of the lower house's opinion is all the stronger, because it appears less partisan and its opposition appears neutralized.

314. The purpose of the Estates as an institution is not to be an inherent *sine qua non* of maximum efficiency in the consideration and dispatch of state business, since in fact it is only an *added* efficiency that they can supply (see Paragraph 301). Their distinctive purpose is that in their pooled political knowledge, deliberations, and decisions, the moment of formal freedom shall come into its right in respect of those members of civil society who are without any share in the executive. Consequently, it is knowledge of public business above all which is extended by the publicity of Estates debates.

315. The opening of this opportunity to know has a more universal aspect because by this means public opinion first reaches thoughts that are true and attains insight into the situation and concept of the state and its affairs, and so first acquires ability to estimate these more rationally. By this means also, it becomes acquainted with and learns to respect the work, abilities, virtues,

and dexterity of ministers and officials. While such publicity
provides these abilities with a potent means of development and a
theatre of higher distinction, it is at the same time another antidote
to the self-conceit of individuals singly and *en masse*, and another
means—indeed one of the chief means—of their education. [A.]

316. The formal subjective freedom of individuals consists in
their having and expressing their own private judgements, opinions,
and recommendations on affairs of state. This freedom is collec-
tively manifested as what is called 'public opinion', in which what
is absolutely universal, the substantive and the true, is linked with
its opposite, the purely particular and private opinions[68] of the
Many. Public opinion as it exists is thus a standing self-contradiction, knowledge as appearance, the essential just as directly
present as the inessential. [A.]

317. Public opinion, therefore, is a repository not only of the
genuine needs and correct tendencies of common life, but also, in
the form of common sense (i.e. all-pervasive fundamental ethical
principles disguised as prejudices), of the eternal, substantive
principles of justice, the true content and result of legislation, the
whole constitution, and the general position of the state. At the
same time, when this inner truth emerges into consciousness and,
embodied in general maxims, enters representative thinking—
whether it be there on its own account or in support of concrete
arguments about felt wants, public affairs, the organization of the
state, and relations of parties within it—it becomes infected by all
the accidents of opinion, by its ignorance and perversity, by its
mistakes and falsity of judgement. Since in considering such
opinion we have to do with the consciousness of an insight and
conviction peculiarly one's own, the more peculiarly one's own an
opinion may be the worse its content is, because the bad is that
which is wholly private and personal in its content; the rational,
on the other hand, is the absolutely universal, while it is on
peculiarity that opining prides itself.

Hence it is not simply due to a subjective difference of view that we
find it said that *vox populi, vox Dei*, and on the other hand, as Ariosto
has it,

> *Che 'l volgare ignorante ogn' un riprenda*
> *E parli più di quel che meno intenda*

or, as Goethe puts it, 'the masses are respectable hands at fighting, but
miserable hands at judging'.[69]

Both types of assertion are true at one and the same time of public opinion, and since it is such a hotch-potch of truth and endless error, it cannot be genuinely serious about both of these. But about which *is* it serious? The question may seem hard to answer, and it will actually be hard if we cling simply to the words in which public opinion is directly expressed. The substantial, however, is the heart of public opinion, and therefore it is with that alone that it is truly serious. What the substantial is, though, is not discoverable from public opinion, because its very substantiality implies that it is known in and from itself alone. The passion with which an opinion is urged or the seriousness with which it is maintained or attacked and disputed is no criterion of its real content; and yet the last thing which opinion could be made to see is that its seriousness is nothing serious.

A great genius[70] propounded as a problem for a public essay competition the question 'whether it be permissible to deceive a people'. The answer must have been that a people does not allow itself to be deceived about its substantive basis, the essence and specific character of its mind. On the other hand, it is *self*-deceived about the manner of its knowledge of these things and about its corresponding judgement of its actions, experiences, &c. [A.]

318. Public opinion therefore deserves to be as much respected as despised—despised for its concrete expression and for the concrete consciousness it expresses, respected for its essential basis, a basis which only glimmers more or less dimly in that concrete expression. But in itself it has no criterion of discrimination, nor has it the ability to extract the substantive element it contains and raise it to precise knowledge. Thus to be independent of public opinion is the first formal condition of achieving anything great or rational whether in life or in science. Great achievement is assured, however, of subsequent recognition and grateful acceptance by public opinion, which in due course will make it one of its own prejudices. [A.]

319. Freedom of public communication—of the two modes of communication, the press and the spoken word, the first exceeds the second in range of contact but lags behind it in vivacity—satisfaction of the goading desire to say one's say and to have said it, is directly assured by the laws and by-laws which control or punish its excesses. But it is assured indirectly by the innocuous character which it acquires as a result principally of the rationality of the constitution, the stability of government, and secondly of the publicity of Estates Assemblies. The reason why the latter makes free speech harmless is that what is voiced in these Assemblies is a sound and mature insight into the concerns of the state, with the result that members of the general public are left with nothing of much importance to say, and above all are deprived of the opinion that what they say is of peculiar importance and efficacy. A further safeguard of free speech is the indifference and contempt speedily and necessarily visited on shallow and cantankerous talking.

To define freedom of the press as freedom to say and write whatever we please is parallel to the assertion that freedom as such means freedom to do as we please. Talk of this kind is due to wholly uneducated, crude, and superficial ideas. Moreover, it is in the very nature of the thing that abstract thinking should nowhere be so stubborn, so unintelligent, as in this matter of free speech, because what it is considering is the most fleeting, the most contingent, and the most personal side of opinion in its infinite diversity of content and tergiversation. Beyond the direct incitation to theft, murder, rebellion, &c., there lies its artfully constructed expression—an expression which seems in itself quite general and vague, while all the time it conceals a meaning anything but vague or else is compatible with inferences which are not actually expressed, and it is impossible to determine whether they rightly follow from it, or whether they were meant to be inferred from it. This vagueness of matter and form precludes laws on these topics from attaining the requisite determinacy of law, and since the trespass, wrong, and injury here are so extremely personal and subjective in form,[71] judgement on them is reduced equally to a wholly subjective verdict. Such an injury is directed against the thoughts, opinions, and wills of others, but apart from that, these form the element in which alone it is actually anything. But this element is the sphere of the freedom of others, and it therefore depends on them whether the injurious expression of opinion is or is not actually an effective act.

Laws then [against libel, &c.] may be criticized by exhibiting their indeterminacy as well as by arguing that they leave it open to the speaker or writer to devise turns of phrase or tricks of expression, and so evade the laws or claim that judicial decisions are mere subjective verdicts. Further, however, against the view that the expression of opinion is an act with injurious effects, it may be maintained that it is not an act at all, but only opining and thinking, or only talking. And so we have before us a claim that mere opining and talking is to go unpunished because it is of a purely subjective character both in form and content, because it does not mean anything and is of no importance. And yet in the same breath we have the claim that this same opining and talking should be held in high esteem and respect—the opining because it is personal property and in fact pre-eminently the property of mind; the talking because it is only this same property being expressed and used.

But the substance of the matter is and remains that traducing the honour of anyone, slander, abuse, the contemptuous caricature of government, its ministers, officials, and in particular the person of the monarch, defiance of the laws, incitement to rebellion, &c., &c., are all crimes or misdemeanours in one or other of their numerous gradations. The rather high degree of indeterminability which such actions acquire on account of the element in which they are expressed does not annul this fundamental character of theirs. Its only effect is that the subjective field in which they are committed also determines the nature and form of the reaction to the offence. It is the field in which the offence was committed which itself necessitates subjectivity of view, contingency, &c., in the reaction to the offence, whether the reaction takes the form of punishment proper or of police action to prevent crimes. Here, as always, abstract thinking sets itself to explain away the fundamental and concrete nature of the thing by concentrating on isolated aspects of its external appearance and on abstractions drawn therefrom.

The sciences, however, are not to be found anywhere in the field of opinion and subjective views, provided of course that they be sciences in other respects. Their exposition is not a matter of clever turns of phrase, allusiveness, half-utterances, and semi-reticences, but consists in the unambiguous, determinate, and open expression of their meaning and purport. It follows that they do not fall under the category of public opinion (see Paragraph 316). Apart from this, however, as I said just now, the element in which views and their expression become actions in the full sense and exist effectively, consists of the intelligence, principles, and opinions of others. Hence this aspect of these actions, i.e. their effectiveness proper and their danger to individuals, society, and the state (compare Paragraph 218), depends on the character of the ground on which they fall, just as a spark falling on a heap of gunpowder is more dangerous than if it falls on hard ground where it vanishes without trace. Thus, just as the right of science to express itself depends on and is safeguarded by its subject-matter and content, so an illegitimate expression may also acquire a measure of security, or at least sufferance, in the scorn which it has brought upon itself. An offence of this sort is punishable on its own account too, but part of it may be accounted that kind of nemesis which inner impotence, feeling itself oppressed by the preponderating abilities and virtues of others, is impelled to vent in order to come to itself again in face of such superiority, and to restore some self-consciousness to its own nullity. It was a nemesis of a more harmless type which Roman soldiers vented against their generals when they sang scurrilous songs[72] about them in triumphal processions in order in a way to get even with them for all the hard service and discipline they had undergone, and especially for the omission of their names from the triumphal honours. The former type of nemesis, the bad and hateful type, is deprived of its effect by being treated with scorn, and hence, like the public, which perhaps forms a circle of spectators of scurrility, it is restricted to futile malice and to the self-condemnation which it implicitly contains.

320. Subjectivity is manifested in its most external form as the undermining of the established life of the state by opinion and ratiocination when they endeavour to assert the authority of their own fortuitous character and so bring about their own destruction. But its true actuality is attained in the opposite of this, i.e. in the subjectivity identical with the substantial will of the state, the subjectivity which constitutes the concept of the power of the crown and which, as the ideality of the whole state, has not up to this point attained its right or its existence.[73] [A.]

2. *Sovereignty* vis-à-vis *foreign States*

321. Sovereignty at home (see Paragraph 278) is this ideality in the sense that the moments of mind and its actuality, the state, have become developed in their necessity and subsist as the organs of the state. Mind in its freedom is an infinitely negative relation to itself and hence its essential character from its own point of view is its singleness, a singleness which has incorporated these subsistent differences into itself and so is a unit, exclusive of other units. So characterized, the state has individuality, and individuality is in essence an individual, and in the sovereign an actual, immediate individual (see Paragraph 279).

322. Individuality is awareness of one's existence as a unit in sharp distinction from others. It manifests itself here in the state as a relation to other states, each of which is autonomous *vis-à-vis* the others. This autonomy embodies mind's actual awareness of itself as a unit and hence it is the most fundamental freedom which a people possesses as well as its highest dignity.

Those[74] who talk of the 'wishes' of a collection of people constituting a more or less autonomous state with its own centre, of its 'wishes' to renounce this centre and its autonomy in order to unite with others to form a new whole, have very little knowledge of the nature of a collection or of the feeling of selfhood which a nation possesses in its independence.

Thus the dominion which a state has at its first entry into history is this bare autonomy, even if it be quite abstract and without further inner development. For this reason, to have an individual at its head—a patriarch, a chieftain, &c.—is appropriate to this original appearance of the state.

323. This negative relation of the state to itself is embodied in the world as the relation of one state to another and as if the negative were something external.[75] In the world of existence, therefore, this negative relation has the shape of a happening and an entanglement with chance events coming from without. But in fact this negative relation is that moment in the state which is most supremely its own, the state's actual infinity as the ideality of everything finite within it. It is the moment wherein the substance of the state—i.e. its absolute power against everything individual and particular, against life, property, and their rights, even against societies and associations—makes the nullity of these finite things an accomplished fact and brings it home to consciousness.

324. This destiny whereby the rights and interests of individuals are established as a passing phase, is at the same time the positive moment, i.e. the positing of their absolute, not their contingent and unstable, individuality. This relation and the recognition of it is therefore the individual's substantive duty, the duty to maintain this substantive individuality, i.e. the independence and sovereignty of the state, at the risk and the sacrifice of property and life, as well as of opinion and everything else naturally comprised in the compass of life.

An entirely distorted account of the demand for this sacrifice results from regarding the state as a mere civil society and from regarding its final end as only the security of individual life and property. This security cannot possibly be obtained by the sacrifice of what is to be secured—on the contrary.

The ethical moment in war is implied in what has been said in this Paragraph. War is not to be regarded as an absolute evil and as a purely external accident, which itself therefore has some accidental cause, be it injustices, the passions of nations or the holders of power, &c., or in short, something or other which ought not to be. It is to what is by nature accidental that accidents happen, and the fate whereby they happen is thus a necessity. Here as elsewhere, the point of view from which things seem pure accidents vanishes if we look at them in the light of the concept and philosophy, because philosophy knows accident for a show and sees in it its essence, necessity. It is necessary that the finite—property and life—should be definitely established as accidental, because accidentality is the concept of the finite. From one point of view this necessity appears in the form of the power of nature, and everything is mortal and transient. But in the ethical substance, the state, nature is robbed of this power, and the necessity is exalted to be the work of freedom, to be something ethical. The transience of the finite becomes a willed passing away, and the negativity lying at the roots of the finite becomes the substantive individuality proper to the ethical substance.

War is the state of affairs which deals in earnest with the vanity of temporal goods and concerns—a vanity at other times a common theme of edifying sermonizing. This is what makes it the moment in which the ideality of the particular attains its right and is actualized. War has the higher significance that by its agency, as I have remarked elsewhere,[76] 'the ethical health of peoples is preserved in their indifference to the stabilization of finite institutions; just as the blowing of the winds preserves the sea from the foulness which would be the result of a prolonged calm, so also corruption in nations would be the product of prolonged, let alone 'perpetual', peace.'[77] This, however, is said to be only a philosophic idea, or, to use another common expression, a 'justification of Providence', and it is maintained that actual wars require some other justification. On this point, see below.[78]

The ideality which is in evidence in war, i.e. in an accidental relation of a state to a foreign state, is the same as the ideality in accordance with which the domestic powers of the state are organic moments in a whole. This fact appears in history in various forms, e.g. successful wars have checked domestic unrest and consolidated the power of the state at home. Other phenomena illustrate the same point: e.g. peoples unwilling or afraid to tolerate sovereignty at home have been subjugated from abroad, and they have struggled for their independence with the less glory and success the less they have been able previously to organize the powers of the state in home affairs—their freedom has died from the fear of dying; states whose autonomy has been guaranteed not by their armed forces but in other ways (e.g. by their disproportionate smallness in comparison with their neighbours) have been able to subsist with a constitution of their own which by itself would not have assured peace in either home or foreign affairs. [A.]

325. Sacrifice on behalf of the individuality of the state is the substantial tie between the state and all its members and so is a universal duty. Since this tie is a *single* aspect of the ideality, as contrasted with the reality, of subsistent particulars, it becomes at the same time a *particular* tie, and those who are in it form a class of their own with the characteristic of courage.[79]

326. The matter at issue in disputes between states may be only one particular aspect of their relation to each other, and it is for such disputes that the particular class devoted to the state's defence is principally appointed. But if the state as such, if its autonomy, is in jeopardy, all its citizens are in duty bound to answer the summons to its defence. If in such circumstances the entire state is under arms and is torn from its domestic life at home to fight abroad, the war of defence turns into a war of conquest.

The armed force of the state becomes a standing army, while its appointment to the particular task of state defence makes it a class. This happens from the same necessity as compels other particular moments, interests, and activities in the state to crystallize into a given status or class, e.g. into the status of marriage or into the business or civil servant class, or into the Estates of the Realm. Ratiocination, running hither and thither from ground to consequent, launches forth into reflections about the relative advantages and disadvantages of standing armies. Opinion readily decides that the latter preponderate, partly because the concept of a thing is harder to grasp than its single and external aspects, but also because particular interests and ends (the expense of a standing army, and its result, higher taxation, &c.) are rated in the consciousness of civil society more highly than what is necessary in and by itself. In this way the latter comes to count only as a means to particular ends.

327. In itself, courage is a *formal* virtue, because (i) it is a display of freedom by radical abstraction from all particular ends, possessions, pleasure, and life; but (ii) this negation is a negation of externalities, and their alienation, the culmination of courage, is not intrinsically of a spiritual (*geistiger*) character; (iii) the courageous man's inner motive need only be some particular reason or other, and even the actual result of what he does need be present solely to the minds of others and not to his own.[80] [A.]

328. The intrinsic worth of courage as a disposition of mind is to be found in the genuine, absolute, final end, the sovereignty of the state. The work of courage is to actualize this final end, and the means to this end is the sacrifice of personal actuality. This form of experience thus contains the harshness of extreme contradictions: a self-sacrifice which yet is the real existence of one's freedom; the maximum self-subsistence of individuality, yet only as a cog playing its part in the mechanism of an external organization; absolute obedience, renunciation of personal opinions and reasonings, in fact complete *absence* of mind, coupled with the most intense and comprehensive *presence* of mind and decision in the moment of acting; the most hostile and so most personal action against individuals, coupled with an attitude of complete indifference or even liking towards them as individuals.

To risk one's life is better than merely fearing death, but is still purely negative and so indeterminate and without value in itself. It is the positive aspect, the end and content, which first gives significance to this spiritedness. Robbers and murderers bent on crime as their end, adventurers pursuing ends planned to suit their own whims, &c., these too have spirit enough to risk their lives.

The principle of the modern world—thought and the universal—has given courage a higher form, because its display now seems to be more mechanical, the act not of this particular person, but of a member of a whole. Moreover, it seems to be turned not against single persons, but against a hostile group, and hence personal bravery appears impersonal. It is for this reason that thought has invented the gun, and the invention of this weapon, which has changed the purely personal form of bravery into a more abstract one, is no accident.

329. The state's tendency to look abroad lies in the fact that it is an individual subject. Its relation to other states therefore falls to the power of the crown. Hence it directly devolves on the monarch, and on him alone, to command the armed forces, to conduct foreign affairs through ambassadors &c., to make war and peace, and to conclude treaties of all kinds.[81] [A.]

B. *International Law*

330. International law springs from the relations between autonomous states. It is for this reason that what is absolute in it retains the form of an ought-to-be, since its actuality depends on different wills each of which is sovereign. [A.]

331. The nation state is mind in its substantive rationality and immediate actuality and is therefore the absolute power on earth. It follows that every state is sovereign and autonomous against its neighbours. It is entitled in the first place and without qualification to be sovereign from their point of view, i.e. to be recognized by them as sovereign. At the same time, however, this title is purely formal, and the demand for this recognition of the state, merely on the ground that it is a state, is abstract. Whether a state is in fact something absolute depends on its content, i.e. on its constitution and general situation; and recognition, implying as it does an identity of both form and content, is conditional on the neighbouring state's judgement and will.

A state is as little an actual individual without relations to other states (see Paragraph 322) as an individual is actually a person without *rapport* with other persons (see Paragraph 71 and elsewhere[82]). The

legitimate authority of a state and, more particularly, so far as its foreign
relations are concerned, of its monarch also, is partly a purely domestic
matter (one state should not meddle with the domestic affairs of another).
On the other hand, however, it is no less essential that this authority
should receive its full and final legitimation through its recognition by
other states, although this recognition requires to be safeguarded by the
proviso that where a state is to be recognized by others, it shall likewise
recognize them, i.e. respect their autonomy; and so it comes about that
they cannot be indifferent to each other's domestic affairs.

The question arises how far a nomadic people, for instance, or any
people on a low level of civilization, can be regarded as a state. As once
was the case with the Jews and the Mohammedan peoples, religious views
may entail an opposition at a higher level between one people and its
neighbours and so preclude the general identity which is requisite for
recognition.   [A.]

332. The immediate actuality which any state possesses from
the point of view of other states is particularized into a multiplicity
of relations which are determined by the arbitrary will of both
autonomous parties and which therefore possess the formal nature
of contracts pure and simple. The subject-matter of these contracts, however, is infinitely less varied than it is in civil society,
because in civil society individuals are reciprocally interdependent
in the most numerous respects, while autonomous states are principally wholes whose needs are met within their own borders.

333. The fundamental proposition of international law (i.e. the
universal law which ought to be absolutely valid between states, as
distinguished from the particular content of positive treaties) is
that treaties, as the ground of obligations between states, ought
to be kept. But since the sovereignty of a state is the principle of
its relations to others, states are to that extent in a state of nature
in relation to each other. Their rights are actualized only in their
particular wills and not in a universal will with constitutional
powers over them. This universal proviso of international law
therefore does not go beyond an ought-to-be, and what really
happens is that international relations in accordance with treaty
alternate with the severance of these relations.

There is no Praetor to judge between states; at best there may be an
arbitrator or a mediator, and even he exercises his functions contin-
gently only, i.e. in dependence on the particular wills of the disputants.
Kant had an idea for securing 'perpetual peace' by a League of Nations
to adjust every dispute. It was to be a power recognized by each individual state, and was to arbitrate in all cases of dissension in order to

make it impossible for disputants to resort to war in order to settle them. This idea presupposes an accord between states; this would rest on moral or religious or other grounds and considerations, but in any case would always depend ultimately on a particular sovereign will and for that reason would remain infected with contingency.

334. It follows that if states disagree and their particular wills cannot be harmonized, the matter can only be settled by war. A state through its subjects has widespread connexions and many-sided interests, and these may be readily and considerably injured; but it remains inherently indeterminable which of these injuries is to be regarded as a specific breach of treaty or as an injury to the honour and autonomy of the state. The reason for this is that a state may regard its infinity and honour as at stake in each of its concerns, however minute, and it is all the more inclined to susceptibility to injury the more its strong individuality is impelled as a result of long domestic peace to seek and create a sphere of activity abroad.

335. Apart from this, the state is in essence mind and therefore cannot be prepared to stop at just taking notice of an injury *after* it has actually occurred. On the contrary, there arises in addition as a cause of strife the *idea* of such an injury as the idea of a danger *threatening* from another state, together with calculations of degrees of probability on this side and that, guessing at intentions, &c., &c.

336. Since states are related to one another as autonomous entities and so as particular wills on which the very validity of treaties depends, and since the particular will of the whole is in content a will for its own welfare pure and simple, it follows that welfare is the highest law governing the relation of one state to another. This is all the more the case since the Idea of the state is precisely the supersession of the clash between right (i.e. empty abstract freedom) and welfare (i.e. the particular content which fills that void), and it is when states become *concrete* wholes that they first attain recognition (see Paragraph 331).

337. The substantial welfare of the state is its welfare as a particular state in its specific interest and situation and its no less special foreign affairs, including its particular treaty relations. Its government therefore is a matter of particular wisdom, not of universal Providence (compare Remark to Paragraph 324). Similarly, its aim in relation to other states and its principle for justifying wars and treaties is not a universal thought (the thought of philanthropy) but only its actually injured or threatened welfare as something specific and peculiar to itself.

At one time the opposition between morals and politics, and the demand that the latter should conform to the former, were much canvassed. On this point only a general remark is required here. The welfare of a state has claims to recognition totally different from those of the welfare of the individual. The ethical substance, the state, has its determinate being, i.e. its right, directly embodied in something existent, something not abstract but concrete, and the principle of its conduct and behaviour can only be this concrete existent and not one of the many universal thoughts supposed to be moral commands. When politics is alleged to clash with morals and so to be always wrong, the doctrine propounded rests on superficial ideas about morality, the nature of the state, and the state's relation to the moral point of view.

338. The fact that states reciprocally recognize each other as states remains, even in war—the state of affairs when rights disappear and force and chance hold sway—a bond wherein each counts to the rest as something absolute. Hence in war, war itself is characterized as something which ought to pass away. It implies therefore the proviso of the *jus gentium* that the possibility of peace be retained (and so, for example, that envoys must be respected), and, in general, that war be not waged against domestic institutions, against the peace of family and private life, or against persons in their private capacity. [A.]

339. Apart from this, relations between states (e.g. in war-time, reciprocal agreements about taking prisoners; in peace-time, concessions of rights to subjects of other states for the purpose of private trade and intercourse, &c.) depend principally upon the customs of nations, custom being the inner universality of behaviour maintained in all circumstances. [A.]

340. It is as particular entities that states enter into relations with one another. Hence their relations are on the largest scale a maelstrom of external contingency and the inner particularity of passions, private interests and selfish ends, abilities and virtues, vices, force, and wrong. All these whirl together, and in their vortex the ethical whole itself, the autonomy of the state, is exposed to contingency. The principles of the national minds[83] are wholly restricted on account of their particularity, for it is in this particularity that, as existent individuals, they have their objective actuality and their self-consciousness. Their deeds and destinies in their reciprocal relations to one another are the dialectic of the finitude of these minds, and out of it arises the universal mind, the mind of the world, free from all restriction, producing itself as that which exercises its right—and its right is the highest right of all—over these finite minds in the 'history of the world which is the world's court of judgement'.

C. *World History*

341. The element in which the universal mind exists in art is intuition and imagery, in religion feeling and representative thinking, in philosophy pure freedom of thought. In world history this element is the actuality of mind in its whole compass of internality and externality alike. World history is a court of judgement because in its absolute universality, the particular—i.e. the *Penates*, civil society, and the national minds in their variegated actuality—is present as only ideal, and the movement of mind in this element is the exhibition of that fact.[84]

342. Further, world history is not the verdict of mere might, i.e. the abstract and non-rational inevitability of a blind destiny. On the contrary, since mind is implicitly and actually reason, and reason is explicit to itself in mind as knowledge, world history is the necessary development, out of the concept of mind's freedom alone, of the moments of reason and so of the self-consciousness and freedom of mind. This development is the interpretation and actualization of the universal mind.

343. The history of mind is its own act. Mind is only what it does, and its act is to make itself the object of its own consciousness. In history its act is to gain consciousness of itself as mind, to apprehend itself in its interpretation of itself to itself. This apprehension is its being and its principle, and the completion of apprehension at one stage is at the same time the rejection of that stage and its transition to a higher. To use abstract phraseology, the mind apprehending this apprehension anew, or in other words returning to itself again out of its rejection of this lower stage of apprehension, is the mind of the stage higher than that on which it stood in its earlier apprehension.

The question of the perfectibility and *Education of the Human Race* arises here. Those[85] who have maintained this perfectibility have divined something of the nature of mind, something of the fact that it is its nature to have γνῶθι σεαυτόν as the law of its being, and, since it apprehends that which it is, to have a form higher than that which constituted its mere being.[86] But to those who reject this doctrine, mind has remained an empty word, and history a superficial play of casual, so-called 'merely human', strivings and passions. Even if, in connexion with history, they speak of Providence and the plan of Providence, and so express a faith in a higher power, their ideas remain empty because they expressly declare that for them the plan of Providence is inscrutable and incomprehensible.[87]

344. In the course of this work of the world mind, states, nations, and individuals arise animated by their particular determinate principle which has its interpretation and actuality in their constitutions and in the whole range of their life and condition. While their consciousness is limited to these and they are absorbed in their mundane interests, they are all the time the unconscious tools and organs of the world mind at work within them. The shapes which they take pass away, while the absolute mind prepares and works out its transition to its next higher stage.

345. Justice and virtue, wrongdoing, power and vice, talents and their achievements, passions strong and weak, guilt and innocence, grandeur in individual and national life, autonomy, fortune and misfortune of states and individuals, all these have their specific significance and worth in the field of known actuality; therein they are judged and therein they have their partial, though only partial justification. World-history, however, is above the point of view from which these things matter. Each of its stages is the presence of a necessary moment in the Idea of the world mind, and that moment attains its absolute right in that stage. The nation whose life embodies this moment secures its good fortune and fame, and its deeds are brought to fruition.

346. History is mind clothing itself with the form of events or the immediate actuality of nature. The stages of its development are therefore presented as immediate natural principles. These, because they are natural, are a plurality external to one another, and they are present therefore in such a way that each of them is assigned to one nation in the external form of its geographical and anthropological conditions.

347. The nation to which is ascribed a moment of the Idea in the form of a natural principle is entrusted with giving complete effect to it in the advance of the self-developing self-consciousness of the world mind. This nation is dominant in world history during this one epoch, and it is only once (see Paragraph 345)[88] that it can make its hour strike. In contrast with this its absolute right of being the vehicle of this present stage in the world mind's development, the minds of the other nations are without rights, and they, along with those whose hour has struck already, count no longer in world history.

The history of a single world-historical nation contains (a) the development of its principle from its latent embryonic stage until it blossoms into the self-conscious freedom of ethical life and presses in upon world history; and (b) the period of its decline and fall, since it is its decline and fall that signalizes the emergence in it of a higher principle as the pure negative of its own. When this happens, mind passes over into the new principle and so marks out another nation for world-historical significance. After this period, the declining nation has lost the interest of the absolute; it may indeed absorb the higher principle positively and begin building its life on it, but the principle is only like an adopted child, not like a relative to whom its ties are immanently vital and vigorous. Perhaps it loses its autonomy, or it may still exist, or drag out its existence, as a particular state or a group of states and involve itself without rhyme or reason in manifold enterprises at home and battles abroad.

348. All actions, including world-historical actions, culminate with individuals as subjects giving actuality to the substantial (see Remark to Paragraph 279). They are the living instruments of what is in substance the deed of the world mind and they are therefore directly at one with that deed though it is concealed from them and is not their aim and object (see Paragraph 344). For the deeds of the world mind, therefore, they receive no honour or thanks either from their contemporaries (see Paragraph 344) or from public opinion in later ages. All that is vouchsafed to them by such opinion is undying fame in respect of the subjective form of their acts.[89]

349. A nation does not begin by being a state. The transition from a family, a horde, a clan, a multitude, &c., to political conditions is the realization of the Idea in the form of that nation. Without this form, a nation, as an ethical substance—which is what it is implicitly, lacks the objectivity of possessing in its own eyes and in the eyes of others, a universal and universally valid embodiment in laws, i.e. in determinate thoughts, and as a result it fails to secure recognition from others. So long as it lacks objective law and an explicitly established rational constitution, its autonomy is formal only and is not sovereignty.

It would be contrary even to commonplace ideas to call patriarchal conditions a 'constitution' or a people under patriarchal government a 'state' or its independence 'sovereignty'. Hence, before history actually begins, we have on the one hand dull innocence, devoid of interest, and, on the other, the courage of revenge and of the struggle for formal recognition (see Paragraph 331 and Remark to Paragraph 57).

350. It is the absolute right of the Idea to step into existence in clear-cut laws and objective institutions, beginning with marriage and agriculture (see Remark to Paragraph 203), whether this right be actualized in the form of divine legislation and favour, or in the form of force and wrong. This right is the right of heroes to found states.

351. The same consideration justifies civilized nations in regarding and treating as barbarians those who lag behind them in institutions which are the essential moments of the state. Thus a pastoral people may treat hunters as barbarians, and both of these are barbarians from the point of view of agriculturists, &c. The civilized nation is conscious that the rights of barbarians are unequal to its own and treats their autonomy as only a formality.

When wars and disputes arise in such circumstances, the trait which gives them a significance for world history is the fact that they are struggles for recognition in connexion with something of specific intrinsic worth.

352. The concrete Ideas, the minds of the nations, have their truth and their destiny in the concrete Idea which is absolute universality, i.e. in the world mind. Around its throne they stand as the executors of its actualization and as signs and ornaments of its grandeur. As mind, it is nothing but its active movement towards absolute knowledge of itself and therefore towards freeing its consciousness from the form of natural immediacy and so coming to itself. Therefore the principles of the formations of this self-consciousness in the course of its liberation—the world-historical realms—are four in number.

353. In its *first* and immediate revelation, mind has as its principle the shape of the substantial mind, i.e. the shape of the identity in which individuality is absorbed in its essence and its claims are not explicitly recognized.

The *second* principle is this substantial mind endowed with

knowledge so that mind is both the positive content and filling of
mind and also the individual self-awareness which is the living
form of mind. This principle is ethical individuality as beauty.[90]

The *third* principle is the inward deepening of this individual
self-awareness and knowledge until it reaches abstract universality
and therefore infinite opposition to the objective world which in
the same process has become mind-forsaken.

The principle of the *fourth* formation is the conversion of this
opposition so that mind receives in its inner life its truth and
concrete essence, while in objectivity it is at home and reconciled
with itself. The mind which has thus reverted to the substantiality
with which it began is the mind which has returned out of the
infinite opposition, and which consequently engenders and knows
this its truth as thought and as a world of actual laws.

354. In accordance with these four principles, the world-
historical realms are the following: (1) the Oriental, (2) the Greek,
(3) the Roman, (4) the Germanic.

355. (1) The Oriental realm.

The world-view of this first realm is substantial, without inward
division, and it arises in natural communities patriarchically
governed. According to this view, the mundane form of government is theocratic, the ruler is also a high priest or God himself;
constitution and legislation are at the same time religion, while
religious and moral commands, or usages rather, are at the same
time natural and positive law. In the magnificence of this régime
as a whole, individual personality loses its rights and perishes; the
external world of nature is either directly divine or else God's
ornament, and the history of the actual is poetry. Distinctions are
developed in customs, government, and state on their many sides,
and in default of laws and amidst the simplicity of manners, they
become unwieldy, diffuse, and superstitious ceremonies, the accidents of personal power and arbitrary rule, and class differences
become crystallized into hereditary castes. Hence in the Oriental
state nothing is fixed, and what is stable is fossilized; it lives therefore only in an outward movement which becomes in the end an
elemental fury and desolation. Its inner calm is merely the calm
of non-political life and immersion in feebleness and exhaustion.

A still substantial, natural, mentality is a moment in the development
of the state, and the point at which any state takes this form is the
absolute beginning of its history. This has been emphasized and

demonstrated with learning and profound insight in connexion with the history of particular states by Dr. Stuhr in his book *Der Untergang der Naturstaaten*[91]—a work in which he leads the way to a rational treatment of constitutional history and of history generally. The principle of subjectivity and self-conscious freedom is there too shown to be the principle of the Germanic people, but the book goes no further than the decline of natural states, and consequently the principle is only brought to the point where it appears either as a restless mobility, as human caprice and corruption, or in its particular form as emotion, and where it has not yet developed to the objectivity of the self-conscious substantiality or to an organized legal system.

356. (2) The Greek realm.

This realm possesses this substantial unity of finite and infinite, but only as a mysterious background, suppressed in dim recesses of the memory, in caves[92] and traditional imagery. This background, reborn out of the mind which differentiates itself to individual mentality, emerges into the daylight of knowing and is tempered and transfigured into beauty and a free and unruffled ethical life. Hence it is in a world of this character that the principle of personal individuality arises, though it is still not self-enclosed but kept in its ideal unity. The result is that the whole is divided into a group of particular national minds;[93] ultimate decision is ascribed not to the subjectivity of explicitly independent self-consciousness but to a power standing above and outside it (see Remark to Paragraph 279); on the other hand, the due satisfaction of particular needs is not yet comprised in the sphere of freedom but is relegated exclusively to a class of slaves.

357. (3) The Roman realm.

In this realm, differentiation is carried to its conclusion, and ethical life is sundered without end into the extremes of the private self-consciousness of persons on the one hand, and abstract universality on the other.[94] This opposition begins in the clash between the substantial intuition of an aristocracy and the principle of free personality in democratic form. As the opposition grows, the first of these opponents develops into superstition and the maintenance of heartless self-seeking power, while the second becomes more and more corrupt until it sinks into a rabble.[95] Finally, the whole is dissolved and the result is universal misfortune and the destruction of ethical life. National heroes die away into the unity of a Pantheon,[96] all individuals are degraded to the level of private persons equal with one another, possessed of formal rights, and the only bond left to hold them together is abstract insatiable self-will.

358. (4) The Germanic realm.

Mind and its world are thus both alike lost and plunged in the infinite grief[97] of that fate for which a people, the Jewish people, was held in readiness. Mind is here pressed back upon itself in the extreme of its absolute negativity. This is the absolute turning point; mind rises out of this situation and grasps the infinite positivity of this its inward character, i.e. it grasps the principle of the unity of the divine nature and the human, the reconciliation of objective truth and freedom as the truth and freedom appearing within self-consciousness and subjectivity, a reconciliation with the fulfilment of which the principle of the north, the principle of the Germanic peoples, has been entrusted.

359. This principle is first of all inward and abstract; it exists in feeling as faith, love, and hope, the reconciliation and resolution of all contradiction. It then discloses its content, raising it to become actuality and self-conscious rationality, to become a mundane realm proceeding from the heart, fidelity, and comradeship of free men, a realm which in this its subjectivity is equally a realm of crude individual caprice and barbarous manners. This realm it sets over against a world of beyond, an intellectual realm, whose content is indeed the truth of its (the principle's) mind, but a truth not yet thought and so still veiled in barbarous imagery. This world of beyond, as the power of mind over the mundane heart, acts against the latter as a compulsive and frightful force.

360. These two realms[98] stand distinguished from one another though at the same time they are rooted in a single unity and Idea. Here their distinction is intensified to absolute opposition and a stern struggle ensues in the course of which the realm of mind lowers the place of its heaven to an earthly here and now, to a common worldliness of fact and idea. The mundane realm, on the other hand, builds up its abstract independence into thought and the principle of rational being and knowing, i.e. into the rationality of right and law. In this way their opposition implicitly loses its marrow and disappears. The realm of fact has discarded its barbarity and unrighteous caprice, while the realm of truth has abandoned the world of beyond and its arbitrary force, so that the true reconciliation which discloses the state as the image and actuality of reason has become objective. In the state, self-consciousness finds in an organic development the actuality of its substantive knowing and willing; in religion, it finds the feeling and the representation of this its own truth as an ideal essentiality; while in philosophic science, it finds the free comprehension and knowledge of this truth as one and the same in its mutually complementary manifestations, i.e. in the state, in nature, and in the ideal world.[99]

ADDITIONS

1. *Preface, p. 4.*

Laws are of two kinds—laws of nature and laws of the land. The laws of nature simply are what they are and are valid as they are; they are not liable to encroachment, though in certain cases man may transgress them. To know the law of nature, we must learn to know nature, since its laws are rigid and it is only our ideas about them that can be false. The measure of these laws is outside us; knowing them adds nothing to them and does not assist their operation; our knowledge of them can expand, that is all. Knowledge of the laws of the land is in one way similar, but in another way not. These laws too we learn to know just as they exist; the citizen's knowledge of them is more or less of this sort, and the student of positive law equally stops at what is given. But the difference in the case of laws of the land is that they arouse the spirit of reflection, and their diversity at once draws attention to the fact that they are not absolute. Positive laws are something posited, something originated by men. Between what is so originated and man's inner voice there may be an inevitable clash or there may be agreement. Man does not stop short at the existent, but claims to have in himself the measure of what is right. He may be subjected to the compulsion and dominion of an external authority, though never as he is to the compulsion of nature, because his inner self always tells him how things ought to be and he finds within himself the confirmation or denial of what passes as valid. In nature, the highest truth is that there is a *law*; in the law of the land, the thing is not valid simply because it exists; on the contrary, everyone demands that it shall comply with his private criterion. Here then an antagonism is possible between what ought to be and what is, between the absolutely right which stands unaltered and the arbitrary determination of what is to be recognized as right. A schism and a conflict of this sort is to be found only in the territory of mind, and because mind's privilege seems therefore to lead to discontent and unhappiness, men are often thrown back from the arbitrariness of life to the contemplation of nature and set themselves to take nature as an example. But it is precisely in these clashes between what is absolutely right and what arbitrariness makes pass as right that there lies the need for studying the fundamentals of right. In the right, man must meet with his own reason; consequently, he must consider the rationality of the right, and this is the task of our science in contrast with the positive study of law which often has to do only with contradictions.* The world of to-day has in addition a more urgent need to make this study because while amongst

* [i.e. with the inconsistencies in any system of positive law (see, e.g., Hegel's comments on fictions in Roman law in the Remarks to Paragraphs 3 and 180) as well as with contradictory judgements, see, e.g., Remark to Paragraph 211.]

the ancients the existing laws were still respected and reverenced, nowadays the civilization of the age has taken a new turning and thought has placed itself at the head of everything which is to have validity. Theories are set over against the existent and are intended to appear as absolutely correct and necessary. At present there is a rather special need for becoming acquainted with, and understanding, the thoughts of the right. Since thought has risen to be the essential form of things, we must try to grasp the right too as thought. It seems to be opening wide the door to casual opinions to hold that thought is to be pre-eminent over the right, yet true thought is not an opinion about the thing but the concept of the thing itself. The concept of the thing does not come our way by nature. Anyone has fingers and may take a brush and colours, but that does not make him a painter. The same is true about thinking. The thought of the right is surely not the thought that everybody possesses at first hand; on the contrary, exact thinking is cognizing and apprehending the thing, and our apprehension should therefore be scientific.

2. *Paragraph 1.*

The concept and its objective existence are two sides of the same thing, distinct and united, like soul and body. The body is the same life as the soul and yet both may be spoken of as lying outside one another. A soul without a body would not be a living thing, nor would a body without a soul. Hence the determinate existence of the concept is its body, while its body obeys the soul which brought it into being. The seeds have the tree implicit within them and contain the tree's whole strength, although they are not yet the tree itself. The tree corresponds in detail with the simple construction of the seed. If the body does not match the soul, it is a poor sort of thing. The unity of determinate existence and the concept, of body and soul, is the Idea. The unity is not a mere harmony, but rather a complete interpenetration. Nothing is alive which is not in some way or other Idea. The Idea of right is freedom, and if it is to be truly understood, it must be known both in its concept and in the determinate existence of that concept.

3. *Paragraph 2.*

Philosophy forms a circle. It has a beginning, an immediate factor (for it must somehow make a start), something unproved which is not a result. But the *terminus a quo* of philosophy is simply relative, since it must appear in another terminus as a *terminus ad quem*. Philosophy is a sequence which does not hang in the air; it is not something which begins from nothing at all; on the contrary, it circles back into itself.*

4. *Paragraph 4.*

The freedom of the will is best explained by a reference to the

* [See *Science of Logic*, i. 79–90.]

physical world. Freedom, I mean, is just as fundamental a character of the will as weight is of bodies. If we say: matter is 'heavy', we might mean that this predicate is only contingent; but it is nothing of the kind, for nothing in matter is without weight. Matter is rather weight itself. Heaviness constitutes the body and is the body. The same is the case with freedom and the will, since the free entity is the will. Will without freedom is an empty word, while freedom is actual only as will, as subject.

The following points should be noted about the connexion between the will and thought. Mind is in principle thinking, and man is distinguished from beast in virtue of thinking. But it must not be imagined that man is half thought and half will, and that he keeps thought in one pocket and will in another, for this would be a foolish idea. The distinction between thought and will is only that between the theoretical attitude and the practical. These, however, are surely not two faculties; the will is rather a special way of thinking, thinking translating itself into existence, thinking as the urge to give itself existence.

This distinction between thought and will may be described as follows. In thinking an object, I make it into thought and deprive it of its sensuous aspect; I make it into something which is directly and essentially mine. Since it is in thought that I am first by myself, I do not penetrate an object until I understand it; it then ceases to stand over against me and I have taken from it the character of its own which it had in opposition to me. Just as Adam said to Eve: 'Thou art flesh of my flesh and bone of my bone',* so mind says: 'This is mind of my mind and its foreign character has disappeared.' An idea is always a generalization, and generalization is a property of thinking. To generalize means to think. The ego is thought and so the universal. When I say 'I', I *eo ipso* abandon all my particular characteristics, my disposition, natural endowment, knowledge, and age. The ego is quite empty, a mere point, simple, yet active in this simplicity. The variegated canvas of the world is before me; I stand over against it; by my theoretical attitude to it I overcome its opposition to me and make its content my own. I am at home in the world when I know it, still more so when I have understood it. So much for the theoretical attitude.

The practical attitude, on the other hand, begins in thinking, in the ego itself, and it appears first as though opposed to thinking because, I mean, it sets up a sort of diremption. In so far as I am practical or active, i.e. in so far as I do something, I determine myself, and to determine myself simply means to posit a difference. But these differences which I posit are still mine all the same; the determinate volitions are mine and the aims which I struggle to realize belong to me. If I now let these determinations and differences go, i.e. if I posit them in the so-called external world, they none the less still remain mine. They are what I have done, what I have made; they bear the trace of my mind.

* [Genesis ii. 23.]

Such is the distinction between the theorical attitude and the practical, but now the tie between them must be described. The theoretical is essentially contained in the practical; we must decide against the idea that the two are separate, because we cannot have a will without intelligence. On the contrary, the will contains the theoretical in itself. The will determines itself and this determination is in the first place something inward, because what I will I hold before my mind as an idea; it is the object of my thought. An animal acts on instinct, is driven by an inner impulse and so it too is practical, but it has no will, since it does not bring before its mind the object of its desire. A man, however, can just as little be theoretical or think without a will, because in thinking he is of necessity being active. The content of something thought has the form of being; but this being is something mediated, something established through our activity. Thus these distinct attitudes cannot be divorced; they are one and the same; and in any activity, whether of thinking or willing, both moments are present.

5. *Paragraph 5.*

In this element of the will is rooted my ability to free myself from everything, abandon every aim, abstract from everything. Man alone can sacrifice everything, his life included; he can commit suicide. An animal cannot; it always remains merely negative, in an alien destiny to which it merely accustoms itself. Man is the pure thought of himself, and only in thinking is he this power to give himself universality, i.e. to extinguish all particularity, all determinacy. This negative freedom, or freedom as the Understanding conceives it, is one-sided; but a one-sided view always contains one essential factor and therefore is not to be discarded. But the Understanding is defective in exalting a single one-sided factor to be the sole and the supreme one.

In history this form of freedom is a frequent phenomenon. Amongst the Hindus, for instance, the highest life is held to be persistence in the bare knowledge of one's simple identity with oneself, fixation in this empty space of one's inner life, as light remains colourless in pure vision, and the sacrifice of every activity in life, every aim, and every project. In this way man becomes Brahma; there is no longer any distinction between the finite man and Brahma. In fact in this universality every difference has disappeared.

This form of freedom appears more concretely in the active fanaticism of both political and religious life. For instance, during the Terror in the French Revolution all differences of talent and authority were supposed to have been superseded. This period was an upheaval, an agitation, an irreconcilable hatred of everything particular. Since fanaticism wills an abstraction only, nothing articulated, it follows that, when distinctions appear, it finds them antagonistic to its own indeterminacy and annuls them. For this reason, the French Revolutionaries destroyed once more the institutions which they had made themselves, since any institution whatever is antagonistic to the abstract self-consciousness of equality.

6. *Paragraph 6.*

This second moment appears as the moment opposed to the first; it is to be grasped in its general character; it is intrinsic to freedom, although it does not constitute the whole of freedom. Here the ego leaves undifferentiated indeterminacy and proceeds to differentiate itself, to posit a content or object and so to give itself determinacy. My willing is not pure willing but the willing of something. A will which, like that expounded in Paragraph 5, wills only the abstract universal, wills nothing and is therefore no will at all. The particular volition is a restriction, since the will, in order to be a will, must restrict itself in some way or other. The fact that the will wills *something* is restriction, negation. Thus particularization is what as a rule is called finitude. Reflective thinking usually takes the first moment, i.e. indeterminacy, as the higher and absolute moment, while it regards restriction as a mere negation of this indeterminacy.* But this indeterminacy is itself only a negation in contrast with the determinate, with finitude; the ego is this solitude and absolute negation.† The indeterminate will is to this extent just as one-sided as the will rooted in sheer determinacy.

7. *Paragraph 7.*

What is properly called the will includes in itself both the preceding moments. The ego as such is in the first place pure activity, the universal which is by itself. But this universal determines itself and to that extent is no longer by itself but posits itself as an other and ceases to be the universal. Now the third moment is that, in its restriction, in this other, the will is by itself; in determining itself it still remains by itself and does not cease to keep hold of the universal. This moment, then, is the concrete concept of freedom, while the two previous moments have been found to be through and through abstract and one-sided.

Freedom in this sense, however, we already possess in the form of feeling—in friendship and love, for instance. Here we are not inherently one-sided; we restrict ourselves gladly in relating ourselves to another, but in this restriction know ourselves as ourselves. In this determinacy a man should not feel himself determined; on the contrary, since he treats the other as other, it is there that he first arrives at the feeling of his own self-hood. Thus freedom lies neither in indeterminacy nor in determinacy; it is both of these at once. The will which restricts itself simply to a *this* is the will of the capricious man who supposes that he is

---

* [Hegel is thinking e.g. of Spinoza's view that all determination is negation and that only the indeterminate, or the infinite, is real.]

† [i.e. the pure ego of Paragraph 5. It is 'alone' and negative because it is the renunciation of everything determinate and is simply turned in upon itself.]

not free unless he has *this* will. But the will is not tied to something restricted; it must go beyond the restriction, since the nature of the will is other than this one-sidedness and constraint. Freedom is to will something determinate, yet in this determinacy to be by oneself and to revert once more to the universal.

8. *Paragraph 8.*

The consideration of the will's determinacy properly belongs to the Understanding and is in the first instance not speculative. The will is determined in two senses, i.e. in both content and form. Its determinacy in form is its purpose and the fulfilment of its purpose. My purpose is at first only something inward, something subjective, but it should also become objective and cast aside the defect of mere subjectivity. At this point you may ask the why of this defect. If what has a defect does not at the same time stand above its defect, it cannot recognize the defect as a defect. An animal is a defective thing from our point of view, not from its own. My purpose, so far as it is still only mine, is felt by me as a defect since freedom and will are for me the unity of the subjective and objective. Hence the purpose must be established objectively and thereby it attains not a new one-sided character but only its realization.

9. *Paragraph 10.*

The will which is a will only in accordance with its concept is implicitly free but at the same time it is also unfree, for it would first become truly free as truly determinate content. At that point it is free in its own eyes, has freedom as its object, and *is* freedom. What is still only in accordance with its concept, what is merely implicit, is only immediate, only natural. In our ordinary ways of thinking we are familiar with this. The child is man implicit. At first it possesses reason only implicitly; it begins by being the potentiality of reason and freedom, and so is free only in accordance with its concept. Now what exists purely implicitly in this way does not yet exist in its actuality. Man is implicitly rational, but he must also become explicitly so by struggling to create himself, not only by going forth from himself but also by building himself up within.

10. *Paragraph 11.*

An animal too has impulses, desires, inclinations, but it has no will and must obey its impulse if nothing external deters it. Man, however, the wholly undetermined, stands above his impulses and may make them his own, put them in himself as his own. An impulse is something natural, but to put it into my ego depends on my will which thus cannot fall back on the plea that the impulse has its basis in nature.

11. *Paragraph 13.*

A will which resolves on nothing is no actual will; a characterless man never reaches a decision. The reason for indecision may also lie in a faintheartedness which knows that, in willing something determinate, it is engaging with finitude, imposing a barrier on itself and sacrificing the infinite; yet it will not renounce the totality after which it hankers. However 'beautiful'* such a disposition may be, it is nevertheless dead. As Goethe says: 'Whoever wills great achievement must be able to restrict himself.'† Only by resolving can a man step into actuality, however bitter to him his resolve may be. Inertia lacks the will to abandon the inward brooding which‡ allows it to retain everything as a possibility. But possibility is still less than actuality. The will which is sure of itself does not *eo ipso* lose itself in its determinate volition.

12. *Paragraph 15.*

Since it is possible for me to determine myself in this way or that, or in other words since I can choose, I possess the arbitrary will, and to possess this is what is usually called freedom. The choice which I have is grounded in the universality of the will, in the fact that I can make this or that mine. This thing that is mine is particular in content and therefore not adequate to me and so is separate from me; it is only potentially mine, while I am the potentiality of linking myself to it. Choice, therefore, is grounded in the indeterminacy of the ego and the determinacy of a content. Thus the will, on account of this content, is not free, although it has an infinite aspect in virtue of its form. No single content is adequate to it and in no single content is it really at grips with itself. Arbitrariness implies that the content is made mine not by the nature of my will but by chance. Thus I am dependent on this content, and this is the contradiction lying in arbitrariness. The man in the street thinks he is free if it is open to him to act as he pleases but his very arbitrariness implies that he is not free. When I will what is rational, then I am acting not as a particular individual but in accordance with the concepts of ethics in general. In an ethical action, what I vindicate is not myself but the thing. But in doing a perverse action, it is my singularity that I bring on to the centre of the stage. The rational is the high road where everyone travels, where no one is conspicuous. When great artists complete a masterpiece, we may speak of its inevitability, which means that the artist's idiosyncrasy has completely disappeared and no mannerism is detectable in it. Pheidias has no mannerisms; his figures themselves live and declare themselves. But the worse the artist is, the more we see in his work the artist, his singularity, his arbitrariness. If you stop at the consideration that, having an arbitrary

* [An allusion to the 'beautiful soul' of the Moravians, for which see Remark (*f*) to Paragraph 140.]

† [From the sonnet *Natur und Kunst* (Lasson). Hegel quotes inaccurately. Goethe's actual words may be translated: 'Whoever wills great achievement must first collect his energies; it is in restriction that a man first shows his mastery.']

‡ [Taking *der* as a misprint for *dem.*]

will, a man can will this or that, then of course his freedom consists in
that ability. But if you keep firmly in view that the content of his willing
is a given one, then he is determined thereby and in that respect at all
events is free no longer.

13. *Paragraph 17.*

Impulses and inclinations are in the first instance a content of the will,
and reflection alone stands above them. But these impulses begin to
impel themselves, they drive one another, stir each other, and all of them
demand satisfaction. Now if I neglect all the others and put myself in
one of them by itself, I find myself under a restriction which destroys me,
since just by so doing I have surrendered my universality, which is a
system of all impulses. But it is just as little help to make a mere hierarchy of impulses—a device to which the Understanding usually resorts
—since no criterion for so ordering them is available here, and therefore
the demand for such a hierarchy runs out in the tedium of generalities.

14. *Paragraph 18.*

The Christian doctrine that man is by nature evil is loftier than the
other which takes him to be by nature good. This doctrine is to be
understood as follows in accordance with the philosophical exegesis of it :*
As mind, man is a free substance which is in the position of not allowing
itself to be determined by natural impulse. When man's condition is
immediate and mentally undeveloped, he is in a situation in which he
ought not to be and from which he must free himself. This is the meaning of the doctrine of original sin without which Christianity would not
be the religion of freedom.

15. *Paragraph 20.*

In happiness thought has already a mastery over the natural force
of impulses, since the thinker is not content with the momentary but
requires happiness in a whole. This requirement is connected with
education in that it is education which vindicates a universal. In the
ideal of happiness, however, there are two moments: (i) a universal
which is above all particularity; but (ii) since the content of this universal is still only universal *pleasure*, there appears here once again the
singular, the particular, i.e. something finite, and a return must therefore
be made to impulse. Since the content of happiness lies in everyone's
subjectivity and feeling, this universal end is for its part particular, and
consequently there is still not present in it any genuine unity of form and
content.

16. *Paragraph 21.*

Truth in philosophy means that concept and external reality correspond. For example, the body is the external reality, while the soul is the

---

* [For Hegel's exegesis of this doctrine, see Paragraph 139 below and the
Addition to *Enc.*, § 24.]

concept; but soul and body ought to be adequate to one another. Therefore a corpse is still an existent, but its existence is no true existence; the
concept has left it; and for this reason a dead body putrefies. So a will
is truly a will only when what it wills, its content, is identical with itself,
when, that is to say, freedom wills freedom.

17. *Paragraph 22.*

Infinity has rightly been represented figuratively as a circle, because
a straight line goes on and on for ever and denotes the purely negative
and false infinite which, unlike the true infinite, has no return into
itself. The free will is truly infinite, since it is not just a potentiality and a
capacity. On the contrary, its external existence is its own inwardness,
is itself.

18. *Paragraph 26.*

It is usually supposed that subjective and objective stand rigidly in
opposition to one another. But this is not the case; it would be truer
to say that they pass over into each other, since they are not abstract
categories like positive and negative but already have a more concrete
significance.

Consider first the word 'subjective'. We may call 'subjective' an end
which is only the end of one specific individual subject. In this sense a
very bad work of art, one which is not quite the thing, is purely 'subjective'. The word may also be applied, however, to the content of the
will, and it is then almost synonymous with 'arbitrary'; a 'subjective'
content is that which belongs to the subject alone. Hence bad actions,
for example, are purely 'subjective'. But, further, it is just that pure
empty ego which may be called 'subjective', the ego which has itself
alone for its object and possesses the power to abstract from any other
content. Thus subjectivity sometimes means something wholly idiosyncratic, and at other times something with the highest of claims, since
everything which I am to recognize has also the task of becoming mine
and attaining its validity in me. Subjectivity is insatiably greedy to concentrate and drown everything in this single spring of the pure ego.

No less varied are the ways in which we may take 'objective'. We may
understand by it everything which we make an object to ourselves,
whether objective actualities or pure thoughts which we bring before
our minds. We also include under this category the immediacy of
existence in which the end is to be realized; even if the end is itself
wholly singular and subjective, we none the less call it 'objective' on its
appearance. But the 'objective' will is also that in which truth lies, and
thus God's will, the ethical will, is an 'objective' one. Finally, we may
also call 'objective' the will which is entirely absorbed in its object, as
for example the will of the child, which is rooted in trust and lacks
subjective freedom, and the will of the slave, which does not yet know
itself as free and on that account is a will-less will. In this sense any will

is 'objective' which acts under the guidance of an alien authority and has not yet completed its endless return into itself.

19. *Paragraph 32.*

The Idea must further determine itself within itself continually, since in the beginning it is no more than an abstract concept. But this original abstract concept is never abandoned. It merely becomes continually richer in itself and the final determination is therefore the richest. In this process its earlier, merely implicit, determinations attain their free self-subsistence but in such a way that the concept remains the soul which holds everything together and attains its own proper differentiation only through an immanent process. It therefore cannot be said that the concept reaches anything new; on the contrary, its final determination coincides with its first. Even if the concept seems in its existence to have become decomposed, this is nothing but a semblance revealing itself in due course as a semblance, because every single detail reverts at last to the concept of the universal. The empirical sciences are usually analyses of the content of our ideas, and when the single instance has been brought back to the common character, the latter is then called the concept. This is not our procedure; we only wish to look on at the way in which the concept determines itself and to restrain ourselves from adding thereto anything of our thoughts and opinions. What we acquire in this way, however, is a series of thoughts and another series of existent shapes of experience; to which I may add that the time order in which the latter actually appear is other than the logical order. Thus, for example, we cannot say that property *existed* before the family, yet, in spite of that, property must be dealt with first.

Consequently you might raise here the question why we do not begin at the highest point, i.e. with the concretely true. The answer is that it is precisely the truth in the form of a result that we are looking for, and for this purpose it is essential to start by grasping the abstract concept itself. What is actual, the shape in which the concept is embodied, is for us therefore the secondary thing and the sequel, even if it were itself first in the actual world. The development we are studying is that whereby the abstract forms reveal themselves not as self-subsistent but as false.

20. *Paragraph 33.*

In speaking of Right [*Recht*, i.e. *jus*] in this book, we mean not merely what is generally understood by the word, namely civil law, but also morality, ethical life, and world-history; these belong just as much to our topic, because the concept brings thoughts together into a true system. If the free will is not to remain abstract, it must in the first place give itself an embodiment, and the material primarily available to sensation for such an embodiment is things, i.e. objects outside us. This primary mode of freedom is the one which we are to become acquainted with as property, the sphere of formal and abstract right. To this sphere there also belong property in its mediated form as contract, and right in its infringement as crime and punishment. The freedom which we have here is what is called a person, i.e. the subject who is free, free indeed in his own eyes, and who gives himself an embodiment in things.

The sheer immediacy of external fact, however, is not an adequate embodiment of freedom, and the negation of this immediacy is the sphere of morality. I am now free, not merely in this immediate thing, but also after the immediacy has been superseded, i.e. I am free in myself, in my subjectivity. In this sphere the main thing is my insight, my intention, my purpose, because externality has now been established as of no importance. Good, however, which here is the universal end, should not simply remain in my inner life; it should be realized. That is to say, the subjective will demands that what is internal to it, i.e. its end, shall acquire an external existence, that the good shall in this way be consummated in the external world.

Morality and formal right are two abstract moments whose truth is ethical life alone. Hence ethical life is the unity of the will in its concept with the will of the individual, i.e. of the subject. Its first embodiment is again something natural, whose form is love and feeling—the family. Here the individual has transcended his shyness of personality and finds himself and his consciousness of himself in a whole. At the next stage, however, we see substantial unity disappearing along with ethical life proper; the family falls asunder and its members relate themselves to each other as self-subsistent, since their only bond of connexion is reciprocal need. This stage—civil society—has often been looked upon as the state, but the state is first present at the third stage, the stage of ethical life and the stage of mind in which the prodigious unification of self-subsistent individuality with universal substantiality has been achieved. The right of the state therefore stands above the preceding stages; it is freedom in its most concrete shape and as such is subordinate to one thing alone—the supreme absolute truth of the world-mind.

21. *Paragraph 34.*
When I say that 'the absolutely free will at the stage when its concept is abstract has the determinate character of immediacy', what I mean is this: when the concept had fully realized itself and when the embodiment of the concept had become nothing but the unfolding of its own self, then that state of affairs would be the fully developed Idea of the will. But at the start the concept is abstract, which means that all its determinations are contained within it, but still only contained within it; they are only implicit and not yet developed to be a totality in themselves. If I say 'I am free', the ego is still this inwardness, not confronted by an opposite. In morality, on the other hand, there is opposition from the start, since I stand in the moral sphere as a *single* will while the good is the *universal* even though it is within myself. Thus at that level, the will

has in itself the different factors of singularity and universality, and this gives it its specific character. But, to begin with, no such difference is present, since at the first stage, that of abstract unity, there is no advance and no mediation and so the will has the form of immediacy, of mere being. The essential point of view to be taken here then is that this original indeterminacy is itself a determinacy. The indeterminacy lies in the fact that there is as yet no difference between the will and its content; but indeterminacy, opposed to the determinate, acquires the character of being something determinate. It is abstract identity which here constitutes determinacy; the will therefore becomes a single will, a person.

22. Paragraph 35.

The abstract will, consciously self-contained, is personality. Man's chief glory is to be a person, and yet in spite of that the bare abstraction, 'person', is somewhat contemptuous in its very expression. 'Person' is essentially different from 'subject', since 'subject' is only the possibility of personality; every living thing of any sort is a subject. A person, then, is a subject aware of this subjectivity, since in personality it is of myself alone that I am aware. A person is a unit of freedom aware of its sheer independence. As *this* person, I know myself to be free in myself. I can abstract from everything, since nothing confronts me save pure personality, and yet as *this* person I am something wholly determinate, e.g. I am of a certain age, a certain stature, I occupy this space, and so on through whatever other details you like. Thus personality is at once the sublime and the trivial. It implies this unity of the infinite with the purely finite, of the wholly limitless with determinate limitation. It is the sublimity of personality that is able to sustain this contradiction, a contradiction which nothing merely natural contains or could endure.

23. Paragraph 37.

Since, in personality, particularity is not present as freedom, everything which depends on particularity is here a matter of indifference. To have no interest except in one's formal right may be pure obstinacy, often a fitting accompaniment of a cold heart and restricted sympathies. It is uncultured people who insist most on their rights, while noble minds look on other aspects of the thing. Thus abstract right is nothing but a bare possibility and, at least in contrast with the whole range of the situation, something formal. On that account, to have a right gives one a warrant, but it is not absolutely necessary that one should insist on one's rights, because that is only one aspect of the whole situation. That is to say, possibility is being which has the significance of also not being.

24. Paragraph 41.

The rationale of property is to be found not in the satisfaction of needs but in the supersession of the pure subjectivity of personality. In his property a person exists for the first time as reason. Even if my freedom is here realized first of all in an external thing, and so falsely realized, nevertheless abstract personality in its immediacy can have no other embodiment save one characterized by immediacy.

25. *Paragraph 42.*

Since a thing lacks subjectivity, it is external not merely to the subject but tô itself. Space and time are external in this way. As sentient, I am myself external, spatial, and temporal. As receptive of sensuous intuitions, I receive them from something which is external to itself. An animal can intuit, but the soul of an animal has for its object not its soul, itself, but something external.

26. *Paragraph 44.*

All things may become man's property, because man is free will and consequently is absolute, while what stands over against him lacks this quality. Thus everyone has the right to make his will the thing or to make the thing his will, or in other words to destroy the thing and transform it into his own; for the thing, as externality, has no end in itself; it is not infinite self-relation but something external to itself. A living thing too (an animal) is external to itself in this way and is so far itself a thing. Only the will is the infinite, absolute in contrast with everything other than itself, while that other is on its side only relative. Thus 'to appropriate' means at bottom only to manifest the pre-eminence of my will over the thing and to prove that it is not absolute, is not an end in itself. This is made manifest when I endow the thing with some purpose not directly its own. When the living thing becomes my property, I give to it a soul other than the one it had before, I give to it my soul. The free will, therefore, is the idealism which does not take things as they are to be absolute, while realism pronounces them to be absolute, even if they only exist in the form of finitude. Even an animal has gone beyond this realist philosophy since it devours things and so proves that they are not absolutely self-subsistent.

27. *Paragraph 46.*

In property my will is the will of a person; but a person is a unit and so property becomes the personality of this unitary will. Since property is the means whereby I give my will an embodiment, property must also have the character of being 'this' or 'mine'. This is the important doctrine of the necessity of private property. While the state may cancel private ownership in exceptional cases, it is nevertheless only the state that can do this; but frequently, especially in our day, private property has been re-introduced by the state. For example, many states have dissolved the monasteries, and rightly, for in the last resort no community has so good a right to property as a person has.

28. *Paragraph 47.*

Animals are in possession of themselves; their soul is in possession of their body. But they have no right to their life, because they do not will it.

29. *Paragraph 49.*

The equality which might be set up, e.g. in connexion with the distribution of goods, would all the same soon be destroyed again, because wealth depends on diligence. But if a project cannot be executed, it ought not to be executed. Of course men are equal, but only *qua* persons, that is, with respect only to the source from which possession springs; the inference from this is that everyone must have property. Hence, if you wish to talk of equality, it is this equality which you must have in view. But this equality is something apart from the fixing of particular amounts, from the question of how much I own. From this point of view it is false to maintain that justice requires everyone's property to be equal, since it requires only that everyone shall own property. The truth is that particularity is just the sphere where there is room for inequality and where equality would be wrong. True enough, men often lust after the goods of others, but that is just doing wrong, since right is that which remains indifferent to particularity.

30. *Paragraph 50.*

The points made so far have been mainly concerned with the proposition that personality must be embodied in property. Now the fact that the first person to take possession of a thing should also be its owner is an inference from what has been said. The first is the rightful owner, however, not because he is the first but because he is a free will, for it is only by another's succeeding him that he becomes the first.

31. *Paragraph 51.*

A person puts his will into a thing—that is just the concept of property, and the next step is the *realization* of this concept. The inner act of will which consists in saying that something is mine must also become recognizable by others. If I make a thing mine, I give to it a predicate, 'mine', which must appear in it in an external form and must not simply remain in my inner will. It often happens that children lay stress on their prior willing in preference to the seizure of a thing by others. But for adults this willing is not sufficient, since the form of subjectivity must be removed and must work its way beyond the subjective to objectivity.

32. *Paragraph 52.*

Fichte* has raised the question whether the matter too belongs to me

* [*Science of Rights*, § 19 A, pp. 298 ff. (so Lasson and Reyburn). Fichte is there maintaining that the farmer has no right to his land as such but only to its products, to its 'accidents', not to its 'substance'; he may not prevent others from grazing cattle on it after harvest, unless, in addition to cultivation rights, he has grazing rights for cattle of his own.]

if I impose a form on it. On his argument, after I had made a golden cup, it would have to be open to someone else to take the gold provided that in so doing he did no damage to my work. However separable the matter may be in thought, still in reality this distinction is an empty subtlety, because, if I take possession of a field and plough it, it is not only the furrow that is my property, but the rest as well, the furrowed earth. That is to say, I will to take this matter, the whole thing, into my possession; the matter therefore does not remain a *res nullius* nor does it remain its own property. Further, even if the matter remains external to the form which I have given to the object, the form is precisely a sign that I claim the thing as mine. The thing therefore does not remain external to my will or outside what I have willed. Hence there is nothing left to be taken into possession by someone else.

33. *Paragraph 54.*

These modes of taking possession involve the advance from the category of singularity to that of universality. It is only of a single thing that we can take possession physically, while marking a thing as mine is taking possession of it in idea. In the latter case I have an idea of the thing and mean that the thing as a whole is mine, not simply the part which I can take into my possession physically.

34. *Paragraph 55.*

Taking possession is always piece-meal in type; I take into possession no more than what I touch with my body. But here comes the second point: external objects extend further than I can grasp. Therefore, whatever I have in my grasp is linked with something else. It is with my hand that I manage to take possession of a thing, but its reach can be extended. What I hold in my hand—that magnificent tool which no animal possesses—can itself be a means to gripping something else. If I am in possession of something, the intellect immediately draws the inference that it is not only the immediate object in my grasp which is mine but also what is connected with it. At this point positive law must enact its statutes since nothing further on this topic can be deduced from the concept.

35. *Paragraph 56.*

This forming of an object may in practice assume the most various guises. In farming land I impose a form on it. Where inorganic objects are concerned, the imposition of a form is not always direct. For example, if I build a windmill, I have not imposed a form on the air, but I have formed something for utilizing the air, though I am not on that account at liberty to call the air mine, since I have not formed the air itself. Further, the preserving of game may be regarded as a way of forming game, for we preserve it with a view to maintaining the species.

[The same is true of] the taming of animals, only of course that is a more direct way of forming them and it depends on me to a greater extent.

36. *Paragraph 57.*

To adhere to man's absolute freedom—one aspect of the matter—is *eo ipso* to condemn slavery. Yet if a man is a slave, his own will is responsible for his slavery, just as it is its will which is responsible if a people is subjugated. Hence the wrong of slavery lies at the door not simply of enslavers or conquerors but of the slaves and the conquered themselves. Slavery occurs in man's transition from the state of nature to genuinely ethical conditions; it occurs in a world where a wrong is still right. At that stage wrong has validity and so is necessarily in place.

37. *Paragraph 58.*

To take possession by marking a thing is of all sorts of taking possession the most complete, since the mark is implicitly at work to some extent in the other sorts too. When I grasp a thing or form it, this also means in the last resort that I mark it, and mark it for others, in order to exclude them and show that I have put my will into the thing. The notion of the mark, that is to say, is that the thing does not count as the thing which it is but as what it is supposed to signify. A cockade, for instance, signifies citizenship of a state, though the colour has no connexion with the nation and represents not itself but the nation. By being able to give a mark to things and thereby to acquire them, man just shows his mastery over things.

38. *Paragraph 59.*

While in marking a thing I am taking possession in a universal way of the thing as such, the use of it implies a still more universal relation to the thing, because, when it is used, the thing in its particularity is not recognized but is negated by the user.* The thing is reduced to a means to the satisfaction of my need. When I and the thing meet, an identity is established and therefore one or other must lose its qualitative character. But I am alive, a being who wills and is truly affirmative; the thing on the other hand is something physical. Therefore the thing must be destroyed while I preserve myself. This, in general terms, is the prerogative and the principle of the organic.

39. *Paragraph 61.*

The relation of use to property is the same as that of substance to accident, inner to outer, force to its manifestation. Just as force exists

---

* [When I mark a thing as mine, I attribute to it the universal predicate 'mine' and 'recognize' its particular characteristics in the sense that I do not interfere with them. But when I use it I 'negate' its particular characteristics in the sense that I change them to suit my purpose. To mark land as mine by fencing it does not change its character, but to use it, e.g. by planting it, does.]

only in manifesting itself, so arable land is arable land only in bearing crops. Thus he who has the use* of arable land is the owner of the whole, and it is an empty abstraction to recognize still another property in the object itself.

40. *Paragraph 63.*

The qualitative disappears here in the form of the quantitative; that is to say, when I speak of 'need', I use a term under which the most various things may be brought; they share it in common and so become commensurable. The advance of thought here therefore is from a thing's specific quality to a character which is indifferent to quality, i.e. quantity. A similar thing occurs in mathematics. The definition of a circle, an ellipse, and a parabola reveals their specific difference. But, in spite of this, the distinction between these different curves is determined purely quantitatively, i.e. in such a way that the only important thing is a purely quantitative difference which rests on their coefficients alone, on purely empirical magnitudes. In property, the quantitative character which emerges from the qualitative is value. Here the qualitative provides the quantity with its quantum and in consequence is as much preserved in the quantity as superseded by it. If we consider the concept of value, we must look on the thing itself only as a symbol; it counts not as itself but as what it is worth. A bill of exchange, for instance, does not represent what it really is—paper; it is only a symbol of another universal—value. The value of a thing may be very heterogeneous; it depends on need. But if you want to express the value of a thing not in a specific case but in the abstract, then it is money which expresses this. Money represents any and every thing, though since it does not portray the need itself but is only a symbol of it, it is itself controlled by the specific value [of the commodity]. Money, as an abstraction, merely expresses this value.† It is possible in principle to be the owner of a thing without at the same time being the owner of its value. If a family can neither sell nor pawn its goods, it is not the owner of their value. But since this form of property is not in accordance with the concept of property, such restrictions on ownership (feudal tenure, testamentary trusts) are mostly in course of disappearing.

41. *Paragraph 64.*

Prescription rests on the presumption that I have ceased to regard the thing as mine. If a thing is to remain mine, my will must continue in it, and using it or keeping it safe shows this continuance. That public

---

* [i.e. the entire and permanent use of it—see Paragraph 62.]

† ['Prices are regulated by an average price; this in the last resort means that they are regulated by the value of the commodities. I say "in the last resort" because average prices do not (as Adam Smith, Ricardo, and others believed) directly coincide with the value of commodities.' Karl Marx: *Capital*, tr. by E. and C. Paul, London, 1929, p. 153.]

memorials may lose their value was frequently shown during the Reformation in the case of foundations, endowments, &c., for the Mass. The spirit of the old faith, i.e. of these foundations, had fled, and consequently they could be seized as private property.

42. *Paragraph 65.*

While prescription is an alienation with no direct expression of the will to alienate, alienation proper is an expression of my will, of my will no longer to regard the thing as mine. The whole matter may also be so viewed that alienation is seen to be a true mode of taking possession. To take possession of the thing directly is the first moment in property. Use is likewise a way of acquiring property. The third moment then is the unity of these two, taking possession of the thing by alienating it.*

43. *Paragraph 66.*

It is in the nature of the case that a slave has an absolute right to free himself and that if anyone has prostituted his ethical life by hiring himself to thieve and murder, this is an absolute nullity and everyone has a warrant to repudiate this contract. The same is the case if I hire my religious feeling to a priest who is my confessor, for such an inward matter a man has to settle with himself alone. A religious feeling which is partly in control of someone else is no proper religious feeling at all. The spirit is always one and single and should dwell in me. I am entitled to the union of my potential and my actual being.

44. *Paragraph 67.*

The distinction here explained is that between a slave and a modern domestic servant or day-labourer. The Athenian slave perhaps had an easier occupation and more intellectual work than is usually the case with our servants, but he was still a slave, because he had alienated to his master the whole range of his activity.

45. *Paragraph 70.*

A single person, I need hardly say, is something subordinate, and as such he must dedicate himself to the ethical whole. Hence if the state claims life, the individual must surrender it. But may a man take his own life? Suicide may at a first glance be regarded as an act of courage, but only the false courage of tailors and servant girls. Or again it may be looked upon as a misfortune, since it is inward distraction which leads to it. But the fundamental question is: Have I a *right* to take my life? The answer will be that I, as *this* individual, am not master of my life,

---

* [Taking possession is *positive* acquisition. Use is the *negation* of a thing's particular characteristics (see Paragraph 59). Alienation is the synthesis of positive and negative; it is negative in that it involves spurning the thing altogether; it is positive because it is only a thing completely mine which I can so spurn.]

because life, as the comprehensive sum of my activity, is nothing external to personality, which itself is this immediate personality. Thus when a person is said to have a right over his life, the words are a contradiction, because they mean that a person has a right over himself. But he has no such right, since he does not stand over himself and he cannot pass judgement on himself. When Hercules destroyed himself by fire and when Brutus fell on his sword, this was the conduct of a hero against his personality. But as for an unqualified right to suicide, we must simply say that there is no such thing, even for heroes.

46. *Paragraph 71.*

In a contract I hold property on the strength of a common will; that is to say, it is the interest of reason that the subjective will should become universal and raise itself to this degree of actualization. Thus in contract my will still has the character 'this', though it has it in community with another will. The universal will, however, still appears here only in the form and guise of community.

47. *Paragraph 75.*

It has recently become very fashionable to regard the state as a contract of all with all. Everyone makes a contract with the monarch, so the argument runs, and he again with his subjects. This point of view arises from thinking superficially of a mere unity of different wills. In contract, however, there are two identical wills who are both persons and wish to remain property-owners. Thus contract springs from a person's arbitrary will, an origin which marriage too has in common with contract. But the case is quite different with the state; it does not lie with an individual's arbitrary will to separate himself from the state, because we are already citizens of the state by birth. The rational end of man is life in the state, and if there is no state there, reason at once demands that one be founded. Permission to enter a state or leave it must be given by the state; this then is not a matter which depends on an individual's arbitrary will and therefore the state does not rest on contract, for contract presupposes arbitrariness. It is false to maintain that the foundation of the state is something at the option of all its members. It is nearer the truth to say that it is absolutely necessary for every individual to be a citizen. The great advance of the state in modern times is that nowadays all the citizens have one and the same end, an absolute and permanent end; it is no longer open to individuals, as it was in the Middle Ages, to make private stipulations in connexion with it.

48. *Paragraph 76.*

Contract implies two consenting parties and two things. That is to say, in a contract my purpose is both to acquire property and to surrender it. Contract is real when the action of both parties is complete, i.e. when both surrender and both acquire property, and when both remain property owners even in the act of surrender. Contract is formal where only one of the parties acquires property or surrenders it.

49. *Paragraph 78.*

Just as in the theory of property we had the distinction between ownership and possession, between the substance of the matter and its purely external side, so here in contract we have the difference between a common will—covenant—and a particular will—performance. It lies in the nature of contract that it should be an expression of both the common and the particular will of the parties, because in it will is related to will. The covenant, made manifest in a symbol, and its performance are quite distinct from each other amongst civilized peoples, though amongst savages they may coincide. In the forests of Ceylon there is a tribe of traders who put down their property and wait quietly until others come to put theirs down opposite. Here there is no difference between the dumb declaration of will and the performance of what is willed.

50. *Paragraph 80.*

In contract we drew the distinction between the covenant or stipulation (which made the property mine though it did not give me possession) and performance (which first gave me possession). Now if I am already the out-and-out owner of the property, the object of the pledge is to put me simultaneously in possession of the value of the property and thereby to guarantee the covenant's performance at the very time the covenant is made. Surety is a particular kind of pledge whereby someone gives his promise or pledges his credit as a guarantee for another's performance. Here a person fulfils the function which is fulfilled by a mere thing in the case of a pledge proper.

51. *Paragraph 81.*

In contract we had the relation of two wills as a common will. But this identical will is only relatively universal, posited as universal, and so is still opposed to the particular will. In contract, to be sure, making a covenant entails the right to require its performance. But this performance is dependent again on the particular will which *qua* particular may act in contravention of the principle of rightness. At this point then the negation, which was implicitly present in the principle of the will at the start, comes into view, and this negation is just what wrong is. In general terms, the course of events is that the will is freed from its immediacy and thus there is evoked out of the common will the particularity which then comes on the scene as opposed to the common will. In contract the parties still retain their particular wills; contract therefore is not yet beyond the stage of arbitrariness, with the result that it remains at the mercy of wrong.

52. *Paragraph 82.*

The principle of rightness, the universal will, receives its essential determinate character through the particular will, and so is in relation with something which is inessential. This is the relation of essence to its appearance. Even if the appearance corresponds with the essence, still, looked at from another point of view, it fails to correspond with it, since appearance is the stage of contingency, essence related to the inessential. In wrong, however, appearance proceeds to become a show. A show is a determinate existence inadequate to the essence, the empty disjunction and positing of the essence, so that in both essence and show the distinction of the one from the other is present as sheer difference. The show, therefore, is the falsity which disappears in claiming independent existence; and in the course of the show's disappearance the essence reveals itself as essence, i.e. as the authority of the show. The essence has negated that which negated it and so is corroborated. Wrong is a show of this kind, and, when it disappears, right acquires the character of something fixed and valid. What is here called the essence is just the principle of rightness, and in contrast with it the particular will annuls itself as a falsity. Hitherto the being of the right has been immediate only, but now it is actual because it returns out of its negation. The actual is the effectual; in its otherness it still holds fast to itself, while anything immediate remains susceptible of negation.

53. *Paragraph 83.*

Wrong is thus the show of the essence, putting itself as self-subsistent. If the show is only implicit and not explicit also, i.e. if the wrong passes in my eyes as right, the wrong is non-malicious. The show here is a show from the point of view of the right but not from my point of view.

The second type of wrong is fraud. Here the wrong is not a show from the point of view of the principle of rightness. The position is that I am making a show to deceive the other party. In fraud the right is in my eyes only a show. In the first case, the wrong was a show from the point of view of the right. In the second case, from my own point of view, from the point of view of wrong, right is only a show.

Finally, the third type of wrong is crime. This is wrong both in itself and from my point of view. But here I will the wrong and make no use of even a show of right. I do not intend the other against whom the crime is committed to regard the absolutely wrong as right. The distinction between crime and fraud is that in the latter the form of acting still implies a recognition of the right, and this is just what is lacking in crime.

54. *Paragraph 86.*

There is a specific ground for what is inherently right, and the wrong which I hold to be right I also defend on some ground or other. The nature of the finite and particular is to allow room for accidents. Thus here collisions must occur, because here we are on the level ot the finite. This first type of wrong-doing negates the particular will only, while universal rightness is respected. Consequently this is the most venial of the types of wrong-doing. If I say 'a rose is not red', I still recognize that it has a colour. Hence I do not deny the genus; all that I negate is the particular colour, red. Similarly, right is recognized here. Each of the parties wills the right and what is supposed to result to each is the right alone. The wrong of each consists simply in his holding that what he wants is right.

55. *Paragraph 87.*

At this second level of wrong-doing, the particular will is respected, but universal rightness is not. In fraud, the particular will is not infringed, because the party defrauded is saddled with what he is asked to believe is right. Thus the right which he demands is posited as something subjective, as a mere show, and it is this which constitutes fraud.

56. *Paragraph 89.*

In the case of non-malicious wrong and civil suits at law, no punishment is imposed, because in such cases the wrongdoer has willed nothing in opposition to the right. In the case of fraud, on the other hand, punishments come in, because here it *is* an infringement of right which is in question.

57. *Paragraph 90.*

Wrong in the full sense of the word is crime, where there is no respect either for the principle of rightness or for what seems right to me, where, then, both sides, the objective and the subjective, are infringed.

58. *Paragraph 93.*

Once the state has been founded, there can no longer be any heroes. They come on the scene only in uncivilized conditions. Their aim is right, necessary, and political, and this they pursue as their own affair. The heroes who founded states, introduced marriage and agriculture, did not do this as their recognized right, and their conduct still has the appearance of being their particular will. But as the higher right of the Idea against nature, this heroic coercion is a rightful coercion. Mere goodness can achieve little against the power of nature.

59. *Paragraph 94.*

Special attention must be paid at this point to the difference between the right and the moral. In morality, i.e. when I am reflected into myself, there is also a duality, because the good is my aim and I ought to determine myself by reference to that Idea. The good is embodied in my decision and I actualize the good in myself. But this embodiment is purely inward and therefore cannot be coerced. The law of the land therefore cannot possibly wish to reach as far as a man's disposition, because, so far as his moral convictions are concerned, he exists for himself alone, and force in that context is meaningless.

60. *Paragraph 96*.

How any given crime is to be punished cannot be settled by mere thinking; positive laws are necessary. But with the advance of education, opinions about crime become less harsh, and to-day a criminal is not so severely punished as he was a hundred years ago. It is not exactly crimes or punishments which change but the relation between them.

61. *Paragraph 97*.

A crime alters something in some way, and the thing has its existence in this alteration. Yet this existence is a self-contradiction and to that extent is inherently a nullity. The nullity is that the crime has set aside right as such. That is to say, right as something absolute cannot be set aside, and so committing a crime is in principle a nullity: and this nullity is the essence of what a crime effects. A nullity, however, must reveal itself to be such, i.e. manifest itself as vulnerable. A crime, as an act, is not something positive, not a first thing, on which punishment would supervene as a negation. It is something negative, so that its punishment is only a negation of the negation. Right in its actuality, then, annuls what infringes it and therein displays its validity and proves itself to be a necessary, mediated, reality.

62. *Paragraph 99*.

Feuerbach* bases his theory of punishment on threat and thinks that if anyone commits a crime despite the threat, punishment must follow because the criminal was aware of it beforehand. But what about the justification of the threat? A threat presupposes that a man is not free, and its aim is to coerce him by the idea of an evil. But right and justice must have their seat in freedom and the will, not in the lack of freedom on which a threat turns. To base a justification of punishment on threat is to liken it to the act of a man who lifts his stick to a dog. It is to treat a man like a dog instead of with the freedom and respect due to him as a man. But a threat, which after all may rouse a man to demonstrate his freedom in spite of it, discards justice altogether.—Coercion by psychological factors can concern only differences of quantity and quality in crime, not the nature of crime itself, and therefore any legal codes that may be products of the doctrine that crime is due to such coercion lack their proper foundation.

63. *Paragraph 100*.

Beccaria's requirement that men should give their consent to being punished is right enough, but the criminal gives his consent already by his very act. The nature of the crime, no less than the private will of the

* [P. J. A. Feuerbach (1775–1833). See his *Lehrbuch des gemeinen peinlichen Rechts* (1801). (Messineo).]

criminal, requires that the injury initiated by the criminal should be annulled. However that may be, Beccaria's endeavour to have capital punishment abolished has had beneficial effects. Even if neither Joseph II nor the French ever succeeded in entirely abolishing it, still we have begun to see which crimes deserve the death penalty and which do not. Capital punishment has in consequence become rarer, as in fact should be the case with this most extreme punishment.

64. *Paragraph 101.*

Retribution is the inner connexion and the identity of two conceptions which are different in appearance and which also exist in the world as two distinct and opposed events. Retribution is inflicted on the criminal and so it has the look of an alien destiny, not intrinsically his own. Nevertheless punishment, as we have seen, is only crime made manifest, i.e. is the second half which necessarily presupposes the first. Prima facie, the objection to retribution is that it looks like something immoral, i.e. like revenge, and that thus it may pass for something personal. Yet it is not something personal, but the concept itself, which carries out retribution. 'Vengeance is mine, saith the Lord', as the Bible says.* And if something in the word '*re*pay' calls up the idea of a particular caprice of the subjective will, it must be pointed out that what is meant is only that the form which crime takes is turned round against itself. The Eumenides sleep, but crime awakens them, and hence it is the very act of crime itself which vindicates itself.—Now although requital cannot simply be made specifically equal to the crime, the case is otherwise with murder, which is of necessity liable to the death penalty; the reason is that since life is the full compass of a man's existence, the punishment here cannot simply consist in a 'value', for none is great enough, but can consist only in taking away a second life.

65. *Paragraph 102.*

In that condition of society when there are neither magistrates nor laws, punishment always takes the form of revenge; revenge remains defective inasmuch as it is the act of a subjective will and therefore does not correspond with its content. Those who administer justice are persons, but their will is the universal will of the law and they intend to import into the punishment nothing except what is implied in the nature of the thing. The person wronged, however, views the wrong not as something qualitatively and quantitatively limited but only as wrong pure and simple, and in requiting the injury he may go too far, and this would lead to a new wrong. Amongst uncivilized peoples, revenge is deathless; amongst the Arabs, for instance, it can be checked only by superior force or by the impossibility of its satisfaction. A residue of revenge still lingers in comparatively modern legislation in those cases where it is left to the option of individuals whether to prosecute or not.

* [Romans xii. 19.]

66. *Paragraph 104.*

Truth entails that the concept shall be, and that this existence shall correspond with the concept. In the sphere of right, the will is existent in something external, but the next requirement is that the will should be existent in something inward, in itself. It must in its own eyes be subjectivity, and have itself as its own object. This relation to itself is the moment of affirmation, but it can attain it only by superseding its immediacy. The immediacy superseded in crime leads, then, through punishment, i.e. through the nullity of this nullity, to affirmation, i.e. to morality.

67. *Paragraph 106.*

So far as right in the strict sense was concerned, it was of no importance what my intention or my principle was. This question about the self-determination and motive of the will, like the question about its purpose, now enters at this point in connexion with morality. Since man wishes to be judged in accordance with his own self-determined choices, he is free in this relation to himself whatever the external situation may impose upon him. No one can break in upon this inner conviction of mankind, no violence can be done to it, and the moral will, therefore, is inaccessible. Man's worth is estimated by reference to his inward action and hence the standpoint of morality is that of freedom aware of itself.

68. *Paragraph 107.*

This entire category of the subjectivity of the will is once again a whole which, as subjectivity, must also have objectivity. It is in a subject that freedom can first be realized, since the subjective is the true material for this realization. But this embodiment of the will which we have called subjectivity is different from the will which has developed all its potentialities to actuality. That is to say, the will must free itself from this second one-sidedness of pure subjectivity in order to become the fully actualized will. In morality, it is man's private interest that comes into question, and the high worth of this interest consists precisely in the fact that man knows himself as absolute and is self-determined. The uneducated man allows himself to be constrained in everything by brute force and natural factors; children have no moral will but leave their parents to decide things for them. The educated man, however, develops an inner life and wills that he himself shall be in everything he does.

69. *Paragraph 108.*

In morality, self-determination is to be thought of as the pure restlessness and activity which can never arrive at anything that *is*. It is in the sphere of ethical life that the will is for the first time identical with the concept of the will and has this concept alone as its content. In the moral sphere the will still relates itself to its *implicit* principle and consequently its position is that of difference. The process through which this position develops is that whereby the subjective will becomes identified with its concept. Therefore the 'ought-to-be' which is never absent from the moral sphere becomes an 'is' only in ethical life. Further, this 'other' in relation to which the subjective will stands is two-sided: first, it is what is substantive, the concept; secondly, it is external fact. Even if the good were posited in the subjective will, that still would not give it complete realization.

70. *Paragraph 110.*

The content of the subjective or moral will has a specific character of its own, i.e. even if it has acquired the form of objectivity, it must still continue to enshrine my subjectivity, and my act is to count as mine only if on its inward side it has been determined by me, if it was my purpose, my intention. Beyond what lay in my subjective will I recognize nothing in its expression as mine. What I wish to see in my deed is my subjective consciousness over again.

71. *Paragraph 112.*

In dealing with formal right, I said [see Paragraph 38] that it contained prohibitions only, that hence a right action, strictly so called, was purely negative in character in respect of the will of others. In morality, on the other hand, my will has a positive character in relation to the will of others, i.e. the universal will is implicitly present within what the subjective will effects. To effect something is to produce something or to alter what already exists, and such changes have a bearing on the will of others. The concept of morality is the inner relation of the will to itself. But here it is not only *one* will; on the contrary its objectification implies at the same time the cancellation of the single will, and therefore, in addition, just because the character of one-sidedness vanishes, the positing of two wills and a positive bearing of each on the other. So far as rights are concerned, it makes no difference whether someone else's will may do something in relation to mine when I give my will an embodiment in property. In morality, however, the welfare of others too is in question, and this positive bearing cannot come on the scene before this point.

72. *Paragraph 114.*

If an action is to be moral, it must in the first place correspond with my purpose, since the moral will has the right to refuse to recognize in the resulting state of affairs what was not present inwardly as purpose. Purpose concerns only the formal principle that the external will shall be within me as something inward. On the other hand, in the second moment of the moral sphere, questions may be asked about the intention behind the action, i.e. about the relative worth of the action in relation to me. The third and last moment is not the relative worth of the action but its universal worth, the good.

In a moral action, then, there may be a breach first between what is purposed and what is really effected and achieved; secondly, between what is there externally as a universal will and the particular inner determination which I give to it. The third and last point is that the intention should be in addition the universal content of the action. The good is the intention raised to be the concept of the will.

73. *Paragraph 115.*

I am chargeable with what lay in my purpose and this is the most important point in connexion with crime. But responsibility contains only the quite external judgement whether I have or have not done some thing. It does not follow that, because I am responsible, the thing done may be imputed to me.

74. *Paragraph 117.*

The will has confronting it a state of affairs upon which it acts. But in order to know what this state of affairs is I must have an idea of it, and the responsibility is truly mine only in so far as I had knowledge of the situation confronting me. Such a situation is a presupposition of my volition and my will is therefore finite, or rather, since my will is finite, it has a presupposition of this kind. As soon as my thinking and willing is rational, I am no longer at this level of finitude, since the object on which I act is no longer an 'other' to me. Finitude, however, implies fixed limits and restrictions. I have confronting me an 'other' which is only contingent, something necessary in a purely external way; its path and mine may meet or diverge. Nevertheless, I am nothing except in relation to my freedom, and my will is responsible for the deed only in so far as I know what I am doing. Oedipus, who killed his father without knowing it, cannot be accused of parricide. The ancient penal codes, however, attached less weight to the subjective side of action, to imputability, than we do nowadays. That is why sanctuaries were instituted in ancient times for harbouring and protecting the fugitive from vengeance.

75. *Paragraph 118.*

The transition to intention depends on the fact that I accept responsibility only for what my idea of the situation was. That is to say, there can be imputed to me only what I knew of the circumstances. On the other hand, there are inevitable consequences linked with every action, even if I am only bringing about some single, immediate, state of affairs. The consequences in such a case represent the universal implicit within that state of affairs. Of course I cannot foresee the consequences—they might be preventable—but I must be aware of the universal character of my isolated act. The important point here is not the isolated thing but the whole, and that depends not on the differentia of the particular action, but on its universal nature. Now the transition from purpose to intention lies in the fact that I ought to be aware not simply of my single action but also of the universal which is conjoined with it. The universal which comes on the scene here in this way is what I have willed, my intention.

76. *Paragraph 119.*

It happens of course that circumstances may make an action miscarry to a greater or lesser degree. In a case of arson, for instance, the fire may not catch or alternatively it may take hold further than the incendiary intended. In spite of this, however, we must not make this a distinction between good and bad luck, since in acting a man must lay his account with externality. The old proverb is correct: 'A flung stone is the devil's.' To act is to expose oneself to bad luck. Thus bad luck has a right over me and is an embodiment of my own willing.

77. *Paragraph 121.*

In my own eyes, reflected into myself, I am a particular in correlation with the externality of my action. My end constitutes the content of the action, the content determinant of the action. Murder and arson, for example, are universals and so are not the positive content of my action *qua* the action of a subject. If one of these crimes has been committed, its perpetrator may be asked why he committed it. The murder was not done for the sake of murdering; the murderer had in view some particular positive end. But if we were to say that he murdered for the mere pleasure of murdering, then the purely positive content of the subject would surely be pleasure, and if that is the case then the deed is the satisfaction of the subject's will. Thus the motive of an act is, more particularly, what is called the 'moral' factor, and this has in that case the double meaning of the *universal* implicit in the purpose and the *particular* aspect of the intention. It is a striking modern innovation to inquire continually about the motives of men's actions. Formerly, the question was simply: 'Is he an honest man? Does he do his duty?' Nowadays we insist on looking into men's hearts and so we presuppose a gulf between the objectivity of actions and their inner side, the subjective motives. To be sure, the subject's volition must be considered; he wills something and the reason for what he wills lies within himself; he wills the satisfaction of his desire, the gratification of his passion. None the less, the good and the right are also a content of action, a content not purely natural but put there by my rationality. To make my freedom the content of what I will is a plain goal of my freedom itself. Therefore it is to take higher moral ground to find satisfaction *in* the action and to advance beyond the gulf between the self-consciousness of a man and the objectivity of his deed, even though to treat action as if it involved such a gulf is a way of looking at the matter characteristic of certain epochs in world history and in individual biography.

78. *Paragraph 123.*

Since the specifications of happiness are *given*, they are not true specifications of freedom, because freedom is not genuinely free in its own eyes except in the good, i.e. except when it is its own end. Consequently we may raise the question whether a man has the right to set before himself ends not freely chosen but resting solely on the fact that the subject is a living being. The fact that man is a living being, however, is not fortuitous, but in conformity with reason, and to that extent he has a right to make his needs his end. There is nothing degrading in being alive, and there is no mode of intelligent being higher than life in which existence would be possible. It is only the raising of the given to something self-created which yields the higher orbit of the good, although this distinction implies no incompatibility between the two levels.

79. *Paragraph 124.*

In magnis . . . voluisse sat est* is right in the sense that we ought to will something great. But we must also be able to achieve it, otherwise the willing is nugatory. The laurels of mere willing are dry leaves that never were green.

80. *Paragraph 126.*

The famous answer:† *Je n'en vois pas la nécessité*, given to the lampooner who excused himself with the words: *Il faut donc que je vive*, is apposite at this point. Life ceases to be necessary in face of the higher realm of freedom. When St. Crispin stole leather to make shoes for the poor, his action was moral but wrong and so inadmissible.

81. *Paragraph 127.*

Life as the sum of ends has a right against abstract right. If for example it is only by stealing bread that the wolf can be kept from the door, the action is of course an encroachment on someone's property, but it would be wrong to treat this action as an ordinary theft. To refuse to allow a man in jeopardy of his life to take such steps for self-preservation would be to stigmatize him as without rights, and since he would be deprived of his life, his freedom would be annulled altogether. Many diverse details have a bearing on the preservation of life, and when we have our eyes on the future we have to engage ourselves in these details. But the only thing that is necessary is to live *now*, the future is not absolute but ever exposed to accident. Hence it is only the necessity of the immediate present which can justify a wrong action, because not to do the action would in turn be to commit an offence,

---

* ['In great things to have willed is enough' (Propertius, II. x. 6).]
† [By Richelieu (Bolland).]

indeed the most wrong of all offences, namely the complete destruction
of the embodiment of freedom. *Beneficium competentiae* is relevant here,
because kinship and other close relationships imply the right to demand
that no one shall be sacrificed altogether on the altar of right.

82. *Paragraph 129.*

Every stage is really the Idea, but the earlier stages contain it only in
rather an abstract form. Thus for example, even the ego, as personality,
is already the Idea, though in its most abstract shape. The good, therefore, is the Idea further determined, the unity of the concept of the will
with the particular will. It is not something abstractly right, but something concrete whose contents are made up of both right and welfare alike.

83. *Paragraph 131.*

The good is the truth of the particular will, but the will is only that
into which it puts itself; it is not good by nature but can become what it
is only by its own labour. On the other hand, the good itself, apart from
the subjective will, is only an abstraction without that real existence
which it is to acquire for the first time through the efforts of that will.
Accordingly, the development of the good has three stages: (i) The good
should present itself to my volition as a particular will and I should
know it. (ii) I should myself say what is good and should develop its
particular specifications. (iii) Finally, the specification of the good on its
own account, the particularization of the good as infinite subjectivity
aware of itself. This inward specifying of what good is, is conscience.

84. *Paragraph 133.*

From my point of view the essence of the will is duty. Now if my
knowledge stops at the fact that the good is my duty, I am still going no
further than the abstract character of duty. I should do my duty for
duty's sake, and when I do my duty it is in a true sense my own objectivity which I am bringing to realization. In doing my duty, I am by
myself and free. To have emphasized this meaning of duty has constituted
the merit of Kant's moral philosophy and its loftiness of outlook.

85. *Paragraph 134.*

This is the same question as was put to Jesus when someone wished
to learn from him what he should do to inherit eternal life.* Good as a
universal is abstract and cannot be accomplished so long as it remains
abstract. To be accomplished it must acquire in addition the character
of particularity.

86. *Paragraph 135.*

While we laid emphasis above on the fact that the outlook of Kant's
philosophy is a high one in that it propounds a correspondence between
duty and rationality, still we must notice here that this point of view is

---

* [St. Luke x. 25.]

defective in lacking all articulation. The proposition: 'Act as if the maxim of thine action could be laid down as a universal principle', would be admirable if we already had determinate principles of conduct. That is to say, to demand of a principle that it shall be able to serve in addition as a determinant of universal legislation is to presuppose that it already possesses a content. Given the content, then of course the application of the principle would be a simple matter. In Kant's case, however, the principle itself is still not available and his criterion of non-contradiction is productive of nothing, since where there is nothing, there can be no contradiction either.

87. *Paragraph 136.*

We may speak in a very lofty strain about duty, and talk of the kind is uplifting and broadens human sympathies, but if it never comes to anything specific it ends in being wearisome. Mind demands particularity and is entitled to it. But conscience is this deepest inward solitude with oneself where everything external and every restriction has disappeared—this complete withdrawal into oneself. As conscience, man is no longer shackled by the aims of particularity, and consequently in attaining that position he has risen to higher ground, the ground of the modern world, which for the first time has reached this consciousness, reached this sinking into oneself. The more sensuous consciousness* of earlier epochs had something external and given confronting it, either religion or law. But conscience knows itself as thinking and knows that what alone has obligatory force for me is this that I think.

88. *Paragraph 137.*

When we speak of conscience, it may easily be thought that, in virtue of its form, which is abstract inwardness, conscience is at this point without more ado true conscience. But true conscience determines itself to will what is absolutely good and obligatory and is this self-determination. So far, however, it is only with good in the abstract that we have to do and conscience is still without this objective content and is but the infinite certainty of oneself.

89. *Paragraph 138.*

If we look more closely at this process of evaporation and see how all specific determinations disappear into this simple concept and then have to be condensed out of it again, what we find is that it is primarily due to the fact that everything recognized as right and duty may be proved by discursive thinking to be nugatory, restricted, and in all respects not absolute. On the other hand, just as subjectivity evaporates every content into itself, so it may develop it out of itself once more. Everything which arises in the ethical sphere is produced by this activity of

* [For the distinction between sense-consciousness and more highly developed types of consciousness, see Remarks to Paragraphs 21 and 35.]

mind. The moral point of view, however, is defective because it is purely abstract. When I am aware of my freedom as the *substance* of my being, I am inactive and do nothing. But if I proceed to act and look for principles on which to act, I grope for something determinate and then demand its deduction from the concept of the free will. While, therefore, it is right enough to evaporate right and duty into subjectivity, it is wrong if this abstract groundwork is not then condensed out again. It is only in times when the world of actuality is hollow, spiritless, and unstable, that an individual may be allowed to take refuge from actuality in his inner life. Socrates lived at the time of the ruin of the Athenian democracy. His thought vaporized the world around him and he withdrew into himself to search there for the right and the good. Even in our day there are cases when reverence for the established order is more or less lacking; man insists on having the authoritative as his *will*, as that to which he has granted recognition.

90. *Paragraph 139.*

The abstract self-certainty which knows itself as the basis of everything has in it the potentiality either of willing the universality of the concept or alternatively of taking a particular content as a principle and realizing that. The second alternative is evil, which therefore always includes the abstraction of self-certainty. It is only man who is good, and he is good only because he can also be evil. Good and evil are inseparable, and their inseparability is rooted in the fact that the concept becomes an object to itself, and as object it *eo ipso* acquires the character of difference. The evil will wills something opposed to the universality of the will, while the good will acts in accordance with its true concept.

The difficulty of the question as to how the will can be evil as well as good usually arises because we think of the will as related to itself purely positively and because we represent its volition as something determinate* confronting it, as the good. But the problem of the origin of evil may be more precisely put in the form: 'How does the negative come into the positive?' If we begin by presupposing that in the creation of the world God is the absolutely positive, then, turn where we will, we shall never discover the negative within that positive, since to talk of God's 'permitting' evil is to ascribe to him a passive relation to evil which is unsatisfactory and meaningless. In the representative thinking of religious mythology there is no comprehension of the origin of evil; i.e. the positive and the negative are not discovered in one another, there is only a representation of their succession and juxtaposition, so that it is from outside that the negative comes to the positive. But this cannot satisfy thought, which demands a reason and a necessity and insists on apprehending the negative as itself rooted in the positive. Now the solution of the problem, the way the concept treats the matter,

* [Reading *und sein Wollen als ein Bestimmtes*, with Lasson.]

is already contained in the concept, since the concept, or to speak more concretely, the Idea, has it in its essence to differentiate itself and to posit itself negatively. If we adhere to the purely positive, i.e. if we rest in the unmixed good which is supposed to be good at its source, then we are accepting an empty category of the Understanding which clings to abstractions and one-sided categories of this kind and by the very asking of this question makes it a difficult one. If we begin with the standpoint of the concept, however, we apprehend the positive as activity and as self-distinction. Evil and good alike have their origin in the will and the will in its concept is both good and evil.

The natural will is implicitly the contradiction of self-distinction, of being both inwardness and also self-awareness.* To maintain then that evil implies the further point that man is evil in so far as his will is natural would be to contradict the usual idea that it is just the natural will which is guiltless and good. But the natural will stands in opposition to the content of freedom, and the child and the uneducated man, whose wills are only natural, are for that very reason liable to be called to account for their actions only in a less degree. Now when we speak of man, we mean not the child but the self-conscious adult, and when we speak of good, we mean the knowledge of it. It is doubtless true that the natural is inherently innocent, neither good nor bad, but when it is drawn into the orbit of the will which is free and knows that it is free, it acquires the character of not being free and is therefore evil. When man *wills* the natural, it is no longer merely natural, but the negative opposed to the good, i.e. to the concept of the will.

On the other hand, if it is now objected that since evil is rooted in the concept and inevitable, man would be guiltless if he committed it, our reply must be that a man's decision is his own act, and his own act is freely chosen and his own responsibility. In the religious legend it is said that man is as God when he knows good and evil;† and it is true that this likeness to God is present in such knowledge in that the inevitability here is no natural inevitability since on the contrary the decision is really the transcendence of this duality of good and evil. When both good and evil are placed before me, I have a choice between the two; I can decide between them and endow my subjective character with either. Thus the nature of evil is that man may will it but need not.

91. *Paragraph 140.*

Representative thinking may go further and pervert the evil will into a show of goodness. Although it cannot alter the nature of evil, it can invest it with a show of goodness. Since every action has a positive aspect, and since the category of good as opposed to evil is likewise

---

* [i.e. both universal inner principle and also awareness of self as particular, as opposed to the universal.]

† [Genesis, iii. 5, i.e. after doing what had been forbidden.]

reduced to positivity, I may claim that my action in its bearing on my intention is good. Thus evil has good linked with it not only in my consciousness but also if we look at my action on its positive side. When self-consciousness gives out, to others only, that its action is good, this form of subjectivism is hypocrisy. But if it goes so far as to claim that the deed is good in its own eyes also, then we have a still higher peak of the subjectivism which knows itself as absolute. For this type of mind absolute good and absolute evil have both vanished, and the subject is therefore at liberty to pass himself off at discretion as anything he likes. This is the position of the absolute sophistry which usurps the office of lawgiver and rests the distinction between good and evil on its own caprice. The chief hypocrites are the pious ones (the Tartuffes) who are punctilious in every ritual observance and may even be religious to all appearance, while yet they do just as they please. There is little mention of hypocrites nowadays, partly because the accusation of hypocrisy seems to be too harsh; partly, however, because hypocrisy in its naïve form has more or less disappeared. This downright falsehood, this veneer of goodness, has now become too transparent not to be seen through, and the divorce between doing good with one hand and evil with the other no longer occurs, since advancing culture has weakened the opposition between these categories.

Instead, hypocrisy has now assumed the subtler form of Probabilism, which involves the agent's attempt to represent a transgression as something good from the point of view of his private conscience. This doctrine can only arise when the moral and the good are determined by authority, with the result that there are as many reasons as there are authorities for supposing that evil is good. Casuist theologians, Jesuits especially, have worked up these cases of conscience and multiplied them *ad infinitum*.

These cases have now been elaborated to such a high degree of subtlety that numerous clashes have arisen between them, and the opposition between good and evil has become so weak that in single instances they appear to turn into one another. The only desideratum now is probability, i.e. something approximately good, something which may be supported by any single reason or authority. Thus the special characteristic of this attitude is that its content is purely abstract; it sets up the concrete content as something inessential or rather abandons it to bare opinion. On this principle, anyone may have committed a crime and yet have willed the good. For example, if a bad character is murdered, the positive side of the action may be given out to be the withstanding of evil and the will to diminish it.

Now the next step beyond Probabilism is that it is no longer a question of someone else's statement or authority; it is a question only of the subject himself, i.e. of his own conviction—a conviction which alone is able to make a thing good. The defect here is that everything is supposed to fall within the orbit of conviction alone and that the absolutely right, for which this conviction should be only the form, no longer exists. It is certainly not a matter of indifference whether I do something by habit and custom or because I am actuated throughout by the truth which underlies these. But objective truth is still different from my conviction, because conviction lacks the distinction between good and evil. Conviction always remains conviction, and the bad could only be that of which I am not convinced.

Now while this obliteration of good and evil implies a very lofty attitude, there is involved in this attitude the admission that it is subject to error, and to that extent it is brought down from its pedestal into mere fortuitousness and seems undeserving of respect. Now this form of subjectivism is irony, the consciousness that this principle of conviction is not worth much and that, lofty criterion though it be, it is only caprice that governs it. This attitude is really a product of Fichte's philosophy, which proclaims that the Ego is absolute, i.e. is absolute certainty, the 'universal self-hood' which advances through a course of further development to objectivity.* Of Fichte himself it cannot properly be said that he made subjective caprice a guiding principle in ethics, but, later on, this principle of the mere particular, in the sense of 'particular self-hood', was deified by Friedrich von Schlegel with reference to the good and the beautiful. As a result, he made objective goodness only an image of my conviction, receiving support from my efforts alone, and dependent for its appearance and disappearance on me as its lord and master. If I relate myself to something objective, it vanishes at the same moment before my eyes, and so I hover over a pit of nothingness, summoning shapes from the depths and annihilating them. This supreme type of subjectivism can emerge only in a period of advanced culture when faith has lost its seriousness, and its essence is simply 'all is vanity'.

92. *Paragraph 141.*

Each of the two principles hitherto discussed, namely good in the abstract and conscience, is defective in lacking its opposite. Good in the abstract evaporates into something completely powerless, into which I may introduce any and every content, while the subjectivity of mind becomes just as worthless because it lacks any objective significance. Thus a longing may arise for an objective order in which man gladly degrades himself to servitude and total subjection, if only to escape the torment of vacuity and negation. Many Protestants have recently gone over to the Roman Catholic Church, and they have done so because they found their inner life worthless and grasped at something fixed, at

* [For further comments on Fichte's views, with references, see e.g. *History of Philosophy*, iii. 481 ff.]

a support, an authority, even if it was not exactly the stability of thought which they caught.

The unity of the subjective with the objective and absolute good is ethical life, and in it we find the reconciliation which accords with the concept. Morality is the form of the will in general on its subjective side. Ethical life is more than the subjective form and the self-determination of the will; in addition it has as its content the concept of the will, namely freedom. The right and the moral cannot exist independently; they must have the ethical as their support and foundation, for the right lacks the moment of subjectivity, while morality in turn possesses that moment alone, and consequently both the right and the moral lack actuality by themselves. Only the infinite, the Idea, is actual. Right exists only as a branch of a whole or like the ivy which twines itself round a tree firmly rooted on its own account.

93. *Paragraph 144.*

Throughout ethical life the objective and subjective moments are alike present, but both of them are only its forms. Its substance is the good, i.e. the objective is filled with subjectivity. If we consider ethical life from the objective standpoint, we may say that in it we are ethical unselfconsciously. In this sense, Antigone proclaims that 'no one knows whence the laws come; they are everlasting',* i.e. their determinate character is absolute and has its source in the nature of the thing. None the less, however, the substance of ethical life has a consciousness also, though the status of this consciousness is never higher than that of being one moment.

94. *Paragraph 145.*

Since the laws and institutions of the ethical order make up the concept of freedom, they are the substance or universal essence of individuals, who are thus related to them as accidents only. Whether the individual exists or not is all one to the objective ethical order. It alone is permanent and is the power regulating the life of individuals. Thus the ethical order has been represented by mankind as eternal justice, as gods absolutely existent, in contrast with which the empty business of individuals is only a game of see-saw.

95. *Paragraph 149.*

Duty is a restriction only on the self-will of subjectivity. It stands in the way only of that abstract good to which subjectivity adheres. When we say: 'We want to be free', the primary meaning of the words is simply: 'We want abstract freedom', and every institution and every organ of the state passes as a restriction on freedom of that kind. Thus duty is not a restriction on freedom, but only on freedom in the abstract,

---

* [This misquotation of Sophocles: *Antigone*, ll. 450-7, may be due to the transcriber of Hegel's lecture, because the lines are quoted correctly in the **Remark to Paragraph 166.**]

i.e. on unfreedom. Duty is the attainment of our essence, the winning of *positive* freedom.

96. *Paragraph 150.*

To conform to the ethical order on this or that particular occasion is hardly enough to make a man virtuous; he is virtuous only when this mode of behaviour is a fixed element in his character. Virtue is rather like ethical virtuosity,* and the reason why we speak of virtue less nowadays than formerly is that ethical living is less like the form of a particular individual's character. The French are *par excellence* the people who speak most of virtue, and the reason is that amongst them ethical life in the individual† is more a matter of his own idiosyncrasies or a natural mode of conduct. The Germans, on the other hand, are more thoughtful, and amongst them the same content acquires the form of universality.

97. *Paragraph 151.*

Just as nature has its laws, and as animals, trees, and the sun fulfil their law, so custom (*Sitte*) is the law appropriate to free mind. Right and morality are not yet what ethics (*Sitte*) is, namely mind. In right, particularity is still not the particularity of the concept, but only that of the natural will. So, too, at the standpoint of morality, self-consciousness is not yet *mind's* consciousness of itself. At that level it is only the worth of the subject in himself that is in question, i.e. the subject who determines himself by reference to good in contrast with evil, who still has self-will as the form of his willing. Here, however, at the standpoint of ethics, the will is mind's will and it has a content which is substantive and in conformity with itself.

Education is the art of making men ethical. It begins with pupils whose life is at the instinctive level and shows them the way to a second birth, the way to change their instinctive nature into a second, intellectual, nature, and makes this intellectual level habitual to them. At this point the clash between the natural and the subjective will disappears, the subject's internal struggle dies away. To this extent, habit is part of ethical life as it is of philosophic thought also, since such thought demands that mind be trained against capricious fancies, and that these be destroyed and overcome to leave the way clear for rational thinking. It is true that a man is killed by habit, i.e. if he has once come to feel completely at home in life, if he has become mentally and physically dull, and if the clash between subjective consciousness

---

* [Heroes ('ethical virtuosi') lived in uncivilized conditions (see Addition to Paragraph 93) and there was no ethical life in society as they found it; but since they introduced ethical institutions for the first time (see Remarks to Paragraphs 167 and 203), they displayed virtue as a kind of virtuosity. Nowadays, ethical life is common to everyone and consists in conformity to the existing order, not in divergence from it.]

† [Reading *das Sittliche am Individuum*, with Lasson.]

and mental activity has disappeared; for man is active only in so far as he has not attained his end and wills to develop his potentialities and vindicate himself in struggling to attain it. When this has been fully achieved, activity and vitality are at an end, and the result—loss of interest in life—is mental or physical death.

98. *Paragraph 153.*

The educational experiments, advocated by Rousseau in *Émile*, of withdrawing children from the common life of every day and bringing them up in the country, have turned out to be futile, since no success can attend an attempt to estrange people from the laws of the world. Even if the young have to be educated in solitude, it is still useless to hope that the fragrance of the intellectual world will not ultimately permeate this solitude or that the power of the world mind is too feeble to gain the mastery of those outlying regions. It is by becoming a citizen of a good state that the individual first comes into his right.

99. *Paragraph 155.*

A slave can have no duties; only a free man has them. If all rights were put on one side and all duties on the other, the whole would be dissolved, since their identity alone is the fundamental thing, and it is to this that we have here to hold fast.

100. *Paragraph 156.*

Ethical life is not abstract like the good, but is intensely actual. Mind has actuality, and individuals are accidents of this actuality. Thus in dealing with ethical life, only two views are possible: either we start from the substantiality of the ethical order, or else we proceed atomistically and build on the basis of single individuals. This second point of view excludes mind because it leads only to a juxtaposition. Mind, however, is not something single, but is the unity of the single and the universal.

101. *Paragraph 158.*

Love means in general terms the consciousness of my unity with another, so that I am not in selfish isolation but win my self-consciousness only as the renunciation of my independence and through knowing myself as the unity of myself with another and of the other with me. Love, however, is feeling, i.e. ethical life in the form of something natural. In the state, feeling disappears; there we are conscious of unity as law; there the content must be rational and known to us. The first moment in love is that I do not wish to be a self-subsistent and independent person and that, if I were, then I would feel defective and incomplete. The second moment is that I find myself in another person, that I count for something in the other, while the other in turn comes to count for something in me. Love, therefore, is the most tremendous contradiction; the Understanding cannot resolve it since there is nothing more stubborn than this point (*Punktualität*) of self-consciousness which is negated and which nevertheless I ought to possess as affirmative. Love is at once the propounding and the resolving of this contradiction. As the resolving of it, love is unity of an ethical type.

102. *Paragraph 159.*

The right of the family properly consists in the fact that its substantiality should have determinate existence. Thus it is a right against externality and against secessions from the family unity. On the other hand, to repeat, love is a feeling, something subjective, against which unity cannot make itself effective. The demand for unity can be sustained, then, only in relation to such things as are by nature external and not conditioned by feeling.

103. *Paragraph 161.*

Marriage is in essence an ethical tie. Formerly, especially in most systems of natural law, attention was paid only to the physical side of marriage or to its natural character. Consequently, it was treated only as a sex relationship, and this completely barred the way to its other characteristics. This is crude enough, but it is no less so to think of it as only a civil contract, and even Kant does this. On this view, the parties are bound by a contract of mutual caprice, and marriage is thus degraded to the level of a contract for reciprocal use. A third view of marriage is that which bases it on love alone, but this must be rejected like the other two, since love is only a feeling and so is exposed in every respect to contingency, a guise which ethical life may not assume. Marriage, therefore, is to be more precisely characterized as ethico-legal (*rechtlich sittliche*) love, and this eliminates from marriage the transient, fickle, and purely subjective aspects of love.

104. *Paragraph 162.*

Amongst peoples who hold the female sex in scant respect, marriages are arranged by the parents at will without consulting the young people. The latter raise no objection, since at that level of culture the particularity of feeling makes no claims for itself. For the woman it is only a matter of getting a husband, for the man, of getting a wife. In other social conditions, considerations of wealth, connexions, political ends, may be the determining factor. In such circumstances, great hardships may arise through making marriage a means to other ends. Nowadays, however, the subjective origin of marriage, the state of being in love, is regarded as the only important originating factor. Here the position is represented to be that a man must wait until his hour has struck and that he can bestow his love only on one specific individual.

105. *Paragraph 163.*

The distinction between marriage and concubinage is that the latter is chiefly a matter of satisfying natural desire, while this satisfaction is made secondary in the former. It is for this reason that physical experiences may be mentioned in married life without a blush, although outside the marriage tie their mention would produce a sense of shame. But it is on this account, too, that marriage must be regarded as in principle indissoluble, for the end of marriage is the ethical end, an end so lofty that everything else is manifestly powerless against it and made subject to it. Marriage is not to be dissolved because of passion, since passion is subordinate to it. But it is not indissoluble except in principle, since as Christ says, only 'for the hardness of your heart'* is divorce established. Since marriage has feeling for one of its moments, it is not absolute but weak and potentially dissoluble. Legislators, however, must make its dissolution as difficult as possible and uphold the right of the ethical order against caprice.

106. *Paragraph 164.*

Friedrich von Schlegel in his *Lucinde,*† and a follower of his in the *Briefe eines Ungenannten,*‡ have put forward the view that the wedding ceremony is superfluous and a formality which might be discarded. Their reason is that love is, so they say, the substance of marriage and that the celebration therefore detracts from its worth. Surrender to sensual impulse is here represented as necessary to prove the freedom and inwardness of love—an argument not unknown to seducers.

It must be noticed in connexion with sex-relations that a girl in surrendering her body loses her honour. With a man, however, the case is otherwise, because he has a field for ethical activity outside the family. A girl is destined in essence for the marriage tie and for that only; it is therefore demanded of her that her love shall take the form of marriage and that the different moments in love shall attain their true rational relation to each other.

107. *Paragraph 166.*

Women are capable of education, but they are not made for activities which demand a universal faculty such as the more advanced sciences, philosophy, and certain forms of artistic production. Women may have happy ideas, taste, and elegance, but they cannot attain to the ideal.§ The difference between men and women is like that between animals and plants. Men correspond to animals, while women correspond to plants because their development is more placid and the principle that underlies it is the rather vague unity of feeling. When women hold the

---

* [St. Matthew, xix. 8, St. Mark, x. 5.]

† [Berlin. 1799.]

‡ Lübeck and Leipzig, 1800. [' *Anonymous Letters* ', i.e. Schleiermacher's anonymously published defence of *Lucinde* against the charge of immorality.]

§ [*Ideale*. By this word Hegel means 'the Beautiful and whatever tends thither' (*Science of Logic*, i. 163, footnote). It is to be distinguished, therefore, from *Ideelle*, for which see Note 36 to Paragraph 7.]

helm of government, the state is at once in jeopardy, because women regulate their actions not by the demands of universality but by arbitrary inclinations and opinions. Women are educated—who knows how?—as it were by breathing in ideas, by living rather than by acquiring knowledge. The status of manhood, on the other hand, is attained only by the stress of thought and much technical exertion.

108. *Paragraph 168.*

A sense of shame—to go no farther—is a bar to consanguineous marriage. But this repugnance finds justification in the concept of the thing. What is already united, I mean, cannot be united for the first time by marriage. It is a commonplace of stock-breeding that the offspring is comparatively weak when animals of the same stock are mated, since if there is to be unification there must first be division. The force of generation, as of mind, is all the greater, the greater the oppositions out of which it is reproduced. Familiarity, close acquaintance, the habit of common pursuits, should not precede marriage; they should come about for the first time within it. And their development has all the more value, the richer it is and the more facets it has.

109. *Paragraph 172.*

In many legal codes the wider circle of the clan is adhered to, and this is regarded as the essential bond, while the other bond, that of each particular family, appears less important in comparison. Thus in the older Roman law, the wife in the easily dissolved type of marriage stood in a closer relation to her kinsfolk than to her husband and children. Under feudal law, again, the maintenance of the *splendor familiae* made it necessary for only the males of the family to be reckoned members and for the clan as a whole to count as the important thing, while the newly founded family disappeared in comparison. Nevertheless, each new family is the essential thing in contrast with the more remote connexions of clan-kinship, and parents and children form the nucleus proper as opposed to the clan, which is also in a certain sense called a 'family'. Hence an individual's relation to his wealth must have a more essential connexion with his marriage than with the wider circle of his kin.

110. *Paragraph 173.*

The relation of love between husband and wife is in itself not objective, because even if their feeling is their substantial unity, still this unity has no objectivity. Such an objectivity parents first acquire in their children, in whom they can see objectified the entirety of their union. In the child, a mother loves its father and he its mother. Both have their love objectified for them in the child. While in their goods their unity is embodied only in an external thing, in their children it is embodied in a spiritual one in which the parents are loved and which they love.

111. *Paragraph 174.*

Man has to acquire for himself the position which he ought to attain; he is not already in possession of it by instinct. It is on this fact that the child's right to education is based. Peoples under patriarchal government are in the same position as children; they are fed from central stores and not regarded as self-subsistent and adults. The services which may be demanded from children should therefore have education as their sole end and be relevant thereto; they must not be ends in themselves, since a child in slavery is in the most unethical of all situations whatever. One of the chief factors in education is discipline, the purport of which is to break down the child's self-will and thereby eradicate his purely natural and sensuous self. We must not expect to achieve this by mere goodness, since it is just the immediate will which acts on immediate fancies and caprices, not on reasons and representative thinking. If we advance reasons to children, we leave it open to them to decide whether the reasons are weighty or not, and thus we make everything depend on their whim. So far as children are concerned, universality and the substance of things reside in their parents, and this implies that children must be obedient. If the feeling of subordination, producing the longing to grow up, is not fostered in children, they become forward and impertinent.

112. *Paragraph 175.*

As a child, man must have lived with his parents encircled by their love and trust, and rationality must appear in him as his very own subjectivity. In the early years it is education by the mother especially which is important, since ethical principles must be implanted in the child in the form of feeling. It is noteworthy that on the whole children love their parents less than their parents love them. The reason for this is that they are gradually increasing in strength, and are learning to stand on their own feet, and so are leaving their parents behind them. The parents, on the other hand, possess in their children the objective embodiment of their union.

113. *Paragraph 176.*

It is because marriage depends entirely on feeling, something subjective and contingent, that it may be dissolved. The state, on the other hand, is not subject to partition, because it rests on law. To be sure, marriage *ought* to be indissoluble, but here again we have to stop at this 'ought'; yet, since marriage is an ethical institution, it cannot be dissolved at will but only by an ethical authority, whether the church or the law-court. If the parties are completely estranged, e.g. owing to adultery, then even the ecclesiastical authority must permit divorce.

114. *Paragraph 180.*

In earlier times, a Roman father had the right to disinherit his children and even kill them. Later he lost both these rights. Attempts were made to forge into a legal system this incoherence between un-ethical institutions and devices to rob them of that character, and it is the retention of this incoherence which constitutes the deficiency and difficulty of the German law of inheritance. To be sure, the right to make a will must be conceded; but in conceding it our point of view must be that this right of free choice arises or is magnified with the dispersion and estrangement of the members of the family. Further, the so-called 'family of friends' which testamentary disposition brings with it may be admitted only in defect of members of the family proper, i.e. of spouse and children. To make a will at all entails something obnoxious and disagreeable, because in making it I reveal the names of my favourites. Favour, however, is arbitrary; it may be gained sur-reptitiously by a variety of expedients, it may depend on all sorts of foolish reasons, and as a condition of having his name included in a will, a beneficiary may be required to subject himself to the most abject servilities. In England, the home of all sorts of eccentricity, there is no end to the folly and whimsicality of bequests.

115. *Paragraph 181.*

The starting-point for the universal here is the self-subsistence of the particular, and the ethical order seems therefore to be lost at this point, since it is precisely the identity of the family which consciousness takes to be the primary thing, the divine, and the source of obligation. Now, however, a situation arises in which the particular is to be my primary determining principle, and thus my determinacy by ethical factors has been annulled. But this is nothing but a pure mistake, since, while I suppose that I am adhering to the particular, the universal and the necessity of the link between particulars remains the primary and essential thing. I am thus altogether on the level of show, and while my particularity remains my determining principle, i.e. my end, I am for that very reason the servant of the universal which properly retains power over me in the last resort.

116. *Paragraph 182.*

Civil society is the [stage of] difference which intervenes between the family and the state, even if its formation follows later in time than that of the state, because, as [the stage of] difference, it presupposes the state; to subsist itself, it must have the state before its eyes as something self-subsistent. Moreover, the creation of civil society is the achieve-ment of the modern world which has for the first time given all deter-minations of the Idea their due. If the state is represented as a unity of different persons, as a unity which is only a partnership, then what is really meant is only civil society. Many modern constitutional lawyers have been able to bring within their purview no theory of the state but this. In civil society each member is his own end, everything else is nothing to him. But except in contact with others he cannot attain the whole compass of his ends, and therefore these others are means to the end of the particular member. A particular end, however, assumes the form of universality through this relation to other people, and it is attained in the simultaneous attainment of the welfare of others. Since particularity is inevitably conditioned by universality, the whole sphere of civil society is the territory of mediation where there is free play for every idiosyncrasy, every talent, every accident of birth and fortune, and where waves of every passion gush forth, regulated only by reason glinting through them. Particularity, restricted by universality, is the only standard whereby each particular member promotes his welfare.

117. Paragraph 184.

Here ethical life is split into its extremes and lost; the immediate unity of the family has fallen apart into a plurality. Reality here is externality, the decomposing of the concept, the self-subsistence of its moments which have now won their freedom and their determinate existence. Though in civil society universal and particular have fallen apart, yet both are still reciprocally bound together and conditioned. While each of them seems to do just the opposite to the other and supposes that it can exist only by keeping the other at arm's length, none the less each still conditions the other. Thus, for example, most people regard the paying of taxes as injurious to their particular interest, as something inimical and obstructive of their own ends. Yet, however true this *seems*, particular ends cannot be attained without the help of the universal, and a country where no taxes were paid could not be singled out as invigorating its citizens. Similarly, it might seem that universal ends would be more readily attainable if the universal absorbed the strength of the particulars in the way described, for instance, in Plato's *Republic*. But this, too, is only an illusion, since both universal and particular turn into one another and exist only for and by means of one another. If I further my ends, I further the ends of the universal, and this in turn furthers my end.

118. Paragraph 185.

Particularity by itself is measureless excess, and the forms of this excess are themselves measureless. By means of his ideas and reflections man expands his desires, which are not a closed circle like animal instinct, and carries them on to the false infinite. At the other end of the scale, however, want and destitution are measureless too, and the discord of this situation can be brought into a harmony only by the state which has powers over it. Plato wished to exclude particularity from his state, but this is no help, since help on these lines would contravene the infinite right of the Idea to allow freedom to the particular.

It was in the Christian religion in the first place that the right of subjectivity arose, together with the infinity of self-awareness, and while
granting this right, the whole order must at the same time retain
strength enough to put particularity in harmony with the unity of
ethical life.

119. *Paragraph 187*.

By educated men, we may prima facie understand those who without
the obtrusion of personal idiosyncrasy can do what others do. It is
precisely this idiosyncrasy, however, which uneducated men display,
since their behaviour is not governed by the universal characteristics of
the situation. Similarly, an uneducated man is apt to hurt the feelings
of his neighbours. He simply lets himself go and does not reflect on the
susceptibilities of others. It is not that he intends to hurt them, but his
conduct is not consonant with his intention. Thus education rubs the
edges off particular characteristics until a man conducts himself in
accordance with the nature of the thing. Genuine originality, which
produces the real thing, demands genuine education, while bastard
originality adopts eccentricities which only enter the heads of the
uneducated.

120. *Paragraph 189*.

There are certain universal needs such as food, drink, clothing, &c.,
and it depends entirely on accidental circumstances how these are
satisfied. The fertility of the soil varies from place to place, harvests
vary from year to year, one man is industrious, another indolent. But
this medley of arbitrariness generates universal characteristics by its
own working; and this apparently scattered and thoughtless sphere is
upheld by a necessity which automatically enters it. To discover this
necessary element here is the object of political economy, a science
which is a credit to thought because it finds laws for a mass of accidents.
It is an interesting spectacle here to see all chains of activity leading
back to the same point; particular spheres of action fall into groups,
influence others, and are helped or hindered by others. The most
remarkable thing here is this mutual interlocking of particulars, which
is what one would least expect because at first sight everything seems
to be given over to the arbitrariness of the individual, and it has a
parallel in the solar system which displays to the eye only irregular
movements, though its laws may none the less be ascertained.

121. *Paragraph 190*.

An animal is restricted to particularity. It has its instincts and means
of satisfying them, means which are limited and which it cannot overstep.
Some insects are parasitic on a certain kind of plant; some animals
have a wider range and can live in different climates, but there is always
a restriction preventing them from having the range open to man. The

need of shelter and clothing, the necessity of cooking his food to make it fit to eat and to overcome its natural rawness, both mean that man has less comfort than an animal, and indeed, as mind, he ought to have less. Intelligence, with its grasp of distinctions, multiplies these human needs, and since taste and utility become criteria of judgement, even the needs themselves are affected thereby. Finally, it is no longer need but opinion which has to be satisfied, and it is just the educated man who analyses the concrete into its particulars. The very multiplication of needs involves a check on desire, because when many things are in use, the urge to obtain any one thing which might be needed is less strong, and this is a sign that want altogether is not so imperious.

122. *Paragraph 191.*

What the English call 'comfort' is something inexhaustible and illimitable. [Others can discover to you that what you take to be] comfort at any stage is discomfort, and these discoveries never come to an end. Hence the need for greater comfort does not exactly arise within you directly; it is suggested to you by those who hope to make a profit from its creation.

123. *Paragraph 192.*

The fact that I must direct my conduct by reference to others introduces here the form of universality. It is from others that I acquire the means of satisfaction and I must accordingly accept their views. At the same time, however, I am compelled to produce means for the satisfaction of others. We play into each other's hands and so hang together. To this extent everything private becomes something social. In dress fashions and hours of meals, there are certain conventions which we have to accept because in these things it is not worth the trouble to insist on displaying one's own discernment. The wisest thing here is to do as others do.

124. *Paragraph 195.*

The entire Cynical mode of life adopted by Diogenes was nothing more or less than a product of Athenian social life, and what determined it was the way of thinking against which his whole manner protested. Hence it was not independent of social conditions but simply their result; it was itself a rude product of luxury. When luxury is at its height, distress and depravity are equally extreme, and in such circumstances Cynicism is the outcome of opposition to refinement.

125. *Paragraph 196.*

There is hardly any raw material which does not need to be worked on before use. Even air has to be worked for because we have to warm it. Water is perhaps the only exception, because we can drink it as we find it. It is by the sweat of his brow and the toil of his hands that man obtains the means to satisfy his needs.

126. *Paragraph 197.*

The savage is lazy and is distinguished from the educated man by his brooding stupidity, because practical education is just education in the need and habit of being busy. A clumsy man always produces a result he does not intend; he is not master of his own job. The skilled worker, on the other hand, may be said to be the man who produces the thing as it ought to be and who hits the nail on the head without shrinking (*keine Sprödigkeit in seinem subjektiven Tun gegen den Zweck findet*).

127. *Paragraph 201.*

The ways and means of sharing in the capital of society are left to each man's particular choice, but the subdivision of civil society into different general branches is a necessity. The family is the first precondition of the state, but class divisions are the second. The importance of the latter is due to the fact that although private persons are self-seeking, they are compelled to direct their attention to others. Here then is the root which connects self-seeking to the universal, i.e. to the state, whose care it must be that this tie is a hard and fast one.

128. *Paragraph 203.*

In our day agriculture is conducted on methods devised by reflective thinking, i.e. like a factory.* This has given it a character like that of industry and contrary to its natural one. Still, the agricultural class will always retain a mode of life which is patriarchal and the substantial frame of mind proper to such a life. The member of this class accepts unreflectively what is given him and takes what he gets, thanking God for it and living in faith and confidence that this goodness will continue. What comes to him suffices him; once it is consumed, more comes again. This is the simple attitude of mind not concentrated on the struggle for riches. It may be described as the attitude of the old nobility which just ate what there was. So far as this class is concerned, nature does the major part, while individual effort is secondary. In the business class, however, it is intelligence which is the essential thing, and natural products can be treated only as raw materials.

129. *Paragraph 204.*

In the business class, the individual is thrown back on himself, and this feeling of self-hood is most intimately connected with the demand for law and order. The sense of freedom and order has therefore arisen above all in towns. The agricultural class, on the other hand, has little occasion to think of itself; what it obtains is the gift of a stranger, of nature. Its feeling of dependence is fundamental to it, and

---

* [On the authority of Arthur Young's *Lincolnshire* (1799), Halévy remarks that, if you were in the offices of a certain farm there, 'you could not tell whether you were on a farm or in the heart of a large factory' (*History of the English People in 1815*, Bk. ii, Chap. i).]

with this feeling there is readily associated a willingness to submit to whatever may befall it at other men's hands. The agricultural class is thus more inclined to subservience, the business class to freedom.

130. *Paragraph 207.*

When we say that a man must be a 'somebody', we mean that he should belong to some specific social class, since to be a somebody means to have substantive being. A man with no class is a mere private person and his universality is not actualized. On the other hand, the individual in his particularity may take himself as the universal and presume that by entering a class he is surrendering himself to an indignity. This is the false idea that in attaining a determinacy necessary to it, a thing is restricting and surrendering itself.

131. *Paragraph 209.*

From one point of view, it is through the working of the system of particularity that right becomes an external compulsion as a protection of particular interests. Even though this result is due to the concept, right none the less only becomes something existent because this is useful for men's needs. To become conscious in thought of his right, man must be trained to think and give up dallying with mere sensation. We must invest the objects of our thought with the form of universality and similarly we must direct our willing by a universal principle. It is only after man has devised numerous needs and after their acquisition has become intertwined with his satisfaction, that he can frame laws for himself.

132. *Paragraph 211.*

The sun and the planets have their laws too, but they do not know them. Savages are governed by impulses, customs, and feelings, but they are unconscious of this. When right is posited as law and is known, every accident of feeling vanishes together with the form of revenge, sympathy, and selfishness, and in this way the right attains for the first time its true determinacy and is given its due honour. It is as a result of the discipline of comprehending the right that the right first becomes capable of universality. In the course of applying the laws, clashes occur, and in dealing with these the judge's intelligence has its proper scope; this is quite inevitable, because otherwise carrying out the law would be something mechanical from start to finish. But to go so far as to get rid of clashes altogether by leaving much to the judge's discretion is a far worse solution, because even the clash is intrinsic to thought, to conscious thinking and its dialectic, while the mere fiat of a judge would be arbitrary.

It is generally alleged in favour of customary law that it is 'living', but this vitality, i.e. the identity between the subject and what the law provides, is not the whole essence of the matter. Law (*Recht*) must be known by thought, it must be a system in itself, and only as such can it be recognized in a civilized country. The recent denial that nations 'have a vocation to codify their laws' is not only an insult; it also implies the absurdity of supposing that not a single individual has been endowed with skill enough to bring into a coherent system the endless mass of existing laws. The truth is that it is just systematization, i.e. elevation to the universal, which our time is pressing for without any limit. A similar view is that collections of judgements, like those available in a *Corpus Juris*, are far superior to a code worked out in the most general way. The reason alleged is that such judgements always retain a certain particularity and a certain reminiscence of history which men are unwilling to sacrifice. But the mischievousness of such collections is made clear enough by the practice of English law.

133. *Paragraph 213.*

In the higher relationships of marriage, love, religion, and the state, the only aspects which can become the subject of legislation are those of such a nature as to permit of their being in principle external. Still, in this respect there is a wide difference between the laws of different peoples. The Chinese, for instance, have a law requiring a husband to love his first wife more than his other wives. If he is convicted of doing the opposite, corporal punishment follows. Similarly, the legislation of the ancients in earlier times was full of precepts about uprightness and integrity which are unsuited by nature to legal enactment because they fall wholly within the field of the inner life. It is only in the case of the oath, whereby things are brought home to conscience, that uprightness and integrity must be taken into account as the substance of the matter.

134. *Paragraph 214.*

There is one essential element in law and the administration of justice which contains a measure of contingency and which arises from the fact that the law is a universal prescription which has to be applied to the single case. If you wished to declare yourself against this contingency, you would be talking in abstractions. The measure of a man's punishment, for example, cannot be made equivalent to any determination of the concept of punishment, and the decision made, whatever it be, is from this point of view arbitrary always. But this contingency is itself necessary, and if you argue against having a code at all on the ground that any code is incomplete, you are overlooking just that element of law in which completion is not to be achieved and which therefore must just be accepted as it stands.

135. *Paragraph 215.*

The legal profession, possessed of a special knowledge of the law, often claims this knowledge as its monopoly and refuses to allow any layman to discuss the subject. Physicists similarly have taken amiss

Goethe's theory about colours* because he did not belong to their craft and was a poet into the bargain. But we do not need to be shoe-makers to know if our shoes fit, and just as little have we any need to be professionals to acquire knowledge of matters of universal interest. Law is concerned with freedom, the worthiest and holiest thing in man, the thing man must know if it is to have obligatory force for him.

136. *Paragraph 216.*

Completeness means the exhaustive collection of every single thing pertaining to a given field, and no science or branch of knowledge can be complete in this sense. Now if we say that philosophy or any one of the sciences is incomplete, we are not far from holding that we must wait until the deficiency is made up, since the best part may still be wanting. But take up this attitude and advance is impossible, either in geometry, which seems to be a closed science although new propositions do arise, or in philosophy, which is always capable of freshness in detail even though its subject is the universal Idea. In the past, the universal law always consisted of the ten commandments; now we can see at once that not to lay down the law 'Thou shalt not kill', on the ground that a legal code cannot be complete, is an obvious absurdity. Any code could be still better—no effort of reflection is required to justify this affirmation; we can think of the best, finest, and noblest as still better, finer, and nobler. But a big old tree puts forth more and more branches without thereby becoming a new tree; though it would be silly to refuse to plant a tree at all simply because it might produce new branches.

137. *Paragraph 217.*

Law and the right are identical in the sense that what is implicitly right is posited in the law. I possess something, own a property, which I occupied when it was ownerless. This possession must now further be recognized and posited as mine. Hence in civil society formalities arise in connexion with property. Boundary stones are erected as a symbol for others to recognize. Entries are made in mortgage and pro-perty registers. Most property in civil society is held on contract, and contractual forms are fixed and determinate. Now we may have an antipathy to formalities of this kind and we may suppose that they only exist to bring in money to the authorities; we may even regard them as something offensive and a sign of mistrust because they impair the validity of the saying: 'A man is as good as his word.' But the formality is essential because what is inherently right must also be posited as right. My will is a rational will; it has validity, and its validity should be recognized by others. At this point, then, my subjectivity and that

---

* [Hegel's acceptance of this anti-Newtonian theory, e.g. in *Enc.*, § 320, gave great pleasure to Goethe. For a summary and criticism of the theory, see e.g. G. H. Lewes: *Life of Goethe*, Book V, chap. ix.]

of others must be set aside and the will must achieve the security, stability, and objectivity which can be attained only through such formalities.

138. *Paragraph 218.*

It seems to be a contradiction that a crime committed in society appears more heinous and yet is punished more leniently. But while it would be impossible for society to leave a crime unpunished, since that would be to posit it as right, still since society is sure of itself, a crime must always be something idiosyncratic in comparison, something unstable and exceptional. The very stability of society gives a crime the status of something purely subjective which seems to be the product rather of natural impulse than of a prudent will. In this light, crime acquires a milder status, and for this reason its punishment too becomes milder. If society is still internally weak, then an example must be made by inflicting punishments, since punishment is itself an example over against the example of crime. But in a society which is internally strong, the commission of crime is something so feeble that its annulment must be commensurable with its feebleness. Harsh punishments, therefore, are not unjust in and by themselves; they are related to contemporary conditions. A criminal code cannot hold good for all time, and crimes are only shows of reality which may draw on themselves a greater or lesser degree of disavowal.

139. *Paragraph 221.*

Since any individual has the right *in judicio stare*, he must also know what the law is or otherwise this privilege would be useless to him. But it is also his *duty* to stand his trial. Under the feudal system, the nobles often refused to stand their trial. They defied the court and alleged that the court was wrong to demand their appearance. Feudal conditions, however, contravened the very idea of a court. Nowadays monarchs have to recognize the jurisdiction of the court in their private affairs, and in free states they commonly lose their case.

140. *Paragraph 222.*

A man may be indignant if a right which he knows he has is refused him because he cannot prove it. But if I have a right, it must at the same time be a right posited in law. I must be able to explain and prove it, and its validity can only be recognized in society if its rightness in principle is also made a posited rightness in law.

141. *Paragraph 224.*

It is straightforward common sense to hold that the publicity of legal proceedings is right and just. A strong reason against such publicity has always been the rank* of justices; they are unwilling to sit in public

---

* [In the eighteenth century, judicial authority was often still vested in Lords of the Manor.]

and they regard themselves as a sanctuary of law which laymen are not to enter. But an integral part of justice is the confidence which citizens have in it, and it is this which requires that proceedings shall be public. The right of publicity depends on the fact that (i) the aim of the court is justice, which as universal falls under the cognizance of everyone, and (ii) it is through publicity that the citizens become convinced that the judgement was actually just.

142. *Paragraph 227.*

No grounds can be adduced for supposing that the judge, i.e. the legal expert, should be the only person to establish how the facts lie, for ability to do so depends on general, not on purely legal, education. Determination of the facts of the case depends on empirical details, on depositions about what happened, and on similar perceptual data, or again on facts from which inferences can be drawn about the deed in question and which make it probable or improbable. Here then, it is an assurance which should be required, not truth in the higher sense in which it is always something eternal. Here such assurance is subjective conviction, or conscience, and the problem is: What form should this assurance take in a court of law? The demand, commonly made in German law, that a criminal should confess his guilt, has this to be said for it, that the right of self-consciousness thereby attains a measure of satisfaction; consciousness must chime in with the judge's sentence, and it is only when the criminal has confessed that the judgement loses its alien character so far as he is concerned. But a difficulty arises here, because the criminal may lie, and the interest of justice may be jeopardized. If, on the other hand, the subjective conviction of the judge is to hold good, some hardship is once more involved, because the accused is no longer being treated as a free man. Now the middle term between these extremes is trial by jury, which meets the demand that the declaration of guilt or innocence shall spring from the soul of the accused.*

143. *Paragraph 229.*

In civil society, universality is necessity only. When we are dealing with human needs, it is only right as such which is steadfast. But this right—only a restricted sphere—has a bearing simply on the protection of property; welfare is something external to right as such. This welfare, however, is an essential end in the system of needs. Hence the universal, which in the first instance is the right only, has to be extended over the whole field of particularity. Justice is a big thing in civil society. Given good laws, a state can flourish, and freedom of property is a fundamental condition of its prosperity. Still, since I am inex-

---

* [The verdict of his peers is the verdict of the criminal's own soul or reason because reason is universal and so common to them and to him alike. His crime is his subjective defiance of his reason or his inner universality—see Part i, subsection 3 (c).]

tricably involved in particularity, I have a right to claim that in this association with other particulars, my particular welfare too shall be promoted. Regard should be paid to my welfare, to my particular interest, and this is done through the police and the Corporation.

144. *Paragraph 234.*

Here nothing hard and fast can be laid down and no absolute lines can be drawn. Everything here is personal; subjective opinion enters in, and the spirit of the constitution and the crisis of the day have to provide precision of detail. In time of war, for instance, many a thing, harmless at other times, has to be regarded as harmful. As a result of this presence of accident, of personal arbitrariness, the public authority acquires a measure of odium. When reflective thinking is very highly developed, the public authority may tend to draw into its orbit everything it possibly can, for in everything some factor may be found which might make it dangerous in one of its bearings. In such circumstances, the public authority may set to work very pedantically and embarrass the day-to-day life of people. But however great this annoyance, no objective line can be drawn here either.

145. *Paragraph 236.*

The oversight and care exercised by the public authority aims at being a middle term between an individual and the universal possibility, afforded by society, of attaining individual ends. It has to undertake street-lighting, bridge-building, the pricing of daily necessaries, and the care of public health. In this connexion, two main views predominate at the present time. One asserts that the superintendence of everything properly belongs to the public authority, the other that the public authority has nothing at all to settle here because everyone will direct his conduct according to the needs of others. The individual must have a right to work for his bread as he pleases, but the public also has a right to insist that essential tasks shall be properly done. Both points of view must be satisfied, and freedom of trade should not be such as to jeopardize the general good.

146. *Paragraph 238.*

To be sure, the family has to provide bread for its members, but in civil society the family is something subordinate and only lays the foundations; its effective range is no longer so comprehensive. Civil society is rather the tremendous power which draws men into itself and claims from them that they work for it, owe everything to it, and do everything by its means. If man is to be a member of civil society in this sense, he has rights and claims against it just as he had rights and claims in the family. Civil society must protect its members and defend their rights, while its rights impose duties on every one of its members.

147. *Paragraph 239.*

The line which demarcates the rights of parents from those of civil society is very hard to draw here. Parents usually suppose that in the matter of education they have complete freedom and may arrange everything as they like. The chief opposition to any form of public education usually comes from parents and it is they who talk and make an outcry about teachers and schools because they have a faddish dislike of them. None the less, society has a right to act on principles tested by its experience and to compel parents to send their children to school, to have them vaccinated, and so forth. The disputes that have arisen in France* between the advocates of state supervision and those who demand that education shall be free, i.e. at the option of the parents, are relevant here.

148. *Paragraph 240.*

There was an Athenian law compelling every citizen to give an account of his source of livelihood.† Nowadays we take the view that this is nobody's business but his own. Of course every individual is from one point of view independent, but he also plays his part in the system of civil society, and while every man has the right to demand subsistence from it, it must at the same time protect him from himself. It is not simply starvation which is at issue; the further end in view is to prevent the formation of a pauperized rabble. Since civil society is responsible for feeding its members, it also has the right to press them to provide for their own livelihood.

149. *Paragraph 244.*

The lowest subsistence level, that of a rabble of paupers, is fixed automatically, but the minimum varies considerably in different countries. In England, even the very poorest believe that they have rights; this is different from what satisfies the poor in other countries. Poverty in itself does not make men into a rabble; a rabble is created only when there is joined to poverty a disposition of mind, an inner indignation against the rich, against society, against the government, &c. A further consequence of this attitude is that through their dependence on chance men become frivolous and idle, like the Neapolitan *lazzaroni* for example. In this way there is born in the rabble the evil of lacking self-respect enough to secure subsistence by its own labour and yet at the same time of claiming to receive subsistence as its right. Against nature man can claim no right, but once society is established, poverty immedi-

---

* [Rousseau's *Émile*, published in 1762, is the classic demand for freedom in education. State supervision was advocated by La Chalotais in his *Essai d'Éducation nationale*, published a year later. The Jesuits, the chief educators in France, were expelled in 1764. The revival of family life also helped to stimulate French interest in education in the second half of the eighteenth century.]

† [Herodotus, ii. 177. Plutarch: *Life of Solon*, chap. 22.]

ately takes the form of a wrong done to one class by another. The important question of how poverty is to be abolished is one of the most disturbing problems which agitate modern society.

150. *Paragraph 248.*

Civil society is thus driven to found colonies. Increase of population alone has this effect, but it is due in particular to the appearance of a number of people who cannot secure the satisfaction of their needs by their own labour once production rises above the requirements of consumers. Sporadic colonization is particularly characteristic of Germany. The emigrants withdraw to America or Russia and remain there with no home ties, and so prove useless to their native land. The second and entirely different type of colonization is the systematic; the state undertakes it, is aware of the proper method of carrying it out and regulates it accordingly. This type was common amongst the ancients, particularly the Greeks. Hard work was not the business of the citizens in Greece, since their energy was directed rather to public affairs. So if the population increased to such an extent that there might be difficulty in feeding it, the young people would be sent away to a new district, sometimes specifically chosen, sometimes left to chance discovery. In modern times, colonists have not been allowed the same rights as those left at home, and the result of this situation has been wars and finally independence, as may be seen in the history of the English and Spanish colonies. Colonial independence proves to be of the greatest advantage to the mother country, just as the emancipation of slaves turns out to the greatest advantage of the owners.

151. *Paragraph 255.*

The consideration behind the abolition of Corporations in recent times is that the individual should fend for himself. But we may grant this and still hold that corporation membership does not alter a man's obligation to earn his living. Under modern political conditions, the citizens have only a restricted share in the public business of the state, yet it is essential to provide men—ethical entities—with work of a public character over and above their private business. This work of a public character, which the modern state does not always provide, is found in the Corporation. We saw earlier [Addition to Paragraph 184] that in fending for himself a member of civil society is also working for others. But this unconscious compulsion is not enough; it is in the Corporation that it first changes into a known and thoughtful ethical mode of life. Of course Corporations must fall under the higher surveillance of the state, because otherwise they would ossify, build themselves in, and decline into a miserable system of castes. In and by itself, however, a Corporation is not a closed caste; its purpose is rather to bring an isolated trade into the social order and elevate it to a sphere in which it gains strength and respect.

152. *Paragraph 258.*

The state in and by itself is the ethical whole, the actualization of freedom; and it is an absolute end of reason that freedom should be actual. The state is mind on earth and consciously realizing itself there. In nature, on the other hand, mind actualizes itself only as its own other, as mind asleep. Only when it is present in consciousness, when it knows itself as a really existent object, is it the state. In considering freedom, the starting-point must be not individuality, the single self-consciousness, but only the essence of self-consciousness; for whether man knows it or not, this essence is externally realized as a self-subsistent power in which single individuals are only moments. The march of God in the world, that is what the state is. The basis of the state is the power of reason actualizing itself as will. In considering the Idea of the state, we must not have our eyes on particular states or on particular institutions. Instead we must consider the Idea, this actual God, by itself. On some principle or other, any state may be shown to be bad, this or that defect may be found in it; and yet, at any rate if one of the mature states of our epoch is in question, it has in it the moments essential to the existence of the state. But since it is easier to find defects than to understand the affirmative, we may readily fall into the mistake of looking at isolated aspects of the state and so forgetting its inward organic life. The state is no ideal work of art; it stands on earth and so in the sphere of caprice, chance, and error, and bad behaviour may disfigure it in many respects. But the ugliest of men, or a criminal, or an invalid, or a cripple, is still always a living man. The affirmative, life, subsists despite his defects, and it is this affirmative factor which is our theme here.

153. *Paragraph 259.*

The state in its actuality is essentially an individual state, and beyond that a particular state. Individuality is to be distinguished from particularity. The former is a moment in the very Idea of the state, while the latter belongs to history. States as such are independent of one another, and therefore their relation to one another can only be an external one, so that there must be a third thing standing above them to bind them together. Now this third thing is the mind which gives itself actuality in world-history and is the absolute judge of states. Several states may form an alliance to be a sort of court with jurisdiction over others, there may be confederations of states, like the Holy Alliance for example, but these are always relative only and restricted, like 'perpetual peace'.* The one and only absolute judge, which makes itself authoritative against the particular and at all times, is the absolute mind which manifests itself in the history of the world as the universal and as the genus there operative.

* [See Paragraphs 324, 333, and the Addition and Notes thereto.]

154. *Paragraph 260.*

The Idea of the state in modern times has a special character in that the state is the actualization of freedom not in accordance with subjective whim but in accordance with the concept of the will, i.e. in accordance with its universality and divinity. Immature states are those in which the Idea of the state is still veiled and where its particular determinations have not yet attained free self-subsistence. In the states of classical antiquity, universality was present, but particularity had not then been released, given free scope, and brought back to universality, i.e. to the universal end of the whole. The essence of the modern state is that the universal be bound up with the complete freedom of its particular members and with private well-being, that thus the interests of family and civil society must concentrate themselves on the state, although the universal end cannot be advanced without the personal knowledge and will of its particular members, whose own rights must be maintained. Thus the universal must be furthered, but subjectivity on the other hand must attain its full and living development. It is only when both these moments subsist in their strength that the state can be regarded as articulated and genuinely organized.

155. *Paragraph 261.*

In the state everything depends on the unity of universal and particular. In the states of antiquity, the subjective end simply coincided with the state's will. In modern times, however, we make claims for private judgement, private willing, and private conscience. The ancients had none of these in the modern sense; the ultimate thing with them was the will of the state. Whereas under the despots of Asia the individual had no inner life and no justification in himself, in the modern world man insists on respect being paid to his inner life. The conjunction of duty and right has a twofold aspect: what the state demands from us as a duty is *eo ipso* our right as individuals, since the state* is nothing but the articulation of the concept of freedom. The determinations of the individual will are given an objective embodiment through the state and thereby they attain their truth and their actualization for the first time. The state is the one and only prerequisite of the attainment of particular ends and welfare.

156. *Paragraph 262.*

In Plato's state, subjective freedom does not count, because people have their occupations assigned to them by the Guardians. In many oriental states, this assignment is determined by birth. But subjective freedom, which must be respected, demands that individuals should have free choice in this matter.

* [Reading *er*, with Lasson.]

157. *Paragraph 263.*

The state, as mind, sunders itself into the particular determinations of its concept, of its mode of being. We might use here an illustration drawn from nature. The nervous system is the sensitive system proper; it is the abstract moment, the moment of being by oneself and so of having identity with oneself. But analysis of sensation reveals that it has two aspects and these are distinct in such a way that each of them seems to be a whole system by itself. The first is feeling in the abstract, keeping oneself self-enclosed, the dull movement which goes on internally, reproduction, internal self-nutrition, growth, and digestion. The second moment is that this self-related existence has over against it the moment of difference, a movement outwards. This is irritability, sensation moving outwards. This constitutes a system of its own, and there are some of the lower types of animals which have developed this system alone, while they lack the soul-charged unity of inner sensation. If we compare these natural features with those of mind, then the family must be paralleled with sensibility and civil society with irritability. Now the third is the state, the nervous system as a whole, something inwardly organized; but this lives only in so far as both moments (in this case family and civil society) are developed within it. The laws regulating family and civil society are the institutions of the rational order which glimmers in them. But the ground and final truth of these institutions is mind, their universal end and known objective. The family too is ethical, only its end is not known as such, while it is the separation between one man and another which makes civil society what it is.

158. *Paragraph 265.*

As was remarked earlier on,* the sanctity of marriage and the institutions in which civil society is an appearance of ethical life constitute the stability of the whole, i.e. stability is secured when universal affairs are the affairs of each member in his particular capacity. What is of the utmost importance is that the law of reason should be shot through and through by the law of particular freedom, and that my particular end should become identified with the universal end, or otherwise the state is left in the air. The state is actual only when its members have a feeling of their own self-hood and it is stable only when public and private ends are identical. It has often been said that the end of the state is the happiness of the citizens. That is perfectly true. If all is not well with them, if their subjective aims are not satisfied, if they do not find that the state as such is the means to their satisfaction, then the footing of the state itself is insecure.

159. *Paragraph 267.*

The unity of the freedom which knows and wills itself is present first

* [The reference is probably to Paragraph 255.]

of all as necessity. Here substance is present as the subjective existence of individuals. Necessity's other mode of being, however, is the organism, i.e. mind is a process internal to itself, it articulates itself within, posits differences in itself, and thereby completes the cycle of its life.

160. *Paragraph 268.*

Immature minds delight in argumentation and fault-finding, because it is easy enough to find fault, though hard to see the good and its inner necessity. The learner always begins by finding fault, but the scholar sees the positive merit in everything. In religion, this or that is quickly dismissed as superstitious, but it is infinitely harder to apprehend the truth underlying the superstition. Hence men's apparent sentiment towards the state is to be distinguished from what they really will; inwardly they really will the thing, but they cling to details and take delight in the vanity of pretending to know better. We are confident that the state must subsist and that in it alone can particular interests be secured. But habit blinds us to that on which our whole existence depends. When we walk the streets at night in safety, it does not strike us that this might be otherwise. This habit of feeling safe has become second nature, and we do not reflect on just how this is due solely to the working of special institutions. Commonplace thinking often has the impression that force holds the state together, but in fact its only bond is the fundamental sense of order which everybody possesses.

161. *Paragraph 269.*

The state is an organism, i.e. the development of the Idea to the articulation of its differences. Thus these different sides of the state are its various powers with their functions and spheres of action, by means of which the universal continually engenders itself in a necessary way; in this process it maintains its identity since it is presupposed even in its own production. This organism is the constitution of the state; it is produced perpetually by the state, while it is through it that the state maintains itself. If the state and its constitution fall apart, if the various members of the organism free themselves, then the unity produced by the constitution is no longer an accomplished fact. This tallies with the fable* about the belly and the other members. The nature of an organism is such that unless each of its parts is brought into identity with the others, unless each of them is prevented from achieving autonomy, the whole must perish. By listing attributes, axioms, &c., no progress can be made in assessing the nature of the state; it must be apprehended as an organism. One might as well try to understand the nature of God by listing his attributes, while the truth is that we must intuit God's life in that life itself.

* [The fable recounted by Menenius Agrippa to dissuade the Roman *plebs* from secession. Livy, ii. 32. Shakespeare, *Coriolanus*, Act I, Sc. i.]

162. *Paragraph 270.*

The state is actual, and its actuality consists in this, that the interest of the whole is realized in and through particular ends. Actuality is always the unity of universal and particular, the universal dismembered in the particulars which seem to be self-subsistent, although they really are upheld and contained only in the whole. Where this unity is not present, a thing is not actual even though it may have acquired existence. A bad state is one which merely exists; a sick body exists too, but it has no genuine reality. A hand which is cut off still looks like a hand, and it exists, but without being actual.* Genuine actuality is necessity; what is actual is inherently necessary. Necessity consists in this, that the whole is sundered into the differences of the concept and that this divided whole yields a fixed and permanent determinacy, though one which is not fossilized but perpetually recreates itself in its dissolution.

To a mature state thought and consciousness essentially belong. Therefore the state knows what it wills and knows it as something thought. Now since knowing has its seat in the state, the seat of science must be there too and not in the church. Despite this, it is often said nowadays that the state must grow out of religion. The state is mind fully mature and it exhibits its moments in the daylight of consciousness. Now the fact that what is hidden in the Idea steps forth into objective existence gives the state the appearance of something finite, and so the state reveals itself as a domain of worldliness, while religion displays itself as a domain of the infinite. If this be so, the state seems to be the subordinate, and since what is finite cannot stand on its own feet, the state is therefore said to need the church as its basis. As finite, it lacks justification, and it is only through religion that it can become sacrosanct and pertain to the infinite. This handling of the matter, however, is supremely one-sided. Of course the state is essentially worldly and finite; it has particular ends and particular powers; but its worldly character is only one of its aspects, and it is only to an unintelligent superficial glance that it is finite and nothing more. For the state has a life-giving soul, and the soul which animates it is subjectivity, which creates differences and yet at the same time holds them together in unity. In the realm of religion too there are distinctions and limitations. God, it is said, is triune; thus there are three persons whose unity alone is Spirit (*Geist*). Therefore to apprehend the nature of God concretely is to apprehend it through distinctions alone. Hence in the kingdom of God there are limitations, just as there are in the world, and to hold that mind (*Geist*) on earth, i.e. the state, is only a finite mind, is a one-sided view, since there is nothing irrational about actuality. Of course a bad state is worldly and finite and nothing else, but the rational state is inherently infinite.

Secondly, it is averred that the state must derive its justification from

* [The illustration is from Aristotle's *Politics* 1253ª 19 ff.]

religion. In religion, the Idea is mind in the inwardness of the heart, but it is this same Idea which gives itself a worldly form as the state and fashions for itself an embodiment and an actuality in knowing and willing. Now if you say that the state must be grounded on religion, you may mean that it should rest on rationality and arise out of it; but your statement may also be misunderstood to mean that men are most adroitly schooled to obedience if their minds are shackled by a slavish religion. (The Christian religion, however, is the religion of freedom, though it must be admitted that this religion may become changed in character and perverted from freedom to bondage when it is infected with superstition.) Now if you mean that men must have religion so that their minds, already shackled, may the more easily be oppressed by the state, then the purport of your statement is bad. But if you mean that men ought to respect the state, this whole whose limbs they are, then of course the best means of effecting this is to give them philosophical insight into the essence of the state, though, in default of that, a religious frame of mind may lead to the same result. For this reason, the state may have need of religion and faith. But the state remains essentially distinct from religion, since whatever it claims, it claims in the form of a legal duty, and it is a matter of indifference to it in what spirit that duty is performed. The field of religion, on the other hand, is the inner life, and just as the state would jeopardize the right of that life if, like religion, it made claims on it, so also when the church acts like a state and imposes penalties, it degenerates into a religion of tyranny.

A third difference which is connected with the foregoing is that the content of religion is and remains veiled, and consequently religion's place is in the field of the heart, feeling, and representative thinking. In this field everything has the form of *subjectivity*. The state, on the other hand, actualizes itself and gives its specific institutions a stable, *objective*, existence. Now if religious feeling wished to assert itself in the state in the same way as it is wont to do in its own field, it would overturn the organization of the state, because the different organs of the state have latitude to pursue their several distinct paths, while in religion everything is always referred back to the whole. If this whole, then, wished to engulf all the concerns of the state, this would be tantamount to fanaticism; the wish to have the whole in every particular could be fulfilled only by the destruction of the particular, and fanaticism is just the refusal to give scope to particular differences. Hence to say: 'To the pious man no law is given' is nothing but an expression of this same fanaticism. Once piety usurps the place of the state, it cannot tolerate the determinate but simply shatters it. It is quite consistent with this if piety leaves decisions to conscience, to the inner life, and is not governed by reasons. This inner life does not develop into reasoned argument or give an account of itself. Hence if piety is to pass for the actuality of the state, all laws are cast to the winds and subjective feeling is the legislator. This feeling may be pure caprice, and whether it is or not can only be learnt from its actions. But by becoming actions and precepts, its actions assume the guise of laws, and this is just the very opposite of the subjective feeling with which we started. This feeling has God for its object, and we might make him the determinant of everything. But God is the universal Idea and this feeling can regard him only as the indeterminate, which is too immature to determine what is existent in the state in a developed form. It is precisely the fact that everything in the state is fixed and secure which is the bulwark against caprice and dogmatic opinion. Religion as such, then, ought not to be the governor.

163. *Paragraph 271.*

Just as irritability in the living organism is itself from one point of view something inward, something pertaining to the organism as such, so here again the outward reference is an inward tendency. The inner side of the state as such is the civil power, while its outward tendency is the military power, although this has a fixed place inside the state itself. Now to have both these powers in equilibrium constitutes an important factor in the spirit of the state. Sometimes the civil power is wholly effaced and rests entirely on the military power, as was the case, for instance, in the time of the Roman Emperors and the Praetorians.* At other times, nowadays for example, the military power is a mere by-product of the civil power once all the citizens are conscriptable.

164. *Paragraph 272.*

We should desire to have in the state nothing except what is an expression of rationality. The state is the world which mind has made for itself; its march, therefore, is on lines that are fixed and absolute. How often we talk of the wisdom of God in nature! But we are not to assume for that reason that the physical world of nature is a loftier thing than the world of mind. As high as mind stands above nature, so high does the state stand above physical life. Man must therefore venerate the state as a secular deity,† and observe that if it is difficult to comprehend nature, it is infinitely harder to understand the state. It is a fact of the highest importance that nowadays we have gained a clear-cut intuition into the state in general and have been so much engaged in discussing and making constitutions. But by getting so far we have not yet settled everything. In addition, it is necessary to bring to bear on a rational topic the reason underlying intuition, to know what the essence of the matter is and to realize that the obvious is not always the essential.

* [Under the reforms instituted by Diocletian and Constantine, the Praetorian Prefects, who were originally exclusively military officials, had supreme authority, under the Emperor, in both civil and military affairs. See e.g. Gibbon, chap. xvii—perhaps Hegel's source.]

† [*Irdisch-Göttliches.* Hegel here follows Kant who, e.g. at the end of his essay on Theory and Practice, refers to nation states as *Erden-Götter*.]

The powers of the state, then, must certainly be distinguished, but each of them must build itself inwardly into a whole and contain in itself the other moments. When we speak of the distinct activities of these powers, we must not slip into the monstrous error of so interpreting their distinction as to suppose that each power should subsist independently in abstraction from the others. The truth is that the powers are to be distinguished only as moments of the concept. If instead they subsist independently in abstraction from one another, then it is as clear as day that two independent units cannot constitute a unity but must of course give rise to strife, whereby either the whole is destroyed or else unity is restored by force. Thus in the French Revolution, the legislative power sometimes engulfed the so-called 'executive', the executive sometimes engulfed the legislative, and in such a case it must be stupid to formulate e.g. the moral demand for harmony.

Leave the thing to the heart if you like and be saved all trouble; but even if ethical feeling is indispensable, it has no right to determine the powers of the state by reference to itself alone. The vital point, then, is that since the fixed characters of the powers are implicitly the whole, so also all the powers as existents constitute the concept as a whole. Mention is usually made of three powers, the legislative, the executive, and the judiciary; of these the first corresponds to universality and the second to particularity, but the judiciary is not the third moment of the concept, since the individuality intrinsic to the concept lies outside these spheres.

165. *Paragraph 273.*

The principle of the modern world is freedom of subjectivity, the principle that all the essential factors present in the intellectual whole are now coming into their right in the course of their development. Starting from this point of view, we can hardly raise the idle question: Which is the better form of government, monarchy or democracy? We may only say that all constitutional forms are one-sided unless they can sustain in themselves the principle of free subjectivity and know how to correspond with a matured rationality.

166. *Paragraph 274.*

The state in its constitution must permeate all relationships within the state. Napoleon, for instance, wished to give the Spaniards a constitution *a priori*,* but the project turned out badly enough. A constitution is not just something manufactured; it is the work of centuries, it is the

* [When he expelled the Bourbons from Spain and put Joseph Bonaparte on the throne under the Constitution of Bayonne in 1808. With the breakdown of the Napoleonic régime in 1812–13, the Bourbons were restored together with the old constitution. A liberal document, the Constitution of Cadiz, was drawn up in 1812, but it remained a dead letter. Note that Hegel regards a more *liberal* constitution as a more rational one.]

Idea, the consciousness of rationality so far as that consciousness is developed in a particular nation. No constitution, therefore, is just the creation of its subjects. What Napoleon gave to the Spaniards was more rational than what they had before, and yet they recoiled from it as from something alien, because they were not yet educated up to its level. A nation's constitution must embody its feeling for its rights and its position, otherwise there may be a constitution there in an external way, but it is meaningless and valueless. Isolated individuals may often feel the need and the longing for a better constitution, but it is quite another thing, and one that does not arise till later, for the mass of the people to be animated by such an idea. The principle of morality, of the inner life of Socrates, was a necessary product of his age, but time was required before it could become part and parcel of the self-consciousness of everyone.

167. *Paragraph 275.*

We begin with the power of the crown, i.e. with the moment of individuality, since this includes the state's three moments as a totality in itself. The ego, that is to say, is at once the most individual thing and the most universal. Prima facie, individuality occurs in nature too, but reality, the opposite of ideality, and reciprocal externality are not the same as self-enclosed existence. On the contrary, in nature the various individual things subsist alongside one another. In mind, on the other hand, variety exists only as something ideal and as a unity. The state, then, as something mental, is the exhibition of all its moments, but individuality is at the same time the bearer of its soul and its life-giving principle, i.e. the sovereignty which contains all differences in itself.

168. *Paragraph 276.*

Much the same thing as this ideality of the moments in the state occurs with life in the physical organism. Life is present in every cell. There is only one life in all the cells and nothing withstands it. Separated from that life, every cell dies. This is the same as the ideality of every single class, power, and Corporation as soon as they have the impulse to subsist and be independent. It is with them as it is with the belly in the organism. It, too, asserts its independence, but at the same time its independence is set aside and it is sacrificed and absorbed into the whole.

169. *Paragraph 277.*

The business of the state is in the hands of individuals. But their authority to conduct its affairs is based not on their birth but on their objective qualities. Ability, skill, character, all belong to a man in his *particular* capacity. He must be educated and be trained to a particular task. Hence an office may not be saleable or hereditary. In France, seats in parliament were formerly saleable, and in the English army commissions up to a certain rank are saleable to this day.* This saleability of office, however, was or is still connected with the medieval constitution of certain states, and such constitutions are nowadays gradually disappearing.

170. *Paragraph 279.*

In the organization of the state—which here means in constitutional monarchy—we must have nothing before our minds except the inherent necessity of the Idea. All other points of view must vanish. The state must be treated as a great architectonic structure, as a hieroglyph of the reason which reveals itself in actuality. Everything to do with mere utility, externality, and so forth, must be eliminated from the philosophical treatment of the subject. Now our ordinary ideas can quite well grasp the conception of the state as a self-determining and completely sovereign will, as final decision. What is more difficult is to apprehend this 'I will' as a person. To do so is not to say that the monarch may act capriciously. As a matter of fact, he is bound by the concrete decisions of his counsellors, and if the constitution is stable, he has often no more to do than sign his name. But this name is important. It is the last word beyond which it is impossible to go. It might be said that an organic, articulated, constitution was present even in the beautiful democracy of Athens, and yet we cannot help noticing that the Greeks derived their final decisions from the observation of quite external phenomena such as oracles, the entrails of sacrificial animals, and the flight of birds. They treated nature as a power which in those ways revealed and expressed what was good for men. At that time, self-consciousness had not yet advanced to the abstraction of subjectivity, not even so far as to understand that, when a decision is to be made, an 'I will' must be pronounced by man himself. This 'I will' constitutes the great difference between the ancient world and the modern, and in the great edifice of the state it must therefore have its appropriate objective existence. Unfortunately, however, this requirement is regarded as only external and optional.

171. *Paragraph 280.*

It is often alleged against monarchy that it makes the welfare of the state dependent on chance, for, it is urged, the monarch may be ill-educated, he may perhaps be unworthy of the highest position in the state, and it is senseless that such a state of affairs should exist because it is supposed to be rational. But all this rests on a presupposition which is nugatory, namely that everything depends on the monarch's *particular* character. In a completely organized state, it is only a question of the culminating point of formal decision (and a natural bulwark against

* [In Hegel's day, all officers' commissions from an ensign's to a lieutenant-colonel's were on sale, but there were restrictions on both purchaser and price.]

passion. It is wrong therefore to demand objective qualities in a monarch);* he has only to say 'yes' and dot the 'i', because the throne should be such that the significant thing in its holder is not his particular make-up. (Monarchy in this sense is rational because it corresponds with the concept, but since this is hard to grasp, we often fail to notice the rationality of monarchy. Monarchy must be inherently stable and) whatever else the monarch may have in addition to this power of final decision is part and parcel of his private character and should be of no consequence. Of course there may be circumstances in which it is this private character alone which has prominence, but in that event the state is either not fully developed, or else is badly constructed. In a well-organized monarchy, the objective aspect belongs to law alone, and the monarch's part is merely to set to the law the subjective 'I will'.

172. *Paragraph 281.*

If we are to grasp the Idea of the monarch, we cannot be content with saying that God has appointed kings to rule over us, since God has made everything, even the worst of things. The point of view of utility does not get us very far either, and it is always possible to point out counter-balancing disadvantages. Still less does it help to regard monarchy as a *positive* right. That I should hold property is necessary, but my holding of this particular property is contingent; and in the same way, the right that there must be one man at the head of affairs seems contingent too if it is treated as abstract and as posited. This right, however, is inevitably present both as a felt want and as a requirement of the situation. Monarchs are not exactly distinguished for bodily prowess or intellectual gifts, and yet millions submit to their rule. Now to say that men allow themselves to be ruled counter to their own interests, ends, and intentions is preposterous. Men are not so stupid. It is their need, it is the inner might of the Idea, which, even against what they appear to think, constrains them to obedience and keeps them in that relation.

If then the monarch comes on the scene as the head and a part of the constitution, we are compelled to hold that there is no constitutional identity between a conquered people and its prince. A rebellion in a province conquered in war is a different thing from a rising in a well-organized state. It is not against their prince that the conquered are in rebellion, and they are committing no crime against the state, because their connexion with their master is not a connexion within the Idea or one within the inner necessity of the constitution. In such a case, there is only a contract, no political tie. *Je ne suis pas votre prince, je suis votre maître*, Napoleon retorted to the envoys at Erfurt.†

* [The bracketed passages are translated from Gans's third edition; they did not appear in the first.]

† [When Napoleon met Tsar Alexander at Erfurt in 1808, he was visited by representatives of many German states. This is one of the many stories of his rudeness on that occasion.]

173. *Paragraph 282.*

Pardon is the remission of punishment, but it does not annul the law (*Recht*). On the contrary, the law stands and the pardoned man remains a criminal as before. Pardon does not mean that he has not committed a crime. This annulment of punishment may take place through religion, since something done may by spirit (*Geist*) be made undone in spirit. But the power to accomplish this on earth resides in the king's majesty alone and must belong solely to his self-determined decision.

174. *Paragraph 290.*

The point of special importance in the executive is the division of functions. The executive is concerned with the transition from the universal to the particular and the individual, and its functions must be divided in accordance with the differences between its branches. The difficulty, however, is that these different branches meet again at both the top and the bottom. The police and the judiciary, for instance, move at right angles to one another, but in each particular case they coincide again. The usual expedient adopted to meet this difficulty is to appoint a Chancellor, a Prime Minister, or a Président du Conseil des Ministres to unify control at the top. But the result of this is that once more everything may have its source in the Minister's power, and the business of the state is, as we say, centralized. This entails the maximum of simplification, speed, and efficiency in meeting state requirements. A system of this kind was introduced by the French revolutionaries, elaborated by Napoleon, and still exists in France to-day. On the other hand, France lacks Corporations and local government, i.e. associations wherein particular and universal interests meet. It is true that these associations won too great a measure of self-subsistence in the Middle Ages, when they were states within states and obstinately persisted in behaving like independent corporate bodies. But while that should not be allowed to happen, we may none the less affirm that the proper strength of the state lies in these associations. In them the executive meets with legitimate interests which it must respect, and since the administration cannot be other than helpful to such interests, though it must also supervise them, the individual finds protection in the exercise of his rights and so links his private interest with the maintenance of the whole. For some time past organizations have been framed with a view to controlling these particular spheres from above,* and effort has chiefly been expended on organizations of that type, while the lower classes, the mass of the population, have been left more or less unorganized. And yet it is of the utmost importance that the masses should be organized, because only so do they become mighty and powerful. Otherwise they are nothing but a heap, an aggregate of

* [Hegel is thinking of his own experience in Bavaria in 1807. See *Briefe von und an Hegel*, vol. i, p. 130. (Lasson).]

atomic units. Only when the particular associations are organized members of the state are they possessed of legitimate power.

175. *Paragraph 297.*

The middle class, to which civil servants belong, is politically conscious and the one in which education is most prominent. For this reason it is also the pillar of the state so far as honesty and intelligence are concerned. A state without a middle class must therefore remain on a low level. Russia, for instance, has a mass of serfs on the one hand and a mass of rulers on the other. It is a prime concern of the state that a middle class should be developed, but this can be done only if the state is an organic unity like the one described here, i.e. it can be done only by giving authority to spheres of particular interests, which are relatively independent, and by appointing an army of officials whose personal arbitrariness is broken against such authorized bodies. Action in accordance with everyone's rights, and the habit of such action, is a consequence of the counterpoise to officialdom which independent and self-subsistent bodies create.

176. *Paragraph 298.*

The constitution must in and by itself be the fixed and recognized ground on which the legislature stands, and for this reason it must not first be constructed. Thus the constitution *is*, but just as essentially it *becomes*, i.e. it advances and matures. This advance is an alteration which is imperceptible and which lacks the form of alteration. For example, the wealth of the German princes and their families began by being private property but then without any struggle or opposition it was converted into crown lands, i.e. into public property. This came about because the princes felt the need of integrating their possessions and demanded property guarantees from their country and Estates; and these guarantees were intertwined with such a mode of stabilizing property that it ceased to be at the sole disposal of the princes. An analogous case is that [in the Holy Roman Empire] the Emperor was formerly a judge and travelled the Empire on circuit, and then, owing to the purely superficial results of cultural progress, external reasons made it necessary for him to delegate more and more of his judicial functions to others, with the result that the judicial power was transferred from the person of the monarch to groups of judges. Hence the advance from one state of affairs to another is tranquil in appearance and unnoticed. In this way a constitution changes over a long period of time into something quite different from what it was originally.

177. *Paragraph 299.*

The two sides of the constitution bear respectively on the rights and the services of individuals. Services are now almost entirely reduced to money payments, and military service is now almost the only personal one exacted. In the past, far more claims were made directly on a man's own person, and he used to be called upon for work according to his ability. In our day, the state purchases what it requires. This may at first sight seem an abstract, heartless, and dead state of affairs, and for the state to be satisfied with indirect services may also look like decadence in the state. But the principle of the modern state requires that the whole of an individual's activity shall be mediated through his will. By means of money, however, the justice of equality can be achieved much more efficiently. Otherwise, if assessment depended on concrete ability, a talented man would be more heavily taxed than an untalented one. But nowadays respect for subjective freedom is publicly recognized precisely in the fact that the state lays hold of a man only by that which is capable of being held.*

178. *Paragraph 300.*

The proposal to exclude members of the executive from legislative bodies, as for instance the Constituent Assembly† did, is a consequence of false views of the state. In England, ministers must be members of parliament, and this is right, because executive officers should be linked with and not opposed to the legislature. The idea‡ of the so-called 'independence of powers' contains the fundamental error of supposing that the powers, though independent, are to check one another. This independence, however, destroys the unity of the state, and unity is the chief of all desiderata.

179. *Paragraph 301.*

The attitude of the executive to the Estates should not be essentially hostile, and a belief in the necessity of such hostility is a sad mistake. The executive is not a party standing over against another party in such a way that each has continually to steal a march on the other and wrest something from the other. If such a situation arises in the state, that is a misfortune, but it cannot be called health. The taxes voted by the Estates, moreover, are not to be regarded as a present given to the state. On the contrary, they are voted in the best interests of the voters themselves. The real significance of the Estates lies in the fact that it is through them that the state enters the subjective consciousness of the people and that the people begins to participate in the state.

180. *Paragraph 302.*

The constitution is essentially a system of mediation. In despotisms where there are only rulers and people, the people is effective, if at all, only as a mass destructive of the organization of the state. When the multitude enters the state as one of its organs, it achieves its interests

---

    * [i.e. external goods. See Paragraph 299.]
    † [In France.]
    ‡ [Montesquieu's. See *Esprit des Lois*, xi. 6.]

by legal and orderly means. But if these means are lacking, the voice of the masses is always for violence. Hence, in despotic states, the despot always indulges the mob and keeps his wrath for his entourage. For the same reason too the mob in such states pays only a few taxes. Taxes rise in a constitutionally governed state simply owing to the people's own consciousness. In no country are so many taxes paid as in England.

181. *Paragraph 306.*

This class has a volition of a more independent character. On the whole, the class of landed-property owners is divided into an educated section and a section of farmers. But over against both of these sorts of people there stands the business class, which is dependent on needs and concentrated on their satisfaction, and the civil servant class, which is essentially dependent on the state. The security and stability of the agricultural class may be still further increased by the institution of primogeniture, though this institution is desirable only from the point of view of politics, since it entails a sacrifice for the political end of giving the eldest son a life of independence. Primogeniture is grounded on the fact that the state should be able to reckon not on the bare possibility of political inclinations, but on something necessary. Now an inclination for politics is of course not bound up with wealth, but there is a relatively necessary connexion between the two, because a man with independent means is not hemmed in by external circumstances and so there is nothing to prevent him from entering politics and working for the state. Where political institutions are lacking, however, the foundation and encouragement of primogeniture is nothing but a chain on the freedom of private rights, and either political meaning must be given to it, or else it will in due course disappear.

182. *Paragraph 309.*

The introduction of representation implies that consent is to be given not directly by all but only by plenipotentiaries, since under a representative system the individual, *qua* infinite person, no longer comes into the picture. Representation is grounded on trust, but trusting another is something different from giving my vote myself in my own personal capacity. Hence majority voting runs counter to the principle that I should be personally present in anything which is to be obligatory on me. We have confidence in a man when we take him to be a man of discretion who will manage our affairs conscientiously and to the best of his knowledge, just as if they were his own. Thus the principle of the individual subjective will disappears, since confidence is given to a thing, to a man's principles, or his demeanour or his conduct or his concrete mentality generally. The important thing, then, is that a member of the Estates shall have a character, insight, and will adequate to his task of concentrating on public business. In other words there is no question of an individual's talking as an abstract single person. The point is rather that his interests are made good in an assembly whose business is with the general interest. The electors require a guarantee that their deputy will further and secure this general interest.

183. *Paragraph 315.*

Estates Assemblies, open to the public, are a great spectacle and an excellent education for the citizens, and it is from them that the people learns best how to recognize the true character of its interests. The idea usually dominant is that everyone knows from the start what is best for the state and that the Assembly debate is a mere discussion of this knowledge. In fact, however, the precise contrary is the truth. It is here that there first begin to develop the virtues, abilities, dexterities, which have to serve as examples to the public. Of course such debates are irksome to ministers, who have to equip themselves with wit and eloquence to meet the criticisms there directed against them. None the less, publicity here is the chief means of educating the public in national affairs. A nation which has such public sittings is far more vitally related to the state than one which has no Estates Assembly or one which meets in private. It is only because their every step is made known publicly in this way that the two Houses keep pace with the advance of public opinion, and it then becomes clear that a man's castle building at his fireside with his wife and his friends is one thing, while what happens in a great Assembly, where one shrewd idea devours another, is something quite different.

184. *Paragraph 316.*

Public opinion is the unorganized way in which a people's opinions and wishes are made known. What is actually made authoritative in the state must operate in an organized manner as the parts of the constitution do. But at all times public opinion has been a great power and it is particularly so in our day when the principle of subjective freedom has such importance and significance. What is to be authoritative nowadays derives its authority, not at all from force, only to a small extent from habit and custom, really from insight and argument.

185. *Paragraph 317.*

The principle of the modern world requires that what anyone is to recognize shall reveal itself to him as something entitled to recognition. Apart from that, however, everyone wishes to have some share in discussion and deliberation. Once he has had his say and so his share of responsibility, his subjectivity has been satisfied and he puts up with a lot. In France freedom of speech has turned out far less dangerous than enforced silence, because with the latter the fear is that men bottle up their objections to a thing, whereas argument gives them an outlet and a measure of satisfaction, and this is in addition a means whereby the thing can be pushed ahead more easily.

186. *Paragraph 318.*

Public opinion contains all kinds of falsity and truth, but it takes
a great man to find the truth in it. The great man of the age is the one
who can put into words the will of his age, tell his age what its will is,
and accomplish it.* What he does is the heart and the essence of his
age, he actualizes his age. The man who lacks sense enough to despise
public opinion expressed in gossip will never do anything great.

187. *Paragraph 320.*

Subjectivity has been treated once already [Paragraphs 279 ff.] as
the apex of the state, as the crown. Its other aspect is its arbitrary
manifestation in public opinion, its most external mode of appearance.
The subjectivity of the monarch is inherently abstract, but it should
be something concrete and so be the ideality which diffuses itself over
the whole state. The state at peace is that in which all branches of
civil life subsist, but they possess their subsistence outside and alongside one another as something which issues from the Idea of the whole.
The fact that it so issues must also come into appearance as the ideality
of the whole.

188. *Paragraph 324.*

In peace civil life continually expands; all its departments wall
themselves in, and in the long run men stagnate. Their idiosyncrasies
become continually more fixed and ossified. But for health the unity
of the body is required, and if its parts harden themselves into exclusiveness, that is death. Perpetual peace is often advocated as an ideal
towards which humanity should strive. With that end in view, Kant
proposed a league of monarchs to adjust differences between states,
and the Holy Alliance† was meant to be a league of much the same
kind. But the state is an individual, and individuality essentially implies
negation. Hence even if a number of states make themselves into a
family, this group as an individual must engender an opposite and
create an enemy. As a result of war, nations are strengthened, but
peoples involved in civil strife also acquire peace at home through
making wars abroad. To be sure, war produces insecurity of property,
but this insecurity of things is nothing but their transience—which is
inevitable. We hear plenty of sermons from the pulpit about the insecurity, vanity, and instability of temporal things, but everyone thinks,
however much he is moved by what he hears, that he at least will be
able to retain his own. But if this insecurity now comes on the scene
in the form of hussars with shining sabres and they actualize in real

* [Reading *Wer, was seine Zeit will, ausspricht, ihr sagt und vollbringt*, with
Ziegler in *Kant-Studien*, 1909.]

† [1815, between Russia, Austria, and Prussia; formed on the initiative of
Tsar Alexander in the professed endeavour 'to regulate future conduct by the
principles of the Gospel'.]

earnest what the preachers have said, then the moving and edifying discourses which foretold all these events turn into curses against the invader. Be that as it may, the fact remains that wars occur when the necessity of the case requires. The seeds burgeon once more, and harangues are silenced by the solemn cycles of history.

189. Paragraph 327.

The military class is that universal class which is charged with the defence of the state, and its duty is to make real the ideality implicit within itself, i.e. to sacrifice itself. Courage to be sure is multiform. The mettle of an animal or a brigand, courage for the sake of honour, the courage of a knight, these are not true forms of courage. The true courage of civilized nations is readiness for sacrifice in the service of the state, so that the individual counts as only one amongst many. The important thing here is not personal mettle but aligning oneself with the universal. In India five hundred men conquered twenty thousand who were not cowards, but who only lacked this disposition to work in close co-operation with others.*

190. Paragraph 329.

In almost all European countries the individual head of the state is the monarch, and foreign affairs are his business. Where the Estates have constitutional powers, the question may arise whether they should not decide on war and peace, and in any case they have their influence on the question, particularly in connexion with ways and means. In England, for example, no unpopular war can be waged. If, however, it is supposed that monarchs and cabinets are more subject to passion than parliaments are, and if for this reason an attempt is made to juggle the decision on war and peace into the hands of the latter, then we must point out that whole peoples may often be a prey to excitement or be carried away by passion to a greater extent than their leaders. In England the whole nation has frequently pressed for war and to a certain extent compelled ministers to wage it. The popularity of Pitt was due to his knowing how to fall in with what the people wanted at the time.† It was only later‡ that the people cooled down and so began to reflect that the war was useless and unnecessary and had been undertaken without counting the cost. Moreover, a state stands in relation not with one other state only, but with many. And the complexities of their relations become so delicate that they can be handled only by the head of the state.

* [In 1751 Clive 'led five hundred men to Arcot . . . and there held a crumbling fortress against ten thousand Indians with a stiffening of French troops'. At Plassey 'he brought 3,000 men into action of whom 900 only were Europeans, against a force of 40,000 infantry and 15,000 cavalry and . . . routed his opponents' (Fisher, *History of Europe*, London, 1936, p. 764).]

† [1793.]   ‡ [1797.]

191. *Paragraph 330.*

States are not private persons but completely autonomous totalities in themselves, and so the relation between them differs from a moral relation and a relation involving private rights. Attempts have often been made to regard the state as a person with the rights of persons and as a moral entity. But the position with private persons is that they are under the jurisdiction of a court which gives effect to what is right in principle. Now a relation between states ought also to be right in principle, but in mundane affairs a principle ought also to have power. Now since there is no power in existence which decides in face of the state what is right in principle and actualizes this decision, it follows that so far as international relations are concerned we can never get beyond an 'ought'. The relation between states is a relation between autonomous entities which make mutual stipulations but which at the same time are superior to these stipulations.

192. *Paragraph 331.*

When Napoleon said before the Peace of Campoformio* that 'the French Republic needs recognition as little as the sun requires it', what his words implied was simply the thing's *strength* which carries with it, without any verbal expression, the guarantee of recognition.

193. *Paragraph 338.*

Modern wars are therefore humanely waged, and person is not set over against person in hatred. At most, personal enmities appear in the vanguard, but in the main body of the army hostility is something vague and gives place to each side's respect for the duty of the other.

194. *Paragraph 339.*

The European peoples form a family in accordance with the universal principle underlying their legal codes, their customs, and their civilization. This principle has modified their international conduct accordingly in a state of affairs [i.e. war] otherwise dominated by the mutual infliction of evils. The relations of state to state are uncertain, and there is no Praetor available to adjust them. The only higher judge is the universal absolute mind, the world mind.

* [1797, at the close of Napoleon's first Italian campaign.]

TRANSLATOR'S NOTES

PREFACE

1. As Professor of Philosophy in Berlin. When the *Philosophy of Right* was published in 1821, Hegel had held this appointment for three years. He used this book as a text for lectures in the winter session of 1821, 1822, 1824, and 1830, and had started to use it for a fifth time when he died on 7 November 1831. On each occasion he lectured on the subject for five days a week throughout the session.

2. *Encyklopädie der philosophischen Wissenschaften im Grundrisse.* A second edition was published in 1827 and a third in 1830. Of the three parts, Logic, Nature, and Mind, the first and third were translated by W. Wallace from the third edition; the second has not yet been translated into English. Where Hegel has cited in the *Philosophy of Right* Paragraphs of the first edition, the translator has appended in square brackets references to the corresponding passages of the third edition, although the third often differs substantially from the first. In the third edition Paragraphs 1–244 are devoted to Logic, and Paragraphs 377–577 to Mind. (The Additions to the Paragraphs on Mind are not included in Wallace's translation.) The Paragraphs in that edition which cover the same ground as the *Philosophy of Right* are 483–552. In these Notes references to the *Encyclopaedia* are to the third edition unless the contrary is stated.

3. The intuitive philosophy of Jacobi, Krug, Fries, and their followers, against which Hegel speaks so strongly here and elsewhere in this book, is treated at greater length in *Enc.*, Paragraphs 61 ff., as well as in essays and articles which Hegel published from 1801 onwards—see *Werke*[1], i. 3 ff, and xvi. 33 ff.

4. *Wissenschaft der Logik* (Nuremberg, 1812–16). See especially the introduction to that work and its final section on 'the Absolute Idea'. 'Speculative'—Hegel is fond of the distinction between 'speculative' and 'empirical', and he uses the latter in a pejorative sense. 'Empiricism' was in his view a purely scientific outlook and not a philosophy in the proper sense at all. Compare Kant's words: 'Those who are more especially speculative are . . . hostile to heterogeneity . . .; those who are more especially empirical are constantly endeavouring to differentiate nature' (*Critique of Pure Reason*, B. 683, Kemp Smith's translation). 'Speculative' thinking is thinking in terms of the 'concept'—see Translator's Foreword, § 4, i and ii.

5. St. Luke xvi. 29.

6. 'Positive'—i.e. posited, laid down arbitrarily, as when we speak of 'positive' as distinct from 'natural' law. Notice that Hegel's statement implies that a state has no absolute authority and is not exempt from philosophical criticism.

7. 'The public was through the philosophy of Kant and Jacobi strengthened in its opinion . . . that the knowledge of God is immediate, and that we know it from the beginning and without requiring to study, and hence philosophy is quite superfluous' (*History of Philosophy*, iii. 505). Cf. *Enc.*, § 5 and §§ 61 ff.

8. It is publications by Romantics (e.g. F. von Schlegel) that Hegel has mainly in mind. For a good account of these and other political ideas current in Hegel's day in Germany, see R. Aris: *History of Political Thought in Germany 1789–1815* (London, 1936).

9. The Romantics in their revolt against eighteenth-century rationalism accepted Kant's view that knowledge was of phenomena alone, since reason could not attain knowledge of things in themselves, but they went on to hold that the heart has its reasons that the head knows not of.

10. Cf. *Enc.*, § 19, with Wallace's note *ad loc.*, in which a specific instance of flattery of the young is quoted from Fichte. Wordsworth, referring to this period, writes of a new philosophy finding a ready welcome because it offered a 'tempting region where passions had the privilege to work. . . . The dream flattered the young. How glorious' to build social freedom on the basis of the individual's freedom, 'superior to the blind restraints of general laws' (*Prelude*, xi. 223–44 in *Works*, ed. by W. Knight, London, 1896, vol. iii).

11. Like nearly all Hegel's quotations, this is inaccurate. Psalm cxxvii. 2, in Luther's version, reads, literally translated, 'for He giveth to His beloved in sleep'. The 'wares of sleep' are dreams, cf. *Phenomenology*, pp. 74–5.

12. J. F. Fries, 1773–1843, Professor at Heidelberg (where he was Hegel's predecessor) 1805–16, and thereafter at Jena. In 1819 he was suspended by the government for his participation in the Wartburg Festival (see the next note) and for his ultra-liberal views. In 1824 he was allowed to teach mathematics and physics, and he was restored to his philosophy chair in 1825. 'He turns back to the faith of Jacobi in the form of immediate judgments derived from reason and dark conceptions incapable of utterance. He wished to improve Kant's *Critique* by apprehending the categories as facts of consciousness. Anything one chooses can be introduced by that method' (*History of Philosophy*, iii. 511).

13. The Wartburg Festival of the German Students' Societies on 18 October 1817 (Lasson). This was a liberal demonstration in favour

of German unity and Stein's reforms. Hegel supported both of these, but he held that enthusiastic demonstrations were no substitute for thinking and could only lead to immorality and anarchy. His view received some support in 1819 when Kotzebue, who was suspected of being a Russian spy, was murdered by a student. However well intentioned the student may have been, good intentions were in Hegel's view no excuse for murder. See Paragraph 126 and Remark (d) to Paragraph 140. The book by von Haller, which Hegel attacks in the footnote to Paragraph 258, was burned at this Festival, and Hegel's reference to Fries at this point is simply an indication that he had as little sympathy with Romantics as he had with Reactionaries. See Note 17 below and the Translator's article on 'Hegel and Prussianism' in *Philosophy*, January 1940. See below, Addenda, p. 376.

14. Epicurus measured conduct by the standard of feeling and impulse, and truth by the standard of sense-perception (*History of Philosophy*, ii. 276 ff. and especially 281).

15. The lines in *Faust* to which Hegel refers are

> *Verachte nur Vernunft und Wissenschaft*
> *Des Menschen allerhöchste Kraft. . . .*
> *Und hätt' er sich auch nicht dem Teufel übergeben,*
> *Er müsste doch zu Grunde gehn.*

I. iv. 322–3, 337–8.

> 'Reason and knowledge only thou despise,
> The highest strength in man that lies! . . .
> Had he not made himself the devil's naught could save him,
> Still were he lost for evermore!'

(Tr. Bayard Taylor.)

Hegel misquotes the lines both here and in the *Phenomenology*, p. 384.

16. The piety which Hegel attacks (Schleiermacher is sometimes in his mind) is that which regards the world as God-forsaken and which exalts the sanctities of inner conviction above the wickedness of the world. It forgets, Hegel holds, that God reveals himself *in* the world, in nature and history. Piety of the right sort worships God not as an abstract 'supreme being', but as a loving and self-revealing spirit. Such piety is at home in the world and is reconciled to it, because it has faith that, since the world is the revelation of God, reason must be immanent in it as its law and essential principle. Philosophy differs from such piety, in Hegel's view, only in substituting knowledge for faith.

17. In the footnote to Paragraph 258. The significance of this reference is that this 'shibboleth' is there said to be characteristic of von Haller, the reactionary, as it is here said to be of Fries, the liberal. Their extreme views rest on a common error.

18. Hegel is speaking of the *Existenz* of philosophy, and all that he means is that in Prussia philosophy was confined mainly or entirely to universities, i.e. to state institutions, whose professors were civil servants and so in 'the service of the state'. In Greece, on the other hand, philosophy was not a professional occupation at all.

19. For the wide meaning which Hegel gives to 'police', see Paragraphs 231–49. The action of which he is thinking here is probably the suspension of Fries from his chair, but he may be going so far as to suggest that there is justification for imprisoning philosophers who propound views dangerous to the maintenance of public peace.

20. See e.g. *Protagoras* and *Republic*, 493 ff., where the sophist is contrasted with the true philosopher.

21. The reference is probably to the numerous attacks made by empirical scientists on Schelling's philosophy of nature.

22. Tübingen, 1810–12. All editions read *Teil* viii, *S.* 56 as the reference, but that is an error.

23. This has not been said before, but it may be implied in the assertion that subjectivism adopts the sophistic principles which, in their practical reference, are destructive of established law and order and so bring police action on themselves.

24. The reference may be to the preface to the *Phenomenology*, p. 105, where philosophy's element and content is said to be the actual, or to the first edition of *Enc.*, § 5, where philosophy is described as the science of reason.

25. In the Remark to Paragraph 185.

26. Reading *welche damals die bevorstehende*, for *welche die*, &c., in accordance with *Hegels e. R.*, p. v, note. The 'deeper principle' breaking into the Greek world in Plato's time was the principle of 'subjective freedom', on which Hegel has a good deal to say in the third part of this book. The 'world revolution' then impending was the change in men's ideas due to the Christian revelation, and especially to the Christian doctrine of conscience. According to this doctrine, moral worth depends not simply on the fulfilment of the law (because such fulfilment may be Pharisaical or involuntary), but on the conscientious and willing acceptance of the law; and the demand which conscience makes is that no moral agent shall be required to perform any action in defiance of his conscientious conviction. Such a doctrine has its danger (as Hegel shows in the Remark to Paragraph 140) because it may degenerate into a claim for subjective infallibility, and it was this danger which Plato saw in the moral subjectivism of the Sophists. For Plato the principles of conduct were objective and eternal, obligatory

whether men knew them or not; the Greeks had no word for conscience. For Hegel the principles are objective indeed, but they
are actualized only in men's minds and through their conscientious
actions. In his view, the subjective claims of the Sophists did enshrine
part of the new truth which mankind was shortly to discover through
Christianity; in substance they were claims for freedom of conscience,
though that was not realized. Hence, instead of regarding this subjectivism as something merely 'corruptive', to be stemmed only by a
rigid system of objective laws imposed on the individual from without,
as described in the *Republic*, Plato should have accepted it in its essence
and so have achieved what Hegel attempts in Part III of this book,
namely an integration of the objectivity of law with subjective freedom.
To have done so, however, would have meant anticipating Christian
teaching, as Plato could not have done before it was revealed 'from on
High'. See Paragraphs 185 and 206. Cf. *History of Philosophy*, ii.
90-115.—'Free infinite personality'—see Paragraphs 5, 21, and 35.
For Hegel a person is a thinking being conscious of himself as an ego.
In virtue of this consciousness, a man is free and infinite, because he
can abstract himself, his ego, from any restraints which may be imposed
on his body. Hegel's point is that Plato (*a*) by his purely objective
regulations, and (*b*) by his retention of slavery, fails to recognize this
inviolable sanctity of the inner life.

27. This statement is further explained and defended in *Enc.*, § 6.
Note that Hegel is not saying that what exists or is 'real' is rational.
By 'actuality' (see Translator's Foreword, § 3) he means the synthesis
of essence and existence. If we say of a statesman who accomplishes
nothing that he is not a 'real' statesman, then we mean by 'real' what
Hegel calls 'actual'. The statesman exists as a man in office, but he
lacks the essence constitutive of what statesmanship ought to be, say
effectiveness. Conversely, and in Hegel's view no less important, if
effectiveness were never the quality of an existing statesman, then it
would not be the rational essence of statesmanship, but a mere ideal or
dream. Hegel's philosophy as a whole might be regarded as an attempt
to justify his identification of rationality with actuality and vice versa,
but his doctrine depends ultimately on his faith in God's Providence,
his conviction that history is the working out of His rational purpose.
That purpose, as the purpose of the Almighty, is not so impotent as to
remain a mere ideal or aspiration, and conversely, what is genuinely
actual or effective in the world is simply the working of that purpose.—
It follows that Hegel's identification of the actual and the rational is
not a plea for conservatism in politics. The actualization of God's
purpose is not yet complete. See the Addition to Paragraph 270 and
the closing pages of the *Philosophy of History*.

28. Thought at any stage does not attain full actuality until it passes

over into existence and embodies itself in something objective. E.g. religious convictions are not genuinely actual until they are objectified in institutions, churches, &c. Similarly, the state, as an objectification in the external world of man's rational will, is that in which alone his freedom, the essence of his will, is fully actualized.

29. *Laws*, vii. 789 e. Hegel's citation is not quite accurate, and he seems to have forgotten that Plato is saying that to make such a regulation is unnecessary and would be ridiculous.

30. *Science of Rights*, § 21, p. 379. Fichte limits this requirement to 'important persons who can afford to pay for it'. For the conception of 'construction' and Hegel's criticism of it, see *Enc.*, § 231.

31. The ultimate source of the Greek proverb ('here is Rhodes, here's your jump') is Michael Apostolius viii. 100 (Leutsch: *Paroemiographi Graeci*, Göttingen, 1851, vol. ii). But in its Latin form it is a commonplace of German elementary Latin text-books, and it may have reached them, and Hegel also, from Erasmus, *Adagia*, III. iii. 28. Erasmus quotes the Greek, gives a Latin translation, and continues: 'The proverb will be apt when someone is asked to show on the spot that he can do what he boasts he has done elsewhere.' (Hegel's interpretation seems to have been slightly different.) Cf. Goethe: *Zahme Xenien*, III. ii.

32. Perhaps a reminiscence of Aulus Gellius, *Noctes Atticae*, xii. 11: 'One of the old poets said that truth is the daughter of time.' Cf. Bacon: *Novum Organum*, i. 84: 'Rightly is truth called the daughter of time, not of authority.'

33. Hegel is playing on words. Ῥόδος means not only the island of Rhodes, but also a rose. *Saltus* means a jump, but *salta* is the imperative of the verb 'to dance'. The rose is the symbol of joy, and the philosopher's task is to find joy in the present by discovering reason within it. In other words, philosophy may 'dance' for joy in this world; it need not postpone its 'dancing' until it builds an ideal world elsewhere.

34. If the actual is rational, then however tragic the actual may seem to be, reason will be able to find joy in it, because it will find itself in it as its essence. Hegel uses the same metaphor in *Philosophy of Religion*, i. 284–5. As he indicates in *Werke*[1], xvii. 227, the metaphor was suggested to him by the Rosicrucians. (See Lasson: *Beiträge zur Hegel-Forschung*, Part 2, Berlin, 1910, pp. 49–50.)

35. Cf. Hegel's criticism of Spinoza in, e.g., *Phenomenology*, p. 80, and *Enc.*, § 151. His point is that Spinoza's view of the universe as substance or necessity needs to be supplemented by the Christian doctrine of subjectivity and subjective freedom. God is substance, but

is person or subject as well. Hegel applies this doctrine to the state and holds that although the state is a substance, in modern times it has come to consciousness of itself in its citizens and its monarch, and so has become not a mere external necessity but the embodiment of freedom. Cf. Note 3 to Paragraph 144.

36. See p. 2.

37. Hegel regards religion, especially Protestantism, and philosophy as the same in content, but faith and feeling are the form of religion, while rationality is the form of philosophy (see Remark to Paragraph 270). According to the 'Lutheran faith, it is this specific individual who is related to God. A man's piety, his hope of salvation, &c., all demand that his heart, his subjectivity, should be present in them. His feelings, his faith, in short all that belongs to him is claimed, Man must repent from the heart and be filled with the Holy Ghost. Thus here the principle of subjectivity, i.e. freedom, is recognized' (*History of Philosophy*, iii. 149). The influence of Luther is marked in Hegel's work. Luther preached non-resistance to the temporal power, and the action which he urged was always action within the framework of the existing order. It is a view like this which colours Hegel's conception of the relation between the state and the church.

38. The phrase is from Bacon: *De Aug. Sc.*, i. 5 (Lasson). There is a similar remark in his essay on Atheism.

39. A hit at Kant's 'regulative employment of the Ideas of Reason'. See e.g. *Critique of Pure Reason*, B. 675.

40. Revelation iii. 15–16.

41. 'Grey in grey'—a reminiscence of the words of Mephistopheles:

> My worthy friend, grey are all theories
> And green alone life's golden tree.

(*Faust*, tr. Bayard Taylor, I. iv. 509-14.) Philosophy paints the greyness of theory against the background of an ageing world.

INTRODUCTION

Heading. 1. This summary of the contents of the Introduction is added here from Hegel's original table of contents.

1. 2. The two moments of the Idea are (*a*) form, i.e. the concept—the will in this book—and (*b*) content, i.e. the existence of the concept or its embodiment in the realm of the finite—in this book a series of rights, subjects, and institutions embodying the will. The concept actualizes its potentialities by developing its determinations and embodying them in existence—see Paragraph 32. Now the characteristic of the

external world is its finitude; anything in it is a this, here, and now, connected by external relations with other equally finite entities. Thought, on the other hand, is an organic system of internal relations, and hence it can never be perfectly embodied without remainder in any external sphere. External relations imply accidental as well as necessary connexions, and the presence of accident in the finite is inescapable, although, since the finite as a whole is mind externalized, and so depends for its being on mind, this contingency is confined within limits. The task of the philosophy of nature and the philosophy of history is to ignore the contingency and penetrate through the husk of appearance to the reason, or the concept, at its heart. What it finds then is (a) a series of thoughts, the determinations of the concept, a necessary, organically connected, series, and (b) a series of natural phenomena and human institutions embodying the series of thoughts. To apprehend the Idea is to grasp both these series. Actuality is the synthesis of the two. Besides this actuality there are the accidents and contingencies inseparable from the spatio-temporal sphere; of these the empirical scientist and the historian have to take account, but in Hegel's view they are of no importance to the philosopher. They are irrational and therefore lack actuality.

2. 3. As Hegel points out in Paragraph 29, right is the will determinately existent, or is an embodiment of the will. The concept of the will is a determination of the concept of mind. The stages through which mind passes before will is reached are briefly summarized in Paragraph 4. Any genuine philosophy must in Hegel's view form a systematically and organically developed whole, and his own conception of this whole is summarized in his *Encyclopaedia*. In the *Philosophy of Right* he is expounding in detail one part of that system, and as a part of an organic development, it is like a period of history in presupposing preceding periods and being pregnant with those to follow. It cannot be too often emphasized that Hegel's philosophy culminates not with the state but with art, religion, and philosophy, which lie beyond the state and above it (see the last section of the *Encyclopaedia*).

4. 'In civil law, definition is always hazardous' (*Digest*, LX. xvii. 202). (Messineo.) 'Slave could not be brought under it', sc. without exposing the wrong of slavery. If a slave is a 'man', then his slavery is a denial of his rights.

5. 'Facts of consciousness'—here and in other places where Hegel uses this phrase, his arrow is primarily aimed at Fries (see Note 12 to the Preface). The expressions 'self-evident truths' and 'things intuitively known' are perhaps the modern equivalents of 'facts of consciousness'.

6. See e.g. Remarks to Paragraphs 126 and 140. If feeling or inspiration is made a substitute for law, then any crime may be justified by the convictions or 'moral intentions' of the criminal.

7. Cf. Preface, p. 2 and Note 4 *ad loc.*

3. 8. Right (*Recht*) once posited (*gesetzt*) or laid down is law (*Gesetz*). Now we may raise questions either about natural law, or about what is accepted as right in a given country, i.e. about positive law. In the latter there is an element of brute fact, something merely 'posited', which is important to the lawyer but out of place in a philosophical theory of law. Further, if we consider what is accepted as right in a given country, we can distinguish between its form and its content. The content may consist of specific statutes, of the judgements of various courts, of 'common law', &c.; but the form which all these possess is positedness or legal validity. The lawyer works *a posteriori*; he simply wishes to know what the law is. The philosopher wishes to probe deeper, to see positive law as the embodiment of the determinations of the concept of right, and these determinations form a necessary series, developing by the inner necessity of thought itself. But we must beware of supposing that the philosopher works *a priori*. A knowledge of what even the categories of logic are can be acquired only after an experience of thinking; and *a fortiori*, in the concrete spheres of nature and history, we cannot forecast the specific determinations which thought has given to itself (see Note 2 to Paragraph 1), although we can probe their necessity once we have ascertained what they have been. A study of empirical science must therefore precede the philosophy of nature (see *Enc.*, § 246) and a study of positive law and history must precede the philosophy of right. The philosopher tries to see the meaning of the facts which the historian collects, and to discover the necessity at the heart of their contingency. It is important to notice that Hegel brought to the writing of this book an extensive study of the facts whose inward and moving principle he here professes to expound, and thus he is very far from attempting to deduce the philosophy of the state by *a priori* thinking. For the distinction between *Recht* and *Gesetz* see Paragraphs 211 ff.

9. i.e. by soil, climate, geographical position, &c. On the influence of these, see the section on the 'Geographical Basis of History' in the *Philosophy of History*, pp. 79 ff.

10. e.g. the concept of theft must be applied to a case of literary plagiarism (*Hegels e. R.*, p. 3), a case not visualized when the law against theft was first laid down. See Remarks to Paragraphs 69, 212, 214.

11. Provisions detailing kind and amount of punishment, e.g. imprisonment or fine, and length of imprisonment or amount of fine; or such things as a summons to appear in court in a year and a day, &c. (*Hegels e. R.*, p. 3).

12. Legal rights in any given system of law are regarded by Hegel as an embodiment of the legislator's conception of what is right in the

nature of things. The illustration he chooses is not very happy. The Institutes of Justinian are an elementary text-book of law; the Pandects (or Digest) are a complete codex of case-law to which the Institutes are an introduction. Hegel takes the Institutes to lay down the general principles on which the detailed case-law collected in the Pandects is based, but that is not quite true of the books in question.

13. See *Esprit des Lois*, Book i, chap. 3.

14. See Remark and Addition to Paragraph 180, with Notes *ad loc.*

15. By the 'pragmatic' type of history is usually meant a type which has a utilitarian aim. See *Enc.*, § 140, and Wallace's note *ad loc.* So here the 'pragmatic' conception of law and institutions is that which regards a given law or institution as justified if it is useful, i.e. if it meets the needs of the time. Bentham's *Theory of Legislation* might perhaps be regarded as written from this point of view.

16. *Begreifen*—i.e. pragmatic historians claim by their method to comprehend (*begreifen*) history, although they make no attempt to pierce the veil of fact to the *Begriff* or concept in the light of which alone the facts are really intelligible, since they are its embodiment.

17. This is an allusion to the controversy started by the historical school of jurists—Savigny and his followers—in Hegel's day. They maintained against the rationalists that the law of a people was part and parcel of the national consciousness; conceptions of what was right differed therefore from nation to nation and customary law was of more importance than direct legislation.

18. Hegel's point is that both history and philosophy study the growth of institutions and the rise and fall of empires. But history stops at brute fact while the philosophy of history penetrates to the meaning of the facts. Since the philosophy of history is dependent on the results of historical investigation for its material, philosophy and history can to this extent be at peace with one another because they supplement each other. But they can also be at peace in another way because philosophy, as logic or metaphysics, must study the concept in and by itself, and not merely, as philosophy of history, the concept embodied in historical material; history and this abstract study are indifferent to one another. Hegel agrees with the historical school of jurists against the rationalists in laying emphasis on the historical or positive element in law, but he thinks that they are wrong in ignoring the rational element which is present also, and indeed fundamental, since the historical element is produced by the working of the concept itself. For some of Hegel's criticisms of Savigny, see Paragraph 211.

19. Gustav, Ritter von Hugo, 1764–1844, Professor in Göttingen from 1788 (Lasson). The first edition of his *Text-book of the History*

of Roman Law, was published in 1790. The fifth edition appeared in 1815 and there were many subsequent editions.

20. 'Affectation'—this refers back to the second paragraph of this Remark. The quotation from Hugo is from Paragraph 51 of the seventh edition, which is more easily accessible than the fifth and of which there is a French translation. The reference to Cicero is to *De Oratore*, i. 44; and the remarks of Favorinus are from the passage cited just below from Aulus Gellius.

21. Right principles remain abstract and therefore not fully actual until they are applied to the needs of the hour and posited in law. Law thus acquires of necessity a positive element which arises from the application of the concept to a finite and given material. This element therefore cannot be deduced from the concept and the only justification which it can have is a utilitarian one. Hegel's point is that philosophers (i.e. rationalists) have based many of their criticisms of law on a failure to understand the positive (and so irrational) element which it necessarily contains.

22. 'Favorinus attacks the Twelve Tables, taking his stand on the nature of the thing. Caecilius justifies the law by its efficacy' (*Hegels e. R.*, p. 6). Both Favorinus, the philosopher of Arles, and Caecilius, the African jurist, were historical figures, members of Hadrian's circle, but their conversation is rather imagined than reported by Aulus Gellius. The Latin quoted by Hegel may be translated as follows: 'You must be aware that the advantages and remedies offered by the laws vary and fluctuate in accordance with contemporary customs, types of constitution, considerations of immediate advantage, and the violence of the ills to be remedied. Laws do not persist unchanged in character; on the contrary, the storms of circumstance and chance alter them as storms change the face of the sea and the sky. Has anything ever seemed more salutary than Stolo's proposal . . ., more advantageous than the decree . . . carried by Voconius as tribune? What has been taken to be so necessary . . . as the Licinian law? Yet, now that the state has grown wealthy, all these regulations have been blotted out and buried' (*Noctes Atticae*, xx. i. 22–3).

23. *Vestimentis instrata.*

24. See *History of Philosophy*, iii. 329–30. Hegel is contrasting the method of mathematics which lays down certain axioms, postulates, and hypotheses, and deduces what follows from them, with the method of philosophy whose subject-matter is actuality and not hypotheses, and which develops by its own inner necessity, a necessity lacking, e.g., in the advance from one book of Euclid to the next. Leibniz frequently uses the mathematical method in his philosophical work, e.g. in his *Principles of Nature and Grace* he lays down the supreme perfection of

God, and then goes on, in Paragraphs 10 ff., to deduce what follows therefrom, e.g. that this is the best of all possible worlds, that the perceptions and desires of each monad must be of a certain character, &c. (see *The Monadology &c. of Leibniz*, translated by R. Latta, Oxford, 1925, pp. 417 ff.). Hugo, loc. cit., quotes from Leibniz's letters a passage comparing the Roman jurisconsults and modern mathematicians in respect of *vis* and *subtilitas* (Leibniz, *Opera omnia*, Geneva, 1768, vol. iv, part iii, p. 267).

25. *callide*—'artfully' or 'on the sly' (see Remark to Paragraph 180). The law of inheritance (*hereditas*), laid down by the Twelve Tables, led to much injustice, e.g. children emancipated from *patria potestas* were *eo ipso* excluded from inheritance. Praetorian edicts allowed parties so excluded to obtain their inheritance under another name— *bonorum possessio*. Thus, by a legal fiction, the old law of *hereditas* was maintained unimpaired, while its unpalatable consequences were evaded. See e.g. Gaius: *Institutes*, iii. 25 ff.

26. This example of a legal fiction was withdrawn from later editions of Heineccius's book as a mistake. What he says is that by a legal fiction the Praetors in certain cases treated a daughter as a son in order to give her rights of inheritance from which in strict law she was excluded.

27. Examples of the trichotomies which Hugo mentions are: *actio, petitio, persecutio; habes, tenes, possides; auro, argento, aere; do, lego, testor.*

4. 28. At the end of Hegel's Logic, the Absolute Idea, i.e. the highest category of thought, 'freely releases itself as nature' (see Note 42 to Paragraph 10). Nature, that is to say, is mind objectifying itself in the inorganic and organic. The whole sphere of right similarly is mind objectifying itself in institutions (see Note 28 to the Preface). In speaking of a world of mind, Hegel is not using 'world' in the general sense of a 'sphere' but in the sense of a world in space and time, a mundane world.

29. The hope of producing an ampler exposition was not fulfilled. In the second and third editions of the *Encyclopaedia* this particular section was not much enlarged, though some important changes were made, e.g. Paragraph 482 of the third edition, which describes the absolutely free will as 'finite', prima facie contradicts Paragraph 22 of this book, as Lasson points out (p. xxv). The *Zusätze* added to §§ 440–82 of the *Enc.* by Hegel's editors in the edition published after his death no doubt incorporate material which Hegel had meant to work up and publish separately, but they have not yet been translated into English.

5. 30. Hegel has in mind the ideas and actions of the French revolutionaries. Compare, as Lasson says, the section on 'Absolute Freedom and Terror' in the *Phenomenology*, pp. 599–610.

6. 31. The phrase 'absolute moment' is a surprising one, because what Hegel usually describes as 'absolute' is the synthesis of opposed moments, not either of them by itself. But he uses the phrase in *Hegels e. R.*, p. 88, in connexion with Paragraph 127. He says there that life, as the totality of particular interests, is the 'absolute moment' and has a true right against the abstract or formal right of property. The 'absolute moment', then, is the one which has a content, is concrete, while the first moment is a bare form or abstraction. Cf. *Philosophy of Religion*, ii. 331.

32. 'A = A . . . Ego = Ego, or I am I . . . The ego is that the being whereof consists in positing itself as being' (pp. 63–70)—'Of the understanding'—i.e. the abstract universality and abstract identity in terms of which the understanding, as distinct from reason, thinks; e.g. 'A thing is what it is and not another thing', i.e. is not, as Hegel holds, a unity of opposites; while the universal is supposed to subsist apart and in abstraction from particulars, i.e. is not concrete or self-differentiating (see Note 63 to Paragraph 24).

33. 'Not-A = not-A . . . A non-ego is absolutely "opposed" to the ego' (pp. 75 ff.). The third proposition states that the ego and the non-ego can be thought together only as limits to each other (pp. 81 ff.). See *History of Philosophy*, iii. 486–90.

34. (i) Jacobi in Hegel's day (like Karl Barth in our own) holds the infinite and the finite apart from one another. The infinite transcends the finite and is represented as absolutely sundered from it. (ii) Fichte attempted to overcome this dualism, because he did at least feel the need for a synthesis, as Jacobi did not. The ego for him is in a sense the whole of reality and the non-ego is immanent in the ego. But since he conceives the ego abstractly, not as a synthesis of opposites but as the bare absence of contradiction, the finite is swallowed up in an abstract infinite and his doctrine of immanence is as abstract as Jacobi's doctrine of transcendence. (iii) Hegel professes to have gone beyond both these abstract points of view by his doctrine that negativity is a moment within the infinite, so that the infinite actualizes itself only in positing itself as finite. This doctrine might be described both as a concrete transcendence and as a concrete immanence, because while in creating the finite the infinite transcends it, still what is so created is the realization of what is implicit in the infinite and so is in a sense immanent in it. (The translator owes this note to Professor Richard Kroner.)

7. 35. 'Itself'—i.e. not the ego (as Messineo translates) but negativity, as the Remark which follows makes clear. Both moments of which the ego is a synthesis are negative: the first is abstraction, the flight from or the negation of everything determinate; the second is determination, the negative of the original abstraction. Hence when the ego synthesizes these moments by becoming *self*-determined, it does so by bringing negativity to bear on negativity. What lives is an individual, neither a 'such' nor a 'this', but their synthesis, and life is the process of actualizing individuality, i.e the attempt to make explicit the 'such' by expressing it in the 'this', to make universal and particular correspond. The individual puts away childish things, rejects one achievement after another as unsatisfactory, because no imperfect correspondence between the universal and particular sides of his nature will satisfy him. And it fails to satisfy him because he is self-related negativity, i.e. the synthesis (whether explicit or not) of these two sides. Since it is this synthesis which is always present as the final cause of his efforts, self-related negativity may be described, as it is in the Remark to this Paragraph, as the ultimate spring of all activity.

36. *ideelle*—'The proposition that the finite is "ideal" constitutes idealism. . . . By "ideal" is meant the finite as it is found in true infinity, i.e. as a determination or content, which though distinct does not exist independently but only as a moment. . . . Religion equally with philosophy refuses to recognize in finitude a veritable being or something absolute' (*Science of Logic*, i. 163 and 168).

37. i.e. you are regarding the will as an ego or a substance whose activities or attributes respectively you can enumerate. You have overlooked the process by which the will develops from potentiality to actuality. Once the will as an actuality is before you, you may look back over the process of its development and describe the universal and particular moments which have become explicit through that process. But from that point of view these moments cannot be abstracted from one another without falsification. They are not like the factors of a number, indifferent to one another, but are related organically. A process is intelligible only in the light of its result, and to this result every moment in the process contributes, since each moment is the making explicit of what was present in germ at the start. Hence if you look at the will organically, you can see that its truth is self-determining individuality and that it is therefore aware of its universality only in determining itself, while it determines itself only to actualize its universality. It becomes aware of its universality by means of its particular determination, and since this determination is its own work, the will may be said to be a 'self-mediating' activity, or concrete individuality. Its individuality may be regarded as the conclusion of a syllogism of which the major premiss is its universality and its minor premiss—the middle term or the *means* whereby the conclusion is reached—is its particular determination.

8. 38. With this Paragraph compare the references to it in Paragraphs 25, 28, 108, and 109. Also see *Enc.*, §§ 424–5. The will may be regarded as determinate on two different levels: (*a*) it may be determined as

subjective only and not as objective also; i.e. it may be the self-consciousness which distinguishes itself from the external world. As *will*, this self-consciousness seeks to overcome its subjectivity and to give objectivity to itself, because to be only subjective is to be restricted, and the will's implicitly infinite nature struggles to overcome this restriction. This relation of consciousness to an object in which it finds not itself but only something other than itself is a mode in which the will *appears*, but it is only an appearance, not actuality. (Actuality is the synthesis of subjective and objective. A cleavage between these is only an appearance.) On this point see Paragraph 108 and Note 5 thereto. The first 'form' of the will which Hegel distinguishes here is the will determined in form as subjective. (*b*) The second form of the will is the will determined in content as well, i.e. the will which strives to satisfy some specific desire or to carry out some specific purpose. This form of will—the genuinely determinate will which supersedes the abstract or formal will of mere self-consciousness—Hegel proceeds to treat in the following Paragraphs.

9. 39. The second form of the will is the one whose determinate content is in the first instance given; but since it is also determined in form (i.e. is conscious of being a *will*), this content is its purpose or aim. A jelly-fish may have impulses, but it lacks self-consciousness and so cannot be said to have the purposes which a man can hold before his mind and then strive to attain.

10. 40. 'Object'—i.e. 'content and purpose' (*Hegels e. R.*, p. 12).

41. 'For itself and in itself'—in itself or in its essential nature a child is a man, a rational being. The child exemplifies the generic essence of manhood, and it is only if we know this that we can understand what a child is at all. But this generic essence is only implicit in the child; *in* itself the child is a man, but *for* itself or in its own eyes it is a child and a child only. Childhood is the mode of *existence* correlative to the *concept* of manhood while that concept is still only *implicit*, or, to use Hegel's terminology, in the child, manhood is 'in its concept', or is 'as concept only', or is 'in accordance with its concept'. The potentialities of manhood are realized only when the child grows up, and then, as man, is *for* itself what it is *in* itself. Manhood explicit or for itself as the adult is a different thing, a different type of existent, from the child, despite the inner identity between child and adult in respect of their concept. A man, however, is finite and he may fail adequately to embody the concept of man; he may be a cripple or a lunatic. Here again then there may be a discrepancy between the man's implicit nature and what he explicitly is, and it is the occurrence of such a discrepancy which constitutes finitude. A lunatic exists, is a phenomenon, but because of this discrepancy, he lacks actuality is a 'mere' existent or 'only' a phenomenon.

42. In Hegel's *Encyclopaedia* the section on nature succeeds the section on logic. Logic describes the movement of pure thought from

its most abstract to its most concrete category, from 'pure being' to 'absolute Idea'. All these categories are inwardly interconnected. No thought can be properly described as 'external' to any other. Now the inward and subjective are opposed to the external and objective, and the 'ideality' of thought to the 'reality' of things; and the concept, in order to actualize itself as a synthesis of opposites, posits itself, at the end of the logic, as its own opposite, i.e. not as abstract inwardness but as an external world of objects externally related to one another. This world is nature, and its chief characteristic is absolute externality, i.e. it is both implicitly and explicitly external. As Hegel puts it, nature is external to itself, it is entirely unconscious of its concept (see Addition to Paragraph 42). I cannot be external to myself, because *I* am *self*-conscious; another man may be external to me but he has an inward life or a consciousness of his own and hence externality is not the whole truth about him as it is about a stone. The truth of nature is its concept; *I* can think this concept, but nature cannot, and since therefore it remains outside its concept it remains outside its true self, and 'abstractly' external because the internality to which that externality is relative is mine and not its. Since nature as a whole is thought positing itself as externality and so as the opposite of itself, the categories of logic will have their analogues in nature. The first category of logic is pure being and its analogue in nature is space. Space is thus the first form which the 'reciprocal externality characteristic of nature' takes. Space is pure quantity, parts of space are all external to each other and so each 'negates' the other. But this reciprocal externality is only implicit in space, because the parts of space still remain beside each other and form a continuum. This moment of externality is explicit, on the other hand, in time, which is 'Chronus, devouring his own children', since, when one instant negates its predecessor, that predecessor disappears into the past and exists no longer. In the movement of thought, space precedes time, just as pure being precedes not-being. In the first stage, that of immediacy, the negative moment is implicit, and it becomes explicit at the next stage. Space then is the external formation appropriate to externality implicit (just as the child is the external formation appropriate to manhood implicit), while time is the external formation appropriate to externality explicit. The best account in English of Hegel's philosophy of nature is an article by S. Alexander in *Mind* for October 1886.

43. The natural or implicit will is treated in Paragraphs 11–18. The will which is explicitly free and is the basis of formal rights is treated in Paragraphs 21 ff. The concept of the will is freedom. The natural will is irrational and chained by desire and caprice; this irrationality is only an appearance (see Paragraphs 11 and 19), and the will appears in its irrational form because at the immediate level there is a gulf between what it is in its inherent nature and what it is explicitly.

11. 44. 'It is the element of individuality', i.e. the 'self-determining concept of the will', 'which first explicitly differentiates the moments of the concept. Individuality is the negative reflection of the concept into itself and in that way it is the free differentiation of the concept by which the specific character of the concept is realized' (*Enc.*, § 165). The self-determining individual in the process of realizing his individuality gives his will a specific content and sets up a difference in the will between its universal nature and the particularity of its content. The character of this difference varies with the character of the content and that in turn varies with the stages in the will's advance from immediacy to its full development.

45. i.e. in Paragraphs 19 and 150 with the Remarks thereto.

12. 46. The indeterminacy is twofold because none of these desires is my desire *in particular* and each of the desires is itself indeterminate (e.g. hunger, which all sorts of different foods might satisfy, is not hunger for anything specific).

47. There is no precise parallel in English to that between *beschliessen* and *sich entschliessen*. Both expressions mean 'to decide'. Etymologically, the former implies simply 'closing the matter', while the latter implies that the decision is at the same time the 'unfolding' or 'opening' of the character of the person who makes it.

13. 48. 'In so far as intelligence thinks'—intelligence is either mind theoretical or mind practical (see Paragraph 4). Cf. *Enc.*, § 34, where Hegel compares the doctrine of mind as activity to the Scholastic notion of God as 'pure act'.

49. i.e. by abandoning impulse and by determining itself in accordance with universal and rational laws. This is what the ethical will does in a state with a rational constitution, see Part III.

50. i.e. Kant and his followers.

15. 51. The difference between impulse and purpose is that the latter is made what it is by thought and so is rational and necessary. Impulse is irrational and contingent, though this is only an appearance, because in fact impulse is purpose disguised. See Paragraph 19 and the Remark thereto, and Note 39 to Paragraph 9.

52. Because the contingent is what is defined as possible, i.e. its definition is that it exists but need not (*Hegels e. R.*, p. 14). Since the ego may abstract itself from any content (see Paragraph 5), the content, in the face of this power to abstract, is only a possible one at the level of the arbitrary will as distinct from the genuinely free will.

53. Christian J. Wolff, 1679–1754, the champion of rationalist metaphysics. For Hegel's view of him, see *History of Philosophy*, iii. 348 ff.

For the arguments used in his day to support the freedom of the will, see Remark to Paragraph 4.

16. 54. i.e. if it renounces choice and determinacy altogether, it reverts to the first moment, described in Paragraph 5.

19. 55. In Paragraphs 18 and 19 where Hegel is considering the goodness or badness of human nature and where he mentions the 'demand for the purification of impulses', he probably has in mind the first part of Kant's *Religion within the bounds of reason alone*. This part is translated in *Kant's Theory of Ethics* under the title 'Of the indwelling of the bad principle along with the good, or on the radical evil in human nature'. The demand in question is made there (p. 354). For Hegel's view of the natural goodness or evil of man, see Paragraph 139.

56. e.g. Remarks to Paragraphs 2 and 4.

57. See Paragraphs 148 ff. and especially Remark to Paragraph 150.

20. 58. For happiness as an end, see Paragraph 123. 'Sum of satisfaction', see *Kant's Theory of Ethics*, p. 15. 'Education', i.e. *Bildung*, a central conception in the work of von Humboldt. 'The state', he says, 'is nothing but a means to the furtherance of *Bildung*, or rather to the removal of hindrances which would be in its way in a social state' (*Werke*, Berlin, 1903, i. 69, quoted here from Aris: *History of Political Thought in Germany from 1789–1815*, p. 144). Hegel regards 'civil society' as a sphere of education also (see Paragraph 187), while the institutions of the state too have an educative force (see Paragraphs 268 and 315). '*Bildung* is a more or less untranslatable term; it means the actual process of education and at the same time the cultured state of mind arrived at through education' (Aris, loc. cit.). 'Mental development' and 'culture' have occasionally been used to render the word. *Bildung* is used especially of education in the humanities. The phrase *gebildeter Mensch* (educated man) originates at the Renaissance and means a man of literary attainments, a scholar, not a scientist.

21. 59. The form of the will, as distinct from its content, is described in Paragraph 5. This form Hegel is fond of calling *Fürsichsein*, i.e. the will's existence for itself or in its own eyes, the ego aware of itself as an independent ego and so able to abstract itself from everything. This form is infinite because it is purely self-related and free from all restriction, see Paragraph 5.

60. Consciousness of the most rudimentary type, the type which precedes sense-perception, let alone intelligence, Hegel calls 'sense-consciousness' (*das sinnliche Bewusstsein*)—*Enc.*, §§ 418–19—the abstract pure consciousness of an immediate object, mere sensation, e.g. smell, taste, colour. These sensations, like their objects, fall into the world of the finite; they are natural, not rational, a temporal

series and therefore mutually exclusive. Consciousness here then is self-external (see Note 42 to Paragraph 10). Doubtless the series of externally related sensations implies an enduring self whose sensations they are; but so long as they are only externally related, not an organic system expressive of the self, the self is outside them, is not conscious of itself in them, and hence the ego in sensation is 'outside itself'. Self-consciousness, the truth to which consciousness attains when it climbs from sensation, through sense-perception, to intelligence (*Enc.*, §§ 420–3) begins by being immediate and has the form of a desire or an impulse directed on an external object in which it hopes to find satisfaction. In this experience, self-consciousness is related to an object outside itself; and since implicitly it is the synthesis of subject and object (since it is *self*-consciousness), it is divided against itself when it is a consciousness of an impulse on the one hand and an external object on the other. The implicit unity of subject and object is explicitly realized when the impulse (e.g. hunger) is satisfied by devouring and so destroying the external object (*Enc.*, § 426).

61. 'Essence'—i.e. he has not risen to the stage of reflection, to distinguishing between his essence (manhood, which implies rationality and therefore freedom) and what he is (a slave). For the meaning of essence see *Enc.*, § 112: 'Any mention of essence implies that we distinguish it from being. The point of view of essence is in general the standpoint of reflection. This word "reflection" is originally applied when a ray of light in a straight line, impinging on the surface of a mirror, is thrown back from it. In this phenomenon, we have two things: first, an immediate which is, and secondly, the . . . derived or transmitted phase of the same. Something of this sort takes place when we reflect or think upon an object, not in its immediacy, but as derivative or mediated. The . . . aim of philosophy is often represented as the ascertainment of the essence of things. . . . The immediate being of things is thus conceived under the image of a . . . curtain behind which the essence lies hidden. . . . There is a permanent in things, and that permanent is in the first instance their essence. . . . The essence subsists in independence of its phenomenal embodiment. Thus we say of a people that the great thing is not what they do . . . but what they are. This is correct if it means that a man's conduct should be looked at not in its immediacy but only as a revelation of his inner self or essence.' Cf. 'We know that the individual is free. . . . Personal freedom is the fundamental thing and there is nothing which can do injury to it. . . . If we imagined a conqueror in Europe who acted on caprice and it struck him to make half his subjects slaves, we would realize at once that this was impossible, however great the force behind the project. Everyone knows that he cannot be a slave, and he knows this as the essence of his being. We are so and so old, we live, are officials, but these things we

know to be transient, not our essential being; what is essential is that we cannot be slaves' (*History of Philosophy*, Hoffmeister's edition, Leipzig, 1938, Lief. 2, pp. 233–4).

22. 62. The external, objective, organization of the state, described in Part III, embodies the inwardness of the will, i.e. its universality, particularity, and individuality, in a way appropriate to the concept, because these three moments there form an organic unity. The will has embodied *itself* in institutions, and there is thus established there what Hegel calls an 'identity' between inward and outward.

24. 63. The self-identical universal is altogether abstracted from and indifferent to individuals. 'It is as "all" that the universal is in the first instance encountered by reflection. The individuals form for reflection the foundation, and it is only our subjective action which collects and describes them as "all" (e.g. all metals conduct electricity). So far the universal has the aspect of an external fastening holding together a number of independent individuals which have not the least affinity towards it. This semblance of indifference is however unreal. . . . If we take Caius, Sempronius, and the other inhabitants of a town, the fact that all of them are men is not merely something which they have in common; it is their universal or generic essence without which these individuals would not be at all. . . . The individual man is what he is in particular only in so far as he is before all things a man as man and in general. And that generality is not something external or in addition to other abstract qualities; it is what permeates and includes in it everything particular' (*Enc.*, § 175).

26. 64. The reference here to the 'ethical will' is surprising. As the Addition indicates, a reference to it would have been expected under (α) rather than under (β). Messineo suggests reading *der kindlich-sittliche*, which would mean 'the naïvely ethical will'. The explanation of Hegel's reference, however, is possibly to be found in the *Phenomenology*, pp. 484 ff., where 'ethical action' is used of action done from the unquestioning acceptance of objective laws; there Hegel is thinking especially of ancient Greece, and of actions like Antigone's. In the modern world, however, as described in Part III of this book, the ethical will is not merely objective in the sense that it is 'sunk in its object'; it is at the same time a subjective and conscientious will, though its 'objective' character is even then part of the truth about it.

27. 65. The ultimate destiny of mind which, *qua* rational, is free, is that it shall find in its object nothing but itself and its own freedom. The process whereby this goal is achieved is described in Paragraph 28. Thereafter, mind is at peace with the world; it has fully developed its potentialities and exists as Idea, the unity of subject and object. Such a unity is achieved in a sense when 'the free will wills the free will', but this is only an abstract identity; a genuine content is lacking. Kant's ethics, in Hegel's view, never rises above this abstraction. What is required further is that the object willed shall take a form apparently the opposite of freedom itself (because the concrete is not an abstract identity but a unity of opposites), i.e. the form of concrete laws. Hence, concrete freedom is the will willing, not simply itself, but what is in accordance with laws embodying the intelligence and so the will of the people who live under them, and the Idea of the will is the synthesis of the subjective volition with the system of objective institutions which give content to that volition.

29. 66. Hegel refers, quoting as usual from memory, to Kant's statement that 'every action is right which in itself or in the maxim on. which it proceeds, is such that it can co-exist with the freedom of the will of each and all in action, according to a universal law' (*Philosophy of Law*, Introduction, § C, p. 45). The 'law of reason' to which Hegel refers just below is a reference to the same section of Kant's work. 'Self-will', i.e. *Willkür*, the arbitrary will, caprice.

67. See e.g. *Contrat Social*, i. 6, where the 'fundamental problem' is said to be 'to find a form of association which will defend and protect the person and property of each associate, and wherein each member, united to all the others, still obeys himself alone, and retains his original freedom'. i.e. what is fundamental is the single individual and his natural liberty; the task of the state is merely to protect these.

68. i.e. the French Revolution.

30. 69. Paragraphs 133 ff.

70. i.e. the stage at which mind has become the state—the mind of a nation objectified in its rational and organic institutions.

31. 71. i.e. like the deduction of the concept of right—see Paragraph 2.

72. 'Plato'—it is usually the second half of the *Parmenides* which Hegel has in mind. 'Scepticism of the ancients'—see *History of Philosophy*, ii. 328 ff. 'Approximation'—see Note 39 to the Preface.

32. 73. A caution against the supposition that Hegel is writing a history of institutions. It is not until Paragraph 158 that he begins to deal with the family. The family thus logically presupposes all the 'determinations of the concept', or categories, dealt with in the earlier Paragraphs, but it does not follow that these logical presuppositions are always explicit in actual societies. In certain social conditions families may exist although private property does not.

33. 74. For the presuppositions here mentioned, see *Enc.*, §§ 237-43, and *Science of Logic*, i, 79 ff. For 'immediacy or pure being', see **Note 1 to Paragraph 34.**

75. *Moralität* and *Sittlichkeit*. For the translation here adopted for these words, see Translator's Foreword, § 3. For Hegel's distinction between these see Paragraph 141. *Moralität* is abstract morality; it possesses the form of all genuinely moral action, i.e. conscientiousness, but it lacks a content to correspond with this form. *Sittlichkeit* is the concrete morality of a rational social order where rational institutions and laws provide the content of conscientious conviction.

PART I (ABSTRACT RIGHT)

34. 1. We are tracing the development of the will from concept to Idea. The start of a process of development is abstract in comparison with its end, and what is developing is at the start 'immediate', not yet mediated and made explicit in and through the later stages; e.g. a man's character is built up in the course of his life, but it was implicit and undeveloped in his childhood. In adult life the bare universal, 'character', has been given determinacy in and through his particular actions and so has become something concrete, mediated through the particular instances of actions flowing from that character. In infancy, this character has 'being', though it does not 'exist' as something differentiated and determinate. The concept of the free will begins therefore at the level of immediacy, pure being, and abstraction; and, since it is a *concept* whose advance we are studying, its abstract phase is the phase of pure undifferentiated universality. The point of this Paragraph, which is amplified and explained in Paragraphs 35–9, is to show that although at the start the will is universal and abstract, the other moments of the concept, particularity and individuality, are also present, but, because of the abstractness of this stage, are explicitly different from the universal and are not fused with it into a concrete unity. Such a fusion is not finally achieved until we come to the state.

What is immediate is a unit, while what is mediated is a member of a whole. Hence the free will in its immediacy is the will of a unit, an exclusive or abstract *individual*, free because it is self-related (see Paragraph 5). Persons are free units in this sense, and, as units merely, are not differentiated from one another by special characteristics of their own. Thus personality is something formal, a *universal* form in which all rational beings participate. Form implies content, but at this stage of immediacy, the universal form has not given itself its own content, its own determinacy; and therefore the content, something *particular*, is something other than the form of the will. Content and form must correspond, and hence if the form is immediate, the content must be immediate also; and such a content is available at this stage (*a*) in immediate desires—i.e. desires not rationalized into a system— and (*b*) in the world of external given objects from which the person as a unit distinguishes himself.

35. 2. Knowledge of the self in abstraction from all objects and determinate experiences is the knowledge that 'I am I'. Here the object known, the self, is identical with the knower, the abstract and infinite ego of Paragraph 5. The 'infinity' of such a self is 'simple' because the self is abstract and self-identical, i.e. not the concrete universality of a synthesis of universal and particular, but only the bare form of universality.

3. 'Consciousness' is what Hegel calls the grade of the pheno-menal mind or mind as 'appearance' (*Enc.*, § 413). Self-consciousness is the second stage within that grade. Mind fully explicit is the 'truth of consciousness' (*Enc.*, § 440), and practical mind, the second stage within that higher grade, has for its content and aim its own freedom (*Enc.*, § 480).

37. 4. Formal rights belong to all persons *qua* persons. No such rights belong to me in respect of my advantage, welfare, or private judgement, because these depend on what differentiates me from other persons. For the rights of intention and welfare, see Paragraphs 119 ff.; for the right of private judgement (the right of 'insight') see Para-graph 132.

40. 5. To be conscious of oneself as a unit implies (*a*) distinguishing between one's self and those determinate characteristics which dif-ferentiate one from other people, and (*b*) abstracting the unitary self from these determinate characteristics and ignoring or negating these. Hence to be conscious of oneself as a unit is to 'be related to oneself negatively' or to 'distinguish oneself from oneself'. The inner self-distinction is outwardly manifested as a distinction between oneself and other units. (Thought, or the concept, a system of internal relations is existent or embodied in the world as a system of *external* relations. The concept is a synthesis of opposites, but in the world the opposites 'appear' as sundered from one another. See Note 42 to Paragraph 10 and cf. Notes 19 and 23 to Paragraphs 161 and 165.) To be conscious of what one is (a self-identical unit) is *eo ipso* to be conscious of what one is not; and since the negative of a unit can only be another unit, to be conscious of oneself as a unit is to be conscious that one is distinct from other units. That is, to be conscious that one is a person *eo ipso* implies that there are other persons from whom one's own personality is distinct (see *Enc.*, § 97). Hegel uses the same argument later in connexion with the state—see Paragraphs 323 and 331. Further, my property is my personality objectified; hence when my consciousness of my personality leads me to distinguish myself from other persons, this is *eo ipso* to distinguish my property from theirs. *Qua* persons, however, I and other property owners are identical; our personality is simply the universality of the free will in its immediacy, and our identity with each other, implicit in the fact that we are all persons, becomes explicit when our property—the embodiment of our personality—changes hands.

6. The classification adopted in Justinian: *Institutes*, i. 2. xii. 'Every right exercised by us relates either to persons, things, or actions.' The translator's authority for this and most of the other notes on Roman law is Buckland: *Text-book of Roman Law* (Cambridge, 1921). A reader unfamiliar with Roman Law will find helpful as guides to this section of Hegel's work (*a*) Gibbon, chapter xliv (out of date, but one of Hegel's authorities), (*b*) Maine's *Ancient Law*, with Pollock's notes (London, 1906).

7. *Philosophy of Law*, § 10, p. 84.

8. *Jus ad actiones* is in the main the law of procedure; but it is still a vexed question how exactly *jus ad personas* is discriminated from *jus ad res*. The difficulty is to define the content of the former. Hegel adopts Savigny's view that the law of persons is family law. For objections to this view, see Buckland, op. cit., p. 58.

9. In the passage cited by Hegel, Heineccius says: 'Man and person are quite distinct in law; a man is a being who possesses a human body and a mind endowed with reason; a person is a man regarded as having a certain status.' Except in the very late Roman law, this is not true, because the Roman lawyers generally use *persona* in the untechnical sense of the man who plays any part in life. Hence both slaves and children are persons. Hegel takes 'person' in a technical sense and makes it equivalent to *caput*, and in respect of *caput*, or status, there was indeed a difference between the slave and the free man. *Caput* is a man's civil capacity, his position in regard to family rights and consequently to freedom and citizenship. *Capitis diminutio* is a change in *caput*, amounting to its loss in the case of those sold as slaves, and suffered to some extent by those banished and by those adopted into a new *familia*. On the 'slave-status' of children, see Remarks to Paragraphs 175, 180.

10. *Philosophy of Law*, §§ 22 ff., pp. 108 ff. 'Personal right of a real kind is a right to the possession of an external object as a thing and to the use of it as a person'—e.g. a man's right over his wife, his children, and his domestics.

11. Paragraphs 163, 167–8.

12. *Philosophy of Law*, §§ 18 ff., pp. 100 ff.

42. 13. For the externality of nature, see Note 42 to Paragraph 10. Mere consciousness may take, e.g. my books, as external to me, but mind in its freedom recognizes that they embody my personality and to that extent they are not external. They are external as natural objects, but not as 'mine', and to treat them as purely external, as the furniture remover does, is to ignore most of the truth about them.

43. 14. i.e. the existences just referred to: (*a*) natural endowments, (*b*) external objects.

15. See Paragraphs 65 ff.

16. See Paragraphs 65 ff. Hegel has a note on the use of the word 'alienation' here: 'It would be better to speak here of a mode of externality. Alienation is giving up something which is my property and which is already external, it is not to externalize' (*Hegels e. R.*, p. 29).

44. 17. It is (i) the philosophy of common sense, and (ii) the philosophy of Kant, which Hegel has in mind. For a full discussion of these see *Enc.*, §§ 26–60.

18. The free will by using and destroying 'external' objects shows that these have no subsistence of their own but are only 'ideal' (see Note 36 to Paragraph 7), not real, while the free will does subsist and is their truth because they exist only 'for' it.

46. 19. i.e. the four elements of early Greek cosmology—earth, air, fire, water (see *Enc.*, § 281).

20. i.e. especially the proposals of the Gracchi and their successors in the last century of the Roman Republic to distribute domain lands to individual colonists.

21. i.e. *fideicommissa*; these were originally requests to a regularly instituted heir to allow the estate to accrue to the benefit of another party, e.g. to children debarred from inheriting because they were the children of a Roman father by an exogamous marriage. It is because such trusts imply that the ultimate beneficiary suffers from some disability in connexion with property ownership that Hegel regards them as in part a contravention of the right of personality.

22. 'Natural persons are such as the God of nature formed us. Artificial are such as are created and devised by human laws for the purpose of society and government, which are called corporations or bodies politic' (Blackstone: *Commentaries*, vol. i, p. 123).

23. If Hegel has Plato's *Republic* in mind, then he fails to notice that it is the Guardians only who are there precluded from holding private property. But he may be thinking of *Laws*, v. 739.

47. 24. My body differs in form from other bodies and to that extent its form is particular; but its content is universal, since everything that is mine is grounded in it. 'Real pre-condition'—i.e. *reale*

Möglichkeit, a category of Hegel's logic; for its significance see *Science of Logic*, ii. 179 ff.

48. 25. *Mittel.* Mind, by taking possession of the body, makes the body a means (*Mittel*) to or an instrument of its realization. In this way, the body ceases to be an immediate existent and becomes 'mediated' through the activity of mind. See Addenda, p. 376.

26. A plan or purpose is realized when it ceases to be something merely inward or subjective and becomes embodied in something, i.e. becomes something determinately existent or objective. Before it is realized, my plan is something for me, but it does not exist for others; they cannot apprehend it until I embody it, give it determinacy, in words or actions. Hence to give it determinacy is *eo ipso* to give it an existence from the point of view of others. In Hegel's language, determinate being and being for others are identical (*Science of Logic*, i. 131). Hence I am free for others only because I am free in my determinate existence, i.e. in my body.

49. 27. Of the 'philosophy of identity', often attacked by Hegel, Bishop Butler's phrase is an example: 'Everything is what it is and not another thing.' If this were the whole truth of the matter, Hegel holds, then philosophy, and thought generally, would consist of statements like 'good is good', 'a plant is a plant', &c. But if everything is simply describable as itself, it must also differ from everything else, a self-identical plant differs from a self-identical good. And this difference is just as much a characteristic of the plant as its self-identity. Identity and difference, then, are never found apart; what is identical is also different and vice versa. The Understanding, however, refusing to contemplate a synthesis of opposites and insisting on an identity which excludes difference, has to resort to the category of likeness, or abstract equality, in order to describe the relation between two things which are the same yet not the same—the child is 'like' the man; the child and the man are 'equally' human. (See *Enc.*, §§ 103 and 118. Cf. also Bradley: *Ethical Studies*, Oxford, 1927, p. 167.) 'Reflective thinking' is intellectual mediocrity in two senses. It is mediocre because it is an inadequate type of mental activity and must be superseded by reason; and it is mediocre because it is midway between what Hegel calls the logic of being on the one hand and the logic of the concept on the other. It is the type of thinking which rests in the categories of essence (see Note 5 to Paragraph 108).

28. e.g. by Moravians and Anabaptists in Germany.

29. An abstract universal has no organic connexion with its particulars. Mind, or reason, as a concrete universal, particularizes itself into differences which are interconnected by its universality in the same way in which the parts of an organism are held together by the single life

which they all share. The parts depend on the whole for their life, but on the other hand the persistence of life necessitates the differentiation of the parts.

30. See Paragraphs 199 ff., 230, 237 ff.

50. 31. The technical term for entering into possession of a thing otherwise than by contract or inheritance is *occupatio*, occupancy, and it is with occupancy that Hegel is dealing when he speaks of 'taking possession' of a thing or 'seizing' it. The principle enunciated in this Paragraph is that of Roman law.

51. 32. 'Relation to others'—i.e. the recognition by others that the thing is mine. This recognition depends on my putting my will into the thing (see Note 26 to Paragraph 49), and I cannot do this (except by infringing the rights of others) unless the thing is without an owner (is a *res nullius*) when I do so.

52. 33. See Note 60 to Paragraph 21.

34. Cf. end of the Remark to Paragraph 43.

53. 35. The relation between these three types of judgement is expounded in *Enc.*, §§ 172–3. They represent progressive attempts to attach a predicate to a subject; e.g. (i) since the will is embodied in its property, we may say that 'the will is a particular thing, its property'— 'this property is my will', 'this and my will are identical'. But the will is universal and the thing is particular, and so the thing is the negative of the universal or the will, and (ii) the will is therefore not the thing. By using it the will negates the thing in order to bring it into accordance with itself. Such negation, however, can never completely achieve its end, because the will, as universal, can never be adequately embodied in any one particular. Hence (iii) the will must be asserted to be the will, and the object must be altogether spurned or alienated. This is not a mere negative judgement, but a 'negatively infinite judgement' which asserts a total incongruity between the subject (the will) and the predicate (the thing).

55. 36. *Accessio naturalis* in Roman law included *fetura* (young born to animals in my possession) as well as jetsam, alluvial deposits, islands formed in rivers, &c.

37. As *fetura* is, e.g. by Fichte: *Science of Rights*, § 19 c, 4, p. 306.

59. 38. See Note 35 to Paragraph 53.

39. Its *Bestimmung*, its determinate character as self-less, as a mere 'thing' (see Paragraph 42).

60. 40. To use a stream continually to drive a mill-wheel is to claim possession not of a restricted amount of water but of the 'elemental' basis of that amount, i.e. of the stream itself. So in stock-breeding, although I limit my use of the animals (e.g. limit the number I slaughter) in order to safeguard the renewal of the stock, I claim as mine not merely the head of cattle I possess now, but their 'organic' basis, i.e. the generic essence which lives in them and their progeny (*Hegels e. R.*, p. 39).

61. 41. i.e. it is only 'ideal'. What is genuinely substantial in Hegel's view is mind or reason. Mind is its own end and external things are at its disposal. Instead of the reference just below to Paragraph 42, a reference to Paragraph 44 would be more apposite.

62. 42. 'Usufruct is the right of using another's property, of enjoying its fruits short of waste of its substance. . . . Nevertheless, in order that properties should not remain wholly unused through the entire cessation of usufruct, the law has been pleased to ordain that in certain circumstances the right of usufruct shall be annulled and that the owner proper shall resume the land.'

43. (*a*) Things transferable by mancipation, a formal ceremony before witnesses, and things transferable by simple delivery. (*b*) Quiritarian ownership was originally the only type recognized in law; when the Praetors began to recognize a beneficial ownership in a man whose legal title failed simply from defect in the form of his conveyance, this was called bonitarian ownership, and quiritarian ownership became only a formality which gave its holder no beneficial interest in that over which his right extended (see the index to Muirhead's edition of the *Institutes of Gaius*, Edinburgh, 1880).

44. The distinction is that between ownership in the abstract and usufruct. The overlord's interest in property is *dominium directum*, the vassal's is *dominium utile* (Huber: *Praelectiones juris civilis*, Leipzig, 1735, p. 93). Emphyteusis was a grant of imperial land *in perpetuum* or for a long term on condition of cultivating it properly and paying a stipulated rent.

45. Lords of the Manor are *eo ipso* nobility or gentry, whether their lands are being farmed or not. Use is a stage further on in the dialectic than mere abstract property, or the mere seizure of a possession, and, since it is further on, it is 'rational' in contrast with the lower stage of property in the abstract.

46. e.g. in France since 1789 (Messineo). Feudal tenure still lingered in some of the German states in Hegel's day and was not abolished in the two Mecklenburgs until 1918. For the 'impatience of opinion', compare *History of Philosophy*, i. 36.

63. 47. If a thing is comparable with other things, it must possess some universal character in common with them in virtue of which the comparison may be made. This character is its value; the value of a loaf depends not on the specific quality of this loaf as distinct from another of the same sort, but simply on the fact that the loaf is a particular instance of a universal kind. Value is a concept existing for thought, not sensation, and therefore value, not taste, smell, &c., is the genuine substance of the thing (see Note 41 to Paragraph 61).

64. 48. Positively, prescription is a title or right to the possession of property which has been uninterruptedly used or possessed either from time immemorial or for a period fixed by law. Negatively, it is a limitation of the time within which an action or a claim may be raised, e.g. to recover possession of property after its usufruct has been given to someone else.

49. *Realität.* In Hegel's terminology, a thing has *Realität* or reality when it has objective existence in relation to something subjective. A plan is 'real' when it ceases to be merely subjective and becomes determinate in words or acts (see *Enc.*, § 91). Property is 'real' as embodying my will, and prescription in Hegel's view is a right because, when I use a thing, I embody my will in it and it becomes 'really' mine, while when I withdraw my will from it, it becomes a *res nullius*. Hegel is not here speaking of 'real' property in the usual legal sense.

50. Public memorials become private property through being disregarded and becoming objects of indifference. The content of books becomes public property by the opposite process, i.e. by being studied, assimilated, and used in the writing of new books.

51. In English law, an Act of Parliament is required before land consecrated for a burial ground can be put to any other use.

66. 52. Spinoza begins his *Ethics* with this definition: 'By cause of itself I understand that whose nature cannot be conceived except as existing', and he goes on in Proposition vii to show that substance is such a cause. Hegel applies this definition to mind, or, as he would say, to that which is both substance and subject as well. Mind is actualized only when it passes over from mere abstract being into existence, i.e. into the actualization of its potentialities in a determinate way.

53. i.e. personality, that in virtue of which I possess rights, as distinct from the finite or particular characteristics in virtue of which I may be qualified, e.g. for membership of a club.

67. 54. Reading *an einen Anderen* (*Hegels e. R.*, p. 46).

69. 55. Reading *es* for *er*. The only possible antecedent of *er* is *Gebrauch*, but 'use' could hardly be said to be an *accessio naturalis*. For the view from which Hegel here dissents, cf. the judgement of King Diarmait in the suit brought by St. Finnian against St. Columba who had made a copy of a codex of St. Finnian's without leave (St. Finnian claimed possession of the copy): 'To every book belongs its son-book as to every cow her calf.' (J. T. Fowler's edition of *Adamnani Vita S. Columbae*, Oxford, 1894, p. lxii.)

56. *ihrer d. i. jener* (*Hegels e. R.*, p. 47).

57. The question of copyright was much discussed in Germany at the end of the eighteenth century. Kant wrote an essay on the subject and he refers to it in his *Philosophy of Law*, pp. 129 ff. A copyright law was passed in England in 1709 and in France by the revolutionaries. Some of the German states followed suit, but there was no systematic law in Prussia before 1832.

70. 58. i.e. the state (see Paragraphs 257 and 323 ff.).

71. 59. In Hegel's view reason is the spring of the life of the whole universe, and men are its instruments, whether they know it or not. This point (cf. Paragraph 344) he owed both to his conception of the providence of God and also to his study of Aristotle (see e.g. *Nic. Eth.* 1153[b] 25 ff. and *De Anima* 415[a] 26 ff.). The point of the reference to Paragraph 45 is that property is there described as a substantive end, and what is substantive is reason (see Note 41 to Paragraph 61). In property the will embodies its freedom in an external thing. As a *thing*, this is related to other things; as *property*, i.e. as my will objectified, it exists for or from the point of view of other wills and is related to them. The relation of will to will implicit in property becomes explicit in contract as a relation between my will and another's. Here the subjective and objective sides of the Idea are both of them the free will, and hence the Idea is here realized less inadequately than it is in property. The advance from property to contract is thus a *rational* advance, a step forward in the actualization of the Idea. 'Mind objective' is the second section of Part III of the *Encyclopaedia*. The whole of the *Philosophy of Right* (except most of the introduction, which is in the sphere of mind subjective) falls within it.

73. 60. A castaway on a desert island may have a right to appropriate and alienate 'things'; but these 'things' are property only if we, who imagine the castaway, imagine ourselves as forming with him the society in which alone the right of 'property' has meaning. To say that I am the rightful owner of a property implies that others recognize my right, i.e. they recognize that what I call mine is not merely a thing externally related to other things, but is my property, the external embodiment of my will. The 'thing' I can alienate on my own account, but the property I cannot alienate without the co-operation of someone else's will, because property (and therefore alienation) presupposes recognition (e.g. 'rubbish may not be shot here without permission', and if I drop something in the street, meaning to get rid of it, the chances are that someone will pick it up and return it to me). Hence in the social context of recognized rights, there is an equivalence between my will to alienate and another's will, and my will thus becomes objective to me in the will of the other (see Paragraph 71 with the Remark and the Note thereto).

75. 61. i.e. under feudalism—cf. Paragraphs 277–8 and see e.g. Sabine: *History of Political Theory* (London, 1937), p. 217.

62. i.e. Part III; see especially Paragraphs 258, 278, 294.

77. 63. *Laesio enormis*, excessive damage. The principle that if you sell, e.g., a farm for less than half its value, you have suffered excessive damage, and the contract is voidable, was enunciated in Roman law, though it is very exceptional and seems to apply only to land transactions, and there to sales only, not to purchases.

64. See Paragraph 217.

65. Roman law recognized four main types of contract: contracts *re*, *verbis*, *litteris*, and *consensu*, giving rise to real, verbal, literal, and consensual obligations. Obligations created by verbal and literal contracts are unilateral, those arising out of real and consensual contracts are bilateral or mutual (though sometimes imperfectly bilateral). *Real* obligations arise out of *traditio rei*, the handing over of things by way of loan, deposit, &c. (For their types see Note 71 to Paragraph 80.) *Verbal* obligations arise out of stipulations made by the parties in set terms by word of mouth to each other. *Literal* obligations arise out of an entry made against a debtor (even in his absence, hence the 'unilateral' character of such a contract) by a creditor. *Consensual* obligations arise out of sales, purchases, &c. They could be created by a common understanding without any formality and so could be contracted by letter, messenger, &c. In a verbal contract, the parties are liable only for what they have specifically promised in words to perform. In a consensual contract, they are reciprocally liable for what each in fairness and equity should do for the other. Kant uses the distinction between unilateral and bilateral contracts, and includes loans, deposits, and gifts in the former (*Philosophy of Law*, § 32, p. 122). A stipulation may be regarded as unilateral in that, although I bind myself by it, the other party has not yet received anything. Hegel dissents from this view in Paragraph 79.

79. 66. *Pactum* is the expression of an intention to make a *contractus*. The formula of a pact is 'I am prepared to sell'. Thus contract is enforceable at law, while pact is not. So Heineccius: *Antiquitatum Romanarum Syntagma* (Frankfurt, 1841), iii. 14. 4, an earlier edition of which was probably Hegel's authority. More recent writers on Roman law give a different account of the matter.

67. *Beitrag zur Berichtigung der Urteile des Publicums über die französische Revolution*, *Werke*, Berlin, 1845, vi. 111 ff. (Lasson).

68. For Hegel's distinction between the false and the true infinite, see *Enc.*, §§ 94–5. The true infinite is mind, which returns from its other

into itself, which is self-related and self-determined. The false infinite, on the other hand, is the eternal sameness of an endless progression; we lay down a limit, then we pass it and lay down another, and so on *ad infinitum*, but without ever leaving the finite behind or reaching true infinity. Hegel's point here is that the infinite divisibility of time, &c., makes impossible any clear answer to the question: at what precise point, in Fichte's view, does the contract become legally, as distinct from morally, binding?

80. 69. 'Real' not in the Roman lawyer's sense mentioned in the preceding Remark, but in Hegel's sense defined in Paragraph 76.

70. Transactions in the form: 'I am doing this for you now on the understanding that you will do this for me later', were classed with 'real' contracts by Roman lawyers, and they have been called 'innominate' by modern writers in distinction from the four 'nominate' types enumerated in Note 65 to Paragraph 77.

71. Roman law distinguished four types of 'real' contract, namely *mutuum, commodatum, depositum*, and *pignus*. (*a*) *Mutuum* was a loan not for use but for consumption, i.e. a loan of *res fungibiles*, things returnable in kind. The borrower of a jar of oil would consume the oil and return other oil of the same kind. *Mutuum* was in essence gratuitous, but it was generally accompanied by a separate agreement for the payment of interest. (*b*) *Commodatum* was a loan for use only, the thing itself being returned, a loan therefore of *res non fungibiles*. In this case the loan had to be gratuitous; if a fee were charged, the transaction became *locatio*, letting, hiring. (Hence Hegel's apologetic 'even' in B (2) (β).) (*c*) *Depositum* was deposit and (*d*) *pignus* was pledge. In C Hegel uses *cautio* as a general word to cover pledge, mortgage, bail, &c., but there is no warrant, apart from the reasons he gives there, for regarding such transactions as specially 'complete'.

72. See Paragraphs 179 ff.

82. 73. Hegel distinguishes between *Schein* (show or semblance) and *Erscheinung* (appearance). See *Enc.*, § 131. An appearance is a forth-shining of the reality. A show is the inessential masquerading as the essential, the denial of the essence in its apparent assertion. Although crime is a denial of rights, it is only in a context of rights that there can be a crime at all. Hence crime is a mere 'show', no genuine existence; what it denies is its own essential basis, the right, on which the very being of crime depends. Contract is an 'appearance' of the right and no more than that, because the will in contract is not the universal will in its truth as self-mediating but only a common will, posited by the arbitrary wills of the parties. Since these wills are arbitrary, their correspondence with the rightness whose appearance they are is contingent on their arbitrary choice; and hence they may if they please make an arbitrary choice in defiance of the right. The right is the essence, the embodiment of the freedom of the universal will. When the free will takes the form of a merely *arbitrary* choice, the universality and rationality, which are the essence of the will, are being denied, and the choice is therefore self-destructive because it denies its own essence and basis. Hence the choice is only a show, a semblance, a pretence, and it will be proved to be so by the punishment which follows when right reasserts itself (see Paragraphs 97 ff.).

85. 74. If a man breaks his contract with me, he does not deny my rights in general or my property as a whole; he only denies that I have rightly included this particular property amongst the things called 'mine'. Hence the judgement which he asserts in wronging me is '*this* is not yours (although I admit that other things are)'. For the necessity of the advance from this type of negative judgement to a positively infinite and then to a negatively infinite judgement, see *Enc.*, §§ 172–3.

88. 75. The 'positively infinite judgement' is the expression of a mere identity: the individual is the individual. This, though true, lacks the universality of thought. The predicate should be a universal and tell us something about the subject, but in this case the subject is qualified by itself, and the judgement is bogus, a show, because it professes to be a judgement, to tell us something, and it does not. The same is true of fraud. Fraud as the sale of *this* article, e.g. this share certificate, which the purchaser voluntarily accepts, is prima facie a genuine transaction. But as a sale it should contain a universal element, i.e. value. The seller professes to sell this universality of which the printed paper is supposed to be only a symbol, and the transaction is fraudulent because the universality is absent.

91. 76. My will is embodied in property only if I have an idea of the property as embodying my will. This idea is a 'determination', or a 'content' of my will. Hence the reference to Paragraph 7. where Hegel says that the self-determining will knows its determination to be its own and only 'ideal', an idea from which it may withdraw itself if it wills to do so.

93. 77. The concept is actualized by manifesting itself in the world, in reality (see Note 49 to Paragraph 64). That sphere, however, is the sphere of externality, and hence what is inwardly a clash between two elements in one thing becomes outwardly (or 'really' as distinct from 'ideally'—see Note 98 to Paragraph 256) manifest as a clash between two different things. (Cf. Note 5 to Paragraph 40.)

78. Compare Paragraph 350 (Messineo), and Paragraphs 102 and 150. *Herren* is a misprint for *Heroen* (*Hegels e. R.*, p. 61). 'It is the absolute interest of reason that the state should exist, and herein lies the justification and the merit of heroes who have founded states, however rude these may have been' (*Philosophy of History*, pp. 30, 403); i.e. in accomplishing what they did, heroes were the 'unconscious instruments' (see Note 59 to Paragraph 71) of reason or of God's purpose. Notice Hegel's assertion in the Addition to this Paragraph that the right of heroes disappears once civilized and political conditions have been introduced—a point which Hegel's critics often overlook.

95. 79. See Note 35 to Paragraph 53. The criminal by wronging someone is in effect denying that his victim has any rights, i.e. he asserts a total incompatibility beween his victim and rights. Hence 'you have no rights' is a 'negatively infinite judgement'.

96. 80. 'The Stoics hold that the virtues accompany each other, and if a man has one, he has all' (Diogenes Laertius, vii. 125—Life of Zeno). The single virtue is to live in accordance with nature, and vice is the converse.

81. See Plutarch's life of Solon, ch. 17: In the early history of Athens, Draco prescribed 'one penalty, death, for almost all offences'.

82. On chivalry and the absurdity of its notion of 'honour', see *Aesthetic*, vol. ii, pp. 325 ff.

83. Robbery is 'larceny with violence'; theft is larceny without violence. The amount stolen makes no difference (Blackstone: *Commentaries*, vol. iv, pp. 241 ff.).

84. See Paragraph 218 and Remark to Paragraph 319.

85. See Paragraphs 113 ff.

99. 86. Crime exists as a fact, an event, and it is 'positive' to that extent (see Paragraph 97), but as an *event* it is not differentiated by any criminal character from other events such as accidents. As a *crime* it exists only for those who understand it from the inside, i.e. as a *purposeful* action, and, so considered, it lacks the positivity of a *mere* event (see Paragraph 99); it is made something genuinely positive, a crime and not an accident, by the presence in it of the criminal's will, and in this sense it is 'positive' only because it carries out his conscious purpose. But to the person injured, and to onlookers, it is negative, a wilful attack on rights, a denial of them, and therefore something null and self-destructive (see Note 73 to Paragraph 82).

87. See Paragraph 220. The references to Klein's book have not been checked.

88. Deleting *aber* with *Hegels e. R.*, p. 65.

100. 89. *Dei delitti e dei pene* (Monaco, 1764). Eng. tr. by J. A. Farrer: *Crimes and punishments* (1880). See chapter xvi. For a short summary of Beccaria's views, see e.g. J. W. Gough: *The Social Contract*

(Oxford, 1936), pp. 164–5. In saying just below that the state's primary duty is not the unconditional protection of the citizens and their property, Hegel may again be expressing dissent from Beccaria, as well as from Rousseau (see Note 67 to Paragraph 29).

101. 90. All editions have 'Paragraph 95'. For 'Paragraph 77' just preceding, all editions have 'see above'.

91. A crime is a particular act with a particular character, e.g. it is a theft, and a theft of £15. But it also has an infinite aspect because it is the negation of the right by the free will (see Paragraph 22) and therefore it *deserves* to be punished, i.e. to be negated in its turn. Crime and punishment are alike as equal and opposite negations, and in comparison with this fact their particular characteristics on any given occasion are of no importance.

102. 92. Blackstone draws the distinction (*Commentaries*, vol. iii, p. 2). In English law there are still 'private crimes' which are left to the injured party to prosecute. In later Roman law, a process against theft was treated as a civil action for damages and not as a criminal action.

103. 93. The dialectical movement of thought from property through contract to wrong.

104. 94. The will in its truth is self-determination, the concrete individuality which is the synthesis of universal and particular (see Paragraph 7). At the stage of implicit being or immediacy, with which the sphere of abstract right began, the will is universal, its individuality is abstract and exclusive, and the particular factor falls outside the will altogether as mere irrational desire (see Paragraph 34). The process which we have studied up to this point is the process whereby the will transcends the immediacy of its starting-point; its universality becomes mediated through the particular which has become explicit in the process as a moment within the will itself.

(*a*) In property, the will embodies its universality in things, the things which it calls 'mine'. Here there is no mediation but only the direct grasp of immediate objects.

(*b*) In contract, the universality of the will is posited, and made explicit, as a relation of will to will. Here there is at least the *appearance* of mediation, but there is no more, because the parties to a contract are still only 'property owners', immediate persons, and so mere units; the content of the contract is due to their arbitrariness, and is not the content produced by the self-differentiation of the universal will.

(*c*) Contract comes into being as a result of arbitrary choices and there is therefore implicit in it the moment of contingency, of particular preference. This is the moment which becomes explicit in wrong-doing. The will of the man who does wrong is at variance with *itself*; right, the embodiment of freedom, is its substance, and in doing wrong it is denying its own substance. In this way, the particular moment of the will itself has become explicit; it no longer lies outside the will in the form of mere desire, &c., but is present in the volition itself as *willed* wrong-doing. The will has become aware of itself as particular and in virtue of this awareness is able to oppose itself to, and so to contradict, the universal embodied in rights.

This contradiction is manifest in the world (i.e. in the sphere of external relations) as a contradiction between wrong and vengeance, a contradiction which leads to an infinite series of subjective and finite acts and so to an irrationality which brings us no nearer the infinite, the Right, which these finite acts are attempting to reach. Hence the will as concept, and so as rational, demands that these contradictions be overcome, both the contradiction of right by the criminal in his volition, and the contradiction between wrong and vengeance in the world.

The only way to overcome these contradictions is to recognize that there is something right in the negation of the universally right. (Cf. Preface, p. 10, where Plato is said to have taken a new principle as merely corruptive, while he ought to have taken measures against it by discovering them in the principle itself.) The universally right is abstract and therefore one-sided. Wrong occurs because of this one-sidedness; wrong is the particular moment in the will demanding satisfaction. Now Hegel's point is that it is essential that it should receive such satisfaction, though it must receive it in co-operation with the universal and not in defiance of it. The contradiction in the world between wrong and vengeance is only resolved when a particular subject, the judge, is the mouthpiece of the universal law. Otherwise the criminal would take the judge's sentence as something merely personal and so as a new injury. So also the contradiction of right by the criminal cannot be annulled by a mere regression to bare universality. Mere denial of the 'corruptive invader' will not root it out—*tamen usque recurret*. The only solution is to recognize the claims of the particular by allowing that the universally right must be mediated by the particular conscientious convictions of the subject. We go beyond the criminal's defiance only by substituting for the abstract conception of personality the more concrete conception of subjectivity. A 'subject' is the universal will embodied, no longer in universal rights, but in a particular will; hence from the point of view of the subject, the law which the criminal breaks is *his own* law; i.e. his crime is not a contradiction of a right outside him but a self-contradiction, a defiance of the right embodied *in* him. As soon as the rational agent realizes this he rises above the contradiction simply by keeping the law, the law which is the law of his own conviction, i.e. he has transcended the sphere of right altogether and become a moral agent.

Wrong is an act of the particular will opposing itself to the universal. It is by reflecting on my wrong act that I become aware of my nature as a moral agent, that I discover that in defying the universal law, I have denied my own law. To discover this is to discover that the universal will is embodied in my will—*my* will wills the *universal*. I have determined myself as 'self-related negativity' because in my eyes the opposition is now one between the universal and particular elements within *me*. The particular or arbitrary will is will as contingency (see Paragraph 15). By reflecting on my crime as the act of a particular will, I have discovered my moral agency, and this is contingency 'reflected into itself'. The universal will is one with my private will, and this subjectivity of mine which I have discovered is 'infinite' and self-identical just as the ego was in Paragraph 5, and for the same reasons. Cf. also Paragraph 34. The difference here is that these are characteristics which I know that I possess. A subject is a person conscious of his own particular personality, i.e. contingency reflected into itself is the discovery not only of one's own particularity but also of universal laws which one *ought* to obey, and with this discovery we pass to the sphere of morality, a sphere where particular and universal are both present though there is an explicit difference between them. (See Addition to Paragraph 35 and Note 5 to Paragraph 108.)

PART II (MORALITY)

106. 1. The subject is aware of himself as a single moral agent. Hence subjectivity is distinct from the concept of the will in its immediacy, since that was pure universality. But since the subject's awareness is of a *single* being, the subject is 'immediate', not part of a rational system of moral agents acting in accordance with recognized laws, a system which we shall later know as ethical life. At the level of property, the will was embodied in immediate things. At the level of morality, the will is embodied in immediate wills. This is a higher level, because the embodiment or existence of the concept (or the existential aspect of the Idea) is now adequate to the concept itself; it is not a 'thing', more or less out of control of mind. The will embodied in a thing can be coerced (see Paragraph 90); but the concept of the will, *existent* as a will, eludes all coercion; inner conviction is beyond the reach of all external forces; and hence it is at the moral level that freedom is for the first time actual. The defect of this level is that the subject is only *für sich*; he is conscious of his subjectivity and independence but is conscious of universality only as something different from his subjectivity. We have not yet reached a concrete synthesis of these opposites; that is attained only at the level of ethical life.

2. The moral will is aware of itself (*für sich*), but so long as it is aware of itself as only a unit, i.e. before its moral agency is mediated by the society in which it lives, it is not aware of the universal as identical with itself and so is not aware of what it is *an sich* or implicitly. At the

start, however, there is an *implied* identity between the universal principle of the will and the will of the subject, because the latter does embody the former, though without fully realizing it. This identity becomes
explicit only after the explicit single will has 'sunk deeper and deeper
into itself', i.e. estranged itself further from the universal, entrenched
itself more and more deeply, plumbed the recesses of its own moralizing
—a process which it may carry so far eventually as to defy the universal
altogether and so be explicitly evil. The occurrence of evil is the transition to the higher stage of ethical life, just as the occurrence of wrong
was the transition to morality.

107. 3. A right is the embodiment of the free will (see Paragraph 29),
or is the free will determinately existent. Abstract rights embody the
freedom of personality, the abstract principle of the will. We now come
to more concrete rights, those of subjectivity, which itself is the higher
ground in which the free will is now embodied. Just as personality in
the process of becoming more and more determinate was embodied in a
series of rights, so the development of subjectivity runs *pari passu* with
the development of a series of rights.

4. The process which we are studying in the field of morality is two-
sided : (*a*) the subject gradually comes to a realization of his own universality, i.e. of the objectivity of the universal will which his subjective will
embodies. (*b*) The embodiment of the subject in his action—the right of
the subject—changes in character *pari passu* with the changes in the
character of subjectivity. To start with, the will recognizes its subjectivity in something which it has done; the recognition is immediate
and the action done is immediate too. Next, when the action is seen to
embody the subject's *welfare*, the universality implicit in the subject
begins to be explicit (Paragraph 125). Finally, the action is seen to
embody the good, something explicitly universal. The whole process
may be summed up by saying that the subject gradually determines the
character of his action further and further until it expresses the universal
nature, i.e. the concept, of the subject in concrete detail, and he does this
in the course of discovering what this concept is. See Addenda, p. 376.

108. 5. The formula of all willing is that *I* will so-and-so. Hence
subjectivity is the form which all willing takes. Now the essential
attitude of morality is that so-and-so *ought to be* done. What characterizes morality, in Hegel's view, is always *ought*, not *is*. This failure to
reach *is*, and the consequent *difference* between the universal (the law)
and the particular (what is willed cr done), is a badge of finitude, and
finitude is a mode in which the infinite *appears*. Hence the field of
morality is governed by what Hegel calls in his logic the categories of
'essence'. Each of these is a duality, two terms *related* but not synthesized, e.g. difference and identity, finite and infinite, appearance and

reality, inessential and essential, particular and universal, &c. Truth
lies in the synthesis of these pairs, but this truth cannot be attained until
thought rises above the abstractions of this sphere to a concrete synthesis
of opposites. What Hegel calls the Understanding, or 'reflection', is
confined to this sphere. In the moral sphere the will is *related* to the
good and strives to attain it, to unite itself with it; but it fails to recognize that unity is impossible until the abstraction of mere isolated subjectivity is overcome, i.e. until it realizes that the good is not something
outside itself to which it can be 'related', or to which it can perennially
approximate but never reach, but its own implicit concept with which it
is identical. 'Self-difference': The subject is conscious of himself as a
unit and so as self-identical; but this is an abstract identity. A concrete
identity is a differentiated identity; abstract identity holds difference
outside itself as an 'other' (see Note 27 to Paragraph 49), and hence the
subject, not realizing its concrete identity with the universal, takes the
'other' as outside itself, as a law or a fact. Hence while the will is a concrete identity (see Paragraph 7), here at the level of morality it appears
as divided into (*a*) a subject, and (*b*) an object to which it relates itself.
The inner identity is manifested outwardly as difference, just as the Idea
of mind 'appears' as consciousness aware of an object 'outside' and other
than itself. The subject who relates himself to his object as to something *different* from him is thus characterized by what is in truth *self-
difference*.

109. 6. i.e. the will determined as subject is *eo ipso* an embodiment
of the concept of the will. Implicitly, then, subjectivity is a unity of
objective and subjective; but this unity cannot be made explicit until
the difference of these moments is made explicit and the will triumphs
over that difference (see Remark to Paragraph 32).

　　7. (α) The will determines itself as a *will* by willing something (i.e. it
ceases to be a self-identical ego and reveals itself as a will); i.e. the will
negates its original indeterminacy by limiting itself qualitatively, by
giving itself the quality of a will, and it does this simply by willing something. Such a qualitative limit Hegel calls *Grenze*. (β) The will is aware
of itself and therefore is aware of itself as limited in quality, i.e. it is
aware of itself as only a will, as something subjective. Hence it is aware
of what it is not, namely objective, and thus the limitation under which
it suffers then appears not as a self-limitation but as an other outside
itself, a barrier (*Schranke*) of objectivity which the will tries to overcome by translating what it wills into objectivity, so that objectivity
ceases to be an other to the will and becomes simply the will over again
(see Addition to Paragraph 110). (γ) The *Grenze* and the *Schranke* are
identical. Both of them are particularizations of the will. In fact they
are the purpose willed, the end which the will sets before itself and
attains by transforming objectivity in accordance with its subjective

volition. For the distinction between *Grenze* and *Schranke*, see *Science of Logic*, i. 144 ff.

112. 8. Since in carrying out my purposes I objectify my will in actions, these various actions give my subjectivity a content, mediate it; it ceases to be simply my consciousness of my own abstract single subjectivity. My actions as the embodiment of my subjectivity (and so as more than mere events) exist for others (see Note 26 to Paragraph 48 and Note 60 to Paragraph 73); and just as the 'other' whose co-operation I required in order to alienate property was a property owner, so here the others without whose co-operation my action cannot be moral (cannot be more than an event) are other subjective wills. Now my moral purposes are in fact objective to me only in so far as they exist for me in the wills of others. The *deed* in itself is not moral; there is no morality in writing on a piece of paper, the morality consists in the fact that the cheque is to pay for someone's education, and this fact is not in the situation but in someone else's consciousness and will. A moral action is something achieved in co-operation with someone else's will and its achievement will therefore turn out to be the expression of a common will. Hegel is repudiating 'desert island morality'.

9. All editions read '112'. 'Universal subjectivity'—i.e. my fulfilled aim is objective to me in the sense that it is present not only to me as *this* subject, but to all other subjects as well.

113. 10. Though I may go to law conscientiously, the essential thing is that I shall follow the positive laws determinant of what may be a matter at issue in a legal action. Hence a legal action has only an incidental connexion with moral responsibility.

114. 11. The sphere of reflection or of the categories of essence is a sphere of related but unsynthesized terms. The moral sphere culminates in a repeated *ought*, which claims to be absolute and yet is not (because it is not an *is*), in a universality which remains subjective (see Remark to Paragraph 112) and so no true universality; it is pure self-certitude; the objective world ought to correspond with it but does not. 'This pure self-certitude appears in the two directly interchanging forms, conscience and wickedness. The former is the will of goodness, but a goodness which to this pure subjectivity is the non-objective, the non-universal, and over which the agent is conscious that he in his individuality has the decision. Wickedness is the same awareness that the single self possesses the decision, so far as the single self does not remain in this abstraction but takes up the content of a subjective interest contrary to the good. . . . Here we have a goodness which has no objectivity but is only sure of itself and a self-assurance which involves the nullification of the universal', i.e. we have the contradiction of a purely 'subjective universality' (*Enc.*, §§ 511–12).

115. 12. *Schuld.* This word may be used in German either with or without a moral reference, and hence means either guilt or cause. The criminal has *Schuld* for his crime and the warm wind has *Schuld* for melting the snow. The English word 'responsibility' is perhaps the nearest equivalent since it also is sometimes used in a non-moral sense.

118. 13. From the moral point of view the necessary and the finite (or contingent) are related, not synthesized. But opposed categories turn into each other when thought tries to hold them apart (see Remark to Paragraph 26). Hence what seems necessitated (e.g. the execution of a plan) turns out after all to have been contingent on Cleopatra's nose, &c. Hence the moral agent, unable to unite necessity with contingency, because his exclusive subjectivity excludes him from a rational order, must act in a world of both necessary laws and unforeseeable contingencies and can never escape either (see *Enc.*, §§ 142–7).

119. 14. The meaning seems to be that when we distinguish the intention (*Absicht*) from what is done, we are 'looking away from' (*absehen*) certain aspects of the concrete event. My intention is either (*a*) a universal form under which I have not yet brought any specific content (*Hegels e. R.*, p. 80), e.g. I intend to satisfy my hunger but have not yet decided how to do it; or else (*b*) that particular aspect of the action which gives it worth for me because it satisfies me in some specific way, e.g. my intention to eat bread.

15. In Hegel's terminology, a proposition contains a statement about the subject which does not stand to it in any universal relationship but expresses some single action or some state or the like. Hence 'gold is a metal' is a judgement, but 'Caesar crossed the Rubicon' is a proposition (see *Enc.*, § 167).

16. 'The distinction between *dolus directus* and *indirectus*, in the sense that, in the latter case, the intention of the agent was not to commit the wrong which resulted, but only a slighter one, is now quite obsolete, although it still obtains in Austria' (Holtzendorff: *Rechtslexikon*, Leipzig, 1875, vol. i, p. 402).

123. 17. Hegel refers to the conversation between Croesus and Solon, reported in Herodotus i. 30–3. 'The stage of reflection that we reach in happiness stands midway between mere desire and the other extreme, which is right as right and duty as duty. In happiness the individual enjoyment has disappeared; the form of universality is there, but the universal does not yet come forth on its own account' (*History of Philosophy*, i. 161–3). See also Hegel's treatment of Eudaemonism in *Werke*[1], i. 7, a passage translated by Wallace in a note to *Enc.*, § 54.

124. 18. This passage is important as casting light on what Hegel means by 'subjective freedom'. He does not mean the satisfaction of desire or impulse in itself. He means freedom to find satisfaction of the whole self, i.e. of *rationalized* desires. The least rational form of this satisfaction is love, which is feeling, though not mere instinct, as we shall see when Hegel comes to deal with the family. A higher (i.e. a more rational) form is the satisfaction to be found in work, the satisfaction of the economic needs of life—this is the principle of 'civil society'. A higher form still is the political satisfaction obtainable through parliamentary institutions and in public opinion. Of course there are desires in the immediate sense which are satisfied incidentally in marriage, business, and politics, but to see nothing in rational purpose except the satisfaction of an instinct is to deny that there is any difference between man and an animal and to make all history unintelligible (cf. *Enc.*, § 140).

Hegel was far from supposing that subjective freedom is just freedom to satisfy what Plato called τὸ ἐπιθυμητικόν—desire pure and simple (see Paragraphs 120 ff. which make it clear that the 'subject' who is entitled to freedom is a *thinker*). On the contrary, he held that subjective freedom never came within the Greek purview at all, since the principle of conscience, of self-certainty, on which 'subjective freedom' in all its forms depends, came into the world with the Christian revelation.

19. *mit Abscheu zu tun, was die Pflicht gebeut.* Schiller (*Die Philosophen—Gedichte der dritten Periode*) actually says: *und mit Abscheu alsdann tun, wie die Pflicht dir gebeut.*

125. 20. The background of Hegel's thought here is his doctrine of reflective judgement in *Enc.*, § 175. The advance of thought from 'this metal conducts electricity' to 'all metals conduct electricity' is due to the reflection that the reason for the truth of the first judgement is the presence of some universal quality in this metal in virtue of which it conducts electricity; i.e. it must share the same characteristic with other metals. This universal is made explicit (though in an imperfect form) when we group together all the subjects to which this same predicate can be attached. Reflective thought is characteristic of the logical sphere of essence, which corresponds to the sphere of morality. Reflection on my welfare leads to bringing welfare into the orbit of my inward universality and this inward reference to the universal is posited outwardly as a reference to the welfare of others (cf. Note 5 to Paragraph 40).

126. 21. It is the philosophers of the Illumination (*Aufklärung*) that Hegel has in mind as is evident from his *History of Philosophy*, iii. 362 and 403 ff. Under the influence of, e.g., Shaftesbury and Hutcheson, they made much of 'benevolence', affection, &c. For an analysis and criticism of the 'law of the heart' (the eighteenth-century doctrine exaggerated by Hegel's Romantic contemporaries) see *Phenomenology*, pp. 392 ff.

22. Hegel refers apparently to the *Sturm und Drang* dramas, e.g. to Schiller's *Robbers*, a play in which a young man with good intentions is

expected to obtain the sympathy of the audience when he organizes a band of robbers to fight tyranny.

23. This has not been said above, but it may be implied, as Lasson suggests, in the Remark to Paragraph 29. It is important to notice the emphasis which Hegel himself here places on the word 'absolute'.

127. 24. The *beneficium competentiae* was the right of an unsuccessful defendant in cases of contract and quasi-contract not to be condemned to pay more than a sum which would still leave him enough to live on in reasonable comfort, having regard to his station in life.

128. 25. Right, an abstract universal, and my welfare, an abstract particular, may collide. Both, therefore, are finite and both are contingent on circumstances for their satisfaction. If the contradiction between them is to be overcome, each must lose its abstractness and both must be welded into a single concrete whole in which the opposites, right and welfare, will both be present as subordinate moments 'really' distinct but 'ideally' one. This is not fully achieved until we reach ethical life, but a relative identity between them is reached in the next section.

132. 26. In Paragraph 117 Hegel speaks of the right to know. The right of insight and the right of the objectivity of action are first mentioned in Paragraph 120.—In the next line, 'the latter' refers to 'action as such'.

27. *Sitten.* So elsewhere, as suggested by J. S. Mackenzie in *International Journal of Ethics*, October 1896, though Wallace had anticipated the suggestion in *Hegel's Philosophy of Mind* (Oxford, 1894), see, e.g., p. 104. For the meaning of *Sitten*, see Paragraph 151 and Note 14 *ad loc.*

28. See Remark to Paragraph 120.

29. So D. G. Ritchie in *Mind*, N.S., vol. vi, p. 121. All editions read '120'.

30. All editions read '119'.

31. 'When we can recognize what it is that we perceive or when we can distinguish it from other perceivable things, then the perception which we have is a clear perception' (i.e. idea) . . . 'e.g., when we look at a tree in daylight, we have a clear idea of the tree' (C. J. Wolff: *Psychologia empirica*, Frankfurt and Leipzig, 1732, Paragraph 31).

32. See Paragraph 282.

133. 33. See Paragraph 131. The particular subject distinguishes between the essence of his will and the inessentiality of, e.g., particular desires, and endeavours to make the latter correspond with the former. He 'ought' to do what the essence of his will enjoins, but never gets beyond 'ought' to 'is' or 'does'.

134. 34. Together with Paragraph 125.

135. 35. See, e.g., *Phenomenology*, pp. 654–5. Pure duty is only a form for action; as an abstract form, it is indifferent to the content given to it and hence the agent, convinced that he ought to be cowardly in order to save his life, may claim that cowardice is a duty. If duty is mere conscientiousness, then any content the agent pleases may be given to it without detracting from its formal character as conscientiousness. After showing (e.g., *Critique of Practical Reason*, Analytic, chap. i, sections 1–6) that the moral law presupposes a free will, Kant goes on to answer the question how I know what my duty is. He then further formulates the principle of duty for duty's sake as 'Act so that the maxim of thy will can always at the same time hold good as a principle of universal legislation' (*Kant's Theory of Ethics*, p. 119). Hegel's citation of this formula is careless or at best elliptical. The citation in the Addition to this Paragraph is more accurate. The passage which Hegel actually has in mind is probably the Introduction to the *Metaphysik der Sitten* (*Kant's Theory of Ethics*, p. 281).

136. 36. Throughout his treatment of conscience (*Gewissen*), Hegel makes use of its verbal similarity with *Gewissheit* (certainty). This similarity is not reproducible in English, but Hegel's argument is not intelligible unless the use he makes of it is borne in mind.

137. 37. What is absolutely good is concrete and therefore systematically determinate and differentiated. Hence to will it is to will in accordance with determinate rational principles.

38. This single subjective will, isolated from a rational social order, is mere self-certainty, abstraction from content. It may make the content of the natural will its content, but desires, &c., do not belong to this subject *qua* this subject; they belong to him only *qua* human being.

39. In the state, 'true' conscience takes the form of patriotism (see Paragraph 268). Note, however, that when Hegel says this, it is the state as Idea, the rational state, that he has in mind. Bad states exist, and patriotic acceptance, even if conscientious, of their bad laws would not in Hegel's view be the working of 'true' conscience, which is the conscientious acceptance of rational laws only. For the 'religious' conscience, see *Enc.*, § 552. In Protestantism, Hegel maintains, the religious conscience and true conscience coincide. Religion as a whole is a sphere above the state (see Note 3 to Paragraph 2).

138. 40. The keynote of the teaching of Socrates is the dictum of the Delphic oracle: 'Know thyself', and he described himself as a midwife, bringing to birth the ideas already present in embryo in men's minds. Cf. Paragraphs 279 and 343, and see *History of Philosophy*, i. 397 ff. The Stoic precept was 'live according to nature', i.e. in accordance with reason. 'In this quite formal principle of holding oneself in a pure harmony with oneself as a merely thinking nature, there rests the power of becoming indifferent to every particular enjoyment, passion, and interest' (*History of Philosophy*, ii. 263).

139. 41. With this rather obscurely expressed Remark, compare the fuller treatment of the same topic in *Enc.*, § 24. The argument here is as follows: We all begin life on the natural level; and at that level, i.e. in infancy, there is neither freedom nor morality. Freedom depends on the discovery of the self which is not natural but spiritual, i.e. the inner rational self present in germ, even in the infant, as the inner truth of its apparently purely impulsive life (see Paragraph 11). It is by transcending that life that we attain to freedom, but since there is no breach of continuity, freedom may be said both to arise from the natural life and yet to be something opposed to that life, i.e. to be our inner essence, there all the time.

The natural will comes into existence as a genuine will when it takes the form of the particular will, i.e. of arbitrariness or self-will (see Paragraphs 11–15). This is a contradiction because of the clash between its form and its content. Its 'form' is selfhood, my inner self which chooses, and is *free*, though only abstractly: this is the pure ego or abstract subjectivity described in Paragraph 5; its content is *given* by nature and consists of desires, impulses, &c. (see Paragraph 11).

Desires and impulses in themselves are neither good nor evil. The infant, whose life is governed by them, is innocent, not yet on the level of morality at all. What makes them evil is their choice in *opposition* to the good. Now a choice of this kind is open to the particular will because there is an explicit distinction in that will between form and content and because the reflection which makes that distinction possible may reflect on the ego and so discover the true nature of the ego's essence, i.e. not abstract subjectivity but the good, universality (see Remark to Paragraph 132). Hence it is possible for the abstract subjectivity of arbitrariness to choose either the good, its own essence, or else a natural desire which conflicts with that essence, i.e. it may take as its standard of choice not its genuine truth, its universality, but its particularity, its opposition to the universal. And when it does this it is evil; its inward freedom has made it possible for it to *will* the natural, i.e. to will in contradiction to its own essence, and this is just what evil is.

Hence evil is not nature alone; nor is it reflection alone (evil is not the same as error). Evil is the conjunction of nature and reflection, not mere nature but the *willing* of the natural which reflection makes possible. The precondition of evil is the *knowledge* of good and evil, i.e. of the distinction between the universal essence of the will and what opposes that essence.

42. i.e. the self-will mentioned in Paragraph 139.

140. 43. Section (*d*) of the Remark which follows is an important exegesis of this Paragraph. The wrongdoer has a positive reason for what he does; his action is bad only as the action of a moral agent, i.e. a responsible person who has a *reason* for what he does. We may describe his action as evil if we please, and so attach to it a negative predicate such as 'unmerciful', 'disobedient', 'ungrateful', &c., but we shall fail to treat the action concretely unless we also ascribe to it some positive predicate, if only 'satisfactory'—i.e. satisfactory, not in the sense in which animal gratification may be satisfactory to the animal, but satisfactory from the point of view of the agent's consciously adopted, and so to some extent rational purpose (see Paragraphs 120 ff.). I.e. in all bad, and so negative, actions there is some good and therefore something positive (see Collingwood: *Essay on Philosophical Method*, Oxford, 1933, chap. iii, Paragraphs 26–9). The conscientious man at the level of morality, when duty is a mere abstract universal, can give to it any 'positive' content he pleases (see Paragraph 135). The 'profound concept' referred to in the first paragraph of the following remark is the concept of subjectivity. The modern world has rightly recognized the claims of subjectivity, as Plato did not, but the thinkers whom Hegel attacks here made such claims for subjective conviction as made no allowance for the right of objectivity and so perverted the legitimate claims of the subject into hypocrisy, sophistry, &c.

44. Aristotle distinguishes between actions done 'through ignorance' (δι' ἄγνοιαν when the agent acts οὐκ εἰδώς), and actions done 'in ignorance' (when the agent acts ἀγνοῶν). In the first case the ignorance is unavoidable; there are external circumstances which the agent (e.g. Oedipus) had no means of knowing. In the second case, the ignorance is due to circumstances within the control of the agent, e.g. to drunkenness.

45. *wirksame Gnade*. The problem of the doctrine of grace is to reconcile a belief in man's inability to attain salvation independently of God's grace with a belief in man's individual freedom. In the seventeenth century the Jansenists, who tended to belittle man's freedom, carried on a controversy with the Jesuits on this question; both parties believed in efficacious grace but differed as to how it was obtained. Hegel's point is that if grace—God's power, i.e. the objective—is regarded as given to some men and not others—as both parties to the controversy agreed that it was—then God's power and human freedom are being treated as if they were related only accidentally. For an admirable account of the seventeenth-century disputes (which are the background of Remarks (*a*), (*b*), and (*c*) to this Paragraph), see Morris Bishop: *Pascal* (London, 1937), chap. x.

46. Probabilism—a doctrine of Jesuit moral theology—teaches that 'should there be a solid reason to suppose an action not prohibited, then we are free to follow that opinion, even though the reasons on the other

side are more weighty, provided that the difference is not such as to render the existence of the law' against the action 'not merely probable but morally certain' (Dr. G. H. Joyce in *Enc. of Religion and Ethics*, s.v.). Dr. Joyce explains that 'probable' here means 'very possibly true because supported by weighty reasons', not 'mathematically probable', and he adds that Pascal's attack on the doctrine in his *Lettres Provinciales* (which Hegel is mainly following here) is based on a caricature, not on a true interpretation.

47. Remark (*d*) is an attack not so much on Kant's doctrine itself (see, e.g., *Kant's Theory of Ethics*, p. 10), but on the perversion of that doctrine by the Romantics.

48. Reading with *Hegels e. R.*, p. 103, *auf welche hin*.

49. So Hegel's first edition. All other editions read '111'. Sterrett reads '119'. A reference to Paragraph 120 would have been more apposite than any of these.

50. '*Cum finis est licitus, etiam media sunt licita* (Busenbaum: *Medulla Theologiae Moralis*, iv. 3. 2) (Bolland). This work, published in the first half of the seventeenth century, contains the fundamental precepts of Jesuit ethics and was still current in Hegel's day. Hegel probably took from it the maxim quoted in the text, a maxim in which the principle of what is called Machiavellianism is clearly recognizable' (Messineo).

51. The version here given of (*e*) is, with a few minor changes, that given by Wallace in a note to his translation of *Enc. Logic*, pp. 388 ff.

52. In the first twenty years of the nineteenth century there was a strong Roman Catholic revival in Germany. It began with the sensational conversion of Count Stolberg in 1800 and gathered momentum by the accession of the leaders of the Romantic movement. Their change of faith antagonized Hegel the Lutheran as much as their elevation of emotion above reason disgusted Hegel the philosopher. *Brennus* was a periodical and this reference has not been checked. The letter in question was not reprinted in Jacobi's collected works.

53. In the quotation from Pascal in Remark (*a*) to this Paragraph.

54. 'Socrates's usual irony', of which Thrasymachus speaks in Plato's *Republic*, 337 a, was his profession of ignorance; by questioning Sophists like Thrasymachus and probing their answers in the professed attempt to find enlightenment for himself, Socrates showed the falsity and incoherence of their doctrines although he treated them with an ironical respect.

55. For Hegel, dialectic is the self-creative movement of thought. In its dialectical development, the universal gives itself a content. Plato on the other hand took his Ideas (or Forms) as self-subsistent,

unchanging, and unmoved realities. For him, the dialectical method was a method of inquiry and led towards the truth, but the truth was finally *seen;* it was outside thought and dialectic, an object shining in its own light like the sun. If the dialectical method ended in the contemplation of an unmoved and eternal object, a substance because self-subsistent, then dialectic might be said to be submerged at last in this object. The process whereby the vision was attained contributed nothing to the vision itself.

56. Karl Wilhelm Ferdinand Solger (1780–1819) was a Professor in Berlin from 1811 until his death. Hegel wrote an appreciative review of his correspondence and posthumous papers (*Werke*[1], xvi. 436 ff.). Hegel's further views on Schlegel, who is called 'the father of irony' in that essay, are contained in *History of Philosophy*, iii. 507–8. The citations in this footnote have not been checked.

57. *Guilt*, a play by Adolf Müllner (1774–1829), (Lasson). The play was an immediate success on its production in 1813. Hugo, a Norwegian, loves Elvira, the wife of Carlos, a Spaniard. He kills Carlos and marries Elvira. Carlos turns out to have been his brother and he and Elvira commit suicide because of their guilt.

58. With modern tragedy (i.e. tragedy written in modern languages), which he calls 'romantic tragedy', Hegel deals in *Aesthetic*, iv. 248 ff. In the same volume he discusses in detail the difference between ancient and modern tragedy (pp. 308 ff.). For a summary of his views on tragedy generally, see A. C. Bradley: *Oxford Lectures on Poetry* (London, 1920), pp. 69–95.

59. The type of spiritual life cultivated by the Moravians was an instance of the 'beautiful soul'—a conception popular with sentimentalists in Hegel's day and expounded, for instance, in the writings of Novalis and by Schiller in his tract *Über Anmut und Würde*, published in 1793. 'Its activity consists in yearning . . . in its transparent purity it becomes sorrow-laden . . . its light dims and dies within it and it vanishes as a shapeless vapour dissolving into thin air' (*Phenomenology*, pp. 666–7). Cf. *Aesthetic*, i. 322.

60. In the *Phenomenology*, published fourteen years before the *Philosophy of Right*, the transition is direct from conscience to religion, not as here and in the third edition of the *Encyclopaedia*, from subjective morality to a concrete rational order embodying both subjective convictions and objective institutions, and then later to religion.

141. 61. Right as pure universality and subjectivity as pure particularity are opposites. We can transcend their negation of one another only by denying their exclusive independence and making the transition to a form of experience in which they both take their place as

complementary moments. This is ethical life—a subjective disposition imbued with an objective, determinate, and rational content. As the unity of form and content, this is the Idea, and it is the Idea of freedom, since the moments comprised in it, right and subjectivity, are each of them embodiments of freedom. This Idea comes before us as the *result* of developing what is implicit in the conceptions of right and subjectivity, but since both of them have now been shown to be only moments in a concrete whole, each of them is an abstraction apart from the whole and each of them therefore presupposes the whole. Therefore the process of advance from right through subjectivity to the Idea of ethical life is at the same time a movement backwards to the 'true ground' out of which right and subjectivity both issue, or, as Hegel sometimes puts it, in developing what is implicit in right and subjectivity we have simply been plumbing their depths. I.e. the advance which we have been studying is a circle which now brings us back to what was implicit at the start.

PART III

Sub-sections I and II (*Family and Civil Society*)

142. 1. *bewegenden Zweck* (cf. Paragraph 258). As is clear from Paragraph 152, Hegel is thinking of Aristotle's doctrine that God, himself unmoved, is the mover of the universe, its 'final cause', moving it not by putting forth powers of his own, but simply by *being*, just as the beloved moves the lover. Hegel, however, is denying that the ethical order is purely transcendent; it is not *merely* a substance of which individuals are accidents; it is a substance which has risen to self-consciousness in those very individuals and has become actualized only for that reason (see Paragraphs 146–7). *Sittlichkeit*, the title given to Part III of the book, means the union of a subjective will with the objective order, and it is here generally translated 'ethical life'; but sometimes Hegel emphasizes the objective aspect and hence 'ethical order' and 'ethical principles' are used to render the word in a few places.

143. 2. The moral attitude was purely subjective, and the moral will distinguished itself from a purely objective world confronting it (see Paragraph 109). This distinction is still present in the ethical attitude, but with an important difference, because the subjective and the objective have undergone modification by each other, so that subjective and objective elements are distinguishable within each of them; i.e. each of them is a synthesis of object and subject and so is the 'totality' of the Idea. The two totalities are described respectively in Paragraphs 144–5 and 146–7. The first is ethical life regarded objectively; it is a substance (e.g., the state and its institutions) but, unlike Plato's state—we have learnt the lesson of the moral attitude and are carrying into the ethical order what was valuable in it—its form is subjective, i.e. the force of political institutions depends entirely on the self-consciousness of the citizens whose institutions they are, and who retain in the ethical order their subjective freedom. The second totality is ethical life regarded subjectively, i.e. it is the ethical will of the individual. This is a subjective will, like the moral will, but it is aware of objective duties as enshrining its own inner universality and not as something outside itself. The two totalities are explicitly identified and unified through the political action, as distinct from the knowledge, of the citizens.

144. 3. We have seen (Note 61 to Paragraph 141) that right and morality were both abstractions; the whole from which they are abstracted is therefore that on which they depend. This whole is a unity of universal and particular, of object and subject. Now 'a thing which has subsistence in itself, a thing that upholdeth that which else would fall' (a phrase of Hobbes, quoted here from Laird: *Hobbes*, London, 1934, pp. 92–3) is a substance. And throughout Hegel's account of ethical life, it is with substance that we are dealing; each type of this life—family, civil society, state—is a substantiality, but it is a substantiality of *mind*, and so one of a special sort. 'In my view', says Hegel (*Phenomenology*, p. 80), 'everything depends on grasping and expressing the ultimate truth not as substance but as subject as well.' (*a*) The family is a substance (in Hegel's view a single mind—see Paragraph 156) of which its members are accidents, but the substantiality is not external or visible; it depends solely on the consciousness of its members. The family's bond of union, its substance, is love; and love, in Hegel's view, is reason in its immediacy, i.e. an immature form of reason. Here there is no explicit difference between substance and accident; unity is present and the family members are not conscious that their unity is a unity of differences. (*b*) At the next stage, civil society, difference becomes explicit; the substance (the mind of the nation), 'appears' in particulars and it is their essence even though they may not realize it. They have risen above love to intelligence, but this is concentrated on a private end. (*c*) The third stage is the synthesis of the first two. The substantial mind of the nation, objectified in the state, rises to consciousness of itself in the minds of the citizens; it particularizes itself into rational laws and institutions. It is concrete because, unlike the family, it is particularized consciously and because, unlike civil society, its particulars are not an 'appearance' of its substantial essence, but the differentiation of that essence. It is concrete again because these laws and institutions, like the state itself as the unity of these, are actual in the minds of the citizens who live under them. They regulate their willing deliberately in accordance with rational ends; the members of the family pursue an ethical end, but only under the influence of feeling; members of civil society are intelligent, but pursue the universal end only under the disguise of the particular. The state, then, has acquired the form of subjectivity, and subjectivity as we have seen, is infinite because self-related. Hegel contrasts his state with an oriental despotism, i.e. with a substance which is an absolute power over individual accidents and alien to them. The essence of his state is that it is not only a substance but one which incorporates individual freedom by means of the parliamentary and other institutions which he later describes.

4. What is concrete is self-differentiating (see Paragraph 7). The substantiality which we are now considering is that of mind and therefore of the concept. Hence the institutions and objective duties of the ethical order are the concept's differentiation of itself (see Paragraphs 262, 269-70, 272).

145. 5. *ihre Vorstellung, erscheinende Gestalt und Wirklichkeit haben.* (*a*) *Vorstellung*—representative thought—is the level of thought characteristic of religion. The worshipper 'represents' the Absolute Idea to himself as the God whom he worships. Hegel regards this level of thought as characteristic of the family; the substantiality of mind and the power of ethical principles are 'represented' to the family member as, e.g., the *Penates*, the gods of the household (see Remark to Paragraph 163). (*b*) In civil society, we rise from the immediate to the reflective stage of mind and so to the explicit distinction between appearance and reality (see Note 5 to Paragraph 108). To all appearance, civil society is a riot of self-seeking, but this is only a mode in which the substantiality of the ethical order appears, because below appearances lie the laws of economics which are universal and which regulate appearances and are their essential substance. (*c*) In the state, the might of the ethical order is actualized in and through the conscious and deliberate volition by individuals of universal ends; what the state's compulsive power exacts, the individual also wills, so that freedom is at the same time a 'circle of necessity'. See Addenda, p. 376.

146. 6. See Note 42 to Paragraph 10. Nature *seems* to be self-subsistent; when we use a tool or derive water power from a stream, we recognize and do not annul the particular character of the object which serves our purpose; i.e. we recognize it as an *object* and to that extent as self-subsistent. In fact, however, nature, as the creation of God, embodies his rational purpose, and it is the task first of science and then of the philosophy of nature to discover what that purpose is. From that point of view, nature is not self-subsistent but depends on mind. It is 'real' but not 'ideal' (see Note 36 to Paragraph 7 and Addition to Paragraph 44). Laws and institutions are through and through rational and to that extent they *are* self-subsistent reason. As *laws* and *institutions* they exist solely for mind and their being is inseparable from the mentality of those whose laws and institutions they are; hence they embody rationality in the medium of reason itself. Their self-subsistence, then, is of a higher order than that of nature. Nevertheless, in Hegel's view they are not absolute. The state is the highest of human institutions but it is only an institution, the culmination of 'objective mind' but subordinate to 'absolute mind'. There is still something external about it and therefore something arbitrary and non-rational. Art, Religion, and Philosophy all stand above it as the complete and perfect synthesis of subject and object (see *Enc.*, the concluding section on the Absolute Mind).

148. 7. 'Circle'—see Addition to Paragraph 2. 'Necessity'—i.e. necessitated by the concept, by reason, the animating principle of the ethical order.

8. The last part of Kant's *Metaphysik der Sitten* is a 'doctrine of duties' (i.e. a *De Officiis*), in contrast with the first part, which is a 'doctrine of rights', and the second which is a 'doctrine of virtues'. The third part of Fichte's *System der Sittlichkeit* is explicitly styled a 'doctrine of duties'. For Hegel's view of a 'doctrine of virtues', see Remark to Paragraph 150.

150. 9. *Rechtschaffenheit*—honesty. But 'honesty' has too specifically moral a sense to express Hegel's meaning; 'respectability' would be nearer. Hegel thinks of 'virtue', when virtue is distinguished from duty, as an element in our natural endowment, as an ingrained excellence. From this point of view, it is something essentially individual and idiosyncratic, and as such has its place mainly at a time before there were rational institutions and an established ethical life in which *all* men are trained to participate.

10. See *Aesthetic*, i. 250, where Hegel points out that the 'heroic' virtue of Hercules, whereby he attained Olympus, is quite compatible with his doubtful morals. He was *tugendhaft* but not *moralisch*. For the deeds and the rights of heroes see Note 78 to Paragraph 93.

11. i.e. a history of ingrained or natural excellence, a history of genius.

12. For a fuller statement of Hegel's point here, see *History of Philosophy*, ii. 205–6. For Aristotle, moral virtue consists in imposing a mean or limit on one's feelings and actions. It therefore contains a rational or universal element and a particular or natural element. Nature, for Hegel, is the realm of the external and so of the quantitative. Hence if virtue as such is the ethical order reflected in the individual's natural disposition, then the determination of any specific virtue must depend on something in the disposition, i.e. on something natural and therefore quantitative; and if a virtue is to be determined quantitatively,

the same must be true of a vice. In Aristotle the difference between,
e.g., rashness and cowardice, as the excess and deficiency respectively,
and courage as the mean, is one of quantity of feeling. It does not
follow, however, that Aristotle makes the difference between virtue
and vice a difference in degree only and not in kind as well, or that
Hegel thought he did.

13. A certain action may be done either on impulse or from a sense
of duty. Duty and impulse may thus have the same content or object;
but the object in abstraction from the motive which led to it is a mere
event in nature and so neither good nor bad. Hence it is impossible to
say that the excellence of the thing done makes the impulse behind it
good, for the thing in itself has no excellence at all.

151. 14. Customs (*Sitten*) are ethical (*sittlich*) in the sense that they
embody the rationality of those whose customs they are. As Hegel
himself points out (*Hegels e. R.*, p. 111 and *Werke*[1], i. 396), the relation
between *Sitte* and *sittlich* is that between ἦθος and ἠθικός, and our word
'ethics' means originally the study of the 'ethos' of a people. For the
Greeks, observance of ἦθος was sufficient to make a man ἠθικός, because
'the ancients knew nothing of conscience' (*Hegels e. R.*, loc. cit.).
Hegel's view, on the contrary, is that the highest type of ethical life is
that in which individuals *conscientiously* conform to *rational* institutions
and customs. That the formation of good habits is the foundation of a
good character is a cardinal doctrine of Aristotle's Ethics, and the view
that custom is a second nature, superseding man's original nature as a
result of education, is found, e.g., in Pascal, *Pensée* 93 (Brunschvicg).

153. 15. 'Others—i.e. Socrates' (*Hegels e. R.*, p. 112). The answer
is ascribed to Xenophilus the Pythagorean by Diogenes Laertius (viii.
i. 15), but emphasis on the educational value of good laws and institutions is a commonplace of Greek ethics and politics.

154. 16. The ethical order as appearance is civil society, and it is in
that sphere that individuals attain their 'particular satisfaction', i.e.
their livelihood through work.

157. 17. 'This Idea'—i.e. the union of the independent self-consciousness with its concept. The concept of this Idea is mind, and mind
objectifies itself in the course of its development from one level to
another of this sphere. I.e. it objectifies its moments, universality,
particularity, and individuality, and the objectification of each of these
is a different form of organization—family, civil society, and state.

18. 'Brought back to'—i.e. the state is the 'true ground' of both
family and civil society, the concrete whole from which they are both
abstractions (see Note 61 to Paragraph 141).

161. 19. From the physical point of view, the individual is made what he is by his generic essence (see Note 63 to Paragraph 24), i.e. as a human being he is a member of the human race and a moment in the process of that race's life. Hence marriage, as a tie affecting the substance of his whole life, is intrinsic to the life of the race. From this point of view, the unity in marriage is only the inner unity of the single life-stream of the race, and this unity is external to the married parties, for they remain two human beings. Mind, however, transcends this duality by transforming a physical external tie into the spiritual union of self-conscious love. Love is reason implicit and this spiritual union is thus a union of mind with mind:

> So they loved, as love in twain
> Had the essence but in one;
> Two distincts, division none;
> Number there in love was slain.

162. 20. For Hegel's view of what constitutes genuine dramatic interest, see his footnote to Remark (f) to Paragraph 140. Here it is the *Sturm und Drang* drama that he has in mind again (see Note 22 to Paragraph 126).

163. 21. *pietas*—dutiful conduct, especially to members of one's family, 'family piety'. *Penates*—the guardian deities of the Roman household, regarded here as representing the mind of the family. See Note 3 to Paragraph 144 and Note 5 to Paragraph 145.

164. 22. See the second footnote to the Remark to Paragraph 270.

165. 23. Mind is present in individuals as their generic essence. As concrete, mind returns into itself out of its differentiation of itself, i.e. the vitality of the race is concrete because it is generated out of the opposition between the two sexes into which it is differentiated. This is the rational basis of sex differences, and as a *rational* basis it must have some bearing on ethics as a rationally ordered life (cf. *Phenomenology*, pp. 484 ff.).

166. 24. *Antigone*, ll. 450–7. Hegel regarded this play as the perfect and most satisfying exemplar of tragedy (*Aesthetic*, iv. 324). Antigone kept family law—the law of the ancient gods—by burying her brother in defiance of the king's edict against doing so. On the universal level, there is a conflict between family law and state law, the law of the heart and the law publicly and objectively promulgated. On the individual level, Hegel holds, there is a similar conflict between the nature of woman (the creature of intuition and feeling) and the nature of man (the creature of reason).

169. 25. *Vermögen*—'estate' might be a more suitable rendering but in some places it might falsely be taken to mean 'real estate' only.

170. 26. See Paragraphs 199 ff. and 253.

173. 27. i.e. persons immediately existent (as children). For the view that the infinity of mind when embodied in the finite leads to the false infinite of endless progression, see *Enc.*, §§ 92–4.

175. 28. For a fuller statement of the point made here see *Philosophy of History*, pp. 286 ff. Also see below, Paragraph 180.

29. Cf. Addition to *Enc.*, § 396. The play theory of education was popularized in Germany by J. H. Basedow (1723–90) in the years following the publication of Rousseau's *Émile* (1762). Froebel, with whom the theory is usually associated in this country, did not publish his *Education of Man* until 1826.

176. 30. The married parties are the other two.

178. 31. By Blackstone in his *Commentaries*, vol. ii, pp. 11–12.

179. 32. The ethical justification of inheritance in Hegel's view is that the family's capital is an embodiment of the family unity; it is therefore common property, and when its administrator dies it is distributed to the members of the family which has now been dissolved in the course of nature. Hence bequests to friends can only be justified from the ethical point of view if the testator had cultivated his circle of friendships to such an extent that his friends formed a kind of family and that his property in his lifetime was theirs as much as his.

180. 33. Fichte implies such a view in his *Science of Rights*, § 19, pp. 341 ff.

34. Hegel does not exaggerate the scope of Roman *patria potestas*. To allow to sons private possession even of *peculium castrense* was a revolutionary change, introduced by Augustus, and even then, if the son died intestate, this *peculium* passed to the *paterfamilias*.

35. In a marriage with *manus* (the type which Hegel calls 'slavery'), the wife passed out of the *potestas* of her *paterfamilias* into that of her husband. Her status in that event was the same as that of her daughters. Divorce in such a marriage was more difficult than in a marriage without *manus*, and marriages with *manus* were rare by the end of the Republic. Hegel's authority for asserting that *materfamilias* means a wife who is, and *matrona* a wife who is not, in *manu* is Aulus Gellius, *Noctes Atticae*, xviii. 6.

36. This titbit of legal lore is culled from an earlier edition of Heineccius: *Antiquitatum Romanarum Syntagma* (Frankfurt, 1841), III. x. i.

37. 'Roman history'—in the last century of the Roman Republic the individual began to count for more than the family. Cases were known of an heir succeeding to the position of *paterfamilias* and the family

obligations, but to only a fraction of its wealth, the remainder having been left to others. This led to attempts to limit the testamentary powers to the *paterfamilias*. 'Lucian'—see, e.g., *Bis Abdicatus*, a speech supposedly delivered in court by a man who was disinherited by his father and studied medicine. His father became insane, the son cured him and was restored to his will. But he was then disinherited a second time on his refusal to treat his stepmother's insanity. He appeals to the court against his father. 'Other writings'—Hegel probably has in mind the rhetoricians. Disinheritance and preposterous imaginary complications arising therefrom made one of their most succulent topics. See, e.g., the elder Seneca: *Controversiae*, i. 1, i. 8, ii. 1, &c.

38. *Fideicommissa*—testamentary trusts, see Note 21 to Paragraph 46. *Substitutiones*—nominations in a will of one or more heirs to inherit as substitutes in the event of the failure of the heir instituted to take possession of the inheritance, whether through death or otherwise.

39. All editions read '356'.

181. 40. The transition from family to civil society corresponds on a higher level to that from right to morality. In each case the transition is the emergence of the particular; in each case we leave behind an undifferentiated universality and arrive at a realm of appearance, i.e. what is visible and obvious is particularity, though universality is its underlying essence. Here, as in the second part, we come upon the categories of 'essence' (see Note 5 to Paragraph 108). Universal and particular, form and content, appear in civil society to fall apart, the Idea appears to be divided, but none the less the pursuit of private ends here turns out to be conditioned by universal laws. These are implicit to start with (as the laws of economics), but they become explicit later as a system of laws and institutions for the protection of private property and as barriers against private selfishness. On the meaning of 'show' see Note 73 to Paragraph 82.

182. 41. Civil Society is the sphere of the particular as opposed to the universal, of men as particulars, not individuals, of men as men, not as Germans, or as David, Jonathan, &c. In other words it is the sphere of the *concrete person*, i.e. not the abstract unit of the sphere of abstract right, nor yet the abstract and isolated subject of the sphere of morality, but the member of civil society, who is like the abstract person in counting as one unit amongst others, but like the subject in consciously pursuing his own private ends (though the ends in question are the satisfaction of the needs common to men as men). He differs from the subject in gradually coming to recognize himself as a member of society and to realize that to attain his own ends he must work in with others. Through working in with others, his particularity is mediated; he ceases to be a mere unit and eventually becomes so socially conscious, as a result of

the educative force of the institutions of civil society (see Paragraphs 230 ff.), that he wills his own ends only in willing universal ends and so has passed beyond civil society into the state. What we watch in studying civil society is a process of mediation; I gain my ends by your means and then by means of a general organization (e.g. the Corporation). In this way particularity loses its exclusiveness, and the universal gradually asserts itself and becomes explicit in the particular consciousness. If we study the process whereby my satisfaction involves yours, we can discern certain universal principles at work—the laws of political economy. These laws are the 'form' or the framework of this sphere; its content is the pursuit of selfish ends. Form and content, however, are explicitly different; the two principles which govern this sphere are the opposite of one another. Hence this is the stage of difference and division; the Idea seems to have fallen asunder (Paragraph 184) and it looks as if ethical life, which is essentially social, were lost in a riot of self-seeking. For the 'mediation' of the particular through the universal, see Hegel's doctrine of syllogism in *Enc.*, §§ 183 ff.

183. 42. See Translator's Foreword, § 5.

184. 43. 'Moment of reality'—'Ideality', Hegel remarks (*Enc.*, § 96) 'must be the ideality of something. But this something is not a mere indefinite this or that, but existence characterized as a reality which, if retained in isolation, has no truth.' In this sense, 'the body is the reality of the soul and the law is the reality of freedom' (*Enc.*, § 91). 'Relative totality'—i.e. the two sides of the Idea as a whole, form and content, are merely related to one another, not integrated here in an organic unity.

Hegel's whole account of civil society, and especially that section of it called the 'system of needs', bears traces of his study of Adam Smith and the *laissez-faire* doctrine that a country best attains commercial prosperity all round if it leaves individual entrepreneurs as far as possible free to pursue their own selfish aims.

185. 44. The two sides of the antithesis are the particular and the universal. Intuition (e.g. in the family) does not distinguish between them but apprehends them only in their immediate unity. 'Reflective self-consciousness', i.e. the Understanding, makes the distinction between them explicit, and, once the distinction is made, intuition by itself is powerless to synthesize them. Unity can be restored only by a further effort of thought, by reason as distinct from the Understanding. The wounds of thought can be healed by thought alone (see *Enc.*, § 24, Addition 3).

45. Hegel regards 'beauty' as the principle of the Greek world. Beauty, he holds, is the Idea appearing in a sensuous form; i.e. beauty and truth are ultimately identical, but truth is an explicit and known synthesis of opposites, while beauty is only a *felt* unity without any

explicit difference. The unity of the family is a 'substantial unity' built on feeling; the substance has not differentiated itself into self-subsistent particulars and then reasserted its unity on a higher and more concrete level by incorporating these particulars into itself like the members of an organism. Plato's state, which Aristotle criticized on the ground that it was too like a family, is substantial in this same sense; its unity, Hegel is holding, is a felt unity based on the 'beauty' of the ethical life there portrayed. Such a state is explicitly defective because it denies subjective freedom, but it is true in essence because it is a genuine unity, not a mere collection of self-subsistent particulars, like a civil society. Hegel's view of beauty as the essence of Greek moral life is doubtless due to his reflection on the fact that the Greeks drew no clear distinction between beauty and goodness, as the meaning of καλός and αἰσχρός shows.

187. 46. *Bürger—bourgeois*, burgher of a town as distinct from the citizen (*citoyen*) of a state—see Remark to Paragraph 190. Civil society (*bürgerliche Gesellschaft*) is a society of burghers or civilians, men interested in civil as distinct from political life. See Addenda, p. 376.

189. 47. All editions read '60'.

48. Three 'classical economists'. Adam Smith's *Wealth of Nations* was published in 1776, J. B. Say's *Traité d'économie politique* in 1803, and D. Ricardo's *Principles of Political Economy and Taxation* in 1817.

190. 49. See Remark to Paragraph 209. We speak of the members of a state not as 'men' but as 'Englishmen', 'Germans', &c. Political institutions may differ, but economic needs are everywhere the same.

192. 50. For the movement of thought in this Paragraph and the next, see Paragraphs 48, 49, and 71. Recognition is termed an 'abstract' relation because two people who recognize each other still preserve their independence. A society bound together by the ties of recognition alone is still a society of independent units and their social tie is only a formal one, unlike the marriage tie, which links the parties in substance.

195. 51. Reading *gebildetem* with Lasson for Hegel's *ungebildetem*. The Remark to the preceding Paragraph is primarily an attack on Rousseau. 'Qualitative limit'—(*Grenze*), i.e. the multiplication of needs never reaches a point when the quantitative alteration simultaneously involves a qualitative change. The savage and Socrates may need different things, but need they share in common. The mere multiplication of needs will never lift you out of the sphere of needs (see *Enc.*, § 92).

52. At the level of morality, the subject had a right of distress. But civil society, as a phase of ethical life, is the *synthesis* of right and welfare, and hence the needy man, with no money to make purchases, may not steal the property of others. It is the task of society in such an event to look after his well-being (see Paragraphs 241-2).

199. 53. As Messineo points out, following Bolland, p. 338, the words in square brackets, which appear in Hegel's table of contents though not in his text, should be supplied here. 'Class-divisions', i.e. *Stände*. A *Stand* is a group of persons with the same status. Hegel uses the word in three senses in this book, and all three of them are found together in the Remark to Paragraph 326: (i) the *status* of marriage; (ii) the *class*, or social position, e.g. of business men; (iii) the *Estates* of the realm assembled in parliament. For the connexion between (ii) and (iii) in fact as well as in language, see Remark to Paragraph 303.

54. The dialectical advance here is based on Hegel's doctrine of the reflective syllogism, for which see *Enc.*, § 190, and Macran: *Hegel's Doctrine of Formal Logic* (Oxford, 1912), p. 301.

202. 55. The class divisions are types of social life, and the basis of division is the concept itself; i.e. the three classes severally correspond to the three main stages in the advance of the concept which is the animating principle of the whole of ethical life. At first we have the stage of immediacy, when thought is sunk in *substance*—the life of feeling for which difference is not explicit. This type of social life is therefore based on the family. Secondly, differences are made explicit; we have advanced from implicit universality to explicit particularity, from feeling to reflection, so that substance now has a particular content and a universal *form* apprehended by reflection. Social life here is based on reflection, i.e. it is the product of education and so is specially characteristic of civil society—the child of the modern world. Thirdly, the synthesis of these; the particular consciously finds himself in the universal; the original unity has been restored, but on a higher plane. Private satisfaction is secured by the deliberate pursuit of *universal* ends. This type of social life prefigures the life of the state. Hegel's point is that the distinction between agriculture, industry, and the civil service is not a matter of accident or convenience, but is based on logical necessities. Civil society, as a type of state, has present in it the relics of patriarchal communities and the promise of the genuinely political life of the state proper. See Addenda, p. 376.

203. 56. G. F. Creuzer, 1771–1858, was appointed Professor at Heidelberg in 1804 and was Hegel's colleague there from 1816 to 1818. There are frequent references in Hegel's lectures to his *Symbolik und Mythologie der alten Völker, besonders der Griechen* (Symbolism and mythology of the ancients, especially the Greeks), 4 vols., Darmstadt, 1810–12.

209. 57. If we reflect on the reciprocity characteristic of society, we may see it as the mirror image of the conception of personality, that in respect of which all men are alike. This conception of personality is embodied in abstract rights. Now if we rise from the abstract conception of person to the concrete conception of a person related to other persons in a society, we must also rise from abstract rights to rights known through their embodiment in law. The sphere of civil society is that of the education of the particular (see Paragraph 187), the sphere of the 'Understanding' as distinct from the 'intuition' of the family and the 'reason' of the state, and it is here therefore where consciousness of man's interrelatedness with other men leads to the creation of positive law as the embodiment of a *known* relatedness. In the Remark to this Paragraph, Hegel is translating into the language of his philosophy, Galatians iii. 28.

211. 58. Throughout this section Hegel has in mind the controversy in his day between the historical and the rationalist schools of jurists. 'The former studied customary law with special interest and regarded it as the genuine manifestation of the popular consciousness. Law in their view could not be treated as dead material to be cast and recast by professional jurists and statesmen in accordance with what they took to be right in the nature of things.' On the contrary, law—as custom—was living, like a language, inextricably intertwined with national tradition. The historical study of national traditions and legal requirements was thus an indispensable prelude to codification; and proposals in Hegel's day to codify were therefore regarded by Savigny, the leader of the historical school and Hegel's colleague in Berlin, as premature (Vinogradoff: *Outlines of Historical Jurisprudence*, Oxford, 1920, vol. i, pp. 128–9).

59. *Landrecht oder gemeines Recht.* Hegel probably has Blackstone in mind: 'The municipal law of England, or the rule of civil conduct prescribed to the inhabitants of this kingdom, may with sufficient propriety be divided into two kinds: the *lex non scripta*, the unwritten or common law, and the *lex scripta*, the written or statute law' (*Commentaries*, vol. i, p. 63). But if *gemeines* has here its ordinary meaning of 'common' and is not intended as a translation of 'municipal', then Hegel has made a bad blunder.

60. Hegel may be thinking of Blackstone (vol. i, pp. 68 ff.) or perhaps Bacon: *De Aug. Sc.* VIII. iii. On the way in which judicature and legislature overlapped in England in the early nineteenth century, see e.g. Halévy: *History of the English People in 1815*, Book i, chap. i.

61. Valentinian III, Emperor of the West, 425–55. The law in question was promulgated in 446 and is given in the Theodosian Code, I. iv. 2. The 'College' consisted of Papinian, Paul, Gaius, Ulpian, and Modestin. When the 'votes' cast on a given point were equal (as they might be, since judgements by all members were not available on all points) Papinian, the 'President', had a 'casting-vote'.

62. This insult is the burden of Savigny's *Vom Beruf unsrer Zeit für Gesetzgebung und Rechtswissenschaft* (Heidelberg, 1815). (Lasson.) Eng. tr. by A. Hayward: *On the vocation of our age to legislation and jurisprudence.* See note 58 to Paragraph 211.

214. 63. The Jamaica Consolidated Slave Law of 1816 (57 Geo. III, c. 25) provided (s. xxvii) that in no case was a slave to suffer more than thirty-nine lashes in one day. Thirty-nine lashes was a not uncommon statutory maximum in slavery legislation, and Hegel was a student of the English press, where such legislation was a good deal discussed. See also Deuteronomy xxv. 3.

215. 64. The translator has been unable to trace this anecdote in any writer on Dionysius.

65. The reformation of Roman jurisprudence was carried out under Justinian's instructions between 527 and 533, and its results were embodied in the Code, the Pandects or Digest, and the Institutes. See Note 12 to Paragraph 3.

216. 66. For the difference between the abstract universal of the Understanding and the concrete self-differentiating universal of reason, see Note 63 to Paragraph 24.

67. So the first edition. Later editions change *meilleur* to *mieux*. The proverb is probably Italian in origin.

68. *Menschenverstand.* For the significance of this word see *Phenomenology*, pp. 127, 176–7. In the *History of Philosophy*, iii. 375 ff., Hegel uses it to describe the philosophy of Reid, Oswald, and Beattie, and he there translates it *sensus communis.* Elsewhere in the same work he says that 'common sense is a way of thinking which is a repository of all the prejudices of the day. It is really controlled by genuine thought but is unconscious of the fact' (i. 379), hence a man of 'true', as distinct from false, common sense is a man of prejudices and opinions which happen to be true, although he does not know their truth.

217. 69. e.g. *mancipium*, a taking by the hand, originally meant the ceremonial transfer of something from one person to another. The ceremony involved an actual transfer by hand and the speaking of certain words. Later, when the ceremony was dropped, the word was used to mean not a transfer but the possession of something acquired by formal transfer.

218. 70. Compare Remarks to Paragraphs 96 and 319.

71. i.e. Greek tragedy. The chorus sometimes (e.g. in the *Agamemnon*, *Oedipus Tyrannus*, &c.) consists of subjects of the royal house with whose misfortune the play is concerned. It sympathizes with the misfortunes of its rulers, and utters appropriate moral maxims, but it does not speak as if their woes were its own.

72. See Note 79 to Paragraph 95 and Note 91 to Paragraph 101.

73. 'It is but reasonable that those crimes should be most severely punished which are most destructive of the public safety and happiness . . . and those which cannot be so easily guarded against as others. . . . Hence it is that . . . to steal a handkerchief . . . privately from one's person is made capital, but to carry off a load of corn from an open field . . . is punished with transportation only' (Blackstone: *Commentaries*, vol. iv, p. 16).

219. 74. See footnote to Paragraph 258.

221. 75. To possess the *jus standi in judicio* is to be the opposite of an 'outlaw'.

223. 76. *Schieds-Friedensgericht.* A *Friedensgericht* is sometimes a court of the first instance, competent in some of the German states to try actions where only small amounts are at issue, sometimes an arbitration tribunal. A *Schiedsgericht* is a court of arbitration. The details in Hegel's text apply only to the judicial organization of some of the German states in his day. The principle of providing for recourse to arbitration in case of dispute is, however, a commonplace of modern commercial contracts, and it is a legal requirement, e.g., in cases where a price is to be fixed for land acquired compulsorily by Act of Parliament.

225. 77. (a) A jury of laymen finds the facts, and (b) the judge declares the law and, in criminal cases, pronounces sentence.

78. Under the *formula* system of trial, the praetor heard the parties informally and prepared an issue which he sent in writing to a panel of *judices* for trial, instructing them to give judgement for A or B in accordance with the evidence. *Judices* were laymen and not magistrates, though they often required and possessed legal knowledge. Greenidge (*The Legal Procedure of Cicero's Time*, Oxford, 1901, p. 150) says that it is a mistake to hold that the work of *judices* was limited to reaching conclusions on points of fact.

79. Hegel seems to be thinking of the fact that in his day a defendant in England was sometimes able to take advantage of technical flaws in the indictment to secure his acquittal. Blackstone (*Commentaries*, vol. iv, p. 333) cites an instance of a man's being charged with feloniously stealing a greyhound. By pleading that to steal a greyhound was a civil trespass and not a felony, he could claim to be acquitted. By an Act of George IV many of these technical pleas were made of none effect.

227. 80. Especially Paragraph 119.

81. The words were used in the formula of the oath of the Roman *judex*; 'I swear to the best of my belief', or 'on my conscience'.

82. The jury attempts to determine objectively and absolutely whether the prisoner is guilty or not. It reasons sincerely from the testimony given on oath, but since this testimony is empirical in content and not rigorously provable in the way that a mathematical theorem is, inferences from it, however sincere, are formally invalid if they claim to be completely and objectively demonstrated. 'Extraordinary punishments'— 'materially, all punishments inflicted as a result of the verdict of a jury are what have been called extraordinary punishments—there may be a confession here too but that is something accidental in these circumstances and outside the essence of the matter' (*Enc.*, edition 2, § 531). Ordinary punishments then are those inflicted, by judges who sit without juries, on criminals who confess their guilt.

229. 83. *Polizei*, translated 'police' here, has a wider sense than that conveyed by 'police' in English. Hence in what follows it is generally translated 'public authority'. The justification for this is that Hegel himself sometimes (e.g. in Paragraph 235) uses *öffentliche Macht* as a synonym for *Polizei*; but the disadvantage of this rendering is that it is less specific than Hegel's word. 'Corporation'—i.e. *Korporation*, a term which originates with the workmen's corporations in ancient Rome. 'Trade guild' is Reyburn's translation of this word (e.g. *Hegel's Ethical Theory*, p. 223) and 'guild corporation' is sometimes used here (in purely economic contexts) in place of 'Corporation'. 'Incorporated trade' would be a suitable rendering in places, since that expression was used in the English literature of Hegel's day (e.g. in the *Wealth of Nations*) to express what he means when he is thinking only of economic organizations. He is of course not thinking of what we know as Trade Unions, since his *Korporationen* are societies of which both employers and employed are members. 'Corporation' has been generally used here to render Hegel's meaning, first, because he is thinking not only of economic organizations but also of religious bodies, learned societies, and sometimes of town councils; and secondly, because 'Corporation' is now used in Hegel's sense of an institution in modern Italy. There, as Professor Finer says (*Mussolini's Italy*, London, 1935, pp. 272–3), 'the Corporations are to act as decentralised administrative bodies, in order to achieve an organisation and a morale half-way between the public irresponsibility and the technical agility of private enterprise and the public responsibility and heavy routine of the ordinary departments of state'. This might almost pass as an exegesis of Hegel's own meaning.

235. 84. i.e. public utility undertakings such as drainage, water supply, &c.

236. 85. Reading with Lasson *dass durch das öffentliche Ausstellen Waren, die*, &c. Messineo rejects this emendation, but if it is not adopted, the plural verb with which the sentence concludes is left without a subject.

242. 86. It is curious to find street-lighting enumerated amongst public charitable institutions. Perhaps the meaning may be that the wealthy could afford servants to carry lanterns to light them through the streets, or that only the poor need to *walk* in the streets at night. At the end of the eighteenth century, in Berlin, one of his friends gave Schleiermacher a lantern to fasten on his coat to guide him home on dark nights (*Schleiermacher and Religious Education*, by A. R. Osborn, Oxford, 1934, p. 40).

243. 87. The *outward* expansion of civil society is considered in Paragraph 246.

244. 88. *Pöbel*, i.e. the *plebs* or proletariat or riff-raff, but no single word is available for a mass of *rebellious* paupers, recognizing no law but their own, and it is this which Hegel means (see the Addition to this Paragraph).

245. 89. This Remark is probably based on Hegel's enthusiastic study of English parliamentary debates on poor-law legislation and newspaper reports of private philanthropy. In his note-books, written during his residence in Frankfurt at the end of the eighteenth century, there were numerous extracts from the English press on these topics (Rosenkranz: *Hegels Leben*, Berlin, 1844, p. 85). The success of the system, or lack of system, in Scotland was much disputed, and a Commission of 1843 led to poor-law legislation there on systematic lines.

247. 90. Cf. *Kant's Critique of Aesthetic Judgment*, translated by J. C. Meredith (Oxford, 1911), p. 122. For an amplified statement of the view here expressed, see, as Messineo suggests, the section on the 'Geographical Basis of History' in *Philosophy of History* (especially pp. 90 ff.). Hegel wrote in the days of bad roads and no aircraft.

251. 91. In this sphere where universal and particular are merely relative to one another and not synthesized, the universal is only an abstract universal, a common character of the particulars, and therefore something determinate in contrast with other similar abstract universals. Hence these universals in turn become particulars with higher universals over them. Thus the study of the sphere of the particulars leads to their distinction into species, which in turn fall under genera. The *truth* about the particulars is that they are differentiations of the concrete universal and so 'identical' with one another, because the life-blood of each of them is the same. In this sphere of relatedness, however, this truth, their identity, is obscured; it *appears* as an inner likeness accompanied by an explicit difference. This inner likeness is made manifest as the common membership of an organization which itself is a specification of the labour organization of civil society as a whole. Civil society is differentiated by the concept into three classes exhaustive of the whole society. The particular, i.e. the business, class—to which Corporations are appropriate because it is the class which specially needs to be brought back to universality—has the universal appearing in it as its classification, i.e. it is a genus divided into species. Reason appears here disguised as the Understanding and hence the classification is not the differentiation of the concept but that used in empirical science, the field where the Understanding is at home. Hence the number of Corporations, unlike the number of classes, is indeterminate.

92. Because the universal purpose of the Corporation is at the same time the particular purpose of its members. In the system of needs, the universal is abstract because the particular in pursuing his end is not clearly conscious of the universal which regulates his activity. In the Corporation the case is otherwise. The difference between the Corporation and the state is that the purpose of the Corporation, though universal for its members, in the sense that it is the same for all of them, is still restricted; it is not the purpose of all the members of society but that of a section only.

252. 93. A *privilegium* (from *privus* and *lex*) is a law affecting an individual only and hence is something exceptional. But the privileges of an order, for example, although peculiar to it, cannot rightly be regarded as exceptional or accidental. The order itself is there because it is a branch of society; as one special branch (i.e. as a particular branch) it is like other branches in being a branch, but is distinct from them in other respects, and its distinction from others is outwardly manifest in its privileges.

253. 94. See Addition to Paragraph 207.

95. The 'ethical ground' presumably consists in the fact that particularity has the *right* in this sphere to seek its own ends (see Paragraph 184) and this leads inevitably to both luxury and poverty (see, e.g., Paragraphs 185, 243).

255. 96. *Momente.* The stability and organic unity of the state are foreshadowed in the family and the Corporation. Civil society is characterized generally by its atomicity, and it is saved from complete disintegration only by these fixed and organic institutions. Hegel is here using a metaphor drawn from the solar system: the sun is a fixed point whose attractive power prevents the dissipation of the heavenly bodies which revolve around it and so confers a unity on the system as a whole. Moreover, the 'fixed points' here are parallel to the 'moment of centrality' in the category of mechanism (see *Enc.*, §§ 196–8).

256. 97. Reflection, the activity of the Understanding, sunders the unity of intuition, and for feeling substitutes judgement. To judge (*urteilen*) is to partition, and the essential task of reflection is in Hegel's view always the making of distinctions which it is powerless to synthesize.

98. 'Ideal'—i.e. moments divergent in 'reality' (the world of outward existence in which the Ideal, the genuinely true, is embodied) but not divergent in actuality because they are distinct yet synthesized moments in the single unity of the concept or the *Idea* (see Note 36 to Paragraph 7). This conception of 'ideality' is frequently used in the section on the state (see especially Paragraph 278). 'True ground'—see Note 61 to Paragraph 141.

Sub-section III (*The State*)

257. 1. *Volksgeist*—see Note 83 to Paragraph 340. With this Remark, compare Remarks to Paragraphs 163 and 166.

258. 2. Hegel's theory of the state has his theory of syllogism for its background. 'The syllogism is the rational and everything rational' (*Enc.*, § 181) because it is a concrete unity of explicit differences, and these differences are the three moments of the concept, universality, particularity, and individuality. 'The state is a system of three syllogisms: (i) The individual or person, through his particularity or physical or mental needs . . . is coupled with the universal, i.e. with society, law, right, government. (ii) The will or action of individuals is the intermediating force which procures for these needs satisfaction in society, law, &c., and which gives to society, law, &c., their fulfilment and actualization. (iii) But the universal, i.e. the state, government, and law, is the permanent underlying mean in which the individuals and their satisfaction have and receive their fulfilled reality, intermediation, and persistence. Each of the moments of the concept, as it is brought by intermediation to coalesce with the other extreme, is brought into union with itself and produces itself. . . . It is only by this triad of syllogisms with the same terms that the whole is thoroughly understood in its organization' (*Enc.*, § 198). What essentially differentiates the state from civil society and makes it rational, is the parliamentary organization which mediates between particulars on the one hand and the individual monarch on the other (see Paragraphs 302-4). The state is the Idea because it is in this way the unity of universal and particular, form and content, and since in the state this is a conscious unity, it may be described as mind in being, since reason is 'essential and actual truth' and 'truth, aware of what it is, is mind' (*Enc.*, §§ 438-9).

3. For references to specific passages of *Le Contrat Social* and a slightly longer statement of Hegel's criticism, see *History of Philosophy*, iii. 400 ff.

4. *Science of Rights*, § 17, pp. 209 ff. See also *History of Philosophy*, iii. 503 ff., and Hegel's essay *Über die wissenschaftlichen Behandlungsarten des Naturrechts* (*Werke*[1], i. 361 ff.).

5. The extent to which the French revolutionaries derived their ideas from *Le Contrat Social* is now disputed (see, e.g., Mornet: *Les Origines*

intellectuelles de la révolution française, Paris, 1934, pp. 95–6). See further for Hegel's view, the section called 'Absolute freedom and terror' in *Phenomenology*, pp. 599 ff.

6. *Restoration of Political Science*—a defence of natural law against man-made civil law, and of conservatism against liberalism (see Note 13 to the Preface). It was published at Winterthür in 1816 in four volumes, and a second edition appeared at the same place from 1820 to 1822. Two further volumes were added later. In the footnote at the end of this Remark, Hegel quotes from the first edition, a copy of which the translator has been unable to see, but the citations are identifiable in the second edition. In almost every instance, however, although Hegel uses von Haller's words and does not misrepresent him, he omits words and sentences without indicating omissions and sometimes he inverts the order of sentences and paraphrases them, despite his use of quotation marks. The translator has inserted references to the second edition in square brackets, both in cases where Hegel gives references and in those where he gives none. In the translation, quotation marks have been used to distinguish von Haller's statements from Hegel's comments, some of which appear within quotation marks in Hegel's first edition.

7. A lawyer who depends on legal technicalities for getting the better of his opponent.

261. 8. Religious duties and their bearing on political life are excluded from consideration for the reason given in the second footnote to the Remark to Paragraph 270. In Hegel's view, religious duties coincide with ethical duties in the Protestant religion and in a Protestant state (see *Enc.*, § 552).

267. 9. Here and in what follows Hegel adopts from Fichte the comparison between the state and a self-reproducing organism. He regards the state as an organism in virtue of its constitution, i.e. its organization. The etymological connexion between 'organization' and 'organism' is seldom present to our minds when we speak of the former, but it is never absent from Hegel's. 'Strictly political state'—cf. Paragraphs 273, 276. Hegel distinguishes between the strictly *political* state, an objective organization, and the state proper (which he calls 'this actual God', &c.). The latter comprises not only the objective side but also the subjective side referred to in Paragraph 267, i.e. it comprises not only the constitution but also the subjective life of the whole community, together with all their moral and legal duties and rights and the whole sphere in which these duties are performed and these rights enjoyed. Hence the state proper is the totality of human life so far as it is the life of moral beings united in a community by tradition, religion, moral convictions, &c. Failure to realize this has been responsible for numerous misrepresentations of Hegel's position and his attitude to 'the state'.

270. 10. Hegel regards ancient states as mere substances—absolute undifferentiated powers imposing their will on their subjects without the intermediation of the subject's own knowledge and will. In civil society, i.e. in the modern world since the Renaissance, particularity is explicit, together with claims made on behalf of private judgement, and is at first, in the system of needs, given free rein. The history of civil society is the history of the education of this private judgement until the particular is brought back to the universal. Corporations and the working of the judicial system are educative institutions helping to produce this result. Hence the modern state which Hegel saw coming into being in his own day is substance and power, but a substance which has come to self-consciousness in its citizens. They recognize its law as their law —if they are educated enough to do so—and hence the state is not an arbitrary will or a blind necessity, but the embodiment of the citizens' freedom.

11. By Friedrich von Schlegel and other Romantics.

12. The state in Hegel's view is the highest and most divine of human institutions, but it is only an institution. It is mind objectified in the way most adequate to mind, but it is still less than, and therefore (see Note 61 to Paragraph 141) is grounded on, 'absolute mind'. The latter is the 'eternally actual truth in which the contemplative reason enjoys freedom' (*Enc.*, § 552) and its three forms are art, religion, and philosophy. The content of religion and philosophy is the same, but what religion believes, philosophy knows. The thinking of philosophy is rational, it knows the concept as the concept, while the thought of religion is only representational (see Note 5 to Paragraph 145). Since this is the general relation between religion and philosophy, there should be no clash in principle between the church, an embodiment of religion, and the state, a 'hieroglyph' of reason. Here Hegel falls back on his Lutheran faith in a co-operation between Protestant churches and a Protestant government. But he modifies the Lutheran doctrine of the subservience of the church to the state so far as to allow freedom of conscience to dissenting sects (see the third footnote to this Remark).

13. i.e. the state 'puts up with them' (*aushalten, tolerare*), endures them. Mennonites were exempt from military service in Prussia until 1868. Prussia granted civil rights to Jews in 1811, but there was an outbreak of anti-Semitism in 1819 when Hegel was writing his book (Rosenzweig: *Hegel und der Staat*, Munich and Berlin, 1920, vol. ii, p. 186).

14. The subject of the debate must have been the slave *trade*, not *Sklaverei*, as Hegel says, since Congress had no jurisdiction over slavery

as such. Quaker petitions against the trade were presented to Congress in 1790 and 1797, and the retort in question may have been made then, or perhaps, if the date is not too late, in 1820 during the debates on the Missouri Compromise.

15. Hegel's original text as printed reads: *führen zwar die innere Durchdringung . . . welche aber durch die Religion . . . erhält; indem die sittlichen*, &c. His list of errata instructs us to delete *aber*. The translation here given assumes that the original *aber* was misplaced and that it should have been inserted between *indem* and *die*. *Zwar* (otherwise left in the air) and *aber* will then point the contrast between *Gesinnung* and *Vernünftigkeit* which is the burden of the two parts of Hegel's sentence.

16. *Geistige*. In English we would say that the 'spiritual' is the domain of religion, rather than the 'mental', but *Geist* means both 'mind' and 'spirit' and to draw a distinction here between mental and spiritual would destroy Hegel's point.

17. This is a reference to the dictum quoted from Kant in the Remark to Paragraph 29 (Messineo).

18. All editions read '358'. The reference a few sentences below to the 'witness of his own spirit and heart' is a reference to the Lutheran doctrine mentioned towards the end of the Preface. Cf. Paragraph 147.

19. Hegel is fond of making the point (e.g. *Philosophy of History*, p. 416) that the distinction between priests and laymen is meaningless in Protestantism. He has in mind Luther's dictum that 'All Christians are really of the priestly class'.

20. So Laplace, from whose work this note has been translated directly. Hegel writes: 'In a man of genius one of the strongest passions is the passion for truth', which may be true, but it is not what Laplace says.

21. Wishes for the unity of church and state were characteristic of Romantics like Friedrich von Schlegel and Adam Müller. In conformity with these wishes, many of them became Roman Catholics (see Addition to Paragraph 141 and Note 52 to Paragraph 140) and longed for the days when an Emperor owed his crown to a Pope.

22. Hegel is thinking of the unity implied by emperor-worship as practised in Persia, the semi-oriental kingdoms of the Near East, and the Roman Empire.

23. See *Philosophy of History*, pp. 412 ff. Hegel there traces how the denial of the authority of the church at the Reformation led to ecclesiastical dissensions; the basis of this change was the discovery of the principle of subjectivity and the right of private judgement. This gradually paved the way for the triumph of the Understanding (univer-

sality of thought) in the eighteenth century, and so to the discovery of thought as the heart of law as well as of nature. This in turn makes possible a transition to the rational state. Thought, the universal *essence* of political life, must come into *existence* as a rational constitution. For the transition of being (or essence) to existence, see *Enc.*, especially §§ 122 ff.

24. It is as a convinced Lutheran—'I am a Lutheran and will remain the same' (*History of Philosophy*, i. 73)—that Hegel condemns the Roman Catholic Church as superstitious and so inimical to freedom of thought.

272. 25. The constitution, as rational, is a unity of explicit differences, i.e. of individuality, particularity, and universality (see Note 2 to Paragraph 258), i.e. of the crown, the executive, and the legislative. Since these form a concrete unity, each one of them has reflected into it the characteristics of the other two. This point Hegel works out for monarchy in Paragraph 275 and for the legislative in Paragraph 300. So far as the executive is concerned, the laws which it administers are the universal element and the monarch who appoints civil servants and gives final decisions is the individual element. 'These powers'—i.e. the differentiations just referred to. See Paragraph 269.

26. See Notes 8 and 12 to the Preface. It is no doubt Fries and the Romantics whom Hegel has in mind as well as von Haller.

27. Kant and his followers.

28. A cardinal point in Montesquieu. See *Esprit des Lois*, xi. 6.

29. Lasson reads: *Dämme auszuklügeln, die Einheit als eine Wirksamkeit nur gegenseitiger Dämme zu begreifen* ('to construct dikes, to apprehend the unity of the state as only an agency of opposed dikes, is characteristic of', &c.). The sense of Hegel's text is obscure, but the emendation is perhaps hardly justified. The point seems to be that the rabble makes distrust of the state its starting-point. It then interprets state action as the building of one dike after another to stem the wishes of the people. And then once state action is so interpreted, the policy of the rabble is to build corresponding dikes against the state, i.e. to resist state action as much as possible. Hegel obviously has in mind again the phrase quoted from Kant in the Remark to Paragraph 29, which implies that society involves mutual restrictions on individual freedom. In that passage he specifically refers to the 'negative' implication of what Kant says.

30. The French Revolution.

273. 31. All editions read '82', but that is probably the perpetuation of a misprint in Hegel's first edition. Read: 52 [3rd edn. § 99].

32. See, e.g., Aristotle's *Politics* 1279ᵃ 26 ff., where three types of constitution are distinguished on the basis of the number of those who govern.

33. In, e.g., Paragraph 214. See also *Enc.*, § 99.

34. For Hegel's further criticisms of Fichte's ideas, see his essay *Über die wissenschaftlichen Behandlungsarten des Naturrechts* (*Werke*[1], i. 365 ff.). (Lasson.) The 'forms' to which Fichte refers are monarchy, aristocracy, and democracy. The name and the idea of the ephorate were derived by Fichte from the constitution of Sparta, where the power of the two kings, who held office for life, was checked by the five ephors, who were elected annually. Fichte distinguished his ephors from the Spartan, however, and likened them rather to the Roman tribunes, because his ephors were to have a veto only and no executive power. See *Science of Rights*, § 16, pp. 259–60.

35. *La vertu* (*Esprit des Lois*, iii. 3. The quotations which follow immediately are from the same chapter), i.e. *Virtus*, 'readiness to sacrifice oneself for an Idea realized in one's fatherland' (*Hegels Theologische Jugendschriften*, Tübingen, 1907, p. 223). In chapter i of the same book, Montesquieu says that the nature of a government differs from its principle: 'The former makes it what it is, the latter makes it act. The former is its special structure, the latter is the human passion which makes it move.' His belief is that while the state is held together by law in limited monarchy, and by force in a despotism, democracy will not subsist unless the citizens are virtuous, i.e. possessed of a sentiment for law and order. Hegel's view is that though the heart of a democracy may be sound, sentiment is not strong enough to withstand the onset of difference, i.e. the onset of reflection (see Remark to Paragraph 185).

36. Montesquieu remarks (iii. 5) that, while virtue is not excluded from monarchy, it is not its spring.

37. *La modération* (iii. 4).

38. The constitution of the Roman Republic was still in essence aristocratic in the second century B.C., and was tottering into anarchy or despotism in the first century B.C. Hegel assumes that this was due to a defect in the character of aristocratic government as such, not to the inability of the particular form of Roman aristocratic government to adapt itself to the rule of an empire.

39. *L'honneur* (iii. 7).

40. i.e. limited or 'constitutional' monarchy, where the moments of the concept are objectified in different institutions which yet so interlock as to form a single whole (see Paragraph 272).

274. 41. Cf. Montesquieu (i. 3): 'The most natural government is that whose particular character is best related to the character of the people for which it has been established.'

278. 42. Paragraphs 321 ff.

279. 43. This must not be misunderstood. Even logic, the most abstract philosophical discipline, implies in the philosopher an experience of thinking and of past ways of thinking. *A fortiori*, in his more concrete studies, he begins with something given—the investigations of physical scientists, the history of political institutions, &c.—and attempts to find in this material the development of its concept. This concept is the same as that whose early development he has studied in logic, and once again its determinations or stages of advance will be found to be a necessary sequence. These stages the concept, in virtue of its self-creative power, gives to itself, and once so created, they can be understood, but the philosopher cannot foresee them any more than he can forecast the actions of a political genius before they are performed, however intelligible they may be after their performance. It is necessary that the categories of logic should have *an* embodiment in the stages of nature and history—they are not actual without it, not rational, therefore, without it—but *what* embodiment is something which cannot be forecast. Hence the 'derivation of a content of a science from its concept alone' is the *conclusion* of philosophical investigation, the discovery that the diverse phenomena investigated are stages in the growth of the single concept which is their soul. The philosopher does not begin with pure thought and write ethics and politics out of his head. Hegel emphatically repudiates apriorism in philosophical studies both in the Preface to the *Philosophy of Right* and at the beginning of his Philosophy of Nature, see *Enc.*, § 246. Cf. above, Note 8 to Paragraph 3.

44. If a monarch derives his authority from God, he rules by divine right—a claim accompanied with disastrous results when interpreted, as in England for example, as a 'divine right to govern wrong'. Hegel holds, however, that God's will is not inscrutable, but intelligible, and that it is the task of philosophy to understand it both in itself and in its results in the world. Hence, philosophy may admit that a monarch rules 'by divine right' in the sense that monarchy is a rational institution, the apex and basis of the state as a rational and so as a divine institution, and yet deny that a monarch may be absolute or defy the will of the people, because rationality requires a limited and not an absolute monarchy.

45. i.e. at the end of the eighteenth century and the beginning of the nineteenth, largely as a result of Rousseau's work.

46. In the Remark to Paragraph 273.

47. See Plato, *Apology*, 31 c ff. For a discussion of the nature of the 'divine sign' and whether it is to be regarded as an inner voice (which is Hegel's view here—cf. Paragraph 138) or as the voice of God coming

from without, see Riddell's edition of the *Apology* (Oxford, 1877), pp. 109–17.

280. 48. The monarch is on a pinnacle above the rest of the state (see the end of the Remark to Paragraph 279). *Qua* monarch, then, he must be considered in abstraction from the rest of the state. Now an individual, taken in abstraction, is simply a unit and his individuality is immediate, not mediated by his position in society. Further, a man's individuality is immediate in another sense, i.e. when he is a baby—a physical organism not yet conscious of its spiritual character—and hence an 'immediate' individuality belongs to a man in the course of nature before it has become mediated through his consciousness of the external world. Thus the monarch reaches his position through his natural characteristics, i.e. in virtue of his birth. See Addenda, p. 376.

49. Kant's rejection of the ontological argument in the *Critique of Pure Reason* was often criticized by Hegel, see, e.g., *Enc.*, § 51. And Hegel is here referring to Kant's assertion that though he had denied that there could be any proof or knowledge of God's existence, still he had 'found it necessary to deny knowledge to make room for faith' (*Critique of Pure Reason*, B. xxx).

50. It is of the French Revolution that Hegel is thinking again. If kingship is irrational, then the king may be guillotined, and Terror, the breakdown of political life, may follow. Cf. the reference to *salut du peuple* in the Remark to the next Paragraph.

281. 51. *des von der Willkür Unbewegten*—'unmoved by caprice'. But 'unmoved by' is ambiguous in English and might mean that the monarch was never actuated by caprice of his own, which Hegel denies (see, e.g., Paragraph 283). He is here thinking again (see Note 1 to Paragraph 142) of Aristotle's doctrine of God as the unmoved mover. The monarch's 'I will'—*le Roi le veult* would seem less satisfactory to Hegel, because less personal—sets the machinery of government in motion though it is not grounded in that machinery, but is its unmoved mover.

52. See Remark to Paragraph 301.

53. In the section on Civil Society; see, e.g., Paragraphs 183 and 206.

54. *Wahl-Kapitulation.* In the sixteenth century, by compelling the man of their choice to accept such a compact as a condition of election, the Electors acquired a distinct preliminary control of both the internal government of the Holy Roman Empire and its foreign policy, and so circumscribed the Emperor's authority.

55. In this treatment of elective monarchy, Hegel has in mind both the Holy Roman Empire and the Kingdom of Poland (see *Philosophy of History*, p. 427).

282. 56. Pardon (forgiveness) belongs essentially to the sphere of religion. See the end of the Remark to Paragraph 137, and Note 12 to Paragraph 270. For the translation of *Geist* here by 'mind', although 'spirit' would be more natural English, see Note 16 to Paragraph 270.

286. 57. See Remarks to Paragraphs 279 and 281.

58. See Paragraph 280.

289. 59. The actions of the players are chosen by the players and therefore are free 'in form', but in substance they subserve universal ends, are restricted by universal laws, and to that extent are not free. See Paragraphs 182 ff.

290. 60. The organized body of officials is said to have an 'abstract' task because its main duty is to construct a skeleton organization for subsuming the particular under the universal (see Paragraph 287). The difficulty which Hegel finds in the construction of a civil service organization springs from the fact that he wishes to combine (*a*) administrative efficiency with (*b*) private freedom. To attain (*a*), he prescribes (i) the division of the civil service into distinct departments, Treasury, Post Office, Ministry of Health, &c., and (ii) the unified control of these departments at the top in the person of the Prime Minister or other supreme official. To attain (*b*), he prescribes that civil life with its concrete business of buying and selling, and the concrete individuals who compose it, shall be governed 'from below', i.e. by officials elected at least partly by themselves. These are the corporation officers (see Remark to Paragraph 288) and probably Mayors also (see *Philosophy of History*, p. 454, where Hegel criticizes adversely the French system where every Maire is appointed by the central government). These popularly elected officers are at the same time the lowest rung of the official hierarchy; it is they and not civil servants proper who directly control the man in the street; in them again the different branches of the civil service converge, in the sense that Treasury, Post Office, &c., issue their orders not directly to private individuals, but to the Mayor or Corporation official who is thus at the same time the lowest of the treasury officials, post office officials, &c. (see Paragraph 295).

295. 61. For a full and entertaining account of this famous case which dragged on from 1770 to 1780, when Frederick the Great overrode the lawyers and found in the miller's favour, see Carlyle's *Frederick the Great*, book xxi, chap. 7. The miller in question was sued for arrears of rent which he could not pay because a nobleman had cut off part of his water power to construct a fish-pond. 'Barrow loads of pleadings' attempted to justify the nobleman's right to do so by reference to Grotius, a law of 1556, &c.

299. 62. i.e. before war breaks out. War-time services are considered in Paragraphs 324 ff.

63. See Paragraphs 42 ff.

300. 64. *das ständische Element*, i.e. the States General, or the Estates of the Realm. Not simply Parliament but also the Estates or classes (*Stände*) assembled therein. The Estates are the classes of civil society given a political significance. See Remark to Paragraph 303. For the interpretation of Paragraphs 300–13 see Note 67 to Paragraph 312.

305. 65. Landed gentry inherit their estates and so owe their position to birth, and since they live from their estates, their choice of what they do to satisfy their private interests has no bearing on the life of the neighbouring gentry. *Per contra*, in industry, the actions of one entrepreneur have a direct bearing on the actions of others, because in that sphere no one is independent of his neighbour (see, e.g., Paragraph 199).

308. 66. An abstract individual is what he is because manhood is his generic essence. But his manhood, the universal immanent within him, is actualized only when the individual loses his abstract individuality and becomes a member of a general group, i.e. when he participates in the generic essence of, e.g., the class of civil servants. In so doing he is possessed of a higher generic essence than that of manhood because in becoming a civil servant he has actualized what formerly was only a potentiality and hence has become more concrete.

312. 67. See Paragraph 304. If we consider in abstraction the monarch and the classes constitutive of civil society, then they are opposed to one another as the one and the many, or as the abstract individual and the abstract universal. The latter Hegel calls the universal of all-ness (see Remark to Paragraph 24) or 'empirical universality' (Paragraphs 301, 304). These opposites become fused into a unity only if some middle term comes into existence to mediate between them and so to produce the concrete unity of syllogism (see Note 2 to Paragraph 258). The executive is such a middle term from the point of view of the crown, because it carries out the crown's will and so particularizes it in the classes of civil society. But the classes do not feel their unity with the crown until they acquire political significance as the Estates and until one of the Estates, in virtue of its likeness in certain respects to the crown, is able to mediate between the crown and civil society as a whole. The agricultural class, or the nobility, shares certain characteristics in common with the crown (see Paragraph 305) and is thus in a position to be such a mediator. But it can act as such in the constitution only if its political function is embodied in an institution separate both from the crown on the one hand and industry (or its embodiment in a lower house of Parliament) on the other; i.e. it must be embodied in an upper house. The upper house then mediates between civil society and the crown; and if the upper house on any given issue sides with the lower house, this helps the lower house and obviates the impression that the latter is a mere faction against the crown and not genuinely devoted to the interest of the state (see Paragraph 313).

316. 68. Hegel always regards 'opinion' (*Meinung*) as something peculiarly 'mine' (*mein*), and this accounts for his general attitude to it. None the less, there is no more etymological affinity between *Meinung* and *mein* than there is between 'mind' and 'mine'.

317. 69. Ariosto's lines ('the ignorant vulgar reproves everyone and talks most of what it understands least') are from *Orlando Furioso*, Canto xxviii, Stanza i. Goethe's lines are:

> *Zuschlagen muss die Masse,*
> *Dann ist sie respektabel;*
> *Urteilen gelingt ihr miserabel.*

(*Sprichwörtlich*, ll. 398–400). Hegel substitutes *kann* for *muss* and *da* for *dann*. The translation given here of both quotations is taken from Bosanquet: *Philosophical Theory of the State* (London, 1930), p. 266.

70. *Geist*—i.e. Frederick the Great, who set as a question for the Berlin Academy prize in 1778: *S'il peut être utile de tromper un peuple?* (Lasson). Hegel misquotes the question both here and in the *Phenomenology*, p. 570. As Lasson remarks, the question was commonly raised, and answered affirmatively, in the eighteenth century.

319. 71. The injury done by libel or by written or spoken incitations to crime or rebellion, is one done to someone's opinions. There is no injury unless someone's *thoughts* are affected. Hence the injury is a subjective one and is committed in a subjective 'field' or 'element'.

72. These *ioci militares* were no doubt permitted in order to avert the evil eye. Examples of them are given in, e.g., Velleius Paterculus, ii. 67, and Suetonius: *Life of Caesar*, 49.

320. 73. So far, the state has been treated, not as a single whole, but as a group of parts, each of which has been separately described. We now ignore their 'real' difference and concentrate on the true and 'ideal' unity of the state as a whole.

322. 74. As Rosenzweig points out (*Hegel und der Staat*, Munich and Berlin, 1920, vol. ii, p. 168), the allusion is to the wishes of Prussians in Hegel's day to sacrifice the autonomy of Prussia on the altar of union with other German states to form a new whole called 'Germany'.

323. 75. See *Enc.*, §§ 96–8 and Note 5 to Paragraph 40 above.

324. 76. In his essay *Über die wissenschaftlichen Behandlungsarten des Naturrechts* (*Werke*[1], i, p. 373). (Lasson.)

77. This is an allusion to Kant's proposals which had appeared in 1795 in his tract *On Perpetual Peace*. See an English translation by M. Campbell Smith (London, 1903).

78. Paragraphs 334–7 and 343.

325. 79. Cf. Plato's *Republic*, where the warriors form a special class distinguished for their courage, as the Guardians are for their wisdom. In war the state is the ideality of the real differences subsistent within it, and one aspect of this unity is that all individuals are bound to sacrifice themselves to it if need be. This aspect is realized objectively in an institution distinct from other institutions, i.e. in a standing army. Hegel is here again criticizing Kant who had proposed the abolition of standing armies (*On Perpetual Peace*, preliminary article 3).

327. 80. This Paragraph must be taken with its successor. Courage is a virtue (*a*) because it is an expression of freedom, (*b*) because the courageous man insists on his freedom to such an extent that he evinces it by renouncing the achievement of particular aims. But 'in itself' (i.e. in abstraction from its intrinsic worth, see Paragraph 328) it is a virtue only in form because (*a*) although it negates the material, it remains negative to the last; such a negation is the formal character of a virtue but there is no intrinsic value in mere negation, even negation of the material. Before we can know whether a given act of courage is merely physical or is of a mental or 'spiritual' character, we must inquire into all the circumstances (see Remark to Paragraph 328). (*b*) The intrinsic worth of courage (see Paragraph 328) is derived from the end it subserves, i.e. from the sovereignty of the state. This sovereignty is both the animating principle and the goal of courageous action, but this may never be present to the courageous man's mind. A courageous man's motive may be not the defence of sovereignty but only devotion to a leader or even personal gain; and of what he achieves (the defence of sovereignty) he may be unconscious and think that he has only captured a particular fort.

329. 81. These are the powers which Blackstone ascribes to the King of England (*Commentaries*, vol. i, pp. 252 ff.).

331. 82. e.g. Paragraph 40. On 'recognition' see Remark to Paragraph 349.

340. 83. As Messineo remarks, the conception of *Volksgeist*, *esprit d'une nation*, seems to be ultimately due to Montesquieu (*Esprit des Lois*, xix. 4–5). It is also used by Kant and Herder and is a commonplace of the historical school of jurists. See Brie: *Der Volksgeist bei Hegel und in der historischen Rechtsschule* (Berlin and Leipzig, 1909).

'World history is the world's court of judgement' is a phrase from Schiller's poem 'Resignation' (*Gedichte der zweiten Periode*). Hegel does not insert quotation marks, and it may be for this reason that the phrase is sometimes falsely attributed to him.

341. 84. Paragraphs 341–60 are a very compressed summary of Hegel's *Philosophy of History*, and, without the commentary which that work supplies, they are perhaps no less hard to understand in German than they are in English.

343. 85. Hegel is primarily referring to Lessing whose *Education of the Human Race* was published in 1780.

86. γνῶθι σεαυτόν 'know thyself', the keynote of the teaching of Socrates (see Note 40 to Paragraph 138). When a man knows his own character, then his mind has risen to a higher level than that on which it was before that knowledge was attained; e.g. if a man knows that he is a sinner, then the very knowledge makes him better than he was when he transgressed without realizing the fact.

87. The reference is probably to Kant, who says (in the first supplementary note to his *Perpetual Peace*) that the guarantee of the progress of man and the eventual end of war lies in Nature, or Providence, inscrutable though the plan of Providence is.

347. 88. All editions read '346'.

348. 89. The deeds of great men are 'subjective in form' simply as being the deeds of self-conscious individuals. But the substance or content of these deeds is the achievement of the world-mind, not of the individual agent. An individual reaps his fame because he imposes a subjective, personal, form on what the world-mind effects. Philosophical history may elicit in detail the genuine substance of actions—a substance for which the agent has and deserves no credit—but public opinion and history in the ordinary sense ignore it.

353. 90. See Note 45 to Paragraph 185.

355. 91. *On the Decline of Natural States* (Berlin, 1812). The book was published under the pseudonym of Feodor Eggo.

356. 92. The reference is presumably to the Eleusinian mysteries.

93. Greece was divided into a plurality of city-states, each possessed of autonomy and so with a 'mind' of its own.

357. 94. In the earlier centuries of the Roman Republic.

95. The end of the Republic from the time of the Gracchi to the time of Augustus.

96. Emperors are deified.

358. 97. *unendlichen Schmerz*: by these words here as elsewhere (e.g.

Werke[1], i. 157) Hegel refers to the Crucifixion, 'the feeling that God is dead'.

360. 98. The medieval church and the medieval empire.

99. i.e. the world of art, religion, and philosophy. See *Enc.*, §§ 553–77.

ADDENDA

Preface. 13. Dr. H. Marcuse in *Reason and Revolution* (New York, 1941), pp. 179–80, says that the Wartburg demonstrators were anti-Semitic, while the 'freedom' of which they said so much was to be a privilege of Teutons alone. They hoped for a 'saviour' to whom 'the people would forgive all sins' and who would achieve German unity. The new state was to be built from below, on the sheer enthusiasm of the masses. Hegel's opposition to these Wartburg ideas is relevant when the relation of his doctrines to National-Socialism is under consideration.

48. 25. As Dr. Marcuse points out (op. cit., p. 199) the 'sophistical reasoning' in the Remark to this Paragraph is Luther's in his tract on Christian Liberty. 'How can it affect the liberty of the soul whether the body be in health? . . . How can a soul in liberty be brought into bondage by ill-health or captivity or hunger or thirst or any external evil'? (*Luthers Werke*, vol. vii, Weimar, 1897, pp. 21, 50).

107. 4. *Gegenstand* means 'object' in the sense of 'what confronts us', i.e., in this context, the action done. For the meaning of *objektiv*, see Paragraphs 26 and 112.

145. 5. Hegel here adopts Ricardo's belief, abandoned by modern economists, that economic laws are not merely observed uniformities within a given economic system but universal and inexorable necessities.

187. 46. Hegel lived in a country where most citizens were simply 'subjects', without participation in the work of government, and where, therefore, a political life and tradition, like the English, was almost wholly lacking. His book was an attempt to educate Germans beyond 'civil' to 'political' life.

202. 55. In the second half of Paragraph 203, there is no subject for *behält* which will give good sense. The translator takes the text to be corrupt, and his rendering is simply an attempt to convey what he believes Hegel's meaning to be.

280. 48. For the connexion between 'immediacy' and 'nature', cf. Paragraphs 11, 34, 43, 158, and the Additions to Paragraphs 10 and 18.

INDEX

The Index supplements the Table of Contents. Where the material of an Addition is similar to that of the relevant Paragraph, only the latter has been indexed. Those passages in the Translator's Foreword and Notes which explain Hegel's more important technicalities have been indexed, but no others.